The World of Athens

Classical Athens boasted one of the most impressive flowerings of civilisation that the
world has ever known, with original and influential achievements in literature, art,
philosophy, medicine and politics. This best-selling undergraduate textbook, now issued
in a second edition, provides a comprehensive and highly illustrated introduction to its
history, society, culture and values aimed at the student. The text has been extensively
revised from the first edition and the bibliography updated. An introduction to the
sources has also been added. A wide range of topics is discussed, but the book refuses to
divide up the Athenian world neatly into separate compartments, insisting that sense
can only be made of the society by making connections between its history, institutions,
values and environment. The book can be used either on its own or as an
accompaniment to students learning Greek with the *Reading Greek* course.

JOINT ASSOCIATION OF CLASSICAL TEACHERS' GREEK COURSE

The World of Athens
An Introduction to Classical Athenian Culture

SECOND EDITION

Revised by Robin Osborne

 **CAMBRIDGE**
UNIVERSITY PRESS

CAMBRIDGE UNIVERSITY PRESS
Cambridge, New York, Melbourne, Madrid, Cape Town, Singapore, São Paulo, Delhi

Cambridge University Press
The Edinburgh Building, Cambridge CB2 8RU, UK

Published in the United States of America by Cambridge University Press, New York

www.cambridge.org
Information on this title: http://www.cambridge.org/9780521698535

First published 1984
Second Edition 2008

Printed in the United Kingdom at the University Press, Cambridge

A catalogue record for this publication is available from the British Library

ISBN 978-0-521-69853-5

Contents

Preface

The World of Athens is an introduction to the history, culture, values and achievements of classical Athens. It requires no knowledge of ancient Greek, but was designed to be used with profit by those learning Greek using *Reading Greek* (*Text* and *Grammar*, 2nd edition, Cambridge University Press, 2007). It begins with a sketch of the history of Athens from earliest times till the destruction of Athenian democracy in 322 BC. There are then seven chapters on different aspects of the Athenian world, and the main text closes with a chapter on the way in which the Athenians situated themselves with regard to other worlds and the way in which they themselves pictured their own world. The main text is followed by a Greek alphabet with a simplified English transliteration and pronunciation guide, a glossary of terms used, suggestions for further reading keyed in to chapters and paragraphs of the text, a bibliography of the works referred to, and an index.

The first edition of this book was produced by a scholarly team presided over by Peter Jones and including Paul Cartledge, George Cawkwell, John Gould, Desmond Lee, Jeremy Paterson, Brian Sparkes, Virginia Webb and John Wilkins. The revisions for the second edition have been entirely my responsibility. I have reviewed the whole original text, substantially rewriting the historical introduction and some sections of other chapters, but leaving intact both the original structure of the book and substantial discussions. I have replaced the very brief suggestions of 'Further Reading' in the first edition with a bibliography keyed to the numbered paragraphs of each chapter. The illustrations have also been reviewed, and various changes made. I am very grateful to the ancient history graduate students reading the M.Phil. in Classics in the University of Cambridge in 2001–2, who offered detailed views of what they thought needed changing, to the JACT Greek Committee for its initiative and support, and to Michael Sharp of Cambridge University Press, without whose assistance with the pictures my job would have been a great deal more tedious.

Passages from the *Iliad* are taken from the translation by E.V. Rieu, revised and updated by Peter Jones (Penguin, 2003). The passage from the *Odyssey* is taken from the translation by Richmond Lattimore, copyright 1951 and 1965 University of Chicago. Acknowledgement is due to the late Richmond Lattimore and the University of Chicago Press for the use of this material.

Robin Osborne, *King's College, Cambridge, August 2006*

Director's note

Professor Osborne is due all our thanks for his superb updating of what has so far been a very successful complement to the *Reading Greek* series, and is now set fair to become even more so. My thanks also to Dr Janet Watson for the Index.

Peter Jones, *Director, JACT Reading Greek Course, January 2007*

Notes

1   The usual messy-ish compromise has been made in turning Greek words into English, opting sometimes for the traditional form, sometimes for the strict transliteration. Macra have been added where the transliteration is literal (but not in the maps). Note that 'Attica' and 'Sparta' are the Romanised forms of the Greek; we have opted for the Greek transliterated forms 'Attikē' and 'Spartē'. But we have kept e.g. Roman 'Persia' rather than Greek 'Persikē'. We have also used 'z' in transliteration in place of the technically more correct 'sd', producing e.g. 'Zeus' instead of 'Sdeus', etc. For the traditional Romanisation of Greek words in English, see p. 365 and *Reading Greek (Grammar and Exercises)*, pp. 494–5, or Peter Jones, *An Intelligent Person's Guide to Classics* (London, 1999), pp. 138–9.

2   All dates are BC unless stated otherwise.

3   All writers quoted are given a brief pen-sketch in the Glossary. Where inscriptions are quoted, the references are as follows:

IG i^3 = *Inscriptiones Graecae* (3rd edn.).

ML = Meiggs and Lewis *A Selection of Greek Historical Inscriptions to the End of the Fifth Century.* Oxford, 1969.

LACTOR 1^4 = Osborne, R. ed. *The Athenian Empire*. LACTOR 1, 4th edn. London, 2000.

RO = Rhodes R. and Osborne, P.J. *Greek Historical Inscriptions 404–323 BC.* Oxford, 2003.

4   Numbers in brackets in the text indicate chapters and paragraphs of this book (e.g. (4.23)).

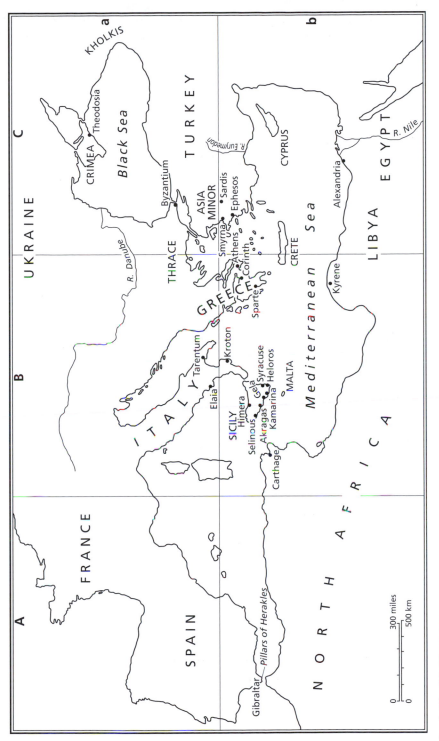

Map 1 The Mediterranean

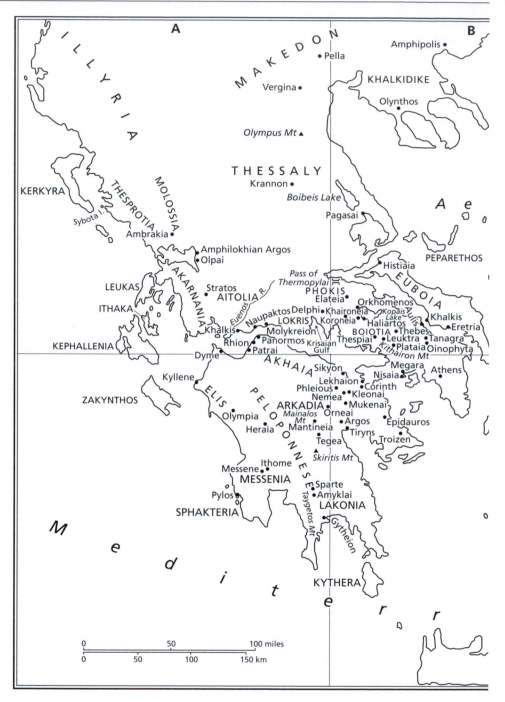

Map 2 Greece and the Aegean Islands

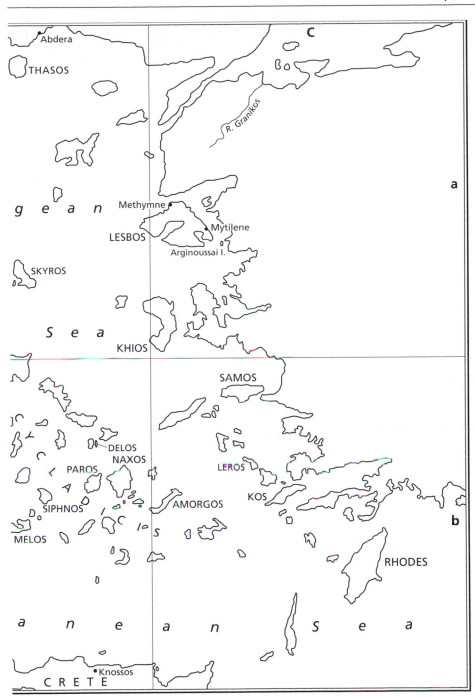

Abdera
THASOS
C
R. Granikos
a
g e a n
Methymne
Mytilene
LESBOS
Arginoussai I.
SKYROS
S e a
KHIOS
SAMOS
DELOS
NAXOS
LEROS
PAROS
KOS
SIPHNOS
AMORGOS
b
MELOS
RHODES
a n e a n S e a
Knossos
C R E T E

Map 3 Attikē

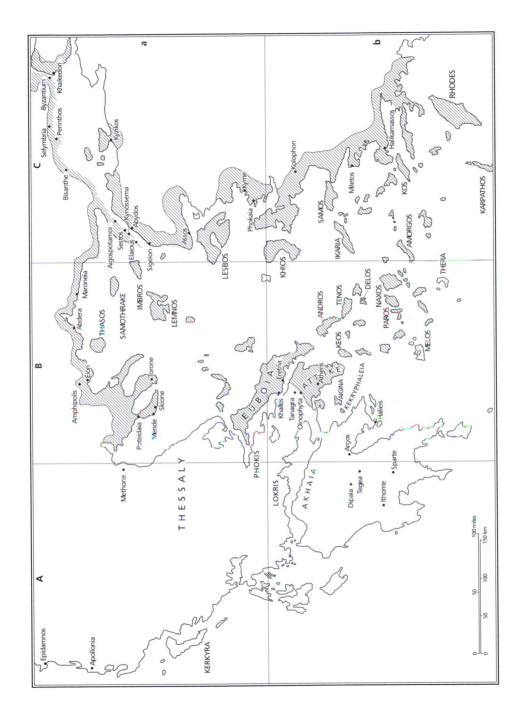

Map 4 The Athenian empire

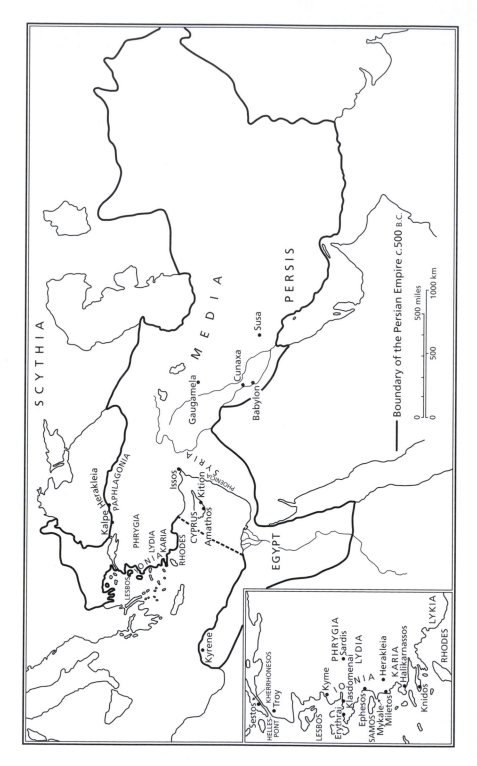

Map 5 The Persian empire

1 An outline history of Athens to the death of Alexander the Great

The basis of Athenian history

1.1 The first incident we are able to recount in the political history of Athens occurs some time after 640. It tells how a one-time Olympic victor called Kylōn attempted a coup during a major religious festival. It failed. Kylōn escaped, but his followers, though promised safe conduct, were killed. From that point on, those who killed them and their descendants were regarded as accursed. We know about this episode because Hērodotos and Thucydides, both writing in the late fifth century (8.41–2), needed to explain the curse to their readers in order to make later events at Athens comprehensible.

1.2 In writing the history of fifth-century Athens, modern scholars effectively repeat the narratives offered to them by Hērodotos, Thucydides, and Xenophōn, supplemented by later writers. Hērodotos, who was not an Athenian but from Halikarnassos (Bodrum, western Turkey), narrated the wars against Persia of 490 and 480–479, in which Athens played a major part. Thucydides, an Athenian who was sufficiently involved in Athenian public and political life to serve as *stratēgos*, dealt with both the so-called *Pentēkontaetia*, the 'fifty years' from the Persian Wars to the outbreak of the 'Peloponnesian War' between Athens and Spartē (431), and the war itself. His narrative breaks off in 410, but another Athenian, Xenophōn, who was also a military man, deliberately started his account of Greek affairs (the *Hellēnika*) from the point at which Thucydides' account ended. Xenophōn provides a narrative of the rest of the war and of the political upheaval in Athens immediately after the end of the war in 404 (8.43).

1.3 In writing the history of Athens *before* the fifth century, however, modern scholars have to piece together a story from accounts handed down *after* the fifth century, like the tradition about Kylōn. This was preserved because, among those who killed his followers, had been members of the controversial Alkmeōnidai family ('sons of Alkmeōn'); and it was politically useful for (some) Athenians (and some other Greeks) to remember that the Alkmeōnidai were accursed. Other figures whose names survive from seventh- and sixth-century Athenian politics do so because their names were attached to laws or institutions which continued in use; or because the story of their political careers could act as a warning about what sort of behaviour to watch out for among the politically ambitious. From the fourth century onwards, it became quite popular to write accounts of the early history of Athens (known as *Atthides*) (8.44), especially among men with an axe to grind who were themselves active in public life (such as Androtiōn and Phanodēmos). Though none of these accounts survives intact, we know of some of them because they were quoted by later writers. These writers picked up such oral stories as were circulating in their time, as Hērodotos and Thucydides had done, but unlike those fifth-century historians they did not subject them to any critical judgement. Instead, they tried to string them together into something which could count as a history. Inevitably this involved systematising what was unsystematic and inventing hypotheses to fill the gaps. Their accounts need therefore to be handled with particular care.

1.4   We can often cross-check the reliability of what Hērodotos or Thucydides says about fifth-century Athenian history by comparing their accounts with other contemporary writing, e.g. the comic dramas of Aristophanēs or the texts of Athenian inscriptions. But when it comes to what they and later writers say about *earlier* Athenian history, we have very few such checks. Scholars therefore argue from what seems most *likely* to have happened. However, while it is unlikely that stories such as that about Kylōn were complete inventions, there is no doubt that they have been elaborated in the telling. Consequently, we are not now in a position to know exactly where truth lies in any particular story. What is important, however, is that the stories which Hērodotos and Thucydides tell about the earlier history of Athens are stories that were *current in the fifth century*. In other words, whether or not Kylōn's attempted coup happened in precisely the way that Hērodotos and Thucydides describe it, fifth-century Athenians told each other that that was how it happened. For the Athenians, these stories *were* their past, and it was in the belief that their past was like this that they took the decisions that they did.

1.5   For us, a different story of Athens' past is also available. This is the story revealed by archaeology. Thucydides shows a faint awareness of the possible importance of archaeology when he claims that the first inhabitants of the Cycladic islands came from Kariā (south-west Turkey). He draws this conclusion because graves discovered on Dēlos during his lifetime contained arms of Karian type and were constructed in the same way as Karian graves of his own time. But this is a rare insight, and to all intents and purposes archaeology is a modern discipline. The story it tells, however, is not the sort of story told by texts. Archaeology reveals something of what was being built or made from non-perishable materials, but working out why what was being built or made took a particular form or changed over time is as difficult as trying to decide which parts of a traditional tale may be true. Nevertheless, we know a great deal more about the history of Athens than was known to the Athenians themselves.

1.6   To understand the world of classical Athens properly, we need to know both what happened in Athens and what the Athenians *thought* had happened. The account that follows will, in consequence, attempt both to summarise what we

1.1 The entrance (*dromos*) of the Mycenaean beehive (*tholos*) tomb at Akharnai.

think we can know of Athenian prehistory and history, and to indicate what the stories were that Athenians themselves told about their past.

Prehistoric Athens

1.7 A single site in Attikē is known to have been occupied in the mesolithic period (9000–7000). At Athens itself, the earliest occupation dates to the early neolithic (7000–6000). At this period, on the basis of the evidence currently available, the most heavily settled part of Greece was not southern Greece but Thessaly. But around 3000, Greece was transformed – from being a peninsula of Balkan Europe into a network of coasts and islands in close connection with each other and with the world of the eastern Mediterranean. This transformation can be associated with the development of sea-transport and consequent improvements in communication. At about the same time, metalworking technology was discovered and developed, and new farming practices arrived from Anatolia (modern Turkey).

1.8 The new technologies and improved communications led to stability, prosperity, and bigger communities. Large settlements – to all intents and purposes 'towns' – grew up shortly before 2000, and soon after 2000 palace complexes appeared in Crete (the so-called Minoan palaces). Comparable developments follow in mainland Greece around 1500, with elaborate palaces constructed at Mycenae, Tiryns, Thebes, Pylos and elsewhere. Modern scholars have come to talk of this period as 'Mycenaean' after the most important site. At Athens itself, the Akropolis was developed as a Mycenaean centre, and extensive tunnelling in the rock secured its water supply. Elsewhere in Attikē (the territory of classical Athens), major Mycenaean burials are known from Akharnai and Thorikos, and traces of buildings with Mycenaean frescoes survive at Eleusīs.

1.9　We know much more about society in the late Bronze Age (2000–1100) than the earlier period because of the development of figurative art (i.e. art depicting human and animal figures) and because the writing system that we call 'Linear B', adopted in the Mycenaean palaces, has been deciphered. This is a syllabic rather than an alphabetic script, but the language which it records is Greek. (The slightly earlier Linear A is undeciphered but does not record Greek.) Palaces kept extensive economic records in this script, and a large number of the clay tablets upon which these records were written, both at Knōssos in Crete and at Pylos, were baked and preserved when the palaces were destroyed by fire. We can justifiably talk of 'palace societies' because these records show how closely palace officials centralised and controlled economic activity, although the precise nature of the political organisation remains obscure.

1.10　Figurative decoration appears in the late Bronze Age on pottery, metalwork, and gems, but above all on painted frescoes. How the scenes relate to life is a topic of much debate, but it seems certain that both religious and political rituals are represented. Since we possess fresco fragments from Egypt depicting Cretan traders and find Cretan goods widely scattered elsewhere, there must have been close and extensive links between Crete and the lands bordering the eastern Mediterranean. Much of that contact was peaceful, involving exchange of goods and ideas; but there is some evidence also for more hostile encounters, reflected in the tradition of a war between Greeks and Trojans which came to be a major theme of Greek epic poetry, above all in Homer's *Iliad* c. 700 BC.

1.11　Excavation of Troy, close by the Hellespont, was undertaken precisely because of this tradition of a Trojan War. It has revealed a city which developed and grew from 3000 to 1100, and had strong links to its east as well as to the west and the Aegean. We cannot be certain which of the city levels revealed by the excavation might have faced attack from invading Greeks, but there is no doubt that this city was indeed an important point of contact between Greek and Anatolian worlds. To that extent, at least, the epic tradition proves to be based on historical reality. So, too, epic tradition describes in some detail, and accurately, some objects known (only) from the late Bronze Age c. 1200, such as the famous boar's tusk helmet worn by Odysseus in *Iliad* 10. Such memories can have survived only if the epics that come down to us stand in a continuous tradition begun at that time. As a result, scholars have attempted to distinguish historical 'layers' within epics in the same way that they distinguish archaeological layers in the soil (this part of Homer seems to reflect the ninth century, this the eighth century, etc.).

1.12　The continuity of epic tradition is important because shortly after 1200, following the destruction (we do not know why) of the Mycenaean palaces,

1.2 An example of so-called 'Protogeometric' pottery from Athens.

there seems to have been massive discontinuity within the Greek world. At Perati on the east coast of Attikē, for example, large numbers of people seem to have settled for a time with an eye to using it (in part) as a staging post from which to leave Attikē and move east (graves at Perati reveal goods of eastern Mediterranean origin). They did not stay long. Within half a century or so, mainland Greece seems to have become isolated and to have lost the skills of writing, figurative art and many specialised metalworking techniques. Many settlements were abandoned.

1.13 Nevertheless, Athens, which had itself played no special part in late Bronze Age history, and had a modest role in epic poetry to match, is one of relatively few sites which was continuously occupied; and it appears that it was from Athens that the new distinctive pottery style, known as Protogeometric, spread. Between 1100 and 700 the primary working metal changed from bronze to iron, while goods found in Attic graves tell us something of Athens' fortunes at this time: many burials dated 900–800 are remarkably wealthy, and demonstrate new metalworking techniques that can have been learned only from the eastern Mediterranean.

1.3 Athenian monumental wine-mixing bowl (*krātēr*), used as a tomb-marker and showing the laying out of the corpse (see 5.81) and a procession of men in armour.

1.14 Then, following 800, dramatic changes can be seen. Figurative decoration reappeared on Athenian pottery; and around 750 Athenian potters began to produce, in at least one Athens cemetery, very large vases with scenes of funerals, chariot processions, ships, and fighting, to stand on and mark graves. Such outsize vases suggest an attempt by some people in the society to distinguish themselves from others, but at the same time numbers of burials rose sharply. This is partly because the population was increasing, but also because more social classes now partook in formal burial rituals. The increase in burial numbers is seen both in Athens and in cemeteries in Attikē, where a number of new settlements arose. Shortly before the middle of the century, Greeks adopted the alphabet used by the Phoenicians, adapting it to have some signs represent vowel sounds (8.2). By 700 Athenians were using writing to communicate with the gods but also for more frivolous purposes: the earliest substantial Athenian writing occurs on the shoulder of a jug and identifies it as a prize for the dancer who 'sports most elegantly'.

The beginnings of Athenian history

1.15 In both Protogeometric (1000–900) and middle Geometric (850–760) periods, Athenian pottery was widely distributed, but late Geometric (760–700) Athenian pottery seems rarely to have been sold abroad. Some containers for olive oil manufactured in Attikē did get widely exported around the Mediterranean in the period 750–700, but it is not at all certain that Athenians travelled with them. But while Athens seems to have turned inwards (for reasons to be discussed), other Greeks, and particularly men from Corinth and from Euboia, seem to have been busy not only sailing throughout the Mediterranean but settling on the coasts of Sicily and southern Italy. Tracing these settlements is much easier than understanding how they came about. Scholars have disputed whether Greeks were attracted abroad by opportunities to gain better agricultural land; or were compelled to leave Greece because of the threat of starvation; or were sent abroad by a community decision; or were involved in exchange of goods with non-Greeks and realised that this could be more profitably and securely achieved if they had staging posts abroad and permanently resident agents. Whatever lay behind their foundation, these settlements abroad (once misleadingly entitled 'colonies') kept close ties with one, sometimes two, cities – but never, until just before 600, with Athens.

1.16 There may have been both positive and negative reasons why groups of Athenians did not lead settlements abroad. The positive reasons include the size of Attikē (2,500 sq. km) (2.3). Athenian tradition held that Attikē had once had a number of independent cities, but that these had been brought together by Athens' mythical king Thēseus in an act of *sunoikismos* ('unification'). But archaeology, on the other hand, suggests that during this period Athens itself was founding new settlements in Attikē. During the period 800–700 further new villages were settled, and even after this there was significant scope for further settlement. The negative reasons may include some sort of Athenian crisis shortly after 700. The number of graves from Attikē that can be dated between 700 and 600 is very much smaller than the number of graves from Attikē that can be dated between 750 and 700. This is likely to represent exclusion from formal burial – surely for some significant reason – rather than catastrophic population decline. At the same time the style and subject matter of painting on Athenian pottery changed markedly, and the new fashion was for scenes which involved individual rather than communal endeavour.

1.17 What kind of political régime Athens enjoyed in the eighth and seventh centuries is not clear. The Homeric *Iliad* and *Odyssey*, now often thought to have reached more or less the form in which we have them only after 700, imply familiarity with monarchic government, but also seem to understand situations where, as on Odysseus' Ithaka, a son did not necessarily inherit his father's throne. The city of peace pictured on the shield that Hēphaistos made for Akhilleus (*Iliad* 18) has justice dispensed by elders upon the decision of the people. By contrast, in the more or less contemporary *Works and Days* of the Boiotian poet Hesiod, justice was in the hands of *basileis* (traditionally translated 'kings'), who were not necessarily hereditary rulers but were certainly officials of some sort. Also, tradition held that, by 650, Athens had acquired her first 'archons' (*arkhontes*, s. *arkhōn*) – annually appointed office-holders. In the classical period Athens had nine of these, each with distinct duties (6.23). The archons included one named the *basileus* and one named *polemarkhos* ('leader in war'). The *polemarkhos* retained some military responsibility until the battle of Marathōn in 490, but subsequently had only judicial duties. The year was named after one of the archons, the 'eponymous' archon, and all who served as archons automatically became members of a council which met on the Areopagus hill, just north-west of the Akropolis (6.38). Thucydides' account of Kylōn's conspiracy makes reference to the nine archons, Hērodotos' to the 'presidents of the naucraries' (apparently some sort of finance division). Contemporary inscriptions from elsewhere sometimes reveal complex bureaucratic structures, in which successive officials were made responsible for seeing that officials below them in the hierarchy did their job properly.

1.18   This suggests that, by about 600, Athens was developing a non-hereditary governmental system of some sophistication, an impression confirmed by the text of a law ascribed to one Drakōn. This law survives because it was reinscribed on stone as part of a review of the Athenian law-code at the end of the fifth century. The law concerned procedure in cases of accidental killing. It reveals the existence of plural *basileis* and of a body of fifty-one *ephetai* ('hearers of appeals'?) who made the final decision. Drakōn's law left an important judicial role for the family of the victim (potentially including cousins as well as the direct line) and for the kinship group known as the phratry (3.53–4; 5.14) – though it has often been thought that one of the important advances made by Drakōn was *reducing* the jurisdiction of family and kin and increasing the role of the state.

1.19   The attempted coup by Kylōn, the cursing of those responsible for the death of some of his followers, and Drakōn's laws – all this suggests that there was some discontent in Athenian society in the late seventh century, and that the community attempted to do something about it. In other Greek communities in the seventh century, we have evidence that people were worried that officials were turning their office into a permanent power base and that individuals were setting themselves up above the constitution. They became known, in a term which the Greeks perhaps borrowed from Lȳdiā, as *turannoi* ('tyrants'). That individuals could do this implies that they were able to call on support from outside the ranks of those involved in running these cities. We do not know what the issues were which divided these other communities, though flagrant injustice is likely to have been one cause. But, in the case of Athens, authors writing after 400 believed that the root of the problem was that 'the poor had become enslaved to the rich', and that the problem had been sorted out in the 590s by one Solōn.

1.20 Nothing is heard of Solōn in Thucydides, while Hērodotos calls him a wise man, but tells us nothing substantial about his achievements. He came into the spotlight only in the local fourth-century histories of Athens; and our best source for this fourth-century view of Solōn comes from *The Constitution of the Athenians*, written as part of an Aristotelian research project on the constitutions of Greek cities. The author of this research work painted a general picture of Solōn's political achievements and then sought to support his views by quoting from Solōn's own poems. The poetic language that Solōn employed to advertise his ideas and defend his actions does not make it easy to understand exactly what he did. He talks of 'freeing the black earth', of pulling up boundary stones, and of bringing back to Athens men who had been sold into slavery and no longer spoke the Attic tongue. He paints himself as a man of moderation:

> To the People (*dēmos*) I have given such privilege as is enough,
> Neither taking away nor adding to their honour;
> While those who had power and were famed for their wealth,
> For them I took care they should suffer no injury.
> I stood, holding out my strong shield over both,
> And I did not allow either to triumph unjustly. (Solōn, fr. 5)

For all the obscurity of detail, however, some of Solōn's principles and achievements are clear. He made it impossible for men to agree to be enslaved if they could not pay their debts. He distributed political power according to wealth, leaving some official posts to the wealthy but giving even the poor some political and judicial role. He introduced a law-code that was far more comprehensive than the laws of Drakōn, and showed a particular concern for property rights. Whether this legislation followed a more general abolition of debt or redistribution of land is much disputed. Nevertheless, it is certainly the case, first, that debt never became a political problem in classical Athens; second, that property in land seems to have been much more evenly distributed in classical Athens than in most other societies; and finally that, after Solōn, the 'sixth-parters' (*hektēmoroi*, peasants who had to give a sixth of their produce to their overlord), were never heard of again. (This is a subject of great concern for *The Constitution of the Athenians*.) Some form of citizen Assembly (*ekklēsiā*) probably already existed in Solōn's time, but he seems to have given it a more formal role in matters of state, with regular meetings. He also invented a formal Council (*boulē*) of 400 – a sort of steering committee – to prepare business for it. The *ekklēsiā*'s actual powers and working relationship with the *arkhontes* at this time remain obscure.

1.21 If Solōn's economic reforms changed Athens for ever, his political reforms did not prevent civil conflict. *The Constitution of the Athenians*, again, told

1.4 Panathenaic *amphorā*. This example dates to c. 530 BC.

of a series of problems, culminating in attempts by Peisistratos to take power as *tyrannos*. The story of Peisistratos' three attempts to seize power was told by Hērodotos as a text-book warning against the deceitful tricks played by the politically ambitious. First, Peisistratos got himself a body-guard by claiming to be in danger from his enemies, and then used that to seize power. Next, he deceived the Athenians into thinking that he had the particular favour of their patron goddess Athēnē, and tricked one of the other major political leaders into thinking he wished genuinely to collabo-rate with him. Finally, he bought military support from outside, and attacked the Athenian army when it was not expecting it. *The Constitution of the Athenians*, while repeating these stories from Hērodotos, also retailed the tradition that Peisistratos was a mild and wise ruler. Both traditions reflected the uses to which stories of a 'tyrant' were put in subsequent history – on the one hand to frighten people about the political ambitions of certain individuals, and on the other to point to the virtues of strong government.

1.5 The foundations of the late sixth-century temple of Athēnē Polias on the Athenian Akropolis, with the late fifth-century Erekhtheion immediately to its north.

1.22 The truth seems to be that Athens flourished in the sixth century, before, during and after Peisistratos' tyranny. In 566, before even the first of Peisistratos' coups, the Athenians had reorganised their major festival, the *Panathēnaia* ('All-Athenian'). Inspired by the Olympic games and the look-alike festivals recently established at Delphi, Nemeā and the Isthmus of Corinth, the Athenians made the *Panathēnaia* a much grander occasion; indeed, this festival came to attract competitors from all over the Greek world (3.42ff.). Such festivals represented a proud statement of confidence, and the victors were rewarded with *amphorā*s of Athenian olive oil, her most famous agricultural product. A building programme may have been begun at more or less the same time, to provide Athēnē with a stone temple on the Akropolis; and later in the century, a major rebuilding programme was undertaken (8.87). The Akropolis attracted more and more lavish sculptural dedications as the century went on; and from the final decades of the century, a large number of extremely ornate statues survive of young women (*korai*) (8.86). Athenian craftsmanship became known all over the Mediterranean world from c. 560, when fine Attic black-figure pottery replaced Corinthian pottery as the tableware of choice, particularly among the Etruscans (8.88 and fig. 3.13).

1.6 An example of an Athenian pot exported to Etruria. A mid-sixth-century 'eye-cup' by the potter and painter Exēkiās (see 8.89), showing hoplites lined up against one another over the corpse of a fallen warrior.

Kleisthenēs and the invention of democracy

1.23   When Peisistratos died, his sons, Hippiās and Hipparkhos, assumed power. Even more than their father, they left a reputation for sympathy for and involvement with poetry and culture. They took, for example, an interest in the performance of the Homeric epics at the *Panathēnaia* and invited the great lyric poet Anakreōn to Athens. But more than their father, they also gained a

1.7 Marble copies of the statues of the 'tyrannicides', Harmodios and Aristogeiton the assassins of Hipparkhos, by the sculptors Kritios and Nēsiōtēs (see 8.92).

reputation for political violence. For example, they had Kīmōn, son of Stēsagorās, killed because his repeated victories in chariot races at the Olympic games gave him a dangerously high public profile. As a result, plots against Hippiās and Hipparkhos multiplied. An attempt to get rid of them by force failed, but at the *Panathēnaia* of 514 Hipparkhos was assassinated. Hippiās, however, was still left in power, and his opponents decided to seek help from outside Athens.

1.24 Among the city-states of sixth-century Greece, one stood out for its desire to secure itself alliances. This was Spartē. Spartē was unlike any other city-state. It had a huge territory, more than three times the size of Attikē; and this territory was worked by 'helots' (Greek *heilōtai*, 'captives'), the name given to Spartē's serf population. These were probably surrounding peoples whom the Spartans had conquered earlier and brought in to work the land. To keep these helots in subjection, the Spartans maintained themselves as a standing army, and ensured that none of their neighbours would support helots against the Spartans themselves. They did this by enlisting as allies the majority of states in the northern half of the Peloponnese, as far away as Corinth and Megara. The more allies Spartē acquired, the more it was worth allying with her. But the more allies Spartē acquired, the greater her responsibility to deal with trouble on her allies' borders. Spartē's willingness to put itself about was well illustrated by Hērodotos. The (accursed: see 1.3) Athenian family of the Alkmaionidai, who had once paid to have the temple of Apollo at Delphi rebuilt, had chosen exile rather than life under Peisistratos and his sons. So they used their credit at Delphi to have the oracle advise the Spartans to 'set Athens free'. The first force sent by Spartē failed to dislodge Hippiās, but a subsequent expedition in 510 succeeded. Hippiās fled, and the Athenians were faced with reconstructing political life after tyranny.

1.25 With Hippiās removed, Athenian politics turned into a battle between different groupings. One Isagorās succeeded in having himself elected to the archonship, and his main opponent, the Alkmeōnid Kleisthenēs, decided to try a new tactic. He mobilised popular support. In a striking phrase, Hērodotos says that Kleisthenēs 'joined the People [*dēmos*] to the company of his followers' (*Histories* 5.66). What attracted general support was a massive programme of constitutional reform. Kleisthenēs created ten new artificial geographical *phūlai* (tribes). These cut across the natural boundaries of the four old kinship-based tribes and probably enabled men who had previously been refused citizenship to be enrolled. Each new tribe was composed of a number of village units, *dēmoi* (demes) (s. *dēmos*), some of them from the coastal region, some from the inland countryside, and some from close to or inside the town of Athens itself. These *dēmoi* had their own chief official (the *dēmarkhos*) and became the focus of the citizen's loyalties and attention. Each deme produced a quota of representatives to serve for each year on the new 'steering-committee' of 500 (the *boulē*). Such formalised involvement in the central organ of government gave the ordinary Athenian a new sense of participation, and a new feeling of self-confidence. Kleisthenēs presumably got his measures through the Assembly of the Athenian citizens (*ekklēsiā*), which (as we have seen) had existed in a formal manner since at least the time of Solōn. Here may be the clue to the real significance of his programme of reform. He gave the citizen *ekklēsiā* a new sense of power with which it could come to expect, and eventually to demand, that all matters of significance should be submitted to it for discussion and then decision. Although this opened the way for the radical democracy of the later fifth century, Kleisthenēs himself may well have expected that the old political élite would continue to exercise a predominant influence on the Assemby – as indeed it did. For the next eighty years, nearly all the leaders of the people came from established propertied families.

1.26 The Spartans were used to creating friendly alliances with states by having friends in those states in positions of power. Isagorās seems to have been the man they expected to take charge, and when Kleisthenēs' reforms threatened to leave Isagorās out in the cold, the Spartans prepared to invade again. However, Spartē could not gain sufficient support from her allies, and the invasion collapsed; further, in 506 the Athenians defeated further threats from the pro-Spartan Boiotians and Khalkidians. 'This proved', claimed Hērodotos, 'if proof were needed, how noble a thing it is to have equal rights to speak' (*Histories* 5.78). As far as Hērodotos was concerned, the effects of the new democracy were heady, invigorating and immediate. As it turned out, they needed to be.

Facing Persia: the Persian Wars

1.27 Up till now, the cities of the Greek mainland had had to face no threats other than those that arose internally or were posed by the ambitions of neighbouring Greek cities. Not so the Greeks who had settled on the coasts of Asia Minor. From c. 570 on, these cities faced successive threats from the major powers to their east – first Lȳdiā and then Persia. Under the vigorous leadership of Cyrus (Kūros) from 558, the Persians had taken over the kingdom of the Medes and gradually moved west. In 546 Cyrus defeated Kroisos, king of Lȳdiā, and followed up his victory by annexing the Greek cities of the coast. Hērodotos tells us that when the Spartans responded to this by sending an embassy to Cyrus to tell him to keep off the Greek communities, Cyrus replied in puzzlement, 'Who are the Spartans?' (*Histories* 1.152–3).

1.28 Cyrus' successors continued conquering the eastern Mediterranean, and in 512 Dareios crossed into Thrace and Makedōniā, the region north of the Greek mainland. The Persians ruled the Greek cities there by supporting tyrants who were effectively their puppets. But Persian financial demands were severe, and one of those tyrants, Aristagorās from Mīlētos, observing other cities being prepared to throw off tyranny elsewhere, saw the opportunity to gain general support for a revolt that was both anti-Persian and anti-tyrant. In 499 the Ionian cities threw out their tyrants and revolted from Persia; and Aristagorās went to Greece to get support for them. Hērodotos tells how Aristagorās failed to persuade the Spartans to help after he revealed that Susa, the Persian administrative capital, was three months' journey away. But Aristagorās had greater success at Athens and Eretriā, which sent ships (*Histories* 5.49–50, 97). The Athenians may have been influenced by the fact that their ex-tyrant Hippiās was in contact with the Persian court, perhaps hoping for support for an eventual restoration. The campaign that followed succeeded in burning Sardis, the old Lydian capital and local base for Persian administration. But when Persians arrived in force, the Greeks were defeated at sea. In 494 Mīlētos was destroyed, and the revolt collapsed. The interference of Athens and Eretriā may well have caused Dareios to become even more determined to bring about a scheme which he had probably been

1.8 A relief from the Persian city of Persepolis showing Dareios seated on his throne with Xerxēs standing beside him.

contemplating for many years – the subjugation of the European Greeks. He demanded from the Greek cities the signs of submission, gifts of earth and water. Some felt their interests lay in giving in. Others, including Athens, were defiant. Dareios, Hērodotos claims, had a servant who constantly reminded him 'Do not forget the Athenians' (*Histories* 5.105).

1.29 In 490 the Persians dispatched a fleet, said by Hērodotos to have numbered 600 ships, across the Aegean. Eretriā, on the island of Euboia, was betrayed to them and was burned. From there the Persians crossed to the nearest convenient landing place in north-east Attikē, the bay of Marathōn. The Athenians had to decide whether to await the enemy at Athens or to march out to meet them. The ten Athenian generals, one for each of the new Kleisthenic tribes, were under the nominal leadership of the *polemarkhos*, Kallimakhos. They decided to march. At the same time they sent one Pheidippidēs to Spartē to beg for help, but according to Hērodotos the Spartans claimed that they could not march out before the full moon; they eventually arrived just too late for the battle.

1.30 When the Athenians reached Marathōn, they waited for a few days. The most influential of the Athenian generals was Miltiadēs, son of the Kīmōn killed by the Peisistratids. This Miltiadēs was the veteran of a colourful career, who had spent much of his life as the ruler of the Thracian Kherronēsos (the Gallipoli peninsula), the vital strategic area commanding the entrance to the Hellēspont. It was he who urged the Athenians to attack at Marathōn. The Athenians, their line extended to avoid being enveloped by the superior numbers of the Persian forces, advanced at the double to close as swiftly as possible with the enemy. Although worsted in the centre, the Athenians on the right wing and their Plataian allies on the left were able to break down the Persian resistance. The Persians fled in confusion to their ships. It was a famous victory. The 192 Athenian dead were buried on the field under a vast mound. The remarkable achievement of the Athenians was extolled in song and painting; and for those

1.9 That the Kalliās against whom this *ostrakon* is written was being accused of Persian sympathies is clear from the drawing of a Persian archer which appears on one side of the sherd.

who were there, it was the high point of their lives. Aiskhylos, the tragic poet, whose brother died in an act of heroism during the battle, is said to have been proud of nothing in his life so much as having served at Marathōn on that day, as one of the *Marathōnomakhai*, 'Marathōn-fighters'.

1.31 The Persians were bound to be back. So the Athenians took action on two important fronts: first, to prevent internal squabbling weakening the city and giving the Persians a chance to intervene; and second, to increase their military strength. In 487 two political changes were made, designed to reduce the threat of the powerful individual: first, the nine *arkhontes* would in future be chosen not by election but by lot (6.23); and, second, the *ekklēsiā* could use the device of ostracism to rid the city of a man whose loyalty was suspect (4.12, 6.16). Ostracism, which some ancient sources say was invented by Kleisthenēs, was a negative election in which the person who got most votes had to leave the city for ten years. It got its name from the voting method: it was on sherds of pottery (*ostraka*, s. *ostrakon*) that Athenians wrote the names of those they wished to see banished. The first victim, Hipparkhos, was a relative of the Peisistratids, and confirmed people's fears by fleeing to Persia. That ostracism was resorted to regularly during the rest of the decade says much about Athenian nervousness.

1.32   One way the Athenians increased their military strength was to use the income from the silver mines at Laureion in southern Attikē (cf. 2.7). They had enjoyed significant revenue from these mines from the later part of the sixth century, but it appears that in this decade rich new veins were discovered. Traditionally, Greeks had distributed the profits from such a windfall among the citizen body; but the Athenians were persuaded to use the money to create the greatest fleet in Greece. By 480 this fleet was to number 200 ships. The author of this proposal was Themistoklēs, son of Neoklēs; and Thucydides tells us that, as *arkhōn* in 493/2, he had already displayed his interest in Athens' naval potential by beginning to transform the Peiraieus into a fortified dockyard and port for Athens (*Peloponnesian War* 1.93). Now, ten years later, he committed the Athenians to the development of the fleet. The decision to increase the fleet to ten times the number of ships sent to help in the Ionian revolt was not only important for the renewed war with Persia, but had a decisive effect on the future of Athenian foreign policy.

1.33   Dareios, delayed by revolts within the Persian empire, was never to get his revenge. He died in 486 and was succeeded by his son Xerxēs, who promptly made preparations for an overwhelming land force, to be accompanied closely by a large navy. No single Greek state on its own could expect to face up to such numbers. In the autumn of 481 and again in the spring of 480, a number of Greek states met at the Isthmus of Corinth to set aside their quarrels and create a league to defeat Persia. Many communities, particularly those in the north who were most vulnerable to Xerxēs' attacks, held aloof or submitted without a fight to Persia. In the end the names of just thirty-one of the many Greek states appeared on the victory monument dedicated at Delphi. At the first meetings of the new alliance it was agreed that Spartē, who with her extensive allies contributed the bulk of the land army, should assume overall command on both land and sea.

1.34   The strategic problem for the Greeks was to find a place at which to resist the invading Persian army where their own forces would not be hopelessly outnumbered by the enemy. They thought initially of making a stand in Thessaly, but failed to find a suitable site. In the end they decided on the narrow pass between the sea and mountain in central Greece, at the point on the mainland opposite the north of the island of Euboia. The peculiar geography and the presence of hot sulphur springs gave the place the name Thermopylai ('Hot Gates'). At sea the Greek fleet took up position nearby off Cape Artemision, at the north end of Euboia. They hoped that they would be able to prevent the Persian fleet making contact with the army as it moved south.

1.10 A bronze statuette of a hoplite.

1.35   The Greeks at Thermopylai were commanded by the Spartan king Leōnidās, although the Spartan contingent numbered only 300, raising doubts about how wholehearted was Spartan support for the expedition. Initially the site proved well chosen: Xerxēs' attempt to take the Greek position by frontal assault was a disastrous failure. For two days the Persians could not make any headway. A Greek traitor then informed them of a mountain track which led round to the rear of the Greek forces. The crack Persian forces, the Immortals, were sent round by this path and defeated the Phokian contingent who were guarding the way. Leōnidās, warned of the impending arrival of the Persians in his rear, dismissed most of the Greek forces, but remained in the pass with the Spartans and contingents from Thespiai and Thebes. Leōnidās' whole force was overwhelmed after a heroic defence. Acts of gallantry so often serve no long-term purpose except to inspire others by the remembrance of them. For Leōnidās and the Spartans, the lyric poet Simōnidēs produced a famous epitaph:

> Stranger, go tell the Spartans that here
> We lie, obedient to their orders. (Quoted in Hērodotos, *Histories* 7.228)

On sea the Greeks were aided by the weather. The Persian naval forces lost large numbers in a series of storms. They were then surprised by the Greek ships, which captured a number of ships off Artemision. After several further, indecisive engagements, news arrived of the defeat at Thermopylai. At that the Greek fleet set off south.

1.36 Themistoklēs managed to persuade the Athenians, faced with the imminent arrival of the Persians, to abandon their city and cross over to Troizēn, Aigīna and Salamīs. He argued that a Delphic oracle declaring that the Athenians were to put their trust in a 'wooden wall', meant that they were to trust their fleet. He then bullied the Greeks into stationing their fleet by the island of Salamīs. The Persians could not ignore or bypass the Greek fleet, and their fleet was lured into the narrow channel between Salamīs and the mainland where it was crushed after a fierce battle, but not before the Persians had sacked Athens itself.

1.37 It was now late September 480; so Xerxēs decided to retire the largest part of his army to the north of Greece to find supplies for the winter. He himself returned to Asia Minor, perhaps fearing that the news of his defeat at Salamīs would inspire revolts among the Ionian Greeks. The army was left in the control of his son-in-law, Mardonios, who, in the following spring, tried through diplomacy to detach Athens from the Greek alliance. Hērodotos records that the Athenians made a resolute reply: 'So long as the sun keeps his present course in the sky, we Athenians will never make peace with Xerxēs.' To the Spartans Hērodotos has the Athenians explain their determination to resist with words which indicated both their determination to avenge the damage that the Persians had done to their city and also their pride in what it meant to be a *Hellēn* (a Greek):

> If we were offered all the gold in the world, or the most beautiful and fertile land imaginable, we would never be willing to join our common enemy and be party to the enslavement of Greece . . . first, there is the burning and destruction of our temples and the images of our gods which compels us to exact from the perpetrators the greatest vengeance we can rather than come to terms with them. Then there is our Greek heritage – the bond of blood and language, our holy altars and sacrifices, and our common way of life, which it would ill become Athens to betray . . . as long as a single Athenian survives there will be no terms with Xerxēs. (Hērodotos, *Histories* 8.144)

The costs of loyalty were paid immediately: Athens was evacuated once more and reoccupied by the Persians, who sacked the city once again and then retired into Boiōtiā.

1.38 The desperate appeals of the Athenians to Spartē eventually had their effect. Despite initial wavering, the Spartans put together the largest force ever to be sent out of the Peloponnese. It included 5,000 Spartans and was commanded by Pausaniās, who was acting as regent for Leōnidās' young son Pleistarkhos. This Peloponnesian force linked up with the Athenians and eventually faced the

Persians in the territory of the Boiotian town of Plataia, where Mount Kithairōn slopes down to the river Asōpos. For nearly two weeks the Greek troops manoeuvred under constant attacks of Persian cavalry. Finally Pausaniās attempted a complex night march to a better position closer to the town of Plataia. Dawn found the Greek units in confusion, and Mardonios was tempted to attack. The Spartans and the troops from Tegeā bore the brunt and with impressive discipline drove the Persians back. Mardonios was killed, the Persians turned and fled, and the Persian threat to the Greek mainland was over.

1.39 A Greek fleet, much smaller than the one assembled in the previous year, and commanded by the Spartan king Leōtykhidās, took the fight across the Aegean. Hērodotos tells how an envoy from Samos on a secret mission encouraged the thought that the very appearance of a Greek fleet would cause Greeks in Asia to revolt from Persia. The Greeks sailed to Samos but the Persians, with the memory of Salamīs too fresh in their minds, were unwilling to face the Greek ships at sea: they had beached their ships at Mykalē, a promontory on the mainland opposite Samos, and joined the land forces already stationed there. Leōtykhidās landed his own forces and stormed the Persian position. Persian resistance collapsed. Many of the Ionian contingents in the Persian forces deserted and helped the Greeks. Hērodotos described it as a second Ionian revolt.

Athens, the continuing struggle with Persia, and the Delian League

1.40 The war with Persia did not end with the victories of 480/79; it continued for decades (see further 6.71–4). After Mykalē, the Greeks held a debate at Samos over what was to be done. The Spartans, anxious not to be committed to the long-term defence of the Greeks of Asia, suggested that the Ionians should be transported back to mainland Greece and resettled. However, the Athenians opposed such radical action and began to form an alliance of Aegean states against Persia. During the winter of 479 the Athenians laid siege to Persian-controlled Sestos in the Hellespont. Hērodotos ends his *Histories* (9.114–20) with the account of how they took the town and crucified the Persian commander. The story is taken up by Thucydides, who begins his account of the growth of Athenian power at this point. He tells how in the following summer, 478, the Spartan Pausaniās took control of the Greek fleet and sailed to Cyprus. He won over most of the island from the Persians and then returned to the Hellespont, where he succeeded in driving the Persian garrison from Byzantion. However, the Ionian Greeks found his behaviour extravagant and dictatorial, and appealed to the Athenians to take on the leadership of the campaign. So in the winter of 478/7, at a meeting on the island of Dēlos, Athens and the other allies from the Aegean founded a voluntary league, which modern scholars have dubbed the 'Delian League', and of which Athens emerged as the effective head. One of the avowed objects of the new League was 'to compensate themselves for their losses by ravaging the territory of the king of Persia' (Thucydides, *Peloponnesian War* 1.96). To this end each member was expected to contribute each year either ships or a cash payment (tribute – *phoros*) which was to be supervised by Athenian officials called *Hellēnotamiai* ('treasurers of the Greeks'). The deviser of this scheme was the Athenian leader Aristeidēs. To him fell the task of drawing up an assessment of the contributions to be made by each state and deciding which states should contribute ships, and which tribute in money. Meanwhile, Spartan Pausaniās was doing secret deals with the Persians . . .

1.41   The question of the leadership of the continuing campaign was not the only one which caused tension between the Athenians and the Spartans. The Athenians set about the immediate repair of their city walls, using for the purpose whatever stone came to hand, including sculptures thrown down by the Persians (8.91). Spartē had always been unfortified, and the Spartans protested and proposed that all city fortifications in Greece should be dismantled as a gesture of goodwill between the Greek states. Themistoklēs used various delaying tactics to divert the Spartans until the work of rebuilding was well under way. He then presented them with a *fait accompli*, and stated defiantly that the Spartans should recognise that the Athenians were capable of making up their own minds about their own interests and those of people in general (2.31). The walls built at this time encompassed only the town of Athens itself, but twenty years later the walls were extended to join the city of Athens to the harbour at the Peiraieus. From that point on, the Athenians could supply themselves from the sea whatever hostile army might occupy their territory.

1.42   The two episodes, taking over leadership of the Greek campaign against Persia and fortifying Athens itself, reveal two rather different foreign policy priorities: the former, aggressive use of the fleet against Persia, the latter, suspicion of Spartē and the power of its Peloponnesian League. When Athens decided to concentrate on its anti-Persian policy in the 470s, Themistoklēs (who also wanted actively to oppose Spartē) was ostracised; when Spartē decided to let Athens pursue that policy and not intervene, Pausaniās was recalled to Spartē and died in disgrace in mysterious circumstances. The historian Diodōros of Sicily, writing more than four centuries later but probably on the basis of the work of the fourth-century historian Ephoros of Kȳmē, relates a story not told by Thucydides that the Spartans were close to declaring war on Athens at this time. But they were dissuaded by one of their elders, named Hetoimaridās. He urged the view that Athens' naval role and Spartē's role on land could be complementary, not in competition one with another (Diodōros 11.50). Whether or not that debate took place in Spartē, both sides effectively decided to live and let live – at least for the immediate future.

1.43 The forces of the Delian League were soon in action. The leader and inspiration of the League's war against Persia was Kīmōn, son of Miltiadēs, the Athenian general at Marathōn. Half a millennium later Plutarch would claim that 'No one humbled the Great King more than Kīmōn. He gave him no rest when he had been driven from Greece, but followed hard on his heels before the barbarian could recover his breath and make a stand' (*Life of Kīmōn* 12). About 476 he captured Ēiōn near the mouth of the river Strȳmōn, the last major Persian stronghold west of the Hellēspont. Perhaps in the following year, 475, Kīmōn captured the island of Skȳros in the north Aegean, a pirate base. A huge skeleton, discovered on the island, was claimed to be the bones of the Athenian hero Thēseus; and soon after, Athenians were settled there. But this campaign had nothing to do with the Persians, and the allies might well have wondered whether removing and punishing the Persians was Athens' sole aim. When in the late 470s Athens used force to compel the city of Karystos, on the island of Euboia, to join the League, it became clear that Athens had targets other than Persia in view. One island, Naxos, proceeded to try to leave the League before it was too late. Thucydides comments that it became the first allied city to be enslaved, 'contrary to established custom' – because the Delian League was supposed to be a union of the free (Thucydides, *Peloponnesian War* 1.98).

1.44 At some time after 469 Kīmōn carried the fight against the Persians to Asia Minor. He drove them from the coastal regions of Kariā and Lykiā and then at the river Eurymedōn, which flows through Pamphȳliā to the south coast of Asia Minor, he decisively defeated the Persian forces on land and sea. 200 Phoenician ships, which constituted the main part of the Persian Mediterranean fleet, were destroyed. They represented Xerxēs' last real attempt to restore his fortunes. But this battle did not bring about the disbanding of the Delian League. When in 465 Thasos tried to leave the League because the Athenians wanted control over a gold mine they owned on the Greek mainland, the Athenians defeated Thasos' fleet, laid siege to the town, imposed a massive fine and destroyed its walls.

Athenian politics, Spartē, and the growth of Athenian imperialism

1.45 Themistoklēs' ostracism was not the only ostracism in the 470s – a sign that the aggressive foreign policy did not command universal support at home. That there was much disagreement in domestic politics emerges only at the end of the 460s (and from rather poor sources, because Thucydides does not mention many of these events). In rapid succession, Ephialtēs took away some of the powers of the highly influential Areopagus Council, Kīmōn was ostracised, and Ephialtēs was assassinated. In Aiskhylos' play *Eumenides*, performed in 458, the Areopagus plays an important role. This suggests that

1.11 On this cup from the end of the first quarter of the fifth century Thēseus is seen being greeted by Athēnē. Thēseus was the only hero of whom Athens made significant political use.

relatively minor judicial reforms like Ephialtēs' that increased the powers of the People's law-courts caused a great deal of public excitement. The sources often depict Ephialtēs as an associate of Periklēs, the man with whom the achievements of classical Athens are most strongly associated. Whatever Periklēs' role in Ephialtēs' reforms or the attack on Kīmōn, it is certainly the case that in the 450s Periklēs pursued three further constitutional reforms, at least two of which are linked to Ephialtēs' actions: the introduction of pay for juries; the abolition of the ban on men in the third rank of Solōn's wealth classes, *zeugītai*, serving as archons; and the law requiring Athenian citizens in future to have a mother, as well as a father, who was an Athenian citizen. This last reform is the hardest to understand. Some have seen this as aimed at the Athenian élite, who were inclined to seek out wealthy women from other cities to be their brides. But since Athenian soldiers and archons were increasingly mingling with people from the Delian League, this ruling would surely affect the non-élites as well.

1.46   The tensions in Athens which led to Kīmōn's ostracism were not purely about constitutional matters. In the late 460s Spartē had suffered a disastrous earthquake, followed by a revolt of the helot population. Spartē called on her allies for support, but when Kīmōn led an Athenian contingent to help, the assistance was dismissed. The Athenians took offence, broke all formal links with

Spartē, and sought alliance with Spartē's old enemy, Argos, and with the Thessalians. This constituted a major policy defeat for Kīmōn, who had named one of his sons Lakedaimonios ('Spartan') and who seems to have been the Athenian champion of the idea of 'dual hegemony', i.e. that both Athens and Spartē should live and let live and not interfere in each other's 'empire'.

1.47   After splitting with Spartē, Athens almost immediately took action against Spartē's allies. They fought the Peloponnesians both by land, in the Argolid and then at Megara, and by sea, in the Saronic Gulf. There they laid siege to the island of Aigīna, eventually taking it and incorporating it into the Delian League. In 457/6 the Athenians faced a force including Spartan troops at Tanagra in Boiōtiā and were defeated; but as soon as the Peloponnesian force had withdrawn, they marched out against the Boiotians again, beat them, and proceeded to take over both Boiōtiā and Phōkis. So Athens too had now acquired a land empire, together with a confidence sufficient for them to launch an expedition against the Spartan heartland. Under their general Tolmidēs they sailed round the Peloponnese, set fire to the Spartan port of Gytheion and made raids on numerous other spots. Periklēs led a further expedition in 454, attacking areas in and around the Corinthian Gulf.

1.48   These activities in Greece itself did not reduce Athenian attacks against the Persians. A casualty list probably to be dated to 460 or 459 lists 175 casualties from just one of the ten Athenian tribes, and identifies the theatres of war in which they had died as Cyprus, Egypt, Phoenicia, Halieis, Aigīna and Megara. Athens became involved with Egypt after it revolted from Persian control. A force of 200 ships of the Delian League sailed to the Nile Delta, and to start with they had significant success. For six years they maintained a hold in the Delta; but in 454 the Persians destroyed the whole force, a major disaster for the Athenians.

1.49   Up until that point the League's anti-Persian activity had been exclusively directed at liberating Greek communities from Persian rule. So involvement in Egypt can be seen as a new policy for the Delian League. It is true that there had long been Greeks settled in Egypt, in particular at Naukratis, but the intervention in the 450s was not closely targeted at them. Like the action in the 470s at Karystos and in the 450s at Aigīna, the action in Egypt looks to be an attempt to extend the area of the League's influence – and increasingly this meant the area of Athenian influence. One indication of this shifting emphasis is that in 454 the Delian League treasury was moved from Dēlos to the Akropolis in Athens. From that date a quota of one-sixtieth of the cities' money tribute was dedicated to the goddess Athēnē. The lists of the amounts were inscribed on stone, and fragments of many of these lists have survived. They testify to the extent of the League, which now included most of the islands of the Aegean and the cities of the northern coast of the Aegean and down the coast of Asia Minor. They also almost certainly testify to unrest among the League members. The reason is that the names of certain allies are absent from the earliest lists, in a pattern that cannot be put down to incomplete preservation of those lists. There was never a single point at which the voluntary league became an empire sustained by force, and many Athenian allies long continued to support her, but by fits and starts the balance of power had shifted – to Athens.

1.50   In 451/0 Kīmōn returned from his ten-year banishment and was immediately elected general. He led a further campaign against the Persians in Cyprus but died fighting there in 449. After this, Thucydides provides no further account of hostilities against Persia. But, oddly, although he indicates that there was a truce between the Athenians and the Peloponnesians in 451, he never mentions a *formal* peace treaty with the Persians. From the fourth century onwards, however, historians debated whether a formal agreement had in fact been made. The balance of probabilities is that the Athenian Kalliās did indeed negotiate a peace treaty – 'the peace of Kalliās' – under which the Persians agreed to keep out of the Aegean, and the Athenians not to intervene in the eastern Mediterranean.

1.51   In all this there seems to be a link between Athenian discussions about their constitution – who should actually make the decisions in the state? – and their growing imperial power (see further 6.70ff.). Perhaps the most significant aspect of this connection was the creation of a belief in the minds of ordinary citizens of Athens on two important issues: first, that they were entitled to enjoy the prosperity which came with the fruits of empire; second, that the success of the self-confident, radical democratic system which emerged at Athens in the middle of the century was intimately bound up with the possession of the empire. This belief, justified or unjustified as it might be, dominated Athenian thinking for over a century. It also brought about a building programme which has dominated the Athenian skyline ever since. The Parthenōn, begun in 447, was the first, the largest, the most expensive and the most elaborately decorated building in the lavish construction project. This provided the Akropolis with a monumental gateway (Propylaia) and a suite of new temples (those of Athēnē Nīkē and of Athēnē Polias – the so-called Erekhtheion (see fig. 1.5) – as well as the Parthenōn itself); the *agorā* with a new stoā (of Zeus); and the Athenians with enhanced cultural facilities through building in the theatre of Dionȳsos and construction of the Ōdeion of Periklēs. Ancient sources name the architects of some of these buildings, in particular Iktīnos for the Parthenōn and Mnēsiklēs for the Propylaia; and we are able to gain some impression of their particular artistic signatures from the buildings they constructed. Ancient sources also associate Pheidiās with the sculptures of the Parthenōn. But the major item, the gold and ivory cult statue which set a new standard for images of the gods, is lost, and the degree of Pheidiās' responsibility for the architectural sculpture is much debated. There is little doubt that, from the first, these buildings made a statement about Athenian power and superiority. Through them, Athens presented herself as a city fit to be the leader of an empire. This was not an uncontro-

1.12 The Athenian Akropolis seen from the west.

versial matter, even in Athens itself. Although Thucydides the historian makes no allusion to it, later sources tell of strong opposition to the policy from another Thucydides (son of Melēsiās), ending in his ostracism. It is notable that the Athenians seem to have been careful not to take the funds to finance the project directly from the tribute which came from her allies.

1.52   The superiority asserted by the new buildings and their sculpture was in reality repeatedly challenged. In 447 the Boiotians defeated the Athenians at the battle of Korōneia, and Athens' control over Boiōtiā and Phōkis was lost for good. The island of Euboia revolted in 446 and, when Periklēs crossed with a force, Megara on the mainland seized the opportunity to massacre the Athenian garrisons there. At the same time the Spartan king Pleistoanax led a Spartan army into Attikē. In response, Periklēs rushed back from Euboia. A major battle seemed imminent. But Pleistoanax seems to have been primarily concerned to prevent Athens intervening in Megara's revolt, and once this had been achieved, he retired without coming near Athens itself. This withdrawal enabled Periklēs to return to Euboia and put down the rebellion there. There were those in Spartē who felt that Pleistoanax had missed his chance in failing to press home his attack. Perhaps the Spartan king had already begun the negotiations with Periklēs which in the winter of 446 were to lead to the signing of a thirty years' peace between Spartē and Athens. The basis of the peace was that both sides accepted the status quo. Athens gave up her claims to a land empire in central Greece and ceased to interfere directly in the Peloponnese. Nevertheless, she did hold on to Aigīna and a base in the Corinthian Gulf at Naupaktos. That in reality the peace settled nothing was immediately clear to at least some at Spartē, who continued to resent the way in which Athens had muscled them out of the limelight since the Persian Wars. Unable to turn their wrath on Athens, they turned it on their own king. In 445 King Pleistoanax was prosecuted and went into exile for his actions in the previous year's invasion of Attikē; the rumour went round that the only explanation of his failure to follow up his advantage was bribery by Periklēs.

1.53 The Thirty Years' Peace lasted only half that time. When Thucydides came to try to explain the outbreak of war in 432, he pointed to Spartan fear of growing Athenian power. The years from 446 to 432 saw repeated challenges to Athenian control, but from each challenge Athens emerged strengthened. Perhaps the most serious came in 440. Samos, one of the most powerful of all the allies, revolted from Athens. The Athenians sent a major expedition under all ten *stratēgoi* (generals), including Periklēs. Samos was crushed. Later writers alleged that some Samians were executed with extreme cruelty. The Athenians forced the Samians to repay the enormous cost of the campaign. But from that point on, Samos proved extremely loyal and was a vital source of support for the Athenians in the later stages of the Peloponnesian War. Thucydides (*Peloponnesian War* 1.40) reveals just how belligerent the mood still was at Spartē when he has the Corinthians claim that the Spartans themselves voted for war against Athens in support of Samos, but were unable to carry a majority of the members of the Peloponnesian League with them.

1.54 Having survived the Samian crisis, the Athenians proceeded to extend their sphere of influence. They had long attempted to establish a base for themselves on the coast of the north Aegean. In 438/7, they finally succeeded and settled a colony at Amphipolis, at a crucial crossing of the river Strȳmōn. Enigmatic entries in some Athenian tribute lists from the late 430s suggest that various local communities saw that the writing was on the wall, and voluntarily decided to become tributary allies of Athens. More or less at the same time, the Athenians also sent a large fleet under Periklēs into the Black Sea. The expedition not only succeeded in expelling the tyrant of Sinōpē, on the south coast, and settling Athenians there, but also in bringing the city of Olbiā, in the north-west Black Sea, into the empire. Four years later, the island of Kerkȳra (Corcyra, modern Corfu) in north-west Greece, which had become involved in a dispute, and indeed open warfare, with her mother city, Corinth, sought a defensive alliance with Athens. The Athenians accepted. While involved in this area of north-west Greece, the Athenians also entered an alliance with the Akarnanians.

1.55   As long as Athens extended her power to the east, she largely avoided imping-
ing on the world in which Spartē and her allies had particular interests,
though Samos proved sensitive because Spartē had long had a special relationship with that particular Ionian island. But both in the north Aegean and
in north-west Greece, states other than Spartē had interests – particularly
Corinth. Indeed, Athens' defensive alliance with Kerkȳra very nearly brought
direct conflict between them. Then, in the winter of 433/2, Athens and
Corinth clashed on a question of jurisdiction concerning Poteidaia, a city in
Khalkidikē in northern Greece. This was both a colony of Corinth and a
tribute-paying member of the Delian League. Corinth now urged her fellow
members of the Peloponnesian League to join her in making protests against
Athens to the Spartans. Aigīna and Megara, the latter banned by Athens
from her *agorā* and the ports of the empire, added their own complaints to
those of Corinth. What was the use of the Peloponnesian League, if Spartē
was not willing to uphold the interests of its members? Corinth added: 'Do
not force us in despair to join a different alliance.' The threat to the continued existence of the Peloponnesian League was probably unnecessary. The
Spartan king Arkhidāmos did counsel caution; but the Spartans, encouraged
by one of the annually elected chief magistrates (*ephors*), Sthenelāidās,
ignored him. Once Spartē was ready for war, her allies were eager to join in.
It is a curious irony that the king who recognised that this would be a difficult
war to win gave his name to the first ten years of fighting, which are often
known as the Arkhidamian War.

The Peloponnesian War: 1. The Arkhidamian War, 431–421

1.56   Thanks to the work of Thucydides, we have more detailed knowledge of the
Peloponnesian War than of any other Greek war. He says that he took care
to find out about the actions of the war from its very beginning, and questioned eyewitnesses in order to discover an accurate account. He ordered
events by summers and winters, giving a detailed view of how they unfolded.
All ancient and modern accounts of the war essentially reproduce
Thucydides' own account – an account that begins not with action by Spartē
but with action by the Thebans. The town of Plataia, an old ally of Athens,
had stalwartly refused to be incorporated into the Boiotian confederacy. One
night in the early spring of 431, a force of Thebans was let into Plataia by
sympathisers. However, the surprise attack failed, and the Plataians captured
and subsequently killed the Thebans. In response to urgent appeals, the
Athenians sent a force to help Plataia. Over the next four years the Thebans
continued action against the city, and from 429 they had the help of the
Spartans in besieging it (6.29). Despite the ingenious counter-measures which
the Plataians took to defend their city, they were eventually forced to capitu-
late in 427. Curiously, Athens had done little to aid them. At Theban

insistence, revenge was exacted upon the defenders. Each prisoner was asked 'Have you done anything to aid the Spartans and allies in the present war?' When, inevitably, he could offer no answer, he was taken off to execution. The city was destroyed. The fate of Plataia illustrates one of the most unpleasant aspects of this war. Plataia stands at the head of a lengthy roll call of small communities which were caught up in the fighting and suffered grievously at the hands of the protagonists. If the Plataians suffered at the hands of the Spartans, others, like the people of Skiōnē and Mēlos, suffered equally at the hands of the Athenians.

1.57   There could be no question of besieging Athens: its Long Walls linked the town with the Peiraieus and access to the sea, so it could not be starved out. The Spartans therefore decided on regular invasions of Athenian territory in early summer to cut down the ripening grain and devastate the countryside. The longest of these invasions, in 430, lasted probably no more than 40 days; yet 'at the beginning of the war some thought that the Athenians might survive a year; others reckoned two; no one reckoned they would last more than that' (Thucydides, *Peloponnesian War* 7.28). Thucydides suggests that the Spartan tactic almost paid off: many Athenians were distressed to have to leave their villages and frustrated by being forced to stay within the walls, watching their territory being devastated (2.21). Thucydides implies that, had it not been for the influence of Periklēs, the Athenians would have met in *ekklēsiā* and voted to go out and fight the invaders. But Periklēs' strategy was to avoid combat in the field, and to rely on command of the sea and maintaining the loyalty of the Delian League allies. Sailing round the Peloponnese, landing, causing damage, and departing, was acceptable since it carried little risk; facing up to the full infantry forces of the Peloponnesian League was not. But this policy became even more difficult to maintain when the quality of life for the Athenians in the city deteriorated further: at the time of the second invasion in 430, a virulent plague, the medical identity of which has been long debated, broke out in Athens, and spread rapidly through the population. Thucydides himself caught the plague, but survived to give a vivid account of the suffering. Very large numbers of Athenians died, and the imminence of death led to something close to a collapse of law and order. The disaster almost broke the Athenian spirit. There was a reaction against Periklēs, who was tried and fined. An attempt was made to open peace negotiations with Spartē, but nothing came of it.

1.58   In 429 Periklēs died, himself a victim of the plague. The passing of the man who had been a major force in democratic politics for thirty years was bound to have a profound effect on Athens. Contemporary sources present Periklēs' death as marking a sea change, after which things could never be the same, only worse. In the opinion of the historian Thucydides, the leaders who succeeded Periklēs, none being obviously superior to any other, tried to win the favour of the majority by flattering their whims. This view accords closely with that of the comic playwright Aristophanēs, who from 427 produced plays which satirised and ridiculed the leaders of the people during the Peloponnesian War. It is Aristophanēs, also, who provides a clue to the source of this prejudice – snobbishness. The demagogue, Kleōn, is nicknamed the 'Tanner', while Hyperbolos, another leader, is the 'Lamp-maker'. The point of these sneers is that the majority of leaders of the people before Periklēs had been from traditional families whose wealth was in land; but after the death of Periklēs, the new breed of politicians came from more recently enriched families, whose wealth derived from activities other than farming. These new politicians tended to be well educated (particularly in the new, sophisticated skills of rhetoric (8.18–21)), but did not necessarily expect to lead troops in the field as well as voters in the *ekklēsiā*. In the immediate aftermath of Periklēs' death, no radically new strategies emerged for the conduct of the war, but the policy of endurance was no easy vote winner.

1.59   In 428 Mytilēnē led the island of Lesbos in revolt from the Athenian empire (except for the town of Methymnē, which had a democratic government). The Athenians blockaded the island and, despite the promise from Spartē of a fleet to help, in 427 Mytilēnē was forced to surrender. The initial reaction of the Athenian *ekklēsiā* was severe: a vote to execute all adult males and sell the women and children into slavery. However, overnight opinion changed, and on the next day the debate was reopened. Kleōn was intransigent; terror, he argued, was a necessary weapon for an imperial power. One Diodotos, however, a figure not otherwise known, was able to convince the majority that a more moderate policy would be more in Athens' interests. The *ekklēsiā* changed its mind and decided to confine its most severe punishment to the minority in Mytilēnē who could be proved to have encouraged the revolt. News of this change of heart, carried across the Aegean by trireme, reached Mytilēnē just in time to prevent the general massacre (2.20). The whole incident has been used to illustrate the fickleness of the Athenian democratic *ekklēsiā*. We might rather observe that what is exceptional here is that a city should admit to an error of judgement and rectify it.

1.60   While Athenian action in the Aegean was essentially defensive, they continued to extend their interests in north-west Greece – in the Corinthian Gulf, Ambrakiā and Akarnāniā. In 429 the Athenian admiral, Phormiōn, operating from the Athenian base at Naupaktos on the northern shore of the entrance to the gulf, was able to inflict two surprise defeats on larger Peloponnesian fleets (cf. 7.40–1). Although Phormiōn disappeared from the scene in the next year (it is not known what happened to him), the Athenians kept up their probing in the region. In 426 the Athenian general Dēmosthenēs tried to offer greater protection to Naupaktos by invading Aitōliā. He was defeated, and it was only with difficulty that the Athenian survivors struggled back to Naupaktos. Later in the year Dēmosthenēs was able to redeem himself, when a Peloponnesian force first attempted to attack Naupaktos and then attacked Amphilokhian Argos. At Olpai Dēmosthenēs, commanding both Athenian and local troops, outwitted the Peloponnesians and inflicted on them the first major defeat of the war. A significant role in the success was played by light-armed troops.

1.61 Even before the war, Athens seems to have begun looking for support even further west – to Sicily. They had made alliances with Leontīnoi and Rhēgion certainly by 433, and perhaps a decade or more earlier. In 427 Leontīnoi appealed to Athens for help against Syracuse, and Athens responded by sending a small fleet. It may be that she was motivated in part by the hope of cutting grain supplies to the Peloponnese from Sicily. But it is likely that Athens had greater ambitions in this direction, which would explain their frustrated reaction when, in 424, the Sicilian states temporarily settled their disputes and sent the Athenian forces home – all three Athenian generals were punished on their return.

1.62 In 425, when the Athenians sent a new fleet to reinforce their men in Sicily, an incident occurred which, for the first time in this war, gave the Athenians the upper hand against the Spartans. The Athenian fleet under the generals Sophoklēs and Eurymedōn rounded the southern Peloponnese and was forced by bad weather into the great natural harbour of Pylos in Messēniā, where the long island of Sphaktēriā protected the bay. Dēmosthenēs, who had been so active in the north-west in the previous two years, was accompanying the fleet, even though he held no official post. He realised the potential of Pylos as a base from which the Messenian helots might be inspired to revolt from Spartē. He was left behind with a small contingent to build a fort at the northern end of the bay. The Spartans were so disturbed by the news, that they called off their normal invasion of Attikē early and rushed troops to the area. The Spartan forces tried to blockade the Athenians. Four hundred and twenty hoplites and their helots were landed on the island of Sphaktēriā to deny it to the Athenians. They then tried an unsuccessful direct assault on Pylos, during which the Spartan Brasidās, leading a landing party, distinguished himself, was wounded, and lost consciousness and his shield.

1.63 The Athenian fleet turned back to help Dēmosthenēs. They entered the bay and defeated the Peloponnesian fleet. The Spartans, to their horror, now realised that their troops were cut off on the island of Sphaktēriā, and their first reaction was to make an offer of peace. The Athenians rejected this, regarding themselves in a strong position, but their blockade of the Spartan forces on Sphaktēriā was not completely effective and the whole operation dragged on indecisively. In Athens Kleōn attacked the incompetence of the generals, incautiously claiming that he could have done better himself. Nīkiās, one of the board of *stratēgoi*, in an act of complete irresponsibility, said that he could have the job, if he wanted it, and Kleōn was forced to make good his boast. Thucydides, whose contempt for Kleōn was undisguised, claimed that the Athenians calculated that whatever happened they stood to gain: either they did indeed capture the Spartans, or they would be rid of Kleōn (Thucydides, *Peloponnesian War* 4.28.5). Kleōn chose to take the experienced Dēmosthenēs with him, and together they led a successful assault on the island. Two hundred and ninety-two hoplites from the Spartan forces were taken as prisoners, of whom some 120 were Spartiates. This was a most serious loss to Spartē. Until peace was made in 421, their every action was governed by fears about the fate of the Spartan prisoners at Athens. Spartē's first action was to stop the invasions of Attikē and to renew offers of peace.

1.64 The success at Pylos affected both Athenian military actions and her attitude to her own allies. They launched a major expedition against Corinth involving 2,000 men and eighty ships under Nīkiās as general, and the same number of men and sixty ships were then used by Nīkiās to take the island of Kytherā, a key position for controlling shipping into and out of the Spartan port of Gytheion. While these actions were taking place in the field, at home a complete reassessment of the tribute paid by Athens' allies was undertaken. Up until this point tribute levels had remained relatively static, barring changes occasioned by revolt or by the Athenians imposing settlements of Athenian citizens. Now massive tribute increases were imposed – regularly threefold, in some cases fivefold. The sanctions which accompanied these increases were also strict. This increase in tribute followed legislation in the previous year to tighten up on tribute payments, and it was almost certainly accompanied by the introduction of a law obliging allies to use the same weights, measures, and silver coins as the Athenians (6.80). The economic advantage to Athens of this 'Standards Decree' was probably small, but the symbolic force was large: in future it would be Athēnē's owl, not their own city's stamp, that Athens' allies would find on the coins that they used. Together, these decrees mark a clear change in Athens' attitude to her allies – a change which the Athenians themselves detected, though not all welcomed, at least to judge from the critical presentation of the same bullying tone in Aristophanēs' *Knights*, which was put on in 424. Such is Thucydides' single-minded focus on military and diplomatic history, however, that he makes no mention of any of these Athenian dealings with their allies.

1.65 The summer and autumn of 424 saw Athens continue further with its aggressive policies and attacks on its neighbours – but without the same success. The Athenians had been regularly invading the territory of Megara, but now they succeeded in occupying Nīsaia, the port of Megara, though their attempt to take Megara itself or dislodge its oligarchic government was defeated. Then the Athenians entered into secret negotiations with democratic elements in Boiōtiā, who had been excluded from power since 447, with a view to creating rebellions in the cities of Boiōtiā and overthrowing the Boiotian confederacy. But the plan went wrong. In a large-scale battle at Dēlion, in which Sōkratēs was one of the combatants, the Boiotians defeated the Athenians.

1.66 The defeat at Dēlion was a blow to the renewed confidence of Athens, but it required damage to her existing empire, and not just to her ambitions, if

Athens was to be made to seek peace. There was one area of the Athenian empire which was vulnerable to Spartan intervention – the cities in northeast Greece, on Khalkidikē, which could be reached overland from the Peloponnese. In 424 an appeal came to Spartē from cities in this area which were ready to revolt. At Spartē the leading advocate for intervention was the enterprising Brasidās, who had already distinguished himself in action at Pylos and elsewhere. He was given a force of 700 helots, who were armed as hoplites; to them he added another thousand mercenaries. Significantly, no Spartiates were to be sent so far from home. Brasidās marched north and began to win over cities of the Athenian empire by a mixture of personal charm, persuasion and threat. His most notable success was the capture of Amphipolis. The Athenian general, a man put in charge because of his family connections with the region, was the historian Thucydides. He was held responsible for not getting his troops to Amphipolis in time to save it, and was exiled. His exile had the advantage that he was able to tour Greece to gather material from both sides for the history of the war; the circumstances of his own military failure mean that in his history he pays particular attention to the importance of timely action.

1.67   Under the shock of Brasidās' continuing success, the Athenians agreed to a truce for one year in 423. The Spartans at home hoped that this would lead to a more permanent peace. In Khalkidikē the priorities looked different, and the truce was not observed there. At the end of the truce, in 422, Kleōn, as one of the generals, took a force to the north to counter Brasidās. The main goal was Amphipolis. Outside the city Kleōn was drawn into battle. The Athenians were routed and Kleōn killed. Brasidās, who had shown himself to be one of the most vigorous and charismatic of Spartan generals, also died from his wounds. These events served to illustrate something which had been evident since the outbreak of hostilities: this war could not be won. Neither side was likely to lose except by some act of gross stupidity. So in the winter of 422/1, both sides began to think seriously of peace. The Spartans wanted back their men who had been captured at Pylos; Athens wanted Amphipolis returned. In 421, a fifty years' peace was agreed on the basis of the return by both sides of most places which had been captured by fighting. The main Athenian negotiator was Nīkiās who gave his name to the settlement. The Peace of Nīkiās brought an end to the Arkhidamian war.

The Peloponnesian War: 2. From the Peace of Nīkiās to defeat in Sicily, 421–413

1.68   Unfortunately, if the war had been unwinnable, the peace was unworkable. The negotiations had been carried on between Athens and Spartē. It was left to Spartē to persuade her allies to accept the agreement. Although she got a majority vote in favour of the peace in the Peloponnesian League, the major states, like Corinth and Boiōtiā, simply refused to play along. They saw no advantages in the peace for them. In an attempt to emphasise the new position in inter-city relations, Spartē and Athens followed up their peace with an alliance, and there was immense relief at Spartē as Athens returned the men captured at Pylos. At Athens, by contrast, there was increasing irritation that Spartē was not obliging her allies to fulfil her side of the Peace of Nīkiās, and Athens continued to hold onto Pylos itself.

1.69   To the discontent of Spartē's allies there was a new factor in the complex diplomacy of the next few years. The thirty-year peace treaty between Spartē and Argos ran out. Argos, which had not suffered at all in the war, became the natural leader for those groups which were dissatisfied with the actions of the two great powers. For a time it looked as though a new grouping of powers, including Corinth and Argos, might emerge to challenge Spartē. But at Athens the discontent felt at the one-sidedness of the Peace of Nīkiās was brilliantly exploited by the most flamboyant personality in Athens in this period, Alkibiadēs, son of Kleiniās. He persuaded the Athenians that there was an advantage to be had from exploiting the dissatisfaction in the Peloponnese. Alkibiadēs was noble by birth and after his father's death had been brought up in the household of Periklēs. He is presented by Thucydides as a man primarily motivated by the pursuit of personal glory. For Alkibiadēs, the democracy of Athens was the stage on which he was playing the starring role; no one was to be allowed to elbow him from the limelight.

1.70   In 420, without repudiating her agreements with Spartē, Athens made an alliance with Argos, Ēlis and Mantineia. In 419 Alkibiadēs spent the summer in the Peloponnese with a small force, intervening in the affairs of a number of small states, and encouraging Argos to attack Epidauros, a Spartan ally. In 418 King Agis of Spartē led an expedition against Argos. When the Argives, encouraged by Alkibiadēs, broke the truce which they had agreed with Agis, a major confrontation developed between the Spartans and the allies of Argos, including Mantineia and Athens. On the plain of Mantineia in eastern Arkadiā, in a battle of confused movement, the Spartans overwhelmed the forces opposed to them (7.8–15). The battle of (First) Mantineia helped to confirm the myth of Spartan invincibility and enabled her to reassert her control of the Peloponnese.

1.71   Spartē did little to follow up her success or to harass Athens, but Alkibiadēs' Peloponnesian policy was doomed. The Athenians turned their attentions back to their own empire. In 416 they captured the island of Mēlos, one of only two islands in the Cyclades which were not part of the Athenian empire. Mēlos claimed to be a Spartan colony and its sympathies lay with the Spartans. After a siege, the island capitulated and received harsh punishment. All men of military age were put to death and the women and children were sold into slavery. Thucydides used the incident to explore the nature and justification of imperialism.

1.13 Fifth-century marble head of a herm recovered from the Athenian *agorā*.

1.72 In the winter of 416/15 envoys came from one of Athens' allies in Sicily, the city of Egesta, to beg for help in a war against Selīnous, which had called in Syracuse on her side. This appeal revived Athens' long-standing ambitions in the area. The Athenians sent envoys to assess the ability of Egesta to finance Athenian intervention; the envoys were deceived and reported positively. When an expedition was mooted Alkibiadēs was strongly in favour, but Nīkiās counselled caution. The Athenians took Nīkiās seriously and, when he suggested that large numbers of troops would be needed, they voted to send an extremely large fleet and to put Nīkiās, as well as Alkibiadēs and Lāmakhos, in charge. Their brief seems to have been simply to help the allies; but the very size of the fleet encouraged expectations and, to judge by a remarkable account of Athenian negotiations with Mēlos which has become known as the 'Melian Dialogue' (Thucydides, *Peloponnesian War* 5.85–113), most Athenians seemed to be looking forward to new conquests and additions to their empire

1.73 Just before the fleet sailed in early summer 415 (cf. 7.42), Athenians awoke to find that some of the Hermai, busts of Hermēs that stood outside both public and private houses as a symbol of good fortune, had been defaced during the night. This act of sacrilege was taken as a sign of ill omen for the coming expedition. Calls were made for an investigation, which threw up further allegations of sacrilegious, mock celebrations of the sacred Mysteries of Eleusīs – and among those accused of taking part was Alkibiadēs. What lay behind these acts is far from clear. We possess a later speech about the affair by Andokidēs who, having been arrested along with others, confessed all in return for a reduced penalty; but it does little to clarify the events (6.58). The profanation of the Mysteries was probably no more than a blasphemous, private entertainment, though Alkibiadēs' alleged involvement was a gift to his political enemies. But the mutilation of the Hermai was a different matter. Discussed at a dinner party several days before it occurred, it could have been no more than an aristocratic 'dare' (this sort of vandalism had happened before, according to Thucydides). But it may also have been a deliberate political act to try to prevent the fleet sailing. If so, it could be significant that it originated in the dining-clubs of the wealthy men, which in a few years' time were to play a crucial role in the attempt to overthrow the democracy. Whatever the truth of the matter, Alkibiadēs tried to get it cleared up before he sailed, but did not succeed. He departed with the fleet but, before it saw action, the Athenians decided to recall him to face his accusers. In response, Alkibiadēs fled to Spartē, where he proceeded to give his best advice on how to overcome his mother city.

1.74   Nīkiās and Lāmakhos were therefore left in charge of the Athenian fleet. The war did not go well. The response from potential allies in Sicily was disappointing. However, by the winter of 415/14, the Athenian fleet was anchored in the Great Bay of Syracuse and the Athenians had begun siege works around the city. In 414 Lāmakhos was killed, and Nīkiās was left in sole command. Before the siege could be brought to a successful conclusion, the Spartans, acting on the advice of Alkibiadēs, sent a commander, Gylippos, to rally the Syracusan resistance. In 413 Nīkiās was reinforced by the Athenians with troops and ships under the command of Dēmosthenēs and Eurymedōn, but no progress was made. Now the Athenian fleet itself came under siege as the Syracusans blockaded the Athenian ships in the harbour. In a desperate attempt to break out, the Athenian fleet was defeated. Nīkiās and Dēmosthenēs began a retreat by land, constantly harried by the Syracusans. The two commanders lost contact with each other and were defeated separately. Despite assurances which were given when they surrendered, both were executed. The surviving Athenian prisoners were herded into a makeshift prisoner-of-war camp – the stone quarries of Syracuse.

> This was the greatest action of this war, and, in my opinion, the greatest action that we know of in Greek history – to the victors the most brilliant of successes, to the vanquished the most disastrous of defeats. (Thucydides, *Peloponnesian War* 7.87)

The Peloponnesian War: 3. Empire and democracy under threat, 413–404

1.75 After the end of the war, Thucydides reflected on the expedition to Sicily and was critical more of the way in which the Athenians had executed the decision to send the expedition than of the decision itself (Thucydides, *Peloponnesian War* 2.65.11). But he records that, after the defeat, the Athenians themselves not only took against those who had advocated the expedition, but began to lose confidence in the way democracy made decisions. So they appointed a board of ten *probouloi*, men of experience who included the tragic poet Sophoklēs, to give advice to Council and *ekklēsiā*. At the same time Athens faced new challenges. The loss of the fleet and of several thousand men presented Athens' enemies with a remarkable opportunity. Even before the final Athenian defeat in Sicily, Spartē had placed a permanent fort at Dekeleia in Attikē. This restricted Athenian freedom of movement all the year round, and the fort also became a sanctuary for runaway slaves. In particular, slaves fled from the silver mines at Laureion, reducing Athenian income from that source to a minimum. These were tough years for Athens. The citizens had to struggle to raise the funds to continue the war and to keep hold on their empire. They were forced to melt down gold statues and to draw on the 1,000 talents' reserve which at the beginning of the war had been set aside for emergencies. A number of Aegean allies of the Athenians saw that this was the best opportunity they had had yet, and sought Spartan assistance to revolt from Athens. Spartē began building a new fleet to try to exploit discontent in the Aegean, but her problem was that ships cost money to build and to man. As a primarily agricultural state, Spartē had little surplus.

1.76 What happened next was crucial: the Persians, who had largely kept out of Greek affairs since the 450s, reappeared on the scene. Athens had chosen to support the revolt of Amorgēs in Kariā from the Persian empire. But in 414/13, the Persian king Dareios appointed one Tissaphernēs as satrap (Persian governor) of Kariā with a brief to deal with Amorgēs and to bring in tribute from the Greek cities of the coast. Both Tissaphernēs and Pharnabazos, the satrap of Phrygiā based at Daskylion, saw that they would be better off with the Athenians out of the scene, and both made approaches to Spartē to ask for help with this. They discussed at length how much Persian funding might be available and what the Spartans might be willing to do in return. An important role in these negotiations was played by Alkibiadēs. Alkibiadēs had fallen out with the Spartan king Agis and got himself sent to Asia Minor with a small Spartan fleet. But Spartans became increasingly suspicious of his negotiating tactics, and he first took refuge with Tissaphernēs and then began to scheme for a return to Athens.

1.77 In 411 the Athenian fleet was based at Samos (close to supplies of the wood needed for rebuilding it), where their officers were contacted by Alkibiadēs.

1.14 A silver tetradrachm with the head of the Persian satrap Tissaphernēs.

Alkibiadēs said that he would persuade the Persians to stop supporting Spartē if, in return, the Athenian officers would bring about the overthrow of the radical democracy at Athens, so that Alkibiadēs could return home. Peisandros, an oligarchic leader, went with this proposal to Athens. There he proposed only that 'they should not continue democracy in the same way'. He offered a very tempting bait – alliance with Persia. Even though Alkibiadēs proved totally unable to deliver this, it was the moment that many of those critics of the radical democracy had been waiting for. Indeed, many Athenians were so dissatisfied with democracy that people could not clearly distinguish who was and who was not a supporter of it. So the oligarchic coup went ahead, and one radical democratic leader (Androklēs) was assassinated. Documents preserved in the Aristotelian *Constitution of the Athenians* show that there was talk of amending the constitution in various ways in order to increase its efficiency and concentrate political power in the hands of those able to serve as soldiers. The population of Athens was terrorised into the creation of a body of 400 who straightaway took control of the government. The reaction in Samos was immediate. If the democracy had been banished from Athens, it was still alive at Samos among the Athenian citizens who made up most of the naval forces there. Indeed, the absence of so many citizens from Athens may have been the key to the oligarchs' initial success. The democrats at Samos now recalled Alkibiadēs, who wisely counselled that they should wait for their moment and not immediately sail to Athens to overthrow the new régime.

1.78   The news of the reaction at Samos caused a split among the oligarchs at Athens. One of the promises at the beginning of the revolution had been that a body of some 5,000 of the better-off Athenians, who could provide hoplite armour at their own expense, was to have full citizen rights and be eligible for election to state office. This was justified on the principle that those who contributed most to the Athenian war effort should be the ones to direct how their money and energies were to be used. However, not all the members of the 400 were keen on the idea of the 5,000. Those within the oligarchic ruling group – men like Therāmenēs – realised that the oligarchs would have to come to terms with the Athenians at Samos, and pressed for the creation of the 5,000. After only four months, the 400 found themselves unable to bring about peace with Spartē or to fulfil any of their promises. Resistance to them mounted, and one of the more extreme oligarchs, Phrȳnikhos, was assassinated. About September 411, they were overthrown and replaced with the rule of the 5,000. The rule of the 5,000 was a significant move away from extreme oligarchy, and in 410 the traditional democracy was restored in Athens. Some of the members of the 400 sought to save themselves by attacking other members. For the next few years many tried to settle political scores in the Athenian courts. Those who knew they would not be able to clear their names left Athens and awaited a more opportune moment to return. The failure of the oligarchic revolution of 411 taught a powerful lesson. Despite the problems of radical democracy, Athenians had decided that they would not easily surrender the powers and privileges they had gained. Those who wished to bring about a more restrictive system of government would have to enlist the assistance of a foreign power.

1.79   Even before the restoration of the democracy at Athens, the democratic fleet in the north Aegean was winning victories against the Peloponnesian fleet, at Kynossēma in the Kherronēsos in 411 and at Kyzikos in 410. In the years following, under the leadership of Alkibiadēs among others, the Athenians had a series of further successes in the Hellespont region. In 407, Alkibiadēs was able to return to Athens and be rehabilitated. But in the same year the Persian king, Dareios, sent his younger son, Cyrus, to supervise the west of Asia Minor and to help the Spartan war effort; so the policy which Alkibiadēs had persuaded Tissaphernēs to adopt, of letting Athens and Spartē slowly wear each other out, had been abandoned. Cyrus struck up a good relationship with the new commander of the Spartan fleet, Lȳsandros; the result was that, for the rest of the war, Persia financed the Spartan fleet with reasonable efficiency. In the spring of 406, the new team had its first success when it defeated an Athenian fleet near Notion on the coast of Asia Minor. Although Alkibiadēs had not been present at the battle, he was held responsible for the failure. Instead of returning to Athens to face prosecution, he retired to a castle in the Kherronēsos, from where he would make a last dramatic appearance to advise the Athenian fleet just before the battle of Aigospotamoi in 405.

1.80   Later in 406, the Spartan admiral Kallikratidās succeeded in blockading the Athenian fleet, now commanded by Konōn, in Mytilēnē. The Athenians put together a new fleet which met Kallikratidās in battle off the Arginoussai islands near Lesbos. The Peloponnesian fleet was crushed, and Kallikratidās lost overboard. On the Athenian side, 13 ships were sunk and 12 disabled. A squadron under two Athenian trierarchs, Therāmenēs and Thrasyboulos, was ordered to pick up survivors, but a storm blew up and prevented the rescue mission. Several thousand Athenians were left to drown. Eight of the board of ten *stratēgoi* had been present at Arginoussai. Of them, six decided to return to Athens, where they were immediately brought before the *ekklēsiā*. Their victory had been overshadowed by the great loss of Athenian lives. Xenophōn tells how the people's grief was whipped up into a fury by the evidence of a survivor, orchestrated, at least in part, by Therāmenēs, who was intent (as usual) on passing the buck. The proposal was put that the *ekklēsiā* should take a single vote on the collective guilt of the generals. When it was objected that this was unconstitutional, the People insisted that it was intolerable if anyone prevented the people from doing what it wanted to do. The generals were condemned, and the unfortunate six who had come home were executed. There could be no more vivid verification of where power ultimately lay in the radical democracy.

1.81 The next year, 405, saw the centre of action return to the Hellespont. While Lȳsandros and a Peloponnesian fleet were besieging Lampsakos late in the year, an Athenian fleet beached on the opposite side of the Hellespont at Aigospotamoi. For five days, Lȳsandros refused to give battle. But on the final evening, when the Athenians disembarked, Lȳsandros caught them unawares. At a stroke and without resistance, he captured almost the entire Athenian fleet. The Athenian *stratēgos*, Konōn, escaped to Cyprus with nine ships. The state trireme, *Paralos*, was sent to bring the news to Athens that she no longer had the means to continue the war:

> It was night when the *Paralos* arrived in Athens. As news of the disaster spread, a howl of grief rose up first from the Peiraieus, then among the Long Walls and into the city, as one man passed the news to another. That night no one slept. (Xenophōn, *Hellēnika* 2.2.3)

At first, the Athenians were defiant. After all, the likely prospect was that the city would be destroyed and the population killed or enslaved, the sort of treatment which Athens herself had meted out on more than one occasion. But the problem was that Spartē now controlled the Hellespont and could therefore cut off Athens' food supply (6.66). So in spring 404, after long negotiations in which the Athenian Thērāmenēs played a prominent part, the Athenians were prepared to accept the Spartan conditions. Athens was not to be destroyed. Instead she lost her empire; her fleet was cut down to 12 ships; the defences of the Peiraieus and the Long Walls were to be demolished; all exiles were to be recalled; and Athens was obliged to recognise Spartan leadership.

The loss and restoration of democracy, 404–399

1.82 In the spring of 404, Lȳsandros arrived to preside over the demolition of the Long Walls. The architect of Athens' defeat, he was now also architect of a new Spartan empire. All over the Aegean he saw to the installation of puppet governments of ten men (*dekarkhiai*) designed to see that Spartē's (and Lysandros') will was done. Later in the summer of 404, he returned to Athens and obliged the Athenians to establish a board not of ten but of thirty men to look after affairs until a new constitution could be drawn up. The Thirty included the anti-democratic intellectual Kritiās and (naturally) the ubiquitous Therāmenēs. Since the revolution of 411, many men of their sort had been in exile or, like Kritiās, had fallen foul of the democracy in the intervening years; but by the terms of the peace, all such exiles were permitted to return to Athens. To back up their take-over, the Thirty got Spartē to send a garrison of 700 men. Under the eyes of these troops, the Thirty instituted a reign of terror against their political and personal enemies. This grim period is vividly described in a speech *Against Eratosthenēs* (who was one of the Thirty) by one of the victims, the wealthy resident foreigner (*metoikos*) and speech-writer Lysiās, whose brother had been put to death (cf. 2.24, 5.69).

1.83 Although the number of men involved in this régime was much smaller, they (like the 400 in 411) held a variety of views. There were some who took the task of redesigning the constitution seriously, and began by repealing the laws which they saw as at the root of radical democracy, including laws about the powers of the courts. Others did not see what they were doing in constitutional terms at all and were concerned rather to keep power in their own hands. According to Xenophōn, who was in Athens during this period and probably served in the cavalry under the Thirty, there was a stand-off between Therāmenēs and the hard-line Kritiās. Therāmenēs lost and was condemned to death by the new form of self-administered execution introduced by the Thirty – drinking hemlock (3.36)). This was a violent end to an extraordinary career. Therāmenēs, the son of Hagnōn (the distinguished Athenian general and founder of Amphipolis (3.31), had played a full part in the oligarchic revolution of 411, yet had turned against the extreme oligarchs in sufficient time to enable him to remain and participate in the restored democracy. However, after the defeat of Athens, he was still able to become one of the ruling Thirty, probably with greater enthusiasm than his supporters were prepared later to admit. The twists and turns of the career of this Athenian opportunist earned him the nickname *kothornos* (the actor's boot which fitted either foot). They also earned him the lasting admiration of some: the Aristotelian *Constitution of the Athenians* treats him as one of the finest Athenian statesmen of the fifth century.

1.84 Meanwhile democracy-supporting exiles from Athens were taking refuge in a number of Greek cities, including Thebes. There were many politicians there who felt that they and Spartē's other allies had gained too little from the peace settlement; further, they were worried that an already powerful Spartē now had control over the wealth of Athens too. So they would support anyone who might disrupt the new arrangements. From Thebes, therefore, the democrats, led by Thrasyboulos, occupied the Athenian fort of Phȳlē in the winter of 404/3. From there they captured the Peiraieus and in a battle succeeded in killing some of the Thirty, including Kritiās. The Spartan sent one of their kings, Pausaniās, to support the Thirty, but when he arrived he realised that it would be impossible to suppress the democratic revival. So he set about reconciling the two sides. An amnesty was declared. The Thirty themselves and others who had had official positions under the régime, if they wished to remain in Athens, were obliged to give an official account of their actions, but no one who did stay was to 'mention past wrongs'. They also had an option to go to live in Eleusīs, which became virtually a separate state until 401/400, when it was forcibly reincorporated in the Athenian state.

1.85 After this there was much discussion about the nature of the democracy to be re-established. Various schemes for restricting citizenship, or for extending it to all who had helped overthrow the Thirty, were canvassed. In the end what was restored was very like what had been abolished by the Thirty, but there were significant exceptions. The most important was the introduction of a distinction between decrees and laws: in future the *ekklēsiā* would continue to decide about particular individual matters (decrees), but general rules (laws) were to be subject to a much more prolonged procedure.

1.86 For several years after the overthrow of the Thirty the Athenians seem to have been scrupulous about keeping the conditions of the reconciliation, and in particular the terms of the amnesty. But as they became less worried that the Spartans might march in again to enforce the conditions, the Athenians began to look back with some anger. In the year 399 a number of trials took place, all of which have something to do with those linked with the Thirty. The most notorious of these is the trial of the philosopher Sōkratēs. He was brought to court on a charge of 'refusing to recognise the gods of the state and introducing other new gods. He is also guilty of corrupting the youth' (Xenophōn, *Memorābilia* 1.1.1). Half a century later Aiskhinēs would state, as if it were a matter of general knowledge: 'Athenians, you executed the sophist Sōkratēs because he had quite clearly been the teacher of Kritiās, who was one of the Thirty who put an end to democracy' (Aiskhinēs, 1.173). Since Athenian jurors voted immediately after hearing the evidence but without discussing the issues among themselves, no one can have known, even at the time, what motivated his condemnation, but it would be foolish to rule political motivation in or out. On the one hand, Sōkratēs had not only loyally fulfilled the duties of a citizen of the democracy, serving as a hoplite and on the *boulē*, he had even on one notable occasion refused to co-operate with the Thirty in helping to arrest a rich metic. But in the unsettled circumstances after the end of the war (had the gods deserted Athens?), the religious charges were serious in themselves. When Sōkratēs was found guilty, he took a high moral stance, refusing the opportunity to have his sentence commuted to a heavy fine. He was condemned to drink hemlock, and died in the dignified manner which was to be an example to generations of martyrs. The killing of their master and guide inspired in his followers like the philosopher Plato a hatred for the democratic system. However, it is difficult to see Sōkratēs as the victim of the democratic system as such. What the case did show was how profoundly sensitive the Athenian democracy could be at difficult times to innovation and change, and how politics pervaded the whole of Athenian life.

Athens rebuilds her power, 399–360

1.87 If the events of 404–399 were highly revealing about Athens, they were also revealing about Spartē. Spartē's victory in the Peloponnesian War brought about division both within the Peloponnesian League and within Spartē herself. In the League we have already seen how Thebes defied Spartē by giving refuge to Athenian democrats. Spartē's allies, who were already unhappy at a new Spartan imperialism in which they had no part, were further confounded when Spartē chose to take military action against Ēlis. They justified it by raking up an old grievance going back to the Olympic games of 420 – the Ēleans had had a Spartan whipped who competed in the games after the Spartans had been banned – and broke up the state of Ēlis. But among the Spartans themselves there was no agreement as to the wisdom of Lȳsandros' imperialist policy of garrisons and puppet governments, and the demand for even more tribute than Athens had imposed. For example, King Pausaniās, who had not treated Athens like that (1.84), was put on trial on his return to Spartē – but was acquitted. The tradition that came down to Pausaniās, the writer of a *Guide to Greece* in the second century A D, was that the king had been acquitted (by just four votes) because all the *ephors* of the year voted for him. The fact that the chief officials elected for that year were solidly behind Pausaniās indicates that opposition to Lȳsandros had already been strong at the moment of the elections. But if an anti-imperialist policy won that day, it was the imperialists who ended up dictating the general course of Spartan foreign policy over the next thirty years.

1.88 When King Dareios died in 405/4, his eldest son, Artaxerxēs, took over. However, Cyrus, Dareios' younger son, resented this and planned an expedition from his base in the west of Asia Minor. In 401 Cyrus took the field and appealed to Spartē for help. This put Spartē in a difficult position: she owed a great deal to Cyrus' goodwill in the last years of the Peloponnesian War, but if Cyrus lost, she might be drawn into a direct confrontation with Persia. So the Spartans hedged their bets by *unofficially* sending a force to join the other Greek mercenaries in Cyrus' army. Cyrus was killed in battle at Cunaxa, not far from Babylon. The Athenian Xenophōn, keen to be away from an Athens which might not look favourably on his support for the Thirty, had been one of those mercenaries. He vividly describes the march home of the 10,000 Greeks from the very heart of the Persian Empire in his *Anabasis* ('March Up-Country').

1.89 The Greek cities of Asia Minor that had also supported Cyrus now expected Persia to take revenge on them and appealed to Spartē for protection. Despite the fact that, a decade earlier, the Spartans had been quite ready to ignore the interests of Greeks in Asia in return for Persian aid, it now suited their imperialist interests to champion Greek freedom. A series of Spartan commanders and troops were sent out, culminating in the great expedition of the new Spartan king, Agēsilāos, in 396. Agēsilāos tried to claim the venture as a

1.15 The monument to the young cavalryman Dexileos who died in the Corinthian War (see also fig. 7.7).

Panhellenic one, modelled on the Greek expeditions against Troy, but when he tried to offer sacrifice at Aulis, as Agamemnōn had fatally done with his daughter Iphigeneia before the Trojan war (8.54), the Boiotians came and disrupted the sacrifices.

1.90 In the immediate aftermath of 404, Athens had felt obliged to support Spartē. Even for the initial Spartan campaigns in Asia Minor, she responded positively to a request for support – even though by sending cavalry whom, Xenophōn suggests (*Hellēnika* 3.1.4), they were happy to have got rid of because of their oligarchic political sympathies. But little by little the Athenians regained the confidence to resist Spartē. In 395 the Athenians made (and then denied) a secret agreement to send a trireme to the general Konōn, who was now serving for the Persians against the Spartans; and later in the year they made alliances with the Boiotians and Lokrians. War with Spartē followed swiftly. The new alliance scored a notable success in a battle at Haliartos in Boiōtiā against the Spartans, in which Lȳsandros was killed.

Ancient sources dispute whether the war against Spartē was inspired by Persian bribes offered to the Greek states, but there is no doubt about the deep-rooted antagonism which Spartē had stirred up throughout Greece. This new conflict centred on the Isthmus, and so gained the name of the 'Corinthian War'.

1.91 On land, Spartē could still make the skill of her highly trained hoplites tell. The Corinthian War saw two impressive Spartan victories in 394, first at the Nemeā river and then by the returning Agēsilāos, who had been recalled from Asia Minor, at Korōneia in Boiōtiā. By sea the picture was different. In the same year, 394, Spartē suffered a major defeat at the battle of Knidos at the hands of a large Persian fleet, commanded by the Persian satrap Pharnabazos and the Athenian mercenary Konōn. The Persians followed this up by sailing round the Aegean, driving out Spartan garrisons and even installing one of their own on the island of Kytherā. Konōn persuaded Pharnabazos to take the fleet to Athens and help in the task of rebuilding the Long Walls. Here Konōn received a rapturous welcome. He was honoured along with Euagorās, the king of Cyprus, who was hailed as a *Hellēn*. The Athenians also honoured Dionȳsios, the tyrant of Syracuse, in an attempt to keep him from supporting Spartē. The Athenians regained control of the island of Dēlos. Athenian confidence was restored.

1.92 Spartē was far from a spent force, however. She now entered into urgent negotiations with the Persian officials in Asia Minor. She had Konōn arrested, and launched a new policy of persuading Persia to champion peace in Greece. This was unsuccessful, and military action resumed. The Athenians revealed unexpected weaknesses in Spartē's land forces when their general Iphikratēs, with a company of lightly armed troops, defeated a Spartan division at Lekhaion near Corinth in 390 (7.24). But in the same year, Spartē revealed the continuing weakness of the Athenians, by harassing both Athenian shipping and the coasts of Attikē. Nevertheless, in 389 the Athenian general, Thrasyboulos, took an Athenian fleet through the eastern Aegean and succeeded in recovering Thasos, bringing about a pro-democracy revolution at Byzantion, and re-establishing a toll at the Bosporos.

1.93 But the basis of Athenian success was shallow. In 387/6 the Spartan Antalkidās was able to win the backing of the Persian king, Artaxerxēs. Spartē then blockaded the Hellēspont and so forced the Athenians to accept terms dictated by Artaxerxēs – even though this involved handing the recently honoured Euagorās over to Persia. The Greek cities accepted a peace in which Persian control of the Greek cities of Asia Minor was acknowledged, and all the other Greek cities, both small and large, were to be left autonomous. These terms were backed up by a threat that the Persian king would make war on anyone who refused to accept them. This, the 'King's Peace', was the first 'common peace' (*koinē eirēnē*), that is, it did not apply to one group of states only, but was designed to impose a general peace on all the Greek cities. In theory a noble idea, this peace was in practice made

primarily to help Persia and Spartē control Greece. It did not provide any real
basis for continued peace there. There was no accepted idea of how the principle of autonomy was to be defined, and no procedure for arbitration.

1.94   It soon became apparent what Spartē thought of the principle of autonomy.
In 385 she intervened militarily in the affairs of the Arkadian city of
Mantineia, forcing the inhabitants to abandon the city and live in separate
villages. In 383 Spartē insisted that Phleious take back some exiles, and two
years later she invaded Phleious in support of those mercenaries. When there
was talk of Olynthos allying itself with Thebes and with Athens, a Spartan
commander, part of a force on its way to intervene in Olynthos, occupied the
Theban akropolis. However, it is also true that in these years Athens was
seeking to strengthen her links with other parts of the Greek world, and even
parts beyond the Greek world. In 386/5 she had passed honours for
Hebryzelmis, king of the Odrysians in Thrace; in 384/3 she formed an
alliance with the island of Khios.

1.95   In 379, the Thebans managed to remove their Spartan garrison and set about
strengthening their links with the rest of Boiōtiā, reorganising the Boiotian
confederacy. Spartē, alarmed, began a programme of annual invasions of
Theban territory. In 378 one Spartan commander, a man named Sphodriās,
decided that marching on Athens also was a good idea, and attempted a night
raid. Daybreak saw him still several miles short of Athens, but the diplomatic
damage was done. Athens had already decided that she needed a web of allies,
and this event only helped to demonstrate the truth of that. In 378 Athens
and Thebes formed an alliance, and Athens then reorganised her existing
allies, including Thebes, into a new league of states, known to scholars as the
Second Athenian Confederacy, and recruited new allies (*RO* 22, see 6.91).
The decree which advertised this League survives. In it Athens renounces the
features of her fifth-century empire which had proved so objectionable: there
was to be no interference in the internal constitutions of member states, no
tribute, and no Athenian settlements on allied territory. The positive attraction of the League was 'to make the Spartans leave the Greeks to enjoy peace
in freedom and autonomy'. Over the next three years some 70 states joined
the new League. Whatever resentment there was over Athens' behaviour in
the fifth century was quite forgotten in the face of Spartē's current behaviour.

1.96   The new confederacy was no empty undertaking from the Athenians: they
reorganised their own finances, in particular reassessing the property of the
rich for the property tax known as the *eisphorā*; they reopened and reorganised the silver mines; and improved the efficiency with which they extracted
tax from the islands of Lēmnos, Imbros and Skȳros, which they controlled.
But the financial burden of naval activity on a large scale was to prove a constant problem. In 376 the Athenians showed that they had the military muscle
to deliver the security they promised when the Spartan fleet was defeated in
a battle off the island of Naxos. In the following years, action moved to other
theatres. In the Ionian Sea, Kerkȳra, Akarnāniā and Kephallēniā became

Athenian allies, and Spartan attempts to keep hold of Kerkȳra were defeated. On this occasion Athens met the cost of the campaign by a sale of war captives, which brought in 60 talents. In the north Aegean, Athenian activity was diplomatic: in 375, or perhaps 373/2, the Athenians made an alliance with Amyntās III, king of Makedōn. Athens was now in so strong a position that she could take the initiative in trying to renew the Common Peace.

1.97   In 371 the Athenians and Thebans went to Spartē to negotiate peace. The Spartans were prepared to withdraw both garrisons and Spartan commanders from Greek cities. The Athenians agreed to do likewise (and did). But negotiations broke down when the Spartans, who had signed the treaty on behalf of their own allies, refused to let Thebes sign on behalf of the Boiotians. Spartē invaded Boiōtiā, but at Leuktrā the Theban army under Epameinōndās delivered a decisive defeat (7.26, 30). Out of 1,000 dead, some 400 Spartiates were killed, along with their general Kleombrotos. The Spartan defeat was a surprise to the whole of Greece. Thebes had developed the arms and tactics to defeat the Spartan phalanx. Spartan power was broken – and not just because of the fact of defeat. Spartan manpower had been on the decline for years, and the losses of men at Leuktrā removed a high proportion of her army. Without massive allied support, Spartē could achieve nothing militarily, but the resentment and ill will which her actions had inspired in the other Greek states meant that she had forfeited such support. The states of the Peloponnese seized their opportunity to assert their independence from Spartē and were backed up by repeated expeditions into the Peloponnese by Epameinōndās and the Thebans during the 360s. The Thebans freed Messēniā and its helots from Spartan domination and helped to set up a new Messenian capital at Ithōmē; they also encouraged the cities of the central Peloponnese to form a new Arkadian League and a new federal capital at Megalopolis. Yet Spartē itself was left untouched, although on two occasions Epameinōndās did come close to the unwalled city. The myth of Spartan invincibility had not been entirely destroyed.

1.98   The growth of Theban power had been worrying Athens. So by 368 Athens had made an alliance with Spartē, and for much of the decade Athens intervened in the Peloponnese to try to counterbalance Theban influence. In the north Aegean the Athenians continued a vigorous policy by sea to recover influence, but they also had to spend increasing amounts of time dealing with rebellious allies, making a series of interventions on the island of Keā. The Thebans felt sufficiently threatened by this to build their own fleet in 364, but they could not sustain this. The Arkadian League also split between those who favoured Thebes and those who turned to Spartē and Athens to protect them from increasing Theban interference. In 362 Epameinōndās led a force into the Peloponnese to help those states which adhered to Thebes. At Mantineia he met an army of those Arkadian states which opposed him, along with Spartē and Athens. Adapting the tactics which had won at Leuktrā, Epameinōndās and the Thebans were again successful, but

Epameinōndās himself was killed and the Thebans failed to press home their victory. After the battle a new 'common peace' was made on the basis that each state should keep what it had. It mattered little that the Spartans, still vainly demanding their right to Messēnē, refused to sign.

1.99 In the last sentences of his history, Xenophōn summed up the situation after the battle of Mantineia: 'There was even more uncertainty and confusion in Greece after the battle than there had been before' (*Hellēnika* 7.5.27). This gloomy assessment was accurate. No one state could claim to be predominant, but this did not mean stability. There was a constant jockeying for position, a waiting for the new superpower. But during the 360s none emerged. Thebes was a significant power in central Greece, but differences of opinion among its leaders limited the scope of her interventions into the Peloponnese. Athens was the dominant power at sea, but this cost her more than she could afford, and in any case the Athenians could have no pretensions by land. The Arkadians, famous mercenaries, failed to turn their new confederacy into a political union sufficiently united to pursue a consistent foreign policy. Competitive, self-assertive, and deeply suspicious of their neighbours, the cities had no interest in any larger, co-operative, united organisation of Greeks, even though some lone voices urged Panhellenic campaigns against Persia. As early as 380, the Athenian political pamphleteer Isokratēs in his *Panēgyrikos* had been urging a united Greek campaign against Persia. But even he thought in terms of that campaign being led by a single city-state – Athens. Panhellenism was not practical politics.

Athens and Makedōn, 359–323

1.100 Athenian satisfaction at the revival of the city as the major naval power, and the steady growth of Athenian gains in the Aegean, increasingly translated into heavy-handed imperialism. Promises made at the time of the formation of the Second Confederacy were forgotten. The purpose of the Confederacy had become obscure now that Athens had allied to Spartē, but states found that they could not leave. Demands for payments to League funds became more regular. The League fleet was used for Athens' purpose. Eventually, in 357, the major members of the League revolted. The so-called Social War lasted until 355, when Athens allowed those states which wanted to leave the League to do so. In a brave pamphlet *On the Peace* in 355, the speech-writer Isokratēs argues that Athens should give up her imperial aspirations. Xenophōn, in a work produced at the same time, the *Poroi* ('Revenues'), sought to demonstrate that with peace Athens was bound to thrive as a trading centre and had no need of income from an empire. It was left to the politician Euboulos to put these principles into action. In the period after 355, Euboulos, a financial expert, enabled Athens to make a financial recovery by a careful husbanding of resources and an avoidance of major military commitments.

1.101   Whether Athens could avoid all major military commitments became the crucial question dividing Athenian politicians. But the military commitment which began to be urged was one which no Athenian politician active in the 370s or 360s would have predicted: action against Makedōn. King Philip II of Makedōn came to power in 360/59 at the age of twenty-four. The Makedonians were Greek in origin, and though other Greeks tended to sneer at their backwardness and distinctness, the Makedonian élite had long been in close touch with the cultural developments of mainland Greece. (A poet of the stature of Euripidēs had been invited to the Makedonian court; and in recent years the discovery of the tombs of the Makedonian élite at Vergina has vividly demonstrated how closely Makedonian and Greek culture had amalgamated.) Philip had inherited a kingdom threatened by neighbouring tribes and disturbed by the claims of competitors. Philip soon dealt with them, reformed the Makedonian army (7.26–7), defeated the invading tribes, and went about securing the border territories of Makedōn. It was inevitable that these actions should concern Athens in particular, as she had long-standing interests in northern Greece. In 357 Philip took Amphipolis. The Athenians were particularly enraged because they always claimed that Amphipolis was theirs, although they had not controlled it since 424. Some Athenians were under the impression that Philip had promised to return Amphipolis to them. Whatever the truth of the matter, Philip held on to the city and the Athenians declared war on him. They were not in a position to prosecute this war effectively, but it was not clear that they could ignore Makedōn either. By the late 350s, a politician in his thirties was making it his business to try to awaken his fellow Athenians to the threat which he saw in the north. This was Dēmosthenēs, who had made his name through the speeches he made in the law-courts to reclaim from his guardians his own inheritance. The speeches in which he tried to bully the Athenians into action against Philip were practically ineffective, but patriotic politicians in Rome and in modern Western countries have often copied their elaborate phrasing and impassioned invective.

1.102   By 352 Philip had taken control of Thessaly and then turned against the kingdom of Thrace and the league of the cities of Khalkidikē, which was dominated by the state of Olynthos. Dēmosthenēs desperately tried to get the Athenians to intervene, first by his 'Philippic' (i.e. anti-Philip) speech of 352/1 and then in a series of speeches in 349/8 in which he urged Athens to back Olynthos. But Dēmosthenēs was unable to produce an answer to the two basic problems: how could Athens fight effectively in an area where she had no bases, and how could a major campaign be financed? The troops Athens did manage to send to Olynthos failed to prevent Philip destroying the city in 348 and selling the population into slavery. The fate of the Athenian captives taken by Philip was to influence Athenian policy for the following two years.

1.103   Philip saw no future in antagonising Athens unnecessarily, and right from the time of the capture of Olynthos he sent messages offering the prospect of

1.16 A copy of the third-century statue of Dēmosthenēs.

peace. Towards the end of 347 Athens responded by sending an embassy of ten men; these included Philokratēs, who had proposed the mission, Dēmosthenēs, and his political rival Aiskhinēs. Philip produced a proposal not just of peace, but also of alliance, backed up by vague, but tempting, promises of help for Athens. These negotiations were tied up with the question of the so-called 'Sacred War' in central Greece. In 356 Phōkis had seized the oracular shrine of Delphi and for ten years Phōkis had fought off the attacks of her enemies, including Philip. Everyone realised that this peace would mean Philip intervening decisively in this war. The Athenians were caught between the desire to keep Philip out of Greece and the need for a

1.17 A copy of a statue of Aiskhinēs.

peace with Philip. When the Athenian embassy returned from Philip, it was only with difficulty that its leader, Philokratēs, was able to get the Athenians to agree to peace and an alliance between Philip, Athens and her allies. Immediately, Philip entered central Greece and put an end to the Sacred War. He presided over the Pythian games and then returned to Makedōn. Since he now controlled the important north–south route via Thermopylai and was in control of the sanctuary at Delphi, he had both the opportunity and the excuse to intervene in Greece whenever he so chose.

1.104 The question was, why did Philip so choose? Did he have further ambitions with regard to southern Greece, or were his ambitions elsewhere? In Athens

1.18 The memorial to the Makedonian victory at Khairōneia, 338.

the peace of Philokratēs very soon became unpopular, as Athenians felt some guilt at the way Phōkis had been left in the lurch and no great benefits came to them from Philip as promised. Dēmosthenēs managed to climb on this bandwagon of resentment and disassociated himself from the process of peace-making. He led the attack on the politicians involved in peace negotiations. In particular, in 343, he brought a case against Aiskhinēs, his fellow ambassador, over the conduct of the embassy. The speeches by both sides illustrate the formidable difficulties faced by a jury in a highly charged political case in Athens. Dēmosthenēs and Aiskhinēs presented totally incompatible accounts of events which had taken place, often in public, only three or

1.19 A marble head of Alexander found on the Athenian Akropolis.

four years earlier. Aiskhinēs was acquitted by a small margin. Nevertheless the mood of antagonism against Philip, stoked up by Dēmosthenēs and others, prevailed in Athens.

1.105   Reasons for Athenian suspicions grew. In 340 Philip not only laid siege to Byzantion but also seized the grain fleet. Dēmosthenēs got his way, and Athens and her allies declared war on Philip. In 339 Athens secured further alliances, most importantly with Thebes and the Boiotians. Together they faced Philip in the field in northern Boiōtiā in 338. In the battle at Khairōneia, Philip decisively defeated the Greek allies. His young son, Alexander (the Great), played an important part in the victory as a commander of the cavalry (7.26). Philip dealt harshly with Thebes. The Boiotian confederacy was again broken up, and a Makedonian garrison was placed in Thebes. Athens got more lenient treatment. Philip promised to send no troops into Attikē, and although Athens was forced to break up what was left of her alliance, she was left in control of a number of islands. Further, as a present from Philip, she was given Orōpos, a city which had been the source of constant dispute between Thebes and Athens.

1.106 There were many reasons for Philip treating Thebes and Athens differently, including Athens' navy, which he could not match. But one important reason was the very different records of Thebes and Athens in the Persian Wars. Thebes had gone over to Persia; Athens had resisted and been sacked. To treat Thebes badly was consistent with championing Greek interests, but Philip could not treat Athens as the Persians had treated Athens. The reason was that he was already planning a major revenge attack against Persia on behalf of the Greeks. In 337 Philip invited the Greek cities to send delegates to a conference at Corinth. A general peace was agreed. All the mainland states south of Olympos, except Spartē and some island states, became members of a federal union, 'the Greeks'. The so-called League of Corinth promptly allied with Philip and joined him in a declaration of war on Persia, for which Philip was elected *hēgemōn* ('leader'). Philip, however, was not destined to lead the crusade against Persia. On the eve of his departure on the expedition in 336, at the wedding celebrations for his daughter, Philip was stabbed to death by one of his bodyguards.

1.107 Many Greek states could not repress their glee at the death of Philip. They anticipated that Makedōn would fall back into its traditional disunity. But Philip was succeeded by his twenty-year-old son, Alexander, and Alexander realised that he must swiftly assert his authority. When Thebes revolted he immediately marched south and took decisive action. Only the house of the poet Pindar, it is said, was left standing in the city. Turning a blind eye to Athenian support for the Theban revolt, Alexander turned his attention to the attack on Persia. He crossed into Asia Minor and at the battle of the river Granikos in 334, defeated the Persians and went on to liberate most of Asia Minor from Persian control. Alexander carefully sent back captured arms from the Granikos victory to Athens, to indicate the defeat which he and his Greek allies, except the Spartans, had won over the old enemy. In the next year he defeated Dareios, the Persian king, at the battle of Issos. Dareios fled and offered a peace, which Alexander turned down – a sign that he was now intent on the conquest of the whole of the Persian Empire. In 332 and 331, Alexander occupied the countries of the eastern end of the Mediterranean and conquered Egypt, where he laid down plans for a great new city, Alexandria. In 331 Alexander marched into the heart of the Persian Empire. At Gaugamela in Mesopotamia, Dareios was once again defeated by Alexander and fled into the remoter parts of the Persian Empire, where he fell victim to one of his own satraps. Alexander was now the new Persian king, and he began to assume some of the garments and ritual associated with that role. His Makedonian colleagues were not sure that they approved.

1.108 The Greek cities, however, largely carried on with their business as usual in Alexander's absence. The Spartan king, Agis, tried to mount an anti-Makedonian revolt in the Peloponnese, but few other Greeks supported him. Antipatēr, the man Alexander had left in charge in Makedōnia, had no trouble putting the revolt down. Athens remained quiet. The Athenians were absorbed in more domestic matters – including the final round of the competition between Dēmosthenēs and Aiskhinēs. The occasion was the proposal by one Ktēsiphōn to reward Dēmosthenēs for his services to Athens with the grant of a crown. Aiskhinēs claimed that the proposal was illegal, and took Ktēsiphōn to court. The speeches of Aiskhinēs and Dēmosthenēs turned into a review of Athenian policy towards Makedōn. Aiskhinēs failed, and his public career ended. More positively, an Athenian financial expert, Lykourgos, carefully supervised the revenues of the city and presided over a period of prosperity and public building (in particular the rebuilding in stone of the theatre of Dionȳsos at the foot of the Akropolis). Athens had not known so much monumental building since the time of Periklēs.

1.109   The years following saw Alexander's great marches to the east through Persia, past the Caspian Sea, to Kandahar (another 'Alexandriā'), then north through the Hindu Kush to Samarkand and Tashkent, where Alexander found a wife, Roxane. Between 327 and 325, Alexander marched into northwest India and the Punjab. At the river Hyphasis his troops cried 'enough', and Alexander could not persuade them to travel further. There followed a long and agonising march back to Babylon, where the indefatigable Alexander made plans for an Arabian expedition. But, in the middle of 323, he fell ill of a fever and died after thirteen years of hectic conquest and endeavour. His senior officers immediately manoeuvred for position and within months had begun to carve out kingdoms for themselves from the empire which he had won.

1.110   In the last year of his life, Alexander had taken an interest once again in Greek cities. In particular he ordered that every city take back its exiles. Not only did this mean that those exiled for political reasons had to be welcomed back, with all the problems of restoration of property that that involved, but it also meant that the Athenians who had settled on Samos had to welcome back the displaced Samians. There was widespread discontent, and when the news arrived of Alexander's death, Athens joined other northern Greek states in revolt against Makedōn. When the Makedonian commander, Antipatēr, marched south, he was besieged in Lamia near Thermopylai during the winter of 323/2. However, in the summer of 322, Antipatēr defeated the Greeks at the battle of Krannōn. Although the defeat was not severe, the Greek cities' contingents melted away. 'Thus was the cause of freedom most shamefully abandoned' (Plutarch, *Life of Phokiōn* 26).

1.111   Antipatēr imposed hard terms on Athens. A Makedonian garrison was established on Mounykhia hill in the Peiraieus. The democratic system of government was to be abolished, and a new constitution with the vote restricted to the well-off introduced. In 322, Athens' experiment in democracy had been destroyed. Although the procedures of democracy would later be restored, the city-state never again enjoyed the position within Greece that it had enjoyed in the fifth or even fourth century.

1.112 Much of this outline survey of Athenian history has been dominated by war (the subject of ch. 7). In part this is a product of war being what caught ancient historians' attentions: both Hērodotos and Thucydides wrote to explain the causes and course of war. In part, however, it is because war was built into the very nature of the Greek city-states, which were fiercely independent. Their competitiveness made it impossible to unify them, or to devise the proper means for regulating relations between states. Comparative peace could be imposed upon the cities only by the intervention of an external power. That same competitiveness brought conflict within cities, which might be every bit as violent as conflict between cities. But the violence of that conflict and the fierceness of the competitiveness were not simply destructive. Their effect on what Greeks thought and wrote will be traced in the pages that follow.

2   Environment and settlement of Athens and Attikē

The Greek setting

2.1 The peninsula which constitutes the core of the modern state of Greece was never in antiquity politically united. As we have seen at 1.37, when the Athenians wished to assert their Greekness, they did so with reference not to territory but to gods, language, blood and customs. Greece was wherever those who regarded themselves as Greek lived: 'Hellēn' and 'Hellenic' were, and still are, words of pride and power. And following the extensive settlements established in the eighth, seventh, and sixth centuries in South Italy, Sicily, southern France, Spain, Libya, Egypt, and the coasts of Asia Minor, the Hellespont and the Black Sea, Greeks lived in almost every part of the Mediterranean basin. A recent calculation suggests there were 1,035 Greek city-states (*poleis*: see below) in all.

Landscape

2.2 Nevertheless, the mountainous Greek peninsula remained the heart of Greece, and can be seen to have played an important part in shaping the attitudes and expectations, as well as the military fortunes, of the Greeks. The mountains shut off one small area of plain from another and run in complex chains, constantly dominating the horizon. Only a few are high, notably Mt Olympos in the north, 2,917m and the Tāygetos mountains, which overlook Spartē, 2,407m. (For comparison, Ben Nevis in Scotland is 1,342m, and Mt Whitney in California (the highest mountain in the United States, excluding Alaska) is 4,418m.) Because of the mountains and the difficulty of communication over the ridges, the Greeks lived in the small, independent settlements which became the hallmark of classical Greek life. A settlement and its surrounding territory were called a *polis* (pl. *poleis*), a term regularly translated as 'city' or city-state', though the settlement might number only hundreds, rather than thousands, of inhabitants. The low, wooded hills which formed the boundaries of these *poleis* made effective borders to them. This was not so much because they were impenetrable, but because no individual could aspire to control agricultural land on both sides of the rough and uncultivated terrain. As a result the communities, though physically close, developed separately; for a traveller, the *polis* of

Megara lay only 50 km from Athens, that of Thebes 70 km, and that of Corinth 100 km.

2.3 As a result of the natural barriers and the limited resources commanded by any single settlement, it was rare for *poleis* to grow to any great size. Some islands individually comprised one *polis*, but it was not unknown for a large island to consist of more than one (for instance Lesbos, 1,630 sq. km, consisted of five *poleis*). Athens was an unusually large *polis*. It embraced a territory of some 2,500 sq. km known as Attikē (the size of present-day Luxembourg and slightly larger than the American state of Rhode Island), and had an outsize population to match (cf. 5.2–8). The area is a roughly triangular promontory, two sides of which are bordered by sea, while the third to the north-west is marked by the mountains of Kithairōn and Parnēs. These effectively shut Attikē off from Boiōtiā and the rest of central Greece. Although mainly a hilly region, there are three major plains: the Thriasian plain on the west, the plain of Athens and the Mesogeia (see Map 4). These are defined by four more mountainous areas (Aigaleos, Pentelikon, Hymēttos and Laureion).

2.4 Most settlements lay, like Athens, in the plains, where reasonably fertile soil supported various crops. The rivers which made their way through the plains were liable to dry up in high summer and to flood in winter, so were useless for transport. However, as the coastline is deeply indented with gulfs and promontories, no point on the Greek mainland is much more than 60 km from the sea; accordingly, it was the sea which provided waterways. Sailors in these waters were unlikely to lose sight of land for long, and the landmarks and islands offered some security from treacherous conditions. However, those same islands, and the steep cliffs and rugged coastlines, also created dangerous currents and down-draughts. When the winds rose, as they might in summer as well as winter, navigation became a hazardous business.

Climate

2.5 Apart from some mountainous areas of the central Peloponnese and Crete, southern Greece enjoys the type of climate called 'Mediterranean': winter rains and summer droughts. In the winter, rainfall is heavy but intermittent, and there are many days when the sky is clear, the sun warm and the breeze cool. But the north wind occasionally has the bite that characterises it in more northerly countries. In summer there is virtually no rain for two to four months, apart from an occasional thunderstorm or brief mist, and the intense heat of noontime can bring activity to a halt. However, for about forty days in the latter half of summer, the hot air rising over the Sahara regularly draws the cold air from Europe down over the Aegean. The sea then becomes boisterous, sailing is hampered, and navigation northwards well-nigh impossible. These winds are the strong, steady 'Etesians', what the Greeks today call the *meltemi*. But if the pattern is regular, the particular form it takes in any one year is highly unpredictable. Particularly in south-eastern Greece, where Athens lies, levels of rainfall vary very significantly from year to year, and more than once a decade rainfall is insufficient to sustain cereal crops.

2.6 Until modern heavy industrialisation, the atmosphere everywhere had a piercing clarity which sharpened the outline of landscape and buildings, so that even distant landmarks could be seen: Corinth's citadel from the Athenian Akropolis (over 80 km), the island of Mēlos from Cape Sounion (over 100 km). Unlike the cold of northern Europe which invites a private, indoor existence, the Mediterranean climate encouraged an outdoor life. As we shall see below, the possibility of life being public led to the development of distinct gender roles: men lived their lives out of doors, constantly observed by one another and made to feel the need to succeed in front of other men and to fear the open shame of failure (4.9–12); women who wanted to be thought 'respectable' remained publicly invisible, occupied in the interior courtyards and upper rooms of their home (5.25–9). The Greeks themselves were inclined to draw attention to the general effects of climate on the whole character of people. Here is Aristotle on the virtues which, in his view, are connected with the climate of Greece:

> The peoples who live in cold climates and in European areas are full of energy, but rather lacking in intelligence and skill; they therefore in general retain their freedom but lack political organisation and the ability to control their neighbours. The peoples of Asia, on the other hand, are better endowed with intellect and skill, but lack energy and so remain in political subjection. But the people of Greece occupy a middle geographical position and correspondingly have a share of both characteristics, both energy and intelligence. They therefore retain their freedom and have the best of political institutions; indeed, if they could achieve political unity, they could control the rest of the world. (Aristotle, *Politics* 7.7, 1327b) (see 1.99).

Mineral resources

2.7 The three major natural resources of the Athenians were building stone, clay and metals. Limestone of varying quality for building was available in virtually all parts of Greece, but Attikē, and a number of Aegean islands, also had high-grade marble suitable for building and fine stone sculpture. The high-quality marbles from beneath Mt Pentelikon and Mt Hymēttos were used for building to an extent unique in the Greek world. Pentelikon marble was white and crisp, giving precision to the lines of the buildings on which it was used, while marble from Hymēttos had a bluish colour. Of the coarser limestones, there were the hard blue-grey 'Akropolis' limestone; the blue-black Eleusinian; the yellowish-grey Kara from Hymēttos; and the softer limestone from the Peiraieus area, more workable and so more popular. Hymēttos also provided a reddish conglomerate that was a natural concrete, much used in foundations. A brownish, less weighty limestone was imported from the

2.1 The face of an ancient quarry on Mount Pentelikon in Attikē.

nearby island of Aigīna. The Pentelic marble used on the structure, architectural sculpture and even roof-tiles of the Parthenōn temple stands out as a supreme example of what it could do; but its uniqueness is emphasised by the contrast with the buildings of the *agorā*, where even from the ruins one can form a more varied and truer picture of the variety of textures and colours that Attic building stones possess (6.79).

2.8 Clay is most familiar to us for its use in the production of baked pottery, roof-tiles, architectural decoration and small-scale figurines. But there was also a heavy demand for unbaked sun-dried bricks, sometimes used instead of stone in fortification walls and an almost universal building material for houses (the Greek for 'burglar' is *toikhōrukhos*, 'one who digs through a wall'). Again, all over Greece local clay was suitable for cooking wares, storage vessels and other everyday pottery. Athens, however, possessed an unusually fine clay that, when baked, became a distinctive orange colour. It was this that was the

2.2 An ancient washery compound excavated in the Laureion district of Attikē.

material basis for the black- and red-figure pots which dominated the central Mediterranean pottery market for about two hundred years from c. 550 (8.88–9).

2.9 Metal ores are found in only a few areas of Greece. Copper was mainly imported from Cyprus; it was the first metal to be smelted, and *khalkeus* – a 'coppersmith' (from *khalkos* meaning 'copper') – was the word later used for all smiths. Tin was necessary to turn soft copper into hard bronze for armour, statues, containers, etc., but was even rarer, and had to be acquired from outside the Greek world altogether. It was probably one of the things for which the Greeks had relied on the Phoenicians in the archaic period (Cornish tin made its way to the Mediterranean from an early date). But Athens was rich in silver, which was found together with lead in the Laureion district of southern Attikē (see 1.32) and also on the island of Siphnos and in Thrace to the north of the Aegean, where it was found together with gold. Both metals were used in the manufacture of coinage and luxury objects. Athens' silver financed both her building activities and her fleet, and was the basis of her power. Lead was mined as well as silver at Laureion. Iron, however, though it exists in Laureion as it does sporadically on mainland Greece, was mined in only a few places (e.g. Lakōnia) and the Athenians seem to have imported theirs from the islands, Thrace or from the west.

Vegetation

2.10   The plains provided some small areas of high fertility which bore succulent fruits. But the shallow soils amidst the bare rocks of the hillsides supported trees and wild flowers, gorse and scrub, and were generally unsuitable for cultivation (2.15). To increase the area of cultivable land, terracing was adopted. This was less common then than more recently in Greece but, even with terraces, less than half of the total land area was capable of growing the most important crops: cereals, olives and vines. Timber of various qualities was relatively easily available, even in Attikē; great quantities were used in the construction of houses, as a component of larger buildings (public as well as private), and for fuel. It is notable that when people moved into Athens in response to Periklēs' defensive strategy against the Spartans, they took the woodwork of their houses with them; and later, at the time of the plague, there was, understandably, a shortage of wood in Athens for pyres to burn the dead (Thucydides, *Peloponnesian War* 2.14, 42). But for shipbuilding Athens was heavily dependent on outside sources, mainly Makedōnia, where the high mountains produced the necessary pine and fir trees (5.58; 7.3).

2.11   Greeks were all too aware of how unproductive their land was. This can be illustrated by a passage from Xenophōn, who was returning from a year away in Persia as a mercenary (1.88). Here he keenly praises the site of Kalpē (modern Kerpe) on the southern shore of the Black Sea, furnished with natural features and resources that Greeks prized so highly:

> Kalpē harbour lies midway on the voyage between Herakleia and Byzantion. It is a bit of land jutting out into the sea, the seaward side being a precipitous cliff, whose minimum height is 35 m while the neck joining it to the mainland is about 120 m across. The area to the seaward side of this neck is large enough to hold a population of ten thousand. The harbour is right at the foot of the cliff and the beach faces west. There is an abundant spring of fresh water just by the sea and commanded by the headland. There is a lot of timber of various sorts, and in particular a lot of fine ship-timber right down by the sea. The high land extends about 3 km inland and the soil is good and free from stones; the land bordering the sea is thickly wooded with large trees of all kinds for a distance of more than 3 km. There is a lot more good country with many inhabited villages. The land bears barley and wheat, all kinds of vegetables, apples, sesame, beans, plenty of figs, a lot of vines which produce a good sweet wine, and indeed everything else except olives.
> (Xenophōn, *Anabasis* 6.4.36)

Xenophōn might almost be advertising Kalpē as the ideal site for a new Greek settlement, as it afforded nearly all the conditions for peaceful and productive existence, and for trade.

2.12   Attikē, situated in the driest part of Greece, has rather shallow soils on the hills and mountains. Ancient authors could not agree as to whether it was unusually good (so Xenophōn) or unusually bad (so Thucydides) for agriculture. Plato, blaming deluges (evidence for deforestation is very meagre), likened Attikē to 'the skeleton of a body wasted by disease; the rich soft soil has all run away, leaving the land nothing but skin and bone' (*Kritiās* 111b–c). Despite Plato's gloomy picture, Attikē still had a variety of trees: planes, cypresses and elms, and in Athens itself these trees were planted in the *agorā*.

Farming

2.13   Ownership of land, which was often restricted to full members of a community, was fundamental to Greek society. Wealth was generally based on land (either directly from crops or indirectly from rent); and care for the land of one's ancestors, together with the religious associations of their shrines there, was of prime concern (cf. 5.12). For the small farmer with his smallholding and for the wealthy man with his more numerous landholdings alike, security of livelihood and status in the eyes of others were rooted in the maintenance of their inherited property (cf. 5.50).

2.14   For the majority of Greeks, farming was their livelihood. Their year fell into a regular pattern. This was marked not by months of the year but by the seasons (which demanded different tasks), and by the phenomena that marked the onset of changes in the weather, e.g. the appearance and position of the important stars and constellations. Major events in the year were: gathering in the wine-producing grapes in September; ploughing and sowing in October and November; gathering olives in November; and harvesting grain in May (cf. 5.52). Times of busy activity – harvest, vintage, the ploughing season – alternated with times when there was relatively little to do. The various festivals of thanksgiving that punctuated the year were expressions of real gratitude to the gods for assuring that year's food supply; the merry-making reflected an understandable feeling of relief (cf. 3.7). It was on such festive occasions that worshippers sacrificed the animals they bred on their farms to provide an acceptable savour of offering to the gods (cf. 3.28) – and a good meal of meat for themselves into the bargain. This would have been a special treat, since everyday food consisted mainly of bread and vegetables. At times, even such meagre fare might not be available. Apollodōros underlines how serious a bad year could be: 'my land not only produced no crops, but that year, as you all know, even the water dried up in the wells, so not a vegetable grew in the garden' ([Dēmosthenēs], *Against Polyklēs* 50.61). Also, the absence of a citizen farmer on a military campaign, normally fought in the summer, might threaten the very survival of his family at home.

2.15   The range of farming available for Greeks was determined by the division of the countryside into wooded mountainsides; hillsides covered with brush and scrub; and the cultivable plains in the valleys. These arable lands (Latin *arābilis*, 'ploughable') were sown with barley and wheat. Wheat was reckoned

2.3 A late sixth-century terracotta group of a ploughman with his yoke of oxen, made in Boiōtiā (cf. fig. 5.20).

more palatable for human consumption, but barley is more resistant to drought and will grow in relatively poor soils. The other two staple crops were vines and olives, the latter in particular being able to survive in poor soil. If one is to picture the Athenian countryside, there will be a house with its adjacent garden, perhaps artificially irrigated, of vegetables and fruits, its pigs and chickens; and then an irregular pattern of fields fanning outwards, dividing the land into patches of vineyards and olive groves, with perhaps grain growing between the trees. On open spaces exposed to the wind, the farmer lays out his threshing floors. The whole farm is dotted with inconvenient rocks that protrude through the thin covering of soil. A comedy by the Athenian Menander provides a description that is perhaps only marginally exaggerated:

> 'Poor wretch; what a life! He's a typical Attic farmer,
> Struggling with rocks that yield nothing but savory and sage
> And getting nothing out of it but aches and pains.'
> (Menander, *Dyskolos* 604–6)

2.16 Priority was everywhere given to grain land; the poor land was given over to pasture, and this tended to be at a distance from settlements. Large cattle were few, and of these the ox was the most useful for the heavy work on the farm and for the slow and expensive business of haulage. Mules and donkeys, used for carrying lighter loads, would have been a commoner sight in the farms

2.4 Harvesting grapes on a late sixth-century Athenian black-figure *amphorā*.

and on the pathways. Horses were a sign of a rich man, who would use them for hunting and racing (the disabled client of Lysiās, 24.11–12 defends himself against the allegation that he was getting above himself by hiring a horse while claiming a pension). They were expensive to keep, as they needed grain as feed to maintain them in good condition, and grain was usually required for human consumption. Their harness was rudimentary and, if the horse put his head down to pull, soon choked him. The horse was therefore unsuitable for heavy draught work on either farm or road, while the absence of stirrups limited its usefulness in war (stirrup-less riders being easily unseated) (cf. 7.25). It was only in the lusher parts of northern Greece (Thessaly and beyond) that horses were raised in any numbers. The pastures were given over primarily to sheep and goats; both were driven up to the mountains in summer where the shepherds would live a remote and isolated life, and in winter the animals were brought back to the protection of the valleys. Sheep and goats, *not* the cow, provided cheese and milk. Medical writings ascribed to Hippokratēs advised against drinking cows' milk, and modern biological evidence suggests that northern Europeans adapted specially in order to digest it. The short-haired sheep provided valuable soft wool which made very fine cloth. More common were coarser, long-haired sheep. Of the wild animals that roamed the hills, the most common were hares and deer, though wild boars and bears were to be found in the more wooded parts and even lions were not unknown.

2.17 Pasture was particularly scarce in Attikē, and when large teams of draught oxen were required for building projects they seem to have been brought in from Boiōtiā. Athenian farmers had to choose between seeing directly to their own subsistence by growing barley, or risking the vagaries of the market and putting their land largely under olives, which resist drought. Olive oil was the only agricultural product of which the Athenians reckoned regularly to have a surplus. It was given away in *amphorā*s at the festival of the *Panathēnaia* as prizes. Indeed, so closely were the people of Attikē associated with the olive that it was claimed that it had been a gift of Athēnē to the land and that it had first grown in Attikē. From at least the middle of the fifth century onwards, the Athenians regularly imported quite a high proportion of the grain they needed, much of it coming from the lands round the Black Sea, from North Africa and from Sicily (6.65–9).

Travel and communications

2.18 Overland travel was arduous and not lightly undertaken. The terrain was difficult, and although carriage roads existed, they consisted of ruts cut into the stone, and progress along them was slow and uncomfortable. The majority of people stayed near to home, walking or riding a donkey into town or local village for the market, or to the farmlands for their daily tasks. The 7-km walk from Athens to the Peiraieus and the journey back might have been counted by many as an everyday excursion (cf. 2.24). Travelling by cart was a sign of status. Princess Nausikaā took her companions and the royal washing to the shore in a mule-drawn cart (Homer, *Odyssey* 6.36–92). King Lāios was travelling in a horse-drawn cart when he was met at a crossroads by his son Oidipous and killed (Sophoklēs, *Oidipous Tyrannos* 800–13). Kleobis and Bitōn substituted themselves for the oxen that had not arrived in time to take their mother to the festival at the sanctuary of Hērā near Argos where she was a priestess (Hērodotos, *Histories* 1.31). Pots made for weddings showed the bride travelling in a cart. Lighter, more manoeuvrable chariots drawn by horses were what the wealthy used for racing and processions. For heavy haulage, e.g. to transport goods such as farm produce, ox carts were needed, but as they had no swivelling axle for negotiating corners, they were not used outside the plains. Pack animals like donkeys transported goods over longer distances and more rugged terrain.

2.19 For transport of all kinds, the sea was therefore the preferred and more economical choice. Some areas of Greece were more self-sufficient than others,

2.5 A well-laden donkey on an early fifth-century red-figure cup attributed to the Antiphōn Painter.

but few could be completely independent of the sea. In the fifth and fourth centuries Athens was strongly dependent upon what was brought in by sea, for two reasons: first, Attikē did not produce enough cereals for the urban population; and second, Athens and the Peiraieus flourished on a reputation for being the place to which one came to find goods from all over the Greek world (cf. 2.27, 5.58). Few voyages would have been taken for pleasure, as pirates were a constant source of danger until the Athenians cleared them from the Aegean in the 470s. Nor was a sea-voyage possible at all times of the year (3.25). The islands lying within the Aegean basin enabled sailors to chart their course by reference to fixed points, but traders did not avoid the open sea. The slow, broad cargo-ships depended on sail and wind, and travelled at an average speed of five knots. Nelson's *Victory*, a much larger and heavier warship with sails, averaged seven knots. Ships powered by oars were swifter than sailing ships, but were used mainly in time of war. The trireme, with 170 rowers, was the fastest and the finest man-of-war in the classical period. It could reach a speed of seven to eight knots with a continuous power output, or even up to 13 knots for a short burst of ten to twenty minutes. But with their complement of about two hundred and their need to be as light as possible, they carried few provisions and had to put in frequently to enable the rowers to rest and eat (cf. 7.34–5). Greek cargo-ships, however, with their small number of crew and their heavy loads, had no reason for rationing the supply

2.6 A red-figure *loutrophoros* (a vessel used to carry water for the bridal bath) showing a bride in a light-weight wheeled vehicle (compare also figs. 5.2–4).

of food and water. They could sail for many days and nights without putting in to land.

2.20 When information needed to be conveyed quickly, a runner could be used (cf. 2.24), or a beacon fire or fast ship. The most famous runner was Pheidippidēs, who in two days ran the 250 km from Athens to Spartē to ask for help against the Persians who had landed at Marathōn (1.29). Beacon fires were used for signalling messages in time of war, e.g. to alert a town to an attack (2.25). Thucydides relates how a swift ship was used to prevent the slaughter of the people of Mytilēnē on the island of Lesbos (see 1.59):

> Another trireme was at once despatched in haste, for fear that the first might arrive before it and the city be found destroyed . . . the crew made such efforts on the voyage that they took their meals (a mixture of barley, oil and wine) while they rowed, and took it in turns to row and sleep. They were lucky to

meet no contrary wind, and as the first ship made no haste on its monstrous mission, while the second pressed on as described, the first arrived so little ahead that Pakhēs had only just time to read the decree and prepare to carry out its sentence when the second put into harbour and prevented the massacre. (Thucydides, *Peloponnesian War* 3.49)

The settlement of Attikē

2.21 Throughout the period with which this book is concerned, Athens was an independent *polis*. But not all the citizens of Athens the state lived in Athens the town. The territory of Attikē stretched some 60 km from Mt Parnēs to Sounion, and some 40 km from Marathōn to the coast opposite the island of Salamīs, which itself belonged to Athens. The majority of the Athenian citizenry lived in smaller or larger settlements scattered across Attikē. The Athenians told the story that once upon a time the largest of these settlements had been independent communities, and that these had then been unified under Athens' leadership (1.16). Kleisthenēs' reforms at the end of the sixth century (1.25) had given a defined political role to these country towns and villages as 'demes' (*dēmoi*), and throughout the classical period they flourished as local centres. Some of the residents of more outlying demes still had little contact with Athens. As we can deduce from the rich finds of sixth-century sculpture and pottery in local cemeteries, wealthy Athenians continued to live and presumably spend their money in the settlements of Attikē from which they originated, and not simply in the city. Country folk may well have been disinclined to attend political meetings in Athens because of the distance or local loyalties: certainly in the fifth century, men from the town of Athens are peculiarly well represented among state officials. The natural reluctance of residents of Attikē to uproot themselves from ancestral lands and move into town at the beginning of the Peloponnesian War was noted by Thucydides (cf. 1.57):

> They were heavy-hearted and reluctant to leave their homes and the temples with their traditional and time-honoured institutions, to change their way of life, and to leave behind what was to them their native city. (*Peloponnesian War* 2.16)

Major festivals certainly tempted some men from outlying parts into town, but most country centres had their own cults, markets and fairs, and tragedy and comedy could be seen in country theatres as well as in the Theatre of Dionȳsos at Athens (cf. 3.55; 8.46).

2.22 The towns and villages of Attikē had their own character and identity. The small fortified town of Eleusīs, 16 km west of Athens, was noted for its cult of Dēmētēr and Persephonē and for its celebration of the Eleusinian Mysteries in honour of Dēmētēr (3.50–2). This festival attracted thousands

2.7 The late sixth-century grave *stēlē* of Aristion from Velanidesa in eastern Attikē.

of worshippers, not just from Attikē but from other parts of Greece as well. The Hall of the Mysteries there (*Telestērion*) took an architectural form distinct from normal Greek temples since the initiates actually gathered inside it. Both in the fifth and again in the fourth century this building was enlarged and made grander. Akharnai, a few kilometres north of Athens, was noted for its charcoal-burners who derived their wood from the slopes of nearby Mt Parnēs; in his *Akharnians* of 425, Aristophanēs makes fun of the belligerent character of these people, no doubt temporarily enhanced because they were regularly in the path of Spartan invasions (cf. 1.57, 8.72). Thorikos on the east coast lay near the mining installations of Laureion and presented a more industrialised aspect than the country villages: washeries for concentrating minerals from the mined ore have been excavated lying cheek by jowl

2.8 The late sixth-century theatre at Thorikos, with the corner of a restored washery for concentrating silver ore seen in the foreground.

with a cemetery and a late sixth-century theatre, while an architecturally innovative temple of Dēmētēr was built there in the later fifth century. The Thorikos theatre was one of several deme theatres in Attikē; and its fifth-century temple was one of a series built more or less contemporaneously with the Parthenōn, and showing the influence of the Parthenōn in their design. These settlements were not at all dormitories for the town of Athens, but thriving communities in which considerable wealth was invested and expended.

2.23 Both Eleusīs and Thorikos are settlements going back to the late Bronze Age (1.8), but the harbour town of Peiraieus, 7–8 km south-west of Athens, was created only in the fifth century. Up until that time the Athenians relied on beaching ships in Phalēron Bay; but when the navy was enlarged and commercial activity increased, the port of Peiraieus was established on and around the neighbouring promontory of Aktē. There were three harbours. Kantharos on the west was the main harbour and commercial emporium. It had a market on the east side and the *deigma*, a place for displaying goods. Zeā and Mounykhiā on the east were smaller, and for warships. All three were noted for their splendid ship-sheds. The town itself was laid out on a regular grid pattern of streets by Hippodāmos, a native of the Greek city of Mīlētos on the west coast of Asia Minor where a similar street plan was also used. In contrast to Athens, notorious for narrow and winding streets (cf. 1.26), the harbour town must have looked rigidly organised, with straight streets, well-placed houses and open public areas. Besides the naval installations, the town boasted many of the amenities that Athens had, including a set of fortifications that were necessary to protect Athens' trade, and a theatre. By the middle of the fifth century, the harbour was linked to Athens by Long Walls, no mean feat of construction given the distance covered and the marshy character of the terrain at the Peiraieus end. The population of the Peiraieus was mixed. Foreign traders lodged there temporarily, and so did many of Athens' resident aliens (*metoikoi*). Some of them were responsible for Athens' trade and ran businesses such as armouries and banking. The *metoikoi* might also be grain-dealers or carry on such trades as fulling (cleaning and thickening cloth) and baking (cf. 5.4, 57, 67ff.).

2.24 This mixture of population meant that the shrines and sanctuaries that dotted the harbour town boasted a greater variety of worship than places less accessible to foreign influence, and such non-Greek deities as Bendīs and Kybēlē had shrines there. These religious novelties were very attractive to curious Athenians like Sōkratēs and Glaukōn; indeed, it was a festival of the Thracian goddess Bendīs that had drawn them to visit the Peiraieus as described at the beginning of Plato's *Republic* (cf. 3.43):

> I went down yesterday to the Peiraieus with Glaukōn, son of Aristōn. I wanted to say a prayer to the Goddess and also to see what they would make of the festival, as this was the first time they were holding it. I must say that I thought the local contribution to the procession was splendid, though the Thracian contingent seemed to show up just as well. We had said our prayers and seen the show and were on our way back to town when Polemarkhos, son of Kephalos, caught sight of us in the distance making our way home, and sent his slave running on ahead to tell us to wait for him. The slave caught hold of my coat from behind and said, 'Polemarkhos says you are to wait.' I turned and asked where his master was. 'He's coming along behind you,' he said, 'Do wait.' 'We will', said Glaukōn, and soon afterwards Polemarkhos came up. With him were Adeimantos, Glaukōn's brother, Nīkēratos, son of Nīkiās, and others who had all apparently been to the procession. (Plato, *Republic* 1.327)

Although the conversation in the *Republic* is imaginary, the setting is real enough and the characters involved belong to the highest society of late fifth-century Athens. Adeimantos and Glaukōn were Plato's elder brothers, and the family can be traced back to the mid-seventh century. Nīkēratos was the son of the Athenian politician Nīkiās who was one of the military commanders of the disastrous Athenian expedition to Sicily in 415; the family was extremely rich, with slaves hired out to work in mines as a main source of income. Kephalos' family also owned slaves and had a lucrative arms factory in the Peiraieus; Polemarkhos' brother was the speech-writer Lysiās (cf. 1.82). Kephalos himself had been invited from Syracuse to Athens by Periklēs, and the family were not citizens, but *metoikoi*.

2.25   Since the Peiraieus was so vital for Athens' prosperity and safety, there was a system for early warning in the case of attack. Here Thucydides describes a surprise attack by sea on Peiraieus early on during the Peloponnesian War in 429, which, had it been successful, might have brought the war to an end at once:

> Knēmos and Brasidās and the others in command of the Peloponnesian fleet decided on the advice of the Megarians to make an attempt on the Peiraieus, the port of Athens, which the Athenians, reasonably enough because of their superiority at sea, had left open and unguarded. The plan was that each sailor should take his oar, cushion and oar-loop, and that they should then proceed on foot to the sea on the Athenian side, make for Megara as quickly as they could and launch from the docks at Nīsaia forty ships which happened to be there and then sail straight to the Peiraieus . . . They arrived by night, launched the ships from Nīsaia and sailed, not for Peiraieus as they had originally intended, thinking it too risky (and because the wind was unfavourable, it was said later) but to the promontory of Salamīs that fronts Megara . . . Meanwhile beacons were lit to warn Athens of the attack, and the biggest panic of the war ensued. Those in the city thought the enemy had already sailed into Peiraieus, those in Peiraieus thought Salamīs had fallen and that an attack on themselves was imminent. Indeed if the enemy had resolved to be a little bolder this might well have happened, and no wind could have prevented it. But at daybreak the Athenians assembled in force at the Peiraieus, launched their ships, embarked in haste, and sailed in some confusion to Salamīs leaving a garrison to guard the Peiraieus. When the Peloponnesians saw that relief was on the way, they made off in haste to Nīsaia . . . After this the Athenians took stricter precautions for the Peiraieus in the future by closing the harbour and by other suitable measures.
> (Thucydides, *Peloponnesian War* 2.93)

The city of Athens

2.26   The plain of Athens is the largest in Attikē; it is enclosed to the west, north and east by hills (Aigaleos, Parnēs, Pentelikon and Hymēttos) but is open to the sea on the south. About 6 km inland from the Saronic gulf a precipitous limestone rock rises 120 m from the surrounding plain, the Akropolis (lit. 'city-top', 'citadel'). This was a natural refuge in time of trouble and the original site of the settlement that developed into the city of Athens. Rocky outcrops lie in close proximity to it – the Areopagus ('the Crag of Arēs'), where the council of ex-archons met (6.38), the Pnyx (which the Athenians assumed to signify 'the Crowded Place'), where the *ekklēsiā* met, as well as the hills of the Nymphs and the Muses. The plain was watered by two seasonal rivers, destructive in winter, much reduced in summer. These flow close to the Akropolis: the Kēphīsos on the west rising in Mt Parnēs and flowing into the bay of Phalēron, and the Īlīsos on the east rising in Mt Hymēttos and flowing into the Kēphīsos; the brook of the Eridanos is smaller and flows into the

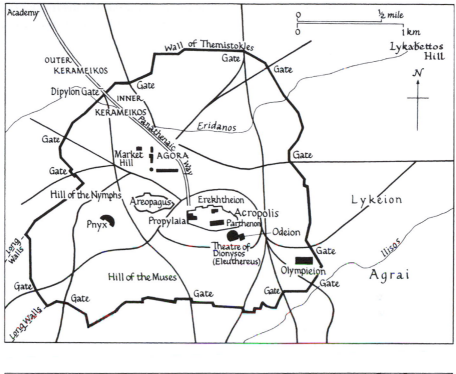

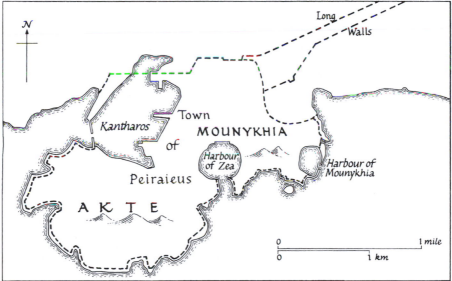

2.9 Plans of the classical city of Athens, showing the line of the Themistoklean Wall, and of the Peiraieus, showing the fourth-century walls.

Īlīsos from Mt Lykabēttos to the north. The Akropolis itself holds water all year round. This issues as natural springs lower down the slope, but there were many man-made wells too. This shows that the natural water supply was never sufficient for the needs of the local inhabitants. Consequently, by the late sixth century fountain-houses were being built to be fed by underground pipelines, bringing in water from outside the city. A traveller ('Hērakleidēs') who first saw Athens in the early third century sets the scene:

> He then comes to the city of the Athenians; the road is pleasant; the ground is cultivated all the way, and has a kindly look. The city is all dry, not well-watered; the streets are badly laid out because of their antiquity. The houses are mostly mean; few are commodious. Strangers visiting the city might be struck by sudden doubt, whether this is really the renowned city of the Athenians; but after a little while one might well believe it. (F. Pfister, *Die Reisebilder des Hērakleidēs* (Vienna 1951) 1.1)

2.27   Athens seems to have been more or less continuously important as a settlement from the late neolithic onwards (1.8). After the fall of the Mycenaean palaces our evidence from Athens between 1100 and 800 is mostly provided by the tombs found to the north-west of the Akropolis. It is very largely from the number of tombs and from their grave goods that we have to reconstruct the history of the Athenian community down to the end of the seventh century (1.13–16). Tombs were usually dug alongside the tracks that led out of a town, beyond the inhabited centres. As a result, their position – they are placed increasingly further and further out along the Eridanos valley – indicates the gradually increasing size of the living area of Athens. As to civic life, our literary sources indicate that in the archaic period the civic centre (*agorā*) lay north-east of the Akropolis, but this area is heavily built over by the modern city and little archaeology has been possible. In the late sixth century, some of the flat ground immediately to the north of the Areopagus, which until c. 600 had been an area of fields, private dwellings and family tombs, was taken over and developed into a new *agorā* (lit. 'gathering-place'). This open ground came to be the arena for many communal activities that made up the life of the town: religious, commercial, political, legal, administrative. It was the heart of the community, and the meanings which other forms of the word *agorā* carry, such as 'address a public meeting' and 'buy', neatly embrace the variety of activities pursued there. The comic poet Euboulos provides a witty list of saleable goods in the fourth century:

> You will find everything sold together in the same place at Athens: figs, witnesses to summonses, bunches of grapes, turnips, pears, apples, givers of evidence, roses, medlars, porridge, honeycombs, chick-peas, lawsuits, milk-puddings, myrtle, allotment-machines [for random jury-selection], irises, lambs, water-clocks [for timing law-court speeches], laws, indictments. (Euboulos, fr. 74)

2.10 One of the improvements to Athens in the sixth century was the provision of a
public fountain-house in the *agorā*. This sixth-century water jug (*hydriā*) shows women
visiting the public fountain.

2.28 Throughout the sixth century the Athenians improved their public facilities.
The temple of Athēnē Polias on the Akropolis underwent two building phases;
there was more temple building on the Akropolis; a massive temple was begun
by the river Īlīsos; and other more minor monuments were put up, including
the first buildings of the classical *agorā* (cf. 1.22). In 522 Peisistratos' grand-
son had an altar to the Twelve Gods (the core pantheon of Olympian deities,
headed by Zeus) erected in the northern part of the *agorā* by the side of the
Panathenaic Way, a place of refuge and asylum.

2.29 The development of the *agorā* gives clear evidence of the radical reordering of
the political life of the whole Athenian state which was put in train by
Kleisthenēs (see 1.23–5), although the precise chronology of the buildings is no
easy matter to settle (see 2.33). At this time, it was marked by boundary stones
(*horoi*) that staked out the public area as a religious precinct and made it closed
to certain types of criminal, a useful reminder of the way in which secular and
religious life were closely linked. A group of statues commemorating the

2.11 Sixth-century boundary stone of the Athenian *agorā*, inscribed 'I am the boundary of the *agorā*'.

tyrant-slayers, Harmodios and Aristogeitōn, was set up near the Panathenaic Way, a symbol for the newly emerging democracy. Because of the increasing amount of political and social life, a number of the public events had to be held away from the *agorā*. For example, the meetings of the *ekklēsiā* were transferred to the Pnyx west of the Akropolis; and the dramatic competitions, instituted perhaps in the 530s, perhaps in the last decade of the sixth century, took place in the sanctuary of Dionȳsos Eleuthereus on the south slope of the Akropolis (8.45–51).

2.30 No trace of an archaic fortification wall has been found, but there is sufficient written evidence to assure its existence. It may have been built in the 560s, when the Akropolis ceased to be a fortress and became a religious sanctuary. The Delphic oracle's advice to the Athenians before the Persian sack of 480, quoted by Hērodotos, is useful here:

'Unhappy people, why stay you here? Leave your homes
And the heights encircled by your city like a wheel
And flee to the ends of the earth.' (Hērodotos, *Histories* 7.140.2)

This suggests the shape of the sixth-century city, with the Akropolis at the centre of a circle of fortification wall. By 500, Peisistratos' establishment of city cults and Kleisthenēs' political reforms had made Athens the centre and indispensable guiding force of all Attikē.

2.31 The victory the Athenians gained over the Persians at Marathōn in 490 inspired them to raise a new temple to Athēnē on the southern part of the Akropolis (the 'Older Parthenōn') and to improve the entrance to the sanctuary on its west side by erecting the first new gateway and forecourt since the Mycenaean period. Neither of these ventures had been completed when the Persians sacked the city in 480. When the Persians had been repulsed in 479 and the Athenians returned to their devastated city, they proceeded to build new defensive walls, despite Spartan opposition (1.41). Thucydides records that Themistoklēs gave instructions to the Athenians:

> The whole population of the city was to work on the wall. No building, private or public, which could provide material was to be spared but all were to be demolished. (Thucydides, *Peloponnesian War* 1.90)

Signs of the hasty construction have been made visible by excavations which show that architectural members, tombstones, statues and statue bases were used alongside the more usual materials. The circuit was roughly 6.5 km in length and made use of such neighbouring low hills as those of the Muses and Nymphs; it was furnished with thirteen gates and an unknown number of towers and posterns. The main gate was located in the north-west where the wall now ran through the old Kerameikos or Potters' Quarter. The classical cemeteries were now firmly fixed outside the wall at the sides of the roads that led to different parts of Attikē; the most important cemetery was still that in the north-west (now the Outer Kerameikos), the site of the earlier main cemetery. By the side of the roads that fan out from there, public grave monuments were set up by the state and family plots were cared for by well-to-do Athenians; it was here too, from a specially constructed platform, that Periklēs gave the traditional Funeral Speech in 431/430 (9.9).

2.32 The Peiraieus had been developed and fortified as the port of Athens from the 490s (cf. 1.32, 2.23). With the development of the Delian League, it became Athens' vital link with its overseas allies. This led in the 460s–450s to the erection of the Long Walls that connected Athens across country to the Peiraieus (Northern Wall) and to the coast at the bay of Phalēron (Phaleric Wall; course uncertain); another (Middle Wall), parallel to the original Peiraieus wall and c. 180 m apart from it, was erected in the 440s at the instigation of Periklēs. The main Athens–Peiraieus road lay outside the walls on the north side; the space between the Northern and Middle Walls (nicknamed 'the Legs') was used for military purposes, but at the beginning of the

Peloponnesian War was a camping-ground for refugees from the country districts of Attikē (cf. 1.57); there was another incursion of refugees after the Spartan occupation of Dekeleia in 413 (Thucydides, *Peloponnesian War* 7.19).

2.33 Within the new circuit wall so hastily erected, the Athenians turned their attention to the task of building the city anew. The private houses and workshops, with walls of unbaked brick on a foundation of small stones and clay, and roofed with tiles of baked clay, were rebuilt piecemeal, and some were still unfinished fifty years later at the outbreak of the Peloponnesian War (431). As a community, the Athenians first concentrated on rebuilding the *agorā*. There was much to do, and old materials were readily used in the reconstruction. A Council Chamber (*bouleutērion*) was constructed for the Council or steering committee (*boulē*) of the Assembly (*ekklēsiā*); a round meeting and dining room (the *tholos*) were built for their standing committee (the *prutaneis*); and a colonnaded building (the Royal Stoā or *Stoā Basileōs*) was put up for the officer of state (the *arkhōn basileus*) whose prime function was justice. It was here that the officers of state stood on a block of stone (*lithos*) to take their oath to abide by the state's laws, and here also that the 'Laws of Solōn', carved on stone, were made accessible to the citizens. Before the middle of the century, work had begun on a further colonnaded building, the *Stoā Poikilē* (the 'Colonnade with the Paintings'), whose walls were decorated with murals, including one of the now legendary battle of Marathōn. The archaeological site of the *agorā* today is an open and largely shade-less place, but Kīmōn, the influential Athenian politician, is said to have embellished the *agorā* during these years with plane trees (some replaced by modern planting). In the middle of the fifth century, a prison (*desmōtērion*) for state debtors and those awaiting trial was erected alongside the road that led southwest from the *agorā* to the Pnyx.

2.34 Soon after the middle of the century, attention turned from civic to religious buildings. These included a temple of Hēphaistos on rising ground known as *Kolōnos Agoraios* above the west side of the *agorā*, built amidst the workshops of the potters and bronze-smiths whose district this was. None the less, it was temple building on the Akropolis to which the Athenians gave priority. No attempt had been made to rebuild the Akropolis temples in the thirty years following the Persian sack. The ruins of the archaic temple had been patched up to provide a safe home for the old wooden image which the Athenians had taken with them when they fled; but the foundations of the 'Older Parthenōn' had been left bare, to act as a reminder of Persian aggression. But after the middle of the century, peace with Persia was a fact (1.50–1), and a new building project, which had the political backing of Periklēs and the artistic supervision of Pheidiās, was inaugurated. Work now started on a new temple to Athēnē which we know as the Parthenōn, built on the highest part of the rock over the foundations of its predecessor, a monument to Athens' imperial position (8.95–7). Like all Greek temples, details were picked out in paint; the temple was not left to stand as the gleaming honeyed marble we know today. It was begun in 447 and completed in 432, a particularly rapid construction for this uniquely intricate and costly building; its massive gold and ivory statue of Athēnē was already in place by 438. In 437, when the major construction work on the Parthenōn was completed, work on new gateway building, the Propylaia, was begun. This architecturally highly innovative building furnished a radically new approach to the whole sanctuary on a different alignment from the earlier gateway. Later in the fifth century, the temple known as the Erekhtheion, named after Erekhtheus, a legendary king of Athens, was built. It stood in the area held to have witnessed the primeval battle of Athēnē and Poseidōn for the land of Attikē, and which had been the site of the Mycenaean palace. The new temple took over many of these holy associations from Athens' sacred past, and employed a uniquely irregular plan to accommodate them. It was to this temple that the old statue of *Athēnē Polias* was moved – the statue to which, every four years, the people of Athens gave a new robe on the occasion of Athēnē's most prestigious festival, the *Panathēnaia*. The buildings of the Akropolis now stand isolated, but in the fifth and fourth centuries, there were many more structures covering the rock as well as altars, statues, stone slabs bearing state decrees, and countless personal offerings.

2.35　Building work continued in the *agorā* even during the time the Parthenōn and Propylaia were being constructed. In addition to the temple of Athēnē, a headquarters for the annually chosen military leaders (*stratēgoi*, 'generals') is known to have been erected during the 440s and 430s. In the last thirty years of the fifth century, further colonnaded buildings were added on the west and south of the *agorā*; the old *bouleutērion* was replaced and converted into a public records office; and the mint and a law-court were erected. Defeat in the Peloponnesian War (404) then halted further building, but activity recommenced in the middle of the fourth century with a new fountain-house. Temples to civic cults and a large altar to *Zeus Agoraios* were also put up at this time; and a fenced pedestal on which stood statues of the ten tribal heroes of Attikē was used as a public notice-board in the *agorā* for new proposed legislation, impending lawsuits and lists of men called up for military service.

　　All this building work emphasises the increasingly democratic bias of Athens and the more extensive involvement of the citizens that it brought in its wake. However, despite the growing formalisation of the *agorā*, the craftsmen of Athens – potters, sculptors, bronze-smiths – continued to live and work on and around the borders of the public area, and excavated remains of their workshops illustrate the variety of life in the city centre. The cobbler's shop belonging to one Simōn, a man mentioned in Plato's dialogues, has been unearthed near the south-west corner of the *agorā*.

2.36　The sixth-century Akropolis had been crowded with statues erected by individuals to commemorate their good fortune and show off their wealth, notably statues of young maidens (*korai*) (8.86). The sixth-century cemetery of the Kerameikos too had featured imposing monuments, including larger than life-sized statues of standing young men (*kouroi*). After the Persian Wars, however, the fifth-century Akropolis seems to have become much less of a place for individual sculptural display, and nothing by way of individual monuments survives from the Kerameikos between 480 and 430. In the fourth century, however, the Kerameikos becomes once more a place in which wealthy Athenians displayed their family achievements, now not with free-standing statues but with broad sculpted reliefs (*stēlai*) displaying one, two, or more figures, sometimes at close to life size (8.98, 102). Elsewhere in Athens, too, the rich put up monuments, notably monuments to victories won by dithyrambic choruses at Athenian festivals. Such monuments were erected along the 'Street of the Tripods' which ran from the *agorā* round the east end of the Akropolis to the theatre of Dionȳsos. The Choregic Monument of Lȳsikratēs is the best-preserved of what must have been a very striking sequence of varied monuments. Public expenditure on buildings and other civic amenities did not preclude private display of individual and family prowess.

2.37   Areas of Athens other than the Akropolis, *agorā* and north-west cemetery have been less thoroughly investigated and give less information. Directly north of the Akropolis may have lain the more strictly commercial area of town, on the east side of the excavated *agorā* and in the adjacent area further east still. On the south slope of the rock, the theatre was rebuilt under Periklēs and again more radically in the middle of the fourth century (8.45, 64); a concert hall (*ōdeion*) was built next to the theatre in the 440s, alleged by Plutarch to be in shape an imitation of the tent of the Persian king and claimed by Vitruvius, the Roman architectural writer, to be roofed with timbers of Persian ships. The Academy, early established in a grove to the north-west near a sanctuary of the Attic hero, Hekadēmos, was used by Plato in the fourth century as a base for his philosophical school; the Lykeion on the east side, on an old foundation, was from the later fourth century onwards linked with the name of Aristotle.

2.38   Even at the end of the fourth century, the size of the city was extremely small by modern standards, one area being within easy walking distance of another. Although large and expensively equipped private houses were not unknown in Athens, most were still basically simple, consisting of a series of small rooms arranged round an inner court. By contrast, private and public money had for generations been spent on public buildings, whether for heated political discussion, athletic or theatrical competitions, legal wrangling or religious celebrations. It was there that the real life of the *polis* had always been lived. Indeed, in the fourth century Athenian politicians, trying to castigate their opponents' indulgence in private comfort and display, nostalgically simplified the more public-spirited attitudes of the fifth-century leaders, as in the following speech ascribed to Dēmosthenēs:

The buildings which they left to adorn our city – the temples and harbours and all that goes with them – are on a scale which their successors cannot hope to surpass; look at the Propylaia, the docks, the colonnades and all the other adornments of the city which they have bequeathed to us. And the private houses of those in power were so modest and in keeping with the title of our constitution that, as those of you who have seen them know, the houses of Themistoklēs, Kīmōn and Aristeidēs, the famous men of those days, were no grander than those of their neighbours. But today, my friends, the city is content to provide roads and springs and stucco and other trivialities by way of public works. I am far from wishing to blame those who pioneered such useful works, but I do blame you for supposing they are all that is required of you. For some of the private individuals who hold any public office have built private houses which are grander not only than those of the ordinary run of citizens but even than our public buildings, and others have bought and cultivate estates on a scale undreamed of before. ([Dēmosthenēs], *On Organisation* 13.28–9)

3 Gods and festivals

Greek polytheism

3.1 Christians and Jews believe that there is one god, who made the world and is external to it. This god, whose characteristic is love, works for good in the world. He demands not only worship but a particular lifestyle, a lifestyle characterised by love, from his adherents. Adherents identify themselves by affirming their belief in a set of propositions about the one god expressed in a creed. They consider that god has communicated to the world through scriptures but may also communicate directly with his adherents by revelation. Worship takes place in church or synagogue and is normally conducted by a cleric. To be a cleric is a vocation, demanding particular ways of life and standards of morality, and is often life-long and paid. The cleric mediates between the god and his adherents and interprets the scriptures to them, to discover the god's will. Because the god of Christianity and Judaism demands particular behaviour, adherence has political and social as well as religious consequences.

3.2 For Greeks there were many gods (the pantheon) and they did not make the world. Hesiod in the *Theogony*, a text which was a foundation stone of Greek 'theological' thought, tells how in the beginning there was only Gaia (Mother Earth), Sky (Ouranos) and Void (Chaos). Gaia and Ouranos mated to produce the physical forms of which the world was made up (mountains, rivers, trees, etc., all thought of as having a divine element) and divine children who were gods. Over time one of these children, Kronos, deposed Ouranos by force, and then Zeus deposed Kronos after a titanic struggle ('Titans' were gods too); indeed, Zeus too might be deposed himself. These new gods were called 'Olympian', because they dwelt on Mt Olympos; but new divinities could always come on the scene. The epic poet Homer (700) is our source for the separate personalities and characteristics of the gods, parallel to the personalities and characteristics of humans. In Homer they are not forces for good, but often behave in ways that are immoral, both towards each other and towards humans.

3.3 The personalities ascribed to the gods helped to define the areas in which they exercised their power, thus enabling humans to know how to appease them properly. Particular gods, like individual humans, might have many interests, and individuals worshipped mainly those gods interested in things

3.1 The goddess Athēnē, on the left, and the god Apollo, on the right, offer support to their respective favourites, Aiās and Hektōr, on this early fifth-century Athenian red-figure cup.

that mattered to those individuals. Zeus, for example, was reckoned to have particular interests in weather, fertility, gold, kings, warfare, counsel, supplication, strangers, beggars, safety, marriage, home and property. These multiple interests might make relations between a human individual or community and a particular god rather complex. Xenophōn records how he had been helped by Zeus as the god of leaders and of safety, but then fell foul of him as god of propitiation. Some gods had purely local associations with places that inspired awe and were considered to have an indwelling divine power – springs, groves and woods, for example, and especially lonely places like hills and mountains, far from human habitation. Other local 'powers' included dead 'heroes', men whose spirit was thought to protect a place (e.g. Thēseus (1.16, 43; 3.31; fig. 1.11)).

3.4 The gods demanded worship only in the sense of human acknowledgement (*nomizein tous theous* does not mean 'believe in the gods', but to 'recognise' or 'acknowledge' them), but they did not love humanity in general, nor did they impose codes of belief or morality. They required to be recognised for the power they wielded and to be respected for it. That done, they would help their favourites. The basis of the relationship between humans and the gods was tit-for-tat, as between humans. Gods, like humans, helped their friends and harmed their enemies.

3.5 Gods manifested themselves to men not in scriptures (so there was nothing equivalent to modern theology) but in person. The images of the gods *were* those gods, and temples were required to house those images. Worship took the form of making or promising an offering and accompanying it with a prayer. Offerings might be durable objects, like small statues of the god, or items of food or drink; the grandest was an animal sacrificed at an altar outside the temple. The function of priests – who might inherit the job within their family, be chosen by lot, or buy the office – was not to interpret (non-existent) scriptures or guide their flock; it was to ensure that the rituals which acknowledged the gods' power were carried out in the way that tradition had handed down. Since there were female and male gods, there were also male and female priests. But there was no centralised religious authority: decisions about religious matters were taken by the same bodies that took decisions about non-religious matters, that is, at Athens, by the *ekklēsiā* (cf. 5.71). Nor did individual priests have roles as confessors, counsellors, or social workers. But gods could offer revelation, and there were human mediators who might assist to make sense of such cases. Those who wished to know the will of the god would go to a seer (*mantis*) or to an oracle (3.17–20) to seek advice. Those who needed healing might go to the shrine of a healing deity and wait there for the god to visit them. There was no general agreement as to whether actions in this life had any influence on any afterlife, but mystery cults associated with Dēmētēr and Dionȳsos (the Eleusinian Mysteries and 'Orphism') offered privileged status in the hereafter to those initiated into them (3.50–2).

3.6 Though the Greek gods could be made fun of, they were not figures of fun. They might be random and fickle; they were certainly awe-inspiring and terrifying. This did not prevent intellectuals criticising them. The complete absence of a ruling priest-caste in Greek (as in Roman) society, linked with the fierce Greek sense of independence, helped Greek thinkers cast off traditional pictures of divine activity in the world. One of the most important contributions of Greek intellectual thought was to minimise the role of gods in 'explaining' the physical world or the meaning of life (cf. 8.12, 15). But this did not mean that they did not continue to acknowledge the gods.

Experience and myth

3.7 Greeks lived with high degrees of uncertainty, not least over agricultural production (2.14); they were, of course, entirely dependent upon the benevolence of nature if life was to continue. Faced with the vagaries of climate, disease, etc., Greeks chose to assume that the decisions and actions of divine powers accounted for things beyond human control. Such powers could explain not only the unpredictability of the weather or of fertility (in both crops and humans) but any strange or incomprehensible event – a meteorite, for example, or an instance of odd behaviour in another person, an unexpected illness, or the arrival of a total stranger. Anything abnormal could indicate the intervention of a divinity and might therefore need careful handling.

3.8   Greek literature was full of examples of unusual events being assumed to herald divine intervention. In Book 1 of Homer's *Iliad*, when a plague struck the Greek army camped outside Troy, Akhilleus' response was to consider how the god responsible (which had to be Apollo, who was god of healing and illness) could be appeased. Akhilleus appealed for a 'seer or priest or reader of dreams' because, although any human being could hope to recognise a god at work, only those especially receptive to the divine will could interpret the reason for the intervention and therefore appease the god concerned.

3.9   Akhilleus' action turned out to have serious consequences for himself and the whole Greek army. The consequences of discovering the will of the gods in relation to unusual incidents could be found in many myths and stories which Greek communities told of their past. Hērodotos related that when Cyrus, King of Persia, was conquering Asia Minor, a Greek community on a peninsula of the west coast tried to halt the invasion of his general Harpagos:

> While Harpagos was reducing Iōniā, the Knidians began to dig through this neck of land, which was about half a mile across, with the object of making their territory into an island. For the isthmus which they were intending to cut through was the link which connected them to the mainland, and bounded their territory. All hands were engaged on this work when the Knidians noticed that the number of injuries, particularly to the eyes, suffered by the workers when the rock was splintered, was unexpectedly and unnaturally large. They therefore sent envoys to Delphi to enquire about this hindrance to the work. The priestess answered them (so their story runs) in iambic verse:
>
> 'Do not fortify the isthmus or dig it through:
> Had Zeus wished he would have made an island.'
>
> The Knidians on receiving this reply gave up their digging and, when Harpagos arrived, gave themselves up without striking a blow.' (Hērodotos, *Histories* 1.174)

This story illustrates both the assumption that the gods indicate their will through making unusual things happen, and the way that divine revelation might conveniently explain political decisions which not all Greeks would admire.

3.10 Besides this understanding, drawn from direct experience of supposed intervention from the supra-human world, the Greeks also drew on the understanding enshrined in myth. Myths were not seen as revealed scriptures, or as

3.2 One Greek myth illustrated the power of the gods by telling how they fought and defeated the Giants. Here an early fifth-century Athenian red-figure cup shows Hēphaistos, with the tongs and a burning coal, and Poseidōn, with a rock, in action.

the 'truth' about the gods (cf. 8.54), but many of them helped to define the human condition in relation to that of the gods. The mythical inheritance was rich and varied, reflecting the presence of the gods in every part of life and almost every place in Greece. The status of myth is well revealed in Hērodotos' famous statement that it was from Homer and Hesiod that the Greeks came to know about the gods (*Histories* 2.53). Since myths, which did not convey authoritative divine revelation, could be retold in any way the teller chose, there could be no such thing as heresy or orthodoxy. The Athenian tragedians, and in particular Euripidēs, exploited the flexibility of myth to present differing interpretations of divine activity in the world.

3.11 Because of the exceptional status which Homer and Hesiod enjoyed in the eyes of classical Greeks, it is useful to look at one particularly important myth as related, in two versions, by Hesiod (c. 700 BC). This is the myth of Promētheus, the thief of fire from heaven. The story is Hesiod's attempt to make sense of human experience by means of a *mūthos*, myth/allegory/story:

> And Iapetos married Klymenē, the Ocean nymph with beautiful ankles, and they went to bed together. And she bore him sons, stout-hearted Atlās, then far-famed Menoitios, Promētheus ['Forethought'], subtle and wily, and misguided Epimētheus ['Afterthought']. Epimētheus was a disaster to busy men, since he was the first to receive from Zeus a virgin wife. Far-seeing Zeus [dealt with the other brothers, and] bound the wily Promētheus in strong

chains from which there was no escape, and which he fastened to a pillar, and set on him a wide-winged eagle which came to feed on his immortal liver; and all that the wide-winged bird had eaten during the day grew again each night [the reason for this will be explained shortly]. The eagle was killed by . . . Hēraklēs, who drove off his tormentor and freed him from his misery. Olympian Zeus did not object, wishing the fame of Hēraklēs to be still greater on the fruitful earth, and showing this respect and honour to his famous son. And he ceased from the rage he had felt against Promētheus who had defied the will of almighty Zeus. For [here comes the explanation for Zeus' treatment of Promētheus] when gods and mortal men came to judgement at Mēkōnē [an incident unknown to us], Promētheus forethoughtfully set out the cut portions of a great ox, intending to deceive Zeus. He put the flesh and the entrails full of fat into the skin on one side and hid them in the ox's stomach; on the other side he put the white bones of the ox, and arranged them with great cunning carefully covering them with shining fat [this would look far bigger than the first portion, which contained all the edible meat]. And the father of gods and men said to him, 'The division you have made is most unequal.' So Zeus, whose counsels are eternal, taunted him. The wily Promētheus answered deceitfully with a gentle smile, 'Zeus, greatest and most glorious of the immortal gods, choose whichever of the two your heart bids you.' He spoke, of course, to deceive. But Zeus . . . took the white fat in both hands, and his blood boiled and rage filled his heart when he saw the white bones and the trick he had been played [i.e. he got the bones, not the meat!]. And from that day, when the races of men sacrifice at their altars to the immortals, they burn the white bones [and keep the good meat for themselves].

But Zeus the cloud-gatherer was enraged and said, 'Promētheus, always cunning, so you are still up to your tricks, my friend.' Zeus whose counsels are eternal spoke thus in anger; and he did not forget the trick which had been played on him, and from then on denied wretched mortals the use of fire. But the brave Promētheus deceived him and stole the far-seen beam of fire, hiding it in a hollow reed. And high-thundering Zeus was cut to the heart and raged within when he saw the far-seen beam of fire again among men, and at once devised a price for men to pay for it. For the famous Hēphaistos, at the will of Zeus, moulded out of earth the image of a modest girl [Hesiod here describes the first woman]. Grey-eyed Athēnē gave her a girdle and silver robe, and over her face drew an embroidered veil, marvellous to look at, and round her head set lovely garlands of spring flowers; and the famous Hēphaistos set on her head a golden tiara, which he made with his own hands, to please father Zeus. On the tiara he modelled many wonderful figures of the creatures which sea and land produce, marvellously life-like, and all breathing with beauty. And when he had made this lovely, evil thing as the price of fire, he led her to a place where gods and men were gathered, and she showed her delight at the finery which Athēnē had given her. And immortal gods and mortal men were amazed when they saw how deep was the trap from which there was no escape for men. For from her the whole female sex is descended, a great curse to mortal men with whom they live, no help in accursed poverty but ready enough to share wealth. They are like

3.3 In the upper frieze of this mid-fifth-century wine-mixing bowl (*krātēr*) we see Pandōra being decked out by Athēnē amid the other Olympian gods. In the lower frieze we see a piper playing for a chorus of men dressed as satyrs in some form of drama. Upper and lower friezes seem to be linked by the idea of dressing up.

drones which are fed by the bees in their roofed hives and are their partners in crime. For the bees are busy all day till the sun goes down and build white honeycombs, while the drones stay at home in the shelter of the hive and fill their bellies with the toil of others. High-thundering Zeus made woman to be a similar curse to mortal men, and partner in vexation.

But Zeus produced a second price for man to pay. If a man avoids marriage and all the mischief women cause, and never takes a wife, he comes to his declining years with no one to look after him in the miseries of old age. He has enough to live on while he lives, and when he dies his distant relatives divide up his property. A man who does marry and has a good wife after his own heart can balance evil with good while he lives; but he who gets one of the hurtful sort of women lives with an open wound in his heart and spirit, and an ill that has no cure. (Hesiod, *Theogony* 507ff.)

Here, then, is one account by Hesiod of how man received fire – the basis of all technology, cooked food and sacrifice – and the price he had to pay for it, i.e. the curse of lazy, spendthrift women. Hesiod returns to this story in another work and produces a slightly different version:

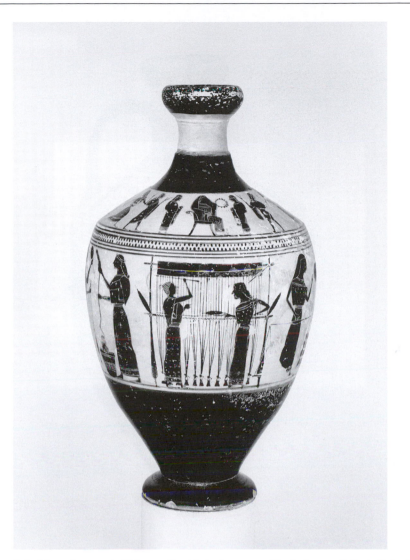

3.4–6 (see also over) This small mid-sixth-century black-figure oil flask (*lekythos*) (from the hand of the Amasis Painter, also responsible for 5.2–4) shows elaborately dressed women engaged in wool craft – spinning, weaving, and folding up the finished products.

The gods keep men's livelihood hidden from them. For you could easily produce in a day enough to keep you in idleness for a year, and hang your rudder up above the smoke and do away with the labour of oxen and hardworking mules. But Zeus hid the way to do so, because his heart was angry at the deception practised on him by the wily Promētheus [i.e. the sacrifice trick, described above]. So Zeus contrived grievous cares for men, first hiding fire from them. But the noble Promētheus secretly stole it back again for men from Zeus the wise, hiding it in a hollow reed. And Zeus the cloud-gatherer was angry and said to him, 'Promētheus, there is none cleverer

3.5

than you, and you are pleased to have stolen fire and tricked me. But you have brought trouble on yourself and on future generations of men, to whom in exchange for fire I will give an evil thing, which will delight their hearts but which they will embrace to their ruin.'

Thus spoke the father of gods and men and laughed. And he told famous Hēphaistos to make a mixture of earth and water, as quickly as he could, and to put in it human voice and strength, to give it features like an immortal god and the lovely shape of a virgin girl. He told Athēnē to teach her the craft of weaving patterned cloth and Aphrodītē to pour golden charm about her head and fierce desire and heavy sorrows; and Hermēs, killer of Argos, his servant, he ordered to give her the mind of a bitch and sly ways.

So he spoke, and they obeyed Zeus. The lame Hēphaistos moulded earth, as Zeus commanded, into the form of a modest virgin; grey-eyed Athēnē

3.6

gave her clothes and girdle; the divine Graces and holy *Peithō* [Persuasion, a god who accompanies Aphrodītē] set golden necklaces about her neck; the fair Seasons crowned her with spring flowers; and, at the will of Zeus, Hermēs put into her heart lies and specious words and sly ways and gave her a voice and called her Pandōra ["All-endowed"], because all the gods who live in Olympos had given her gifts, to be the ruin of man and their business.

And when the deadly and inescapable snare was complete, Zeus sent Hermēs, the swift messenger of the gods, to Epimētheus bearing it as a gift. And Epimētheus forgot that Promētheus had told him never to accept a gift from Olympian Zeus, but to send it back, in case it brought trouble to mortals. But he accepted it and did not perceive the trouble it brought till it was upon him. (Hesiod, *Works and Days* 42ff.)

3.12 Together, these stories of Promētheus contain much of the Greek understanding of man's lot. Sacrifice is presented as a shared act with the gods, and at the same time a symbol of trickery on both sides (reflecting Greek admiration for the weaker party turning the tables on the stronger by cunning on the human side, and on the other the deceptiveness of the words of the gods in oracles, omens and dreams (see 3.14–20)). All the responsibilities and problems of life as males understood them are introduced – women (cf. 4.22–4), marriage, work, property and succession, old age, and sickness. These elements collected together in the form of a story define the Greek understanding of the 'human condition'. Elsewhere in Hesiod, man's lot is clarified by the contrast first with the life of the gods, then with beasts, and finally with the idea of a 'Golden Age', when once upon a time life was easy and man had no need to work.

Human contact with the gods

3.13 Greeks had many gods, many different traditions of worshipping them (cult practices varied widely from city to city) and a rich mythological tradition. So there was no single element in Greek religion that *had* to be accepted if one was to be classed as conventionally pious. But without the hard basis of a creed, or any revealed word, it was extremely difficult to know whether one was keeping the gods happy: only one's good or bad fortune might give a hint. So when it was important that a human enterprise went well, some form of access to the gods' will was required, and the more important the enterprise – e.g. founding a settlement, joining battle or dispatching an expedition – the more important it was to get the best qualified experts to discover what that will was.

Dreams

3.14 A common way in which the gods were thought to contact a person was through dreams. These could be true, or deceitful, as Agamemnōn found to his cost in Homer, *Iliad* 2.1ff., when Zeus sent a deceitful dream to trick him into rash action. If the dream was telling the truth, it was impossible to avoid the consequences, as Kroisos found when he dreamt that his son was to be killed by an iron spear (Hērodotos, *Histories* 1.34–45). If dreams seemed not to be fulfilled, it was because they had been wrongly interpreted. So Hērodotos told how Hippiās, son of Peisistratos, mistakenly believed that he would regain power in Athens because of the misinterpretation of a dream:

> Hippiās, the son of Peisistratos, guided the Persians to Marathōn. The previous night he had had a dream in which he seemed to be in bed with his mother, and he interpreted the dream to mean that he would return to Athens, recover the power he had lost, and die in old age in his own country. That was his interpretation at the time, and he continued to act as guide to the Persians, first landing the prisoners from Eretriā on an island called

Aigiliā belonging to the Styrians, and then leading the fleet to anchorage at Marathōn and disembarking and drawing up the troops. In the course of all this he was seized by an unusually violent fit of sneezing and coughing. He was an elderly man and a good many of his teeth were loose, as is not uncommon at that age, and the violence of his coughing dislodged one of them and it fell into the sand. He tried very hard to find this tooth and when it was nowhere to be seen, turned to the bystanders with a deep groan and said, 'This land is not ours and we shall never be able to subdue it. My tooth has the only share I ever had in it.' This was how Hippiās finally interpreted the meaning of his dream. (Hērodotos, *Histories* 6.107ff.)

3.15 Hippiās' dream seems to have been spontaneous, but god-sent dreams might also be sought by sleeping in a sanctuary. Such dreams proved equally problematic. When, in the face of a threat from the Makedonians (in the fourth century), the Athenian state sent a man to sleep in a shrine in order to receive divine guidance, the resulting dream was subject to charges of fabrication for political ends:

> The people ordered Euxenippos and two others to spend the night in the temple, and he tells us that he went to sleep and had a dream which he duly reported to them. Now, Polyeuktos, if you assumed that he was telling the truth, and that he reported to the people what he actually saw in his dream, what wrong has he done by reporting to the Athenians what the god's instructions had been? But if, as you now allege, you think he misrepresented the god and made a biased report to the people, your right course was not to put forward a decree disputing the dream, but, as the speaker before me said, to send to Delphi and find out the truth from the god. (Hypereidēs, *Euxenippos* 14)

3.16 One particular form of dream which was widely sought was the healing dream (5.73, 8.39). Men had long sought healing by making offerings in temples, but in the classical period a number of sanctuaries became well-known for healing. These sanctuaries built porticoes specially for patients to sleep in, and the expectation was that the patient would dream of being cured and wake up healed. The most famous of these shrines was that of Asklēpios at Epidauros. A record was inscribed there of healing experiences. The following is an example of a cure effected there:

> A man came to the god as a suppliant, so deficient in one eye that he had only eyelids and there was nothing between them but just an empty hole. Some of those in the sanctuary mocked the naïvety of the man, that he should think that he would see when he had none of the makings of an eye, but only the place. A dream appeared to him as he slept in the sanctuary. It seemed to him that the god prepared some drug and then, pulling the eyelids apart, poured it into them. When day came he departed seeing with both eyes.' (RO 102.72–8)

Asklēpios' cult was introduced to Athens only in the late fifth century, following the plague during the Peloponnesian War, and a sanctuary was then

3.7 The ruins of the fourth-century temple of Apollo at Delphi.

built on the south side of the Akropolis. A second important healing shrine developed at much the same time on the borders of Attikē – the shrine of Amphiareōs at Orōpos.

Oracles

3.17 When states as well as individuals needed advice or help, not just in times of national emergency but to cope with everyday occurrences, they would send to an oracle. The Sanctuary of Apollo at Delphi was home to the most influential oracle, but there were many others throughout the Greek world, using different methods of divination – clanging pots, rustling leaves, warbling doves, rushing waters, reflecting mirrors, all supposedly indicating the will of the god. It is important to stress that the function of an oracle was not to foretell the future, but to advise. It is inevitable that, if the advice was good, the oracle would get the reputation for being *able* to foretell the future, but that was not its function. What oracles offered was insight into the will of the gods; and the regular form of consultation involved asking the god which choice of possible policies was better, or what appropriate rituals should attend it. Generally speaking (and discounting for the moment myth and legend), the oracle at, for example, Delphi, spoke directly to questioners in perfectly plain and simple terms. There is no good evidence that in the fifth century the Delphic prophetess (Pȳthiā) was in a state of babbling ecstasy. This is not to deny that the prophetess was inspired, but to note that prophetic inspiration, like poetic inspiration, did not result in incoherence, but rather in heightened lucidity of perception and utterance. The following practical, down-to-earth questions, answered in equally practical, down-to-earth terms, are typical:

> Isyllos the poet asked, in relation to the composition of a paean in honour of Apollo, whether it was better to inscribe the paean. The response was that it was better for both present and future if he inscribe the paean.
>
> The cities of Klazomenai and Kȳmē were disputing possession of Leukē. They asked which city the god wanted to possess Leukē. The response was: 'Let the city which is first to make sacrifice in Leukē have it. On the day agreed, each party should start at sunrise from its own city.'
>
> Poseidōnios of Halikarnassos, concerned for welfare of his family, asked, 'What is it better for him and his sons and daughters to do?' The response came: 'It will be better for them to worship Zeus ["of our ancestors"], Apollo lord of Telmessos, the Moirai (Fates) the Mother of Gods, the Agathos Daimōn ('Lucky Spirit') of Poseidōnios and Gorgis, as their ancestors did; it will be better for them if they continue to perform these rites.' (J. Fontenrose, *The Delphic Oracle*)

3.18 That said, there was a strong *literary* tradition, in both myth and the early history of Greece, that oracles were opaque and tended to deceive. Hērodotos tells of the oracle given to the Athenians as the Persians advanced on the city [see 1.36], that Zeus would grant them a wooden wall as a stronghold for themselves and their children. But what did that mean? The oracle had to be given to special readers of oracles to interpret; and it is notable that the religious experts were in the end ignored when the people were persuaded by the politician Themistoklēs that wooden walls meant the fleet. The question of what to do was a *political* question, and it was settled in a political forum by the political expert (1.36).

3.19 One particularly revealing story is told by Xenophōn of his own consultation of Delphi before joining Cyrus' mercenary army to fight against his brother (1.88):

> Xenophōn went to Delphi, but he asked Apollo to which of the gods he should offer sacrifice and prayer with a view to the successful completion of a journey he had in mind, and to a safe return. In reply Apollo told him to which gods he should sacrifice. On his return Xenophōn told Sōkratēs what the oracle had said. On hearing it Sōkratēs blamed Xenophōn because he had not first asked whether he should make the journey or not, but had taken his own decision and then asked how best he could make the journey successfully. But, he added, as he had put the question in the way he had, he must do whatever the god directed. (Xenophōn, *Anabasis* 3.1.4ff.)

That the oracle was taken seriously, and expected to answer cogently, is clear from this passage of Xenophōn. But what is also clear is that Xenophōn had asked the conventional question one would ask an oracle – how to carry through a policy already decided upon, not about the policy to adopt. It is Sōkratēs who is presented as suggesting that the god should be asked about something other than cultic matters. Nevertheless, one can see why the philosopher Hērakleitos said, 'The lord whose oracle is in Delphi does not speak and does not conceal: instead, he sends a sign.' A sign always needs interpreting.

Divination

3.20 In the course of leading the mercenary troops back from Persia, Xenophōn had many other occasions to consult the gods. But in those circumstances he was not in a position to consult an oracle. Instead he had to rely on seers (*manteis*, s. *mantis*):

> After this Xenophōn stood up and said, 'Fellow soldiers, it looks as if we shall have to complete our journey on foot. There are no ships, and it is time we set out. There are no supplies if we stay here. We then', he went on 'will sacrifice; and you must be ready to fight if ever you did. For the enemy has taken heart again.' The generals then proceeded to sacrifice, the presiding seer being Arexiōn the Arkadian; Silanos from Ambrakiā had by this time deserted on a ship he hired at Hērakleia. But when they sacrificed for their departure, the omens were not favourable, and they therefore gave up sacrificing for the day. There were some impudent enough to say that Xenophōn wanted to found a city at the place and had persuaded the seer to say the omens were not favourable for departure. Xenophōn in consequence made an announcement that anyone who wished could be present at the sacrifice next day and ordered anyone who was a seer to participate in the sacrifice; and so there were a good many present when he made the sacrifice. But though he performed the sacrifice three times for their departure, the omens were not favourable . . . He sacrificed again on the next day, and pretty well the whole army attended the ceremony, as it was of such consequence to them. But there was a shortage of sacrificial victims. Thereupon the generals, though they would not lead them out, assembled them, and Xenophōn said, 'Perhaps the enemy have joined up and we shall have to fight them. If we were to deposit our equipment in the stronghold and set out in battle order, the omens might favour us.' When they heard this the soldiers shouted that there was no need to take things to the stronghold, but that the sacrifice should be made at once. There were no sheep left, but they bought an ox which was yoked to a wagon and sacrificed it. Xenophōn asked Kleanōr the Arkadian to take special note of any favourable sign, but none was forthcoming . . .
>
> [*There follows an unsuccessful plundering raid for supplies, in which they lose 500 men. They spend the night under arms. Eventually . . .*]
>
> A vessel arrived from Hērakleia bringing barley, sacrificial victims and wine. Xenophōn rose early and sacrificed for departure, and the omens were favourable at the first sacrifice. Just as the ceremonies were completed, Arexiōn the Parrhasian saw an eagle in a favourable quarter, and told Xenophōn to lead on. (Xenophōn, *Anabasis* 6.4.12ff.)

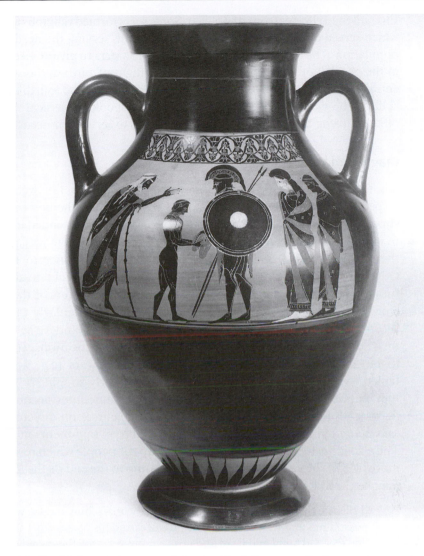

3.8 On this late sixth-century Athenian black-figure *amphorā*, a warrior examines the liver of a sacrificial victim brought to him by a youth, in order to discover whether the gods will look favourably on his fighting.

It is important to draw a distinction between the priest (*hiereus*), who was responsible for correct procedure at sacrifices, and the seer, who deduced the will of the gods from the innards of the sacrificial victim. Priests, male or female, held an official position; but a seer might be simply a person with insight into the interpretation of signs. Hērodotos tells us that the first seer was Melampos, and that he brought the art to Greece. Since the family of Melampos maintained the tradition, it looks as if the practice of the seer went back to time immemorial and was handed down to future generations of the seer's family. There were other famous families of seers, e.g. the Iamides (sons of Iamos) at

Ēlis and the Telliades (sons of Tellias). Some seers formed religious associations which served as oracles; others were independent, serving the needs of a local population. The two most common methods for seers to give advice are related in the passage of Xenophōn: observing the flight of birds and examining the entrails, especially the livers, of slaughtered beasts. By the fourth century, the skill of the *mantis* had become the subject of books. Classical Athens sent officially recognised *manteis* out with its armies to serve their needs in the field.

Magic and curses

3.21   All the forms of contacting the gods discussed so far were perfectly respectable. But there were other forms of consulting the gods or invoking supernatural powers which were less above board. These tended in particular to involve the powers not of the gods but of the dead. There was an oracle of the dead in north-west Greece, supposedly at the entrance to Hādēs, and Odysseus sacrificed and called up the dead in *Odyssey* 11 to discover his future. In classical Athens, the chief way in which the powers of the dead were enlisted was by depositing curse tablets in graves, particularly the graves of those who had died young. These were thought to wander the earth until their 'proper' time had come to die. Other favoured locations were thought to be 'in touch' with chthonic (underground) powers (e.g. wells). These tablets, which are generally inscribed lead, regularly sought to 'bind' those they cursed, leaving them helpless; they were sometimes accompanied by figurines. Surviving Athenian examples include curses on directors of plays (*didaskaloi*) and on actors, on rivals in love and on opponents in law-courts. The also include curses aimed at whole groups of people which reveal no clear motivation. The earliest of all examples, dating to the end of the fifth century may be the following:

> [I bind] Lysaniās the blower from the silver works – him and his wife and possessions and whatever work he produces and his possessions and hands and feet and mind and head and nose . . . curse . . . of the sacred earth.

The line between acceptable and unacceptable use of such curses seems to have been a fine one. The Athenian *ekklēsiā* went in for ritual curses against would-be traitors, for example, and oaths might be accompanied by wax models to whose fate those swearing the oath linked their own. Nevertheless all attempts to link individual fates to material substances were suspect: it is notable that the most prominent figures in mythology who employed such methods were from outside the Greek world (Kirkē in the *Odyssey* and Mēdeia).

Divine intervention with humans

3.22   How far should events be explained by the activity of the gods? Or were events all the result of human activity? Or of natural causes? In the fourth century,

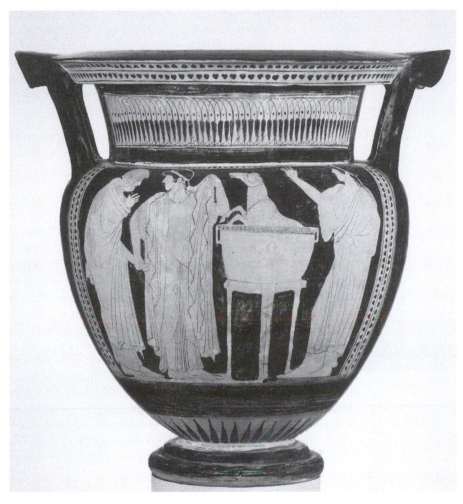

3.9 This Athenian fifth-century red-figure column *krātēr* shows Mēdeia magically rejuvenating a sheep by boiling it, in order to persuade old King Pēliās, on the left, to undergo the same treatment.

Aristotle would attempt to bring some order into the discussion by distinguishing different sorts of human or material cause, and allowing the gods a place only as 'final cause'. But these questions were always open to debate, and were discussed by philosophers with increasing sophistication. For example, while numbers of 'divine' healing sanctuaries were growing, philosophers were criticising the idea of religious cures. The flavour of the debate is well seen in the work *On the Sacred Disease* written around 400 (see further 8.37):

> The facts about the so-called sacred disease are as follows. I don't think it is really any more divine or sacred than any other disease; it has its own symptoms and cause, but because of their inexperience and its extraordinary

and unique character men supposed it had some divine origin. I think that the kind of men who first attributed a sacred quality to this disease were similar to today's magicians, salvationists, quacks and charlatans who all claim to be very religious and to have superior knowledge. Because they felt helpless and had no effective treatment to suggest, they took refuge in the pretence of divinity and treated the disease as sacred to conceal their own ignorance. ([Hippokratēs], *On the Sacred Disease* 1ff.)

3.23　On the other side of the debate, Hērodotos expresses in the mouth of Solōn (addressing the Lydian king, Kroisos) what may have been a widely held view of how human life was shaped by the gods:

> You have asked me about the human condition, Kroisos. I know well that the gods are all envious and disruptive. In the space of a long life you can see and experience much that you would not wish. I reckon the span of human life to be about seventy years. That number of years gives a total of 25,200 days, omitting the intercalary months. If you allow for the addition of an intercalary month every other year, to keep the seasons in step, you get thirty-five additional months and 1,050 additional days. This gives you a total of 26,250 days in your seventy years, and no day is just like another in what it brings. So you see, Kroisos, that human life is a chancy affair. You seem to me to be a very rich man and to rule over a large population, but I still can't call you what you asked until I know that your life has ended well. For the very wealthy man is no happier than the man who has just enough for his daily needs, unless he has the good fortune to end his life in prosperity. Many of the richest men are unhappy, many who have moderate means have good luck. The man who is wealthy but unhappy is better off than the man who has good luck in two respects only, whereas the lucky man is better off than the rich and unhappy in many ways. The rich man can satisfy his desires and is better able to bear great calamities, but the other is better off in the following respects. He may be less well placed to gratify his desires or withstand calamity, but his luck keeps him clear of them, and he has sound physique, good health, freedom from trouble, fine children and good looks. If in addition to all this he prospers till the end of his life, he is the man you are looking for and deserves to be called happy. But till he dies do not call him happy but lucky. It is humanly impossible for one man to combine in himself all good things, just as no country can be entirely self-sufficient but if it has one thing will be short of another; and the country which has most is best. So no single human individual is self-sufficient; if he has one thing he lacks another. But the man who continues to have the most advantages and dies peacefully deserves in my opinion, Kroisos, this title of happiness. In all things look to the end and final result. For god often gives men a glimpse of happiness only to ruin them root and branch. (Hērodotos, *Histories* 1.32ff.)

Note especially the phrase 'envious and disruptive'. Gods are disruptive (*tarakhōdēs*) because it is impossible to forecast what they will do next, and they are envious (*phthoneros*) of good fortune amongst humans (a theme

3.10 The envy, injustice, and disruptive behaviour of the gods is seen in myth when Artemis turns his own hounds upon the hunter Aktaiōn. On this mid-fifth-century red-figure bell *krātēr* the figure of Madness appears alongside the hounds.

which is much developed by tragedians, cf. 4.17; 8.40ff.). The attribution of envy to the gods may seem deeply pessimistic, but it simply attributed to the gods the attitude commonly found among humans: others' successes were to be envied, others' weakness to be scorned and exploited.

3.24 This attribution of envy to the gods did, however, make it hard to enlist the gods on the side of justice (*dikē*). *Dikē* implied justice according to the established rules. For Greeks, rules made to govern human societies were made by *men* (and regularly attributed to famous past law-makers), not handed down to men by the gods (contrast God's giving of the Law to Moses). On the other hand, the rules and order that governed the *world* ('the ordered world' is *ho kosmos*), were in the gods' interests, not men's. Consequently it was extraordinarily difficult to determine exactly what divine justice at any time required. Matters were complicated by the *tīmē* (honour, respect) that gods demanded from men. Since the gods fought for *tīmē* amongst themselves, to honour one god might be to offend another. In Euripidēs' *Hippolytos*, Artemis promises to take revenge on Aphrodītē, who has caused the death of Hippolytos because he honoured Artemis too much, Aphrodītē not at all:

> *Hippolytos:* I wish the gods were subject to men's curse.
> *Artemis:* Be easy. Because of your piety and goodness towards me, though your body lies in earth's darkness, the strokes with which Aphrodītē in her anger struck you down shall not be unavenged. For I will slay in retribution with my unerring arrows her dearest love among mortals. (Euripidēs, *Hippolytos* 1417ff.)

There were, however, some fixed points.

3.25 (1) If a man transgressed his obligation to the gods, if he became *asebēs* ('without piety'), then the gods would be expected to punish him, and might punish the community in which he lived. Thus the orators use safety in a hazardous journey as a proof of innocence:

> I have also been attacked for being a ship-owner and a merchant, and we are asked to believe that the gods have preserved me from the perils of the sea merely in order that I should be ruined by Kēphīsios on my return to Athens. I simply cannot believe, gentlemen, that if the gods thought I had done them wrong they would have been minded to spare me when I was in the utmost danger – for what greater danger is there than a sea-voyage in winter? They had my life in their hands, my person and my property in their power; why should they have preserved me when they could well even have denied my body decent burial? (Andokidēs, *On the Mysteries* 1.137)

But the gods were not generally thought to demand high moral standards of men. Gods certainly expected reverence and worship as of right, but certain sorts of men were thought to be specially in the gods' care and so the gods required that they should be respected. This applied particularly to men in inherently vulnerable positions because they were outside the protection of their own city – suppliants, heralds, strangers and beggars. To spurn or do violence to such people was to spurn the god. But although this in effect constituted a demand for moral behaviour, it was not because morality as such was enforced by the gods.

3.26 (2) Even more important was the gods' concern with homicide and blood-guilt. The death of a man aroused the powers associated with bloodshed, the Erīnyes (Furies). These fearsome goddesses hounded the blood-guilty with madness and terror until the dead man's kin avenged his death. Blood-guilt, like impiety, could pollute the whole city until the murderer had made atonement (cf. 8.13). Sophoklēs has Oidipous consider such pollution (*miasma*) in Thebes at the beginning of *Oidipous Tyrannos*:

> I pronounce that no one in this land, where I hold the power and the throne, shall receive or speak to the murderer, nor share prayer or sacrifice with him, nor dispense to him his portion of holy water. All must ban him from their homes, for he has brought pollution on us, as the oracle of the Pythian god

has just revealed to me. And in this pronouncement I support the god and the murdered man. (Sophoklēs, *Oidipous Tyrannos* 236ff.)

3.27   (3) Finally, in a society where the spoken word was the main means of communication, a man made an agreement *under oath* where we would use a contract and signature. The guarantors of these oaths – both private and public – were the gods. So sworn treaties between cities were regularly deposited in sanctuaries. The theory was that, because the 'contract' was made in the gods' name, to break it was to dishonour them and therefore invoke their wrath. So the Peace of Nīkiās between Athens and Spartē which concluded the Arkhidamian War (1.56–67) includes the following clauses:

> The Athenians shall take an oath to the Spartans and their allies, city by city. Every man shall swear by the most binding oath of his country, seventeen from each city. The oath shall be as follows: 'I will abide by this agreement and treaty honestly and without deceit.' In the same way an oath shall be taken by the Spartans and their allies to the Athenians; and the oath shall be renewed annually by both parties. Inscribed copies shall be erected at Olympiā, Pȳthiā [i.e. Delphi], the Isthmus, at Athens in the Akropolis, and at Spartē in the temple at Amyklai. (Thucydides, *Peloponnesian War* 5.18.9–10)

Worshipping the gods

Sacrifice

3.28   All major communal acts of worship were accompanied by sacrificial offerings. The simplest form of offering was the gift of the products of the earth: placing fruits or cakes made from grain on altars, or pouring out wine or milk or olive oil upon the ground (a practice known as 'libation'). The food was left to decompose or to be taken by animals, the liquid to drain into the earth. Both forms of offering can be seen as withdrawing from human use something made from the produce of the earth, and making it over to the divine powers ('sacrifice' comes from the Latin roots *sacr-* and *fac>fic-* meaning 'make sacred'). It was a sort of tit-for-tat. It is notable that Greeks sometimes pictured the gods themselves pouring libations – so these offerings of the fruits of the earth are to be seen as different from the sacrifice of animals, which is something the gods themselves are never shown performing.

3.29   Animal sacrifice normally involved a very much more elaborate ritual, and there is intense debate about exactly what the Greeks thought they were doing when they engaged in this ritual slaughter. The classic description of the ritual itself is found in Homer:

> The men washed their hands and took up the sacrificial grains . . . When they had made their prayers and thrown the grain over the victims, they first drew back the animals' heads, slit their throats and skinned them. Then, for the

3.11 A group of men and youths bring the sacrificial meat on spits and the innards of the sacrificial animal to the altar for roasting, on this Athenian bell *krātēr* from the third quarter of the fifth century. On the right, behind the altar, is a statue of Apollo.

> god's portion, they cut out the thigh bones, wrapped them in folds of fat and laid raw meat from the rest of the animal above them. These pieces the old priest burnt on wooden spits while he poured libations of red wine over them, and the young men gathered round him with five-pronged forks in their hands. When the god's portion had been consumed by fire, they ate the offal and then carved the rest of the victims into small pieces, pierced them with skewers, roasted them carefully and drew them all off. When their work was done and the meal prepared, they feasted, and no one went without a fair share . . .' (Homer, *Iliad* 1.449ff.)

Note the ceremonial washing (cleanliness and good order are associated in the ancient world); the prayer; the symbolic 'slaying' with barley grain before life was actually taken; the burning of the thigh-bones, with the fat (as in the Promētheus story) and a little meat placed on top to symbolise the whole animal – this the god's portion; the roasting and eating of the entrails (the offal – heart, liver, lungs, kidney, stomach); the kebabing of the good meat, cooking it and – the big treat for humans – consumption of it (2.14). Not all sacrifices followed exactly this form (sometimes small victims were entirely

3.12 This black-figure jug (*hydriā*) shows the various stages of preparing sacrificial meat for consumption.

burnt up and not eaten at all), but throughout the classical period they followed this general, basic pattern.

3.30 Hesiod's myth of the origin of this pattern of sacrifice sets it in the context of Promētheus' tricking Zeus into accepting the fat and bones from a sacrifice (see 3.11) and leaving men with the meat. This is all part of a wider story which explains why men, unlike other animals, do not live off the natural fruits of the earth but have to cultivate the soil to ensure that it yields them their staple foods. Since it was farm animals from meadow and pasture, not wild animals hunted in the hills, which were offered in normal sacrifices, we may guess that sacrifice was somehow felt to forge a link between man and the soil. But how can we explain the act of killing? Some have suggested that sacrifice was an extension of the hunter's pang of guilt at taking a free life; so ritualising the killing removed any sense of individual blame. But Hesiod's account stresses the element of deception in the origins of sacrifice. This suggests that sacrifice is rather a justification for the farmer's necessary deceit when the old working ox must be taken away and 'tricked' into being killed, so that a younger animal can be fed up to replace it. As humans consume the sacrificial animal, they acknowledge that their nourishment depends upon their deceitful relationship to animals, just as it is a product of their deceitful relationship with the gods. On this view, gods were not shown making animal

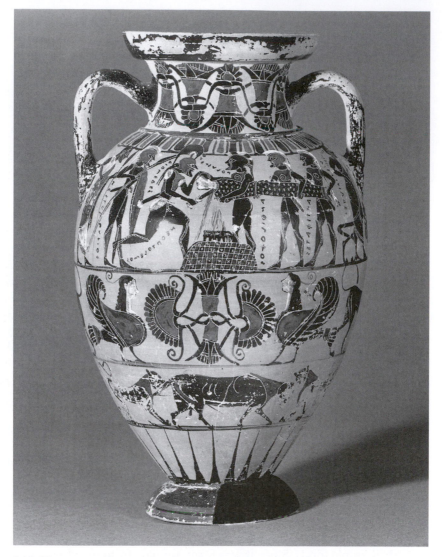

3.13 Human sacrifice seems to have been a feature only of myth and not of life in the classical period. Here a sixth-century *amphorā* painted in Athens for the Etruscan market shows in gory detail the sacrifice of Polyxenē at the tomb of Akhilleus.

sacrifice because, although they were thought to hunt, they were not engaged in agriculture and so had no deceitful relation to the animal world.

3.31   Holocaust [lit. 'whole burnt'] sacrifices were made principally on two occasions. First, in the case of homicide, once the dead man's kin had been appeased, the removal of a whole beast from the secular to the sacred sphere represented a life for a life and might also appease the avenging powers of the underworld (*alastores*, 'Avengers' or Erīnyes, 'Furies'). Second, hero cults. Heroes were local powers, either the great dead of the past, like Thēseus (1.16, 43), or minor deities who had not been assimilated into the Olympian system, or men within

3.14 This small flat late sixth-century oil flask (*askos*) seems to show the spirit of a dead hero rising from his tomb mound.

living memory, especially founders of new cities, e.g. in 437 the Athenians, led by one Hagnōn, founded a new city at Amphipolis in Thrace. By 424 Hagnōn himself was back in Athens, but he was being worshipped as a hero in the city he had founded! When the city was taken by the Spartan force under Brasidās, he was accorded hero-status as the founder of Amphipolis, in Hagnōn's place. Heroes were felt to be weaker gods, literally in need of physical sustenance lest they haunt the community as ghosts. The blood of the holocaust might provide such nourishment (cf. Homer, *Odyssey* 11.23ff.).

3.32 Sacrifices were made not merely by cities, but by smaller communities united through locality or kinship. Sacrifices to retain a god's protection over the family and family property, or to secure protection during a journey or for many other reasons were an important part of religious life. This is nicely illustrated from two law-court speeches from late fifth- and early fourth-century Athens:

> Later on it so happened that Philoneōs had a sacrifice to perform in the Peiraieus to *Zeus Ktēsios* [guardian of family possessions] and my father was

going to sail to Naxos. So Philoneōs decided that the best plan would be to make a single journey of it and see my father (who was a friend of his) as far as the Peiraieus, make the sacrifice, and then entertain him. Philoneōs' mistress accompanied him to attend the sacrifice. When they reached the Peiraieus, Philoneōs carried out the sacrifice, as you would expect. When he had performed it, the woman deliberated whether to give them the drug before or after dinner. After some thought she decided to give it after dinner . . . When they had dined, as you would expect after sacrifice to *Zeus Ktēsios* and the entertainment of a friend who was about to set out on a voyage, they set about making libations and sprinkling frankincense. And it was as she was mixing the libation, and as they were offering prayers – prayers, alas, never to be fulfilled – that his mistress poured in the poison. (Antiphōn, *Against the Stepmother* 1.16ff.)

Moreover, there is other evidence we can cite to show that we are the children of Kirōn's daughter. For as is natural with a daughter's children, he never performed any sacrifice except in our presence; we were present at and took part in all sacrifices, whether the ceremony was great or small. And we were invited not only to such domestic rites but also taken to the Rural Dionysia, and we sat with him at public entertainments and went to his house for all festivals. He attached particular importance to sacrifices to *Zeus Ktēsios*, which he performed himself and to which he admitted neither slaves nor free men who were not members of the family; but we shared in the ceremony, laying our hands on the victims, making our offerings with his and playing a full part in all the rites, while he prayed for our health and prosperity in the way you would expect of a grandfather. (Isaios, *On Kirōn's Estate* 8.15)

Purification

3.33 Ritual purity was both required for, and could be brought about by, sacrifice (cf. 8.13). So before every meeting of the Athenian *ekklēsiā*, a pig was sacrificed and its blood sprinkled to render the place ritually pure. Before a sacrifice, a ceremonial washing of hands was usually all that was needed, together with purification of the place of sacrifice, thenceforth called the *katharma*, 'the purified place'. More elaborate ritual purification was needed in certain cases, particularly for murderers who were excluded from sacred ground, and for those who came into contact with murder or with the dead (5.81). It might be required after sexual intercourse and childbirth. Some cities set up lists of situations that brought impurity and what actions were required to restore purity, and one particularly full list survives from fourth-century Kūrēnē. There were also official bodies of people in Athens to whom one could apply for advice. One such body was the *exēgētai* in Athens, who were official ministers of Apollo. Some of them were named by the oracle at Delphi for this task, others were elected by the Athenian people from one or two noble families with hereditary authority in such matters (one such family was the Eumolpidai). They advised on such matters as temples, cult procedure, sacrifices, and particularly purification following homicide. When this body could not advise, the matter was referred to Delphi (3.17).

Prayers

3.34 Prayers, like sacrifices, were more or less fixed in their general shape. Once more, the first book of the *Iliad* offers a typical example. The old man is Khrȳsēs, priest of Apollo, who prays that the Greeks (Danaans) may suffer for taking his daughter:

> The old man poured out prayers to lord Apollo, son of lovely-haired Lētō: 'Hear me, Apollo, lord of the silver bow, protector of Khrȳsēs and holy Killā, and mighty ruler over Tenedos. Plague-god, if ever I built a temple that pleased you, if ever I burnt you offerings of the fat thighs of bulls or goats, grant me this wish. Make the Greeks pay with your arrows for my tears.' So he spoke in prayer, and Phoibos Apollo heard him . . . (Homer, *Iliad* 1.35ff.)

The god is invoked by name or titles, which are often numerous; he is reminded of past kindnesses, then the request is made. Without some reference to the ties binding a god to his worshippers, there was no ground for expecting divine aid, for the basic assumption was one of reciprocity (cf. 3.4; 4.14). A prayer was made to the Olympians standing, with hands raised, to the underworld with hands lowered towards the earth. If a priest made the prayer, it would probably be at the altar in the temple precinct (*temenos*, 'a sacred ['cut-off'] area'); if it was a private ceremony any male – usually the head of the family – would conduct it.

Supplication

3.35 The safety and position of a man in ancient Greece depended primarily upon himself, his family, friends and possessions. These were all the material means available to him for helping or defending himself. Beyond this, a citizen enjoyed the protection of certain rights by virtue of his membership of a city-state. But a stranger or foreigner had no rights. He would naturally be far from friends, family and possessions (cf. 5.12). Already in Homer and Hesiod, the gods are shown to extend their protection to those outside human legal protection. One method of self-preservation in emergency was the act of supplication.

3.36 To become a suppliant to either a man or a god was to proclaim the abjectness of one's position, and to acknowledge and honour fulsomely the power and position of the other. This was a complete inversion of normal patterns of behaviour and encounters between equals (cf. 4.2). It would then be a slight on the honour and power of the god or man to fail to protect his suppliant. In a simple supplication of a god, the suppliant merely had to *touch* the altar. More formally, a suppliant donned garlands and carried branches,

3.15 On the frieze from the late fifth-century temple of Apollo at Bassai the centaurs are shown trying to tear some women away from the cult statue at which they have sought sanctuary.

decorated with wool, before approaching the altar to grasp it. While contact with the altar was maintained, any violence offered to the suppliant was an offence against the god and a violation of the sanctity of his power and that of Zeus himself, under his title of *Zeus Hikēsios* (protector of suppliants). Consequently, direct force in removing a suppliant from the altar was rarely resorted to, and was all the more shocking when it was used. Less direct methods were sometimes tried; even so the wrath of the gods was not always avoided. Here the politician Therāmenēs takes refuge at the altar, but little good it does him. He has just been struck off the roll of citizens, and Kritiās, the dominant figure among the Thirty Tyrants in power at the time, takes this opportunity to get rid of him (cf. 1.82–3):

> 'I therefore', concluded Kritiās, 'strike the name of Therāmenēs from the roll, with your unanimous agreement, and we condemn him to death.'
>
> When Therāmenēs heard this he jumped onto the altar and cried, 'All I ask is basic justice. You must not allow Kritiās to strike either me or any of you off the roll just as he pleases; they have passed a law about those on the roll, and you and I must be judged in accordance with it. I know very well, I assure you, that this altar will give me no protection, but I wish to demonstrate that this junta has no respect either for justice or religion. But I am surprised that you, good men and true that you are, are reluctant to defend your rights, knowing very well as you do that your names are as easy to strike out as is mine.'
>
> At this the herald of the Thirty ordered the Eleven to seize Therāmenēs; they entered with their attendants, led by Satyros, the most brazen and shameless of the gang. Kritiās said to the Eleven, 'We hand this fellow

Therāmenēs over to you. He has been condemned according to the law; do you take him to the proper place and carry out the sentence.'

At these words Satyros and his attendants dragged Therāmenēs from the altar. He, as was natural, called on gods and men to witness what was being done. But the *boulē* kept quiet. They saw the rail was packed with men of the same sort as Satyros, and that the front of the *bouleutērion* was full of security guards who, they knew, had come armed with daggers. So Therāmenēs was led away through the *agorā*, loudly proclaiming his wrongs. (Xenophōn, *Hellēnika* 2.3.51)

To supplicate *a person*, the suppliant would clasp his or her knee and chin. The person could not refuse the request made of him while contact lasted. It *was* possible to supplicate a human without physical contact, but success was not assured since physical contact between the two parties could not be made. Consider Odysseus' dilemma here: naked, filthy, stranded, he desperately needs help, so he emerges from the bush where he has been sleeping. The girls run in terror from him – all except Nausikaā, daughter of Alkinoos:

> Only the daughter of Alkinoos stood fast, for Athēnē
> Put courage into her heart, and took the fear from her body,
> And she stood her ground and faced him, and now Odysseus debated
> Whether to supplicate the well-favoured girl by clasping
> Her knees, or stand off where he was and in words of blandishment
> Ask if she would show him the city, and lend him clothing.
> Then in the division of his heart this way seemed best to him,
> To stand well off and supplicate in words of blandishment,
> For fear that, if he clasped her knees, the girl might be angry.
> So blandishingly and full of craft he began to address her:
> 'I am at your knees, O queen. But are you mortal or goddess?'
> (Homer, *Odyssey* 6.127ff)

Ironically, the words with which he starts his appeal mean literally 'I seize your knees'!

Coming face to face with the gods

3.37   A sanctuary (*temenos*) was a sacred area, 'cut off' (*temnō* 'I cut') from profane human use, because it was a traditionally holy reservation. Many sanctuaries were furnished with a temple or temples, but the size and importance of *temenos* and temple were not related. Decisions to create sanctuaries and build temples were decisions taken by communities, so that, as in the case of the Parthenōn, the magnificence of a temple could reflect political rather than religious pressures. Consequently, both sanctuaries and temples varied greatly in size and importance. At one extreme a private group, called *orgeōnes*, might honour a little-known hero, at the other, many thousands of worshippers would come to the great festivals – of Athēnē at Athens or of Zeus at the games of Olympiā.

3.16 The *peplos* presented to the statue of Athēnē Polias at the climax of the
Panathenaic procession forms the centrepiece of the east frieze of the Parthenōn
(2.34, 8.95–9).

3.38   Temples existed primarily to house the statue of the god. That statue might
be a small wooden effigy, or even some object bearing no resemblance to the
appearance of the god, or it might be a colossal display statue by a contemporary artist (Athēnē Parthenos created by Pheidiās for the Parthenōn was
12 m high and made of gold and ivory (8.95)). The contrast between cult
image and sacred object shows two aspects of divinity: the first imagines the
god 'humanly', as a physical presence, while the non-human sacred object has
religious power because it evokes mystery and awe. The Athenian Akropolis
had both the statue of Athēnē in the Parthenōn and also the old wooden
image of Athēnē Polias in the Erekhtheion (cf. 2.34). There is some reason to
suppose that initially the Athenians intended to keep the Athēnē Polias statue
in a subsidiary shrine in the colonnade of the Parthenōn, and that they only
later decided to house it in a temple of its own (hence the construction of the
Erekhtheion). Old sacred images were often held not to have been made by
human hands at all. Pausaniās relates the story of the 'mask' of Dionȳsos at
Methymnē on Lesbos:

> My next story comes from Lesbos. Some fishermen at Methymnē drew up
> from the sea in their nets a face made of olive wood. In appearance it bore

3.17 Remains of the fourth-century altar of Zeus Phrātrios and Athēnē Phrātriā from the Athenian *agorā*.

some resemblance to a divinity, but a foreign one, not in the normal style of the Greek gods. The Methymnians accordingly asked the Pythian priestess of what god or hero it was an image, and she told them to worship Phallic Dionȳsos. Accordingly, the Methymnians kept the wooden image from the sea for themselves and honour it with sacrifices and prayers; but they sent a bronze replica to Delphi. (Pausaniās, *Guide to Greece* 10.19.2)

Religion in practice in classical Athens

3.39   By the fifth century, shrines and cults proliferated in Attikē to both heroes and minor deities, and to Athēnē and the other Olympians. Most civic as well as sacred functions were under the patronage of the gods: Zeus, Artemis, Athēnē and Hermēs in particular oversaw the activities of most officials in the *agorā* – so Zeus Boulaios and Artemis Boulaiā in the *boulē*, Zeus and Hermēs Agoraios in the *agorā*, and so on. The presence of the gods, who would grow angry if their areas of interest were not respected, gave these institutions authority and permanence. So too for the citizen body, a temple in the *agorā* to Apollōn Patrōios ('of our ancestors' – Apollo was the mythical ancestor of the Athenian race) and one to Zeus Phrātrios and Athēnē

Phrātriā ('of the phratries') were nuclei of civic life uniting small groups of citizens. Nearly all citizens belonged to one of the *phrātriai*, and many had shrines to Apollōn Patrōios in their homes (cf. 5.14). Indeed, prospective state officials were specifically asked whether they had one or not (see 5.10).

The religious calendar

3.40 Religious festivals came in various shapes and sizes, but the largest were the big public rituals that often lasted several days, and occupied a large part of the civic and sacred year. Some of the major state festivals involved all members of the population, both slave and free, citizen and metic, male and female, adults and children. The gods too were felt to be watching: Pheidiās pictured a group of immortals, all set to watch the spectacle, on the Parthenōn frieze, which represents the procession at the Great *Panathēnaia* (8.96). No doubt their sympathies and interests were felt to be particularly caught by the scale of the celebrations and the quality of the athletic, poetic and dramatic performances (8.76). For although ancient ceremonies to encourage the grain and grape harvest lived on in these festivals, at the same time the celebrants enjoyed every kind of intellectual, religious and physical excitement. Little in the modern world parallels these festivals (though the medieval carnival comes close), for Athenian festivals included not only processions and sacrifices but cultural events such as the performance of dithyramb (see 8.45), tragedy and comedy, and athletic competitions (8.45).

3.41 Every month, certain days were set aside for festivals and sacrifices to particular gods (e.g. the seventh of each month to Apollo). These were relatively minor affairs, but sufficiently important for the *ekklēsiā* not to meet on those days. The major festivals occurred on an annual cycle. Some festivals were peculiar to particular groups, for example demes or phratries, others were festivals of the whole *polis*. Demes had their own calendars, and different demes would be found holding different celebrations on different days (3.55). Phratries all celebrated the same main festival, the *Apatouria*, and since all Athenians belonged to one phratry or another, this became a general holiday (3.53–4). During major state festivals everyone seems to have taken a holiday; demes avoided having local festivities on those days and even the standing committee, the *boulē*, seems to have been dismissed for these days, except for emergencies. The Athenians in the fifth century were noted for the number and magnificence of their festivals. In fact, the number of firmly dated festival days is 130; when the undated festivals are added, about one-half of the days of the year can be shown to have boasted one festival or another. Some sources indicate that the jury-courts may have been expected to work 300 days in the year, leaving some 54 'holidays'; but other indications suggest that the courts sat on a rather smaller number of days, perhaps as few as 150. We also have a contract given to some workmen to work at Eleusīs for a period of 40 days which included the festivals of *Kronia*, *Sunoikia* and the major state festival of *Panathēnaia*. The conclusion must be that while most people would expect to have a real holiday during state festivals, not everyone did or could.

Months of the Athenian calendar, with modern equivalents (Athenian months run from new moon to new moon)

Hekatombaiōn	June–July
Metageitniōn	July–August
Boēdromiōn	August–September
Pyanopsiōn	September–October
Maimaktēriōn	October–November
Poseideiōn	November–December
Gamēliōn	December–January
Anthestēriōn	January–February
Elaphēboliōn	February–March
Mounikhiōn	March–April
Thargēliōn	April–May
Skirophoriōn	May–June

The constituents of public ritual

3.42   Sacrifice we have already discussed (3.28ff.). It formed the climax of many festivals, often on a vast scale. So at the *Panathēnaia*, Athenian communities overseas, and in the fifth century the members of the Delian League, were required to send a cow as a sacrificial victim, and a fourth-century law shows that the rents of some public lands were used to buy more animals (the sum involved was the equivalent of two to three thousand skilled men's wages for a day). The victims were slaughtered at the great altar of Athēnē on the Akropolis. Some of the meat was set aside for the religious and secular officials of the community, and the rest was probably divided up among the Athenians by deme, perhaps in proportion to the number of demesmen that each contributed to the procession. We should not underestimate the expense and complexities of public ritual.

3.43   Processions too were centre-pieces of many festivals, and again on a very considerable scale of solemnity and grandeur. They would include the bearers of ritual objects and offerings, such as *kanēphoroi* (bearers of gold baskets of grain for throwing at the sacrifice), *skaphēphoroi* (resident aliens who carried trays of such gifts as cakes and honeycombs), carriers of silver bowls, jugs and incense burners, of stools for the officiating priests to sit on and of great awnings under which the priests walked. Many in the procession would carry branches of olive or of oak as sacred emblems. In processions to honour Dionȳsos, phalluses were carried (Athenian communities abroad were required to bring one), as well as wine-skins and special loaves of bread called *obeliai* ('spit-loaves' – presumably baguettes). Such processions would wind their way across Athens (from the Kerameikos across the *agorā* to the

3.18 On this Athenian red-figure cup from the first quarter of the fifth century we see the god Dionȳsos in the central tondo and a chorus of boys with their pipe player in the surrounding frieze.

Akropolis at the *Panathēnaia*) or on longer routes across Attikē. At the *Dionȳsia*, the wooden image of the god was brought in procession from the Academy to the god's temple by the theatre, to commemorate his first coming to Athens from Eleutherai on the border between Attikē and Boiōtiā. Participants in the great procession of the Eleusinian Mysteries walked from Athens to Eleusīs (22 km) carrying the 'holy things' of Dēmētēr or escorting the initiates; and at another festival the wooden image of Athēnē was taken in procession from the Akropolis to the sea at Phalēron (7 km) to be washed by its traditional custodians, members of a family called Prāxiergidai.

3.44   More surprising to us as a form of religious worship are the competitions held to honour the gods. These were a recurring part of Greek religious rituals. They might take many forms: athletic contests (in chariot racing, running, wrestling, and throwing the discus and javelin); competitions between choirs and professional reciters of heroic poetry, or between teams of playwrights, actors and managers (*khorēgoi*); and torch-races (held in the dark and in one case on horseback) ending at an altar. Some festivals combined more than one type of contest: the *Panathēnaia* combined athletics and torch-races with competitions between Homeric 'rhapsodes'. Some might

3.19 The reverse side of the Panathenaic *amphorā* shown above (fig. 1.4) shows competing runners, though this does not necessarily mean that the *amphorā* was awarded to a winning runner, since some athletic events are illustrated which seem not to have been part of the Panathenaic programme.

offer only one: the festivals of Dionȳsos featured contests between playwrights and their troupes of actors (cf. 8.45). We can look at all these competitions in two ways: either as shows for the gods to watch and enjoy (as we see them watch and enjoy heroic warfare in the *Iliad*); or as arenas for the conspicuous display of human competitive aggression, giving divine sanction and recognition to an aspect of human behaviour which had in it the seeds of social disruption and conflict (cf. 4.2, 18–19). Just as Greeks imagined their gods as often in conflict with one another, so they imagined them as understanding and enjoying human conflict. As Patroklos (*Iliad* 23.257ff.) was honoured in death by men competing with each other, so the gods were honoured by the competitive display of human excellence in all its forms – even balancing on a greasy wine-skin!

3.45 If the great festivals were primarily religious occasions, they were not solely religious occasions. For example, the Athenians demanded that communities of Athenians that had been established elsewhere contribute sacrificial animals, sets of armour and phalluses to festivals at Athens. This suggests that religious display and political display could not be disentangled. Further, the major festivals that gathered Greeks from many parts of the Mediterranean were great opportunities to interchange goods (big market stalls were common at such events) and ideas as well. For example, the great athletic games held in honour of Zeus at Olympiā every four years provided a venue at which men such as Gorgiās and Lysiās could displayed their rhetorical and intellectual virtuosity (8.20). On one occasion Alexander the Great even used the gathering to issue a proclamation requiring all Greek states to take back their exiles (1.110).

The great Athenian festivals

(a) The Panathēnaia

3.46 This took place every year at the waning of the first moon after the new year in *Hekatombaiōn*. Every fourth year it was celebrated with extra splendour and called the Great *Panathēnaia*. We have already discussed the contests which took place during the festival and said something of the great procession and sacrifices which were the climax (3.42). The procession was to escort up to the Akropolis the new robe (*peplos*), woven every four years with much attendant ritual by girls chosen from Athenian aristocratic families, to be presented to Athēnē Polias, the protecting goddess of Athens. As its name implies, the *Panathēnaia*, like other such festivals elsewhere (the *Paniōnia* and *Pamboiōtia*, for example), was a celebration of the solidarity of the whole (Greek *pan*) Athenian community under the protection of the great goddess, whose birthday it was imagined as being. It reinforced their sense of 'being Athenian', wherever in Attikē or overseas they lived, different from and superior to other, non-Athenian Greeks.

(b) The Anthestēria

3.47 This festival in honour of Dionȳsos gave its name to the month in which it took place (*Anthestēriōn*, January–February). Its name derives from the Greek for 'flowers', and the festival took place at a time when the first signs of life in nature, blossom, began to show. The main concern of the festival was with the new wine (i.e. the reappearance of Dionȳsos) and the spirits of

3.20 On this Athenian red-figure *stamnos* from the second quarter of the fifth century Dionȳsos himself is shown dancing and tearing apart a wild animal.

ill omen (cf. 5.83). The festival lasted three days. On day one (*pithoigia*, 'jar opening'), the new wine was opened and tested; on day two (*khoes*, 'wine-jugs'), there was a procession in which Dionȳsos rode in a ship-chariot and the wife of the king *arkhōn* (*arkhōn basileus*) was 'married' to him in a 'holy marriage'. In the evening, drinking-parties were the order of the day, but each guest brought his own wine and drank it in silence, the very antithesis of community fellowship. The Greek explanation lay in myth. Orestēs, infected with blood-pollution for killing his mother, arrived in Athens on *khoes*. In order that he should not be excluded from the celebrations and that the people should not be polluted, the king ordered that all drink their own wine from their own cups. We may prefer to explain the ritual rather as an attempt to put a boundary around the potentially destructive effects of too much alcohol. The third day was *khutrai*, 'pots', and of a completely different character. Vegetables were boiled in these pots not for the living but for the spirits of the dead. It was a day of ill omen, when these spirits were said to roam abroad. When the day was over, the householders shouted, 'Get out, *kēres* ['evil demons'], the *Anthestēria* is over!'

3.48   This seems an extraordinary hotchpotch of events, but perhaps makes sense in the light of the many-sided character of Dionȳsos. Not only is he god of life, wine and festivities, but he is also god of destruction. Wine itself has distinct potentials: it can create good feeling, but it can also release violent, destructive passions. The destructive side of Dionȳsos is brought out most powerfully by a number of tragedies staging myths in which violence is done under the influence of Dionysiac possession. The most famous and only fully extant example is Euripidēs' *Bacchae* which stages Dionȳsos' power to drive his followers wild with ecstasy in their search for him. They lost all control over themselves and ripped wild animals apart to get the raw, bleeding flesh inside them and with it, the god of life, Dionȳsos himself. Euripidēs has Dionȳsos in that play say of himself that he is a god most awesome and most gentle to men.

3.49   The *Anthestēria* presents a face of Greek religion different from that on display at the *Panathēnaia*. In the latter, we have a civic and political religion which integrated individuals into society, defining them as 'citizen' or 'member of the family' or 'guest' (cf. 3.46); in the former, we have elements in the worship of Dionȳsos which seem to have torn people away from their lives as citizens of the civilised world of the *polis* towards something very different. It should be no surprise that women, disqualified from equal participation with men in social life, should appear to have been prominent in religious life (cf. 5.24, 26, 29). *Anthestēria* was a festival whose deeper purpose may have been to defuse and contain some of these wilder aspects of Dionysiac worship.

(c) The Eleusinian Mysteries

3.50   The Eleusinian Mysteries (2.22), celebrated towards the end of summer, have some points in common with the *Panathēnaia* – processions, sacrifices, Panhellenic involvement – and some with the *Anthestēria* – looking forward to death and life after death. But they are different from both, in that participation was not restricted to Athenians but open to anyone, slave or free, who was a Greek speaker and had been initiated. The emphasis was not upon the community but firmly upon personal revelation and salvation. A character in Sophoklēs is recorded as saying, 'Thrice blessed are those among men who, after beholding these rites, go down to Hādēs. Only for them is there life' (Plutarch, *Morālia* 21f.). The cult, which centred around the myth of Dēmētēr's recovery of her daughter Persephonē from the underworld, was administered by Athens as a state festival. It was overseen by the king *arkhōn*, though its chief priesthood, that of the *Hierophantēs* ('revealer of holy things'), was in the hands of the Eumolpidai family and that of the *Daidoukhos* ('the Torch-holder') in the hands of the Kērykes family. In contrast to practice in other state cults, these priests wore elaborate clothes.

3.51   Initiation was in two stages. The Lesser Mysteries, which were held in *Anthestēriōn* at Agrai near the river Īlīsos just outside the walls of Athens, were dedicated to Persephonē. The initiates (*mustai*) wore wreaths and carried in procession branches of myrtle. A woman bore on her head the sacred vessel (*kernos*) which held a variety of seeds and grains to symbolise Dēmētēr's gifts, as Dēmētēr was goddess of the crops. For the Greater Mysteries in *Boēdromiōn*, a truce of fifty-five days was declared so that people could travel safely from all over Greece to the festival. The *epheboi*, youths of eighteen or nineteen (cf. 7.31), escorted the sacred things (*hiera*) from Eleusīs in boxes (*kistai*) to Athens. These objects were a central part of the ritual, but because of the universal awe and respect for the secrecy of the Mysteries in Greece, we have no evidence at all for suggesting what they might have been. On the 15th was held the *agurmos* (gathering); and on the 16th, the day probably known as *halade mustai* ('seaward initiates'), purification rites were held. The initiates bathed in the sea, each with a sucking pig which they later sacrificed. The 18th was spent indoors by the initiates, while the rest of Athens celebrated the festival of Asklēpios. On the 19th the initiates went in procession to Eleusīs led by Iakkhos, the personified cry ('*Iakkhe!*') of the celebrants approaching Dēmētēr. They wore garlands of myrtle and carried *bakkhoi* (branches of myrtle tied with wool), as well as provisions on a stick, probably bedding and new clothes. On the evening of the 20th the procession reached Eleusīs, lit by torches. The *kernos* was presented to Dēmētēr. On the 21st, sacrifices were made to the two goddesses; a vast offering of ground wheat, enough for 1,000 men, was set aside for this. The revelations which lasted through this night were not made in the open air. For these, uniquely in Greek ritual, took place inside the *Telestērion*, which at the period of its greatest extent could have held as many as 10,000 initiates. Little is known of the central ritual, except that it was divided into 'things said', 'things done' and 'things revealed'. Initiates who were allowed to see the last stage were known as *epoptai* ('viewers'). We can be fairly sure that two things seen by the initiates were light appearing from darkness, and an ear of (Dēmētēr's) wheat being carried round.

3.52   The Mysteries provided an intense personal involvement and an emotional experience of the highest order. Initiation, as the quotation from Sophoklēs shows, was regarded with reverence. The rites were said to 'inspire those who take part in them with sweeter hopes regarding both the end of life and all eternity'. No wonder that such intense feelings were aroused in 415 when claims were made about members of the Athenian élite travestying these rites. The passion of the investigation into these allegations is one more indication of the immense respect in which the Mysteries were held by all Athenians (cf. 1.73).

(d) The phratry festival of the Apatouria

3.53 The *Apatouria*, celebrated in the autumn of each year, was a very old festival which existed also in all the Ionian cities of the Aegean and the coast of Asia Minor. At Athens it was a state festival, but one organised and celebrated by the individual phratries (*phrātriai*, hereditary groups of families). Its chief purpose, apart from renewing the religious and secular solidarity of the phratries, was as a 'rite of passage' (i.e. a transition from one status to another) to register and attest the status of citizen children. Each phratry had a local cult centre. There the members (all of whom were men) celebrated various rituals. For example, on the third day, *koureōtis* (the name might mean either 'Day of Youths' or 'hair-cutting') was the occasion for the presentation of the children of phratry members for public 'legitimisation'. New brides would also be presented to phratries on the third day. There were as well drink-offerings (*khoai*) for deceased phratry members.

3.54 The *Apatouria* thus focused religious feeling upon the traditional phratry grouping and upon the acceptance of children as eligible for citizenship. This emphasises the constant relationship in Athens between the organisation of the institutions of the *polis* and the local loyalties of the people. Phratry membership was not just a practical matter of keeping outsiders out; it combined a positive sense of belonging with a deep feeling of traditional religious values, which could be played on to good effect in the courts (5.140).

(e) Deme festivals

3.55 The demes (*dēmoi*), the local village communities of Attikē, also had their own public rituals. From one of them, Erkhia, we have an inscription which lists more than fifty sacrifices in the year, offered to almost forty different divine powers. The gods most frequently honoured at Erkhia are Zeus, Apollo, Kourotrophos ('she who raises the young') and Athēnē. On a few days in the year, men went from Erkhia to Athens (on the other side of Mt Hymēttos, more than 20 km away) to make offerings to the gods of Athens, to Zeus and Athēnē 'of the city', to Apollōn Lykeios (worshipped in the Lykeion ('Lyceum')) and to Dēmētēr of Eleusis. In the village of Erkhia itself, they had an Akropolis on which were worshipped the same divinities, great or small, as were worshipped in Athens, but also at Erkhia men offered sacrifices to obscure gods such as Zeus Epōpetēs, the nymphs, the Heroines, the *Tritopateres*, and the *Hērakleidai*, and to local heroes such as Leukaspis ('he of the white shield') and Epops. The picture has parallels in Christian practice in many Mediterranean and Latin American countries, where loyalty to the local saints may figure as much in religious feeling as acknowledgements of the great gods in the Greek world. In this, Erkhia seems to be typical of the village communities of the Attic countryside (cf. 2.21).

Conclusion

3.56 When the divinities Greeks worshipped seemed to act irrationally, and there were few if any rules of behaviour which could be adduced to mollify them, one may wonder why the religion continued to be so successful in retaining people's loyalty. A Greek may well have replied that it was a matter of observing the world as it actually *was*, rather than as one would like it to be, and if it was irrational and intractable, one did one's best to live with it. Still, there were fixed points, as we have seen. The orator Lysiās certainly thought so in the following extract, where the politician Andokidēs was indicted on charges of impiety:

> But think again, envisage in your mind's eye what he did, and you will be able to form a better judgement. This man put on a sacred robe, he acted a parody of the sacred rites before the uninitiated and spoke the forbidden words; he mutilated the gods whom we worship, and to whom our devotions and sacrifices and prayers are offered. For this the priests and priestesses stood and cursed him, facing the west and shaking out their crimson robes as is their ancient and time-honoured custom. And he has confessed. What is more, he has broken the law you made debarring transgressors from our holy ceremonies; in defiance of it he has made his way into the city; he has sacrificed at the altars forbidden to him; he has been present at the very rites which he violated; he has entered the Eleusinion and bathed his hands in the holy water. Who can tolerate all this? Can friend or relation or fellow townsmen dare to incur the manifest anger of heaven by showing him indulgence in private? You should indeed today reckon that, in punishing Andokidēs and getting rid of him, you are cleansing the city and freeing it from pollution, expelling a scapegoat and ridding yourselves of a transgressor. For that is what he is. (Lysiās, *Against Andokidēs* 6.50ff.)

3.57 At the same time, criticism of the gods had been a feature of intellectual thought since the sixth century (cf. 8.13); and in the fifth century, Athens had seen a general broadening of the spectrum of attitudes to the gods. In other words, the picture is less coherent than may appear from the above account. Indeed, the time would come when some Greeks started thinking in terms not so much of gods as of a Supreme Being. At the end of the day, a Greek might have said that the very existence of himself and his community was some sort of proof that the gods had heeded their prayers. To that extent, the longer the tradition of worship in *this* way or *that* way (rather than in any other way) had existed, the more acceptable to the gods it must, by definition, have been. Isokratēs sums it up precisely:

In religious matters (for it is right to begin with them), our forefathers were neither inconsistent nor irregular in their worship or celebrations. They did not make a sacrifice of three hundred oxen merely when it seemed a good idea, while neglecting (at whim) the sacrifices instituted by their fathers. They did not celebrate foreign festivals imported from abroad on a grand scale whenever there was a feast attached to them, while performing their own most hallowed rituals at the lowest price possible. Their only concern was not to weaken the religion of their fathers nor to introduce unwanted innovations; for in their eyes, piety consisted not in lavish expenditure, but in leaving untouched what their forefathers had bequeathed to them. So the blessings of heaven were visited on them with unbroken regularity and in due season for ploughing and for harvest. (Isokratēs, *Areopagītikos* 7.29ff.)

4 Human obligations, values and concerns

Introduction

4.1 How should one live one's life? Philosophers attempt to establish a rational basis for how we should behave towards each other; economists attempt to show what behaviour is in our best interests on the assumption that others too are concerned to maximise their interests. But most people derive their moral values from a mixture of parental influence, self-interest, understanding of the law, vague memories of Biblical values, particularly those of the Christian Gospels, and imitation of people known from life or from fiction. It was in classical Athens that philosophers, beginning with Sōkratēs, first debated moral questions in the abstract ('What is justice?' 'What is piety?' 'What is goodness?'), but most Athenians will have derived their values from the same sort of mix that we do. In Plato's dialogue *Prōtagorās*, for example, Prōtagorās says that from early on, children are taught standards at home and at school, and then by the state, in the shape of obedience to the laws. But no single person teaches them: they learn through life. To ask who 'taught' you standards, he concludes, is as pointless as asking who taught you your native tongue. Doubtless literary texts, particularly the Homeric poems which were central to their education, also played a part. Given that we today stress the value of collaboration, the Athenian stress on the value of competition comes as some surprise.

4.2 Aggressive, self-assertive competition, for which the Greek word is *agōn* (cf. 'agony'), encouraged Greeks to make a clear distinction between friends and enemies; to emphasize that you would be treated as an enemy by the opposition, in the same way as you would be treated as a friend by your own side (tit-for-tat, or reciprocal action, again, cf. 3.34); and to understand that the final arbiter of all matters was other people, i.e. what you looked like in the public eye. These constitute three important features of the Greek values as displayed and debated in the Homeric poems, in Athenian tragedy, and in what is said in the Athenian law-courts. These competitive values make a number of common features of Greek life comprehensible. The regular assertion that it was a man's duty to help his friends (*philoi*) and harm his enemies (*ekhthroi*) arises from the principle of reciprocal action. In the tragic theatre, poets competed aggressively against each other under the public gaze to secure a prize. A law-court trial settled disputes by ensuring that one side won and the other lost – it did not necessarily see that justice was done. Indeed, in many court cases the issue before the jurors often seems to be 'Who started it?' or 'How shall we deal with these litigants?' rather than 'Where do right and wrong lie?' Conversely, the institution of *xeniā*, hospitality, shows men helping their *philoi*. Friendship was made tangible by the exchange of gifts, which were visible signs of a relationship. The greater the man, the greater the gift; the greater the gift, the more important to display it.

4.3 Clearly, a society which embraced only these values, and no others, would soon tear itself apart. So in real life, steps were taken to divert aggression into other channels before it came to public confrontation. Solōn (1.20–1), for example, legislated against conspicuous displays of wealth at funerals, prime occasions when families put on lavish shows to demonstrate just how rich they were. The use of the lot in selecting candidates for office in democratic Athens was one way of selecting a candidate without ranking or judging the others (cf. 6.28). Ostracism (1.31, 4.12) was one way of averting open aggression between rival political factions.

4.4 Unlike Greeks, we tend not to analyse our own behaviour in terms of public displays of status and power, or pride in helping friends and harming enemies. By contrast, both in Greek literature and in Greek life, individuals openly acknowledged their competitive ambitions. While Greeks acknowledged the value of reconciliation and compromise, they did not go out of their way to disguise their love of competition either. On the contrary, individuals were expected to compete.

Honour and shame

4.5 In *Iliad* book 12, Sarpēdōn, a great Lykian warrior fighting on the Trojan side, asks his companion Glaukos:

> Glaukos, why are we most of all singled out for honour at home in Lykiā, with pride of place, the choicest meat and never-empty cups? Why do they all look up to us as gods? And why do we cultivate a great estate on the banks of the river Xanthos, with lovely orchards and splendid fields of wheat? All this now obliges us to take our places in the front ranks of the Lykians and fling ourselves into the flames of battle. Only then will our Lykian men-at-arms say of us: 'Well! These are no dishonourable lords of Lykiā that rule over us and eat fat sheep and drink the best sweet wine: they are indomitable and fight in the front ranks of the Lykians.' (Homer, *Iliad* 12.310–21)

The passage neatly illustrates three of the main cornerstones of the Greek value-system: society needs the skill of the warrior, and rewards it with (i) *material gifts*, and (ii) *honour*, or *public acclaim* (*tīmē*, the Greek word often translated 'honour', is derived from a word meaning 'value', 'true assessment', cf. 3.24). These rewards are (iii) *reciprocated* by the warriors' duty of

4.1 Before the eyes of the mourning Priam and Hekabē, Akhilleus has the corpse of Hektōr dragged round the walls of Troy, exacting revenge for the death of Patroklos and shaming the memory of Hektōr. An Athenian black-figure water jug (*hydriā*) of the late sixth century.

fighting in the front line. So, when Akhilleus, the greatest Greek warrior, refuses to fight for the Greeks because of the slight done to him by the king Agamemnōn, his old mentor Phoinix tries to persuade him to return to the fighting and to accept Agamemnōn's compensatory gift as well:

> No; come while gifts are still to be had, and the Greeks will treat you like a god. If you plunge into the killing fields with no such gifts, you will not be so respected, even though you turn defeat into victory. (Homer, *Iliad* 9.602–5)

4.2 This red-figure *skyphos* (deep drinking cup) painted in the second quarter of the fifth century at Athens shows Priam bringing to Akhilleus a large ransom in return for Hektōr's corpse, seen here lying under Akhilleus' couch.

Without the physical evidence of compensation in gifts, any Greek might have assumed that Akhilleus had simply given in.

4.6 Since public approval was the greatest spur to success, public *disapproval* acted powerfully to dissuade individuals from failing to meet their obligations. The technical term for this sense of feeling men's eyes upon you was *aidōs*, often translated as 'shame'. Once more, the Homeric poems put this value clearly on display. In the following passage, Hektōr justifies his decision to fight on against hopeless odds:

> As it is, having sacrificed the army to my own reckless stupidity, I would feel nothing but shame before the Trojan men and the Trojan women in their trailing gowns. I could not bear to hear some second-rater say: 'Hektōr trusted in his own right arm and lost an army.' But it will be said, and then it would be far better for me to stand up to Akhilleus and either kill him and come home alive, or be killed by him gloriously in front of Ilium. (Homer, *Iliad* 22.104–10)

But the Homeric poems showed not only how the 'honour-and-shame' system might work in particular circumstances, but also how problems arose when a whole group of separate individuals all strongly espoused these competitive virtues.

4.7 The *Iliad* started with the public quarrel between Agamemnōn and Akhilleus. The heart of their argument was 'Who deserves public rewards? Those who are the best fighters, or those who are leaders (whether they are right or not)?' In the heat of the moment, Agamemnōn (son of Atreus) decided to take the girl of Akhilleus (son of Pēleus) from him, to make up for the girl whom he (Agamemnōn) had earlier been forced to give up. The wise old Nestōr attempted to find a middle way, addressing Agamemnōn first:

> You, Agamemnōn, though you have the authority, do not rob him of his girl. The Greek army gave her to him first. Let him keep his prize. And you, Akhilleus, give up your desire to cross swords with your leader. Through the authority he derives from Zeus, a leader who holds the sceptre of power has more claim to our respect than anyone else. Even if you, with a goddess for mother, are the better fighter, yet Agamemnōn is your superior since he rules more people. Agamemnōn, cool your fury; I, Nestōr, entreat you to put aside your anger against Akhilleus, who is a mighty tower of strength for every Greek in the hell of battle. (Homer, *Iliad* 1.275–84)

In other words, in Homer's world excellence in fighting was only one of a number of qualities which demanded to be honoured. Wealth, the number of a man's subjects or the quality of advice one gave were all rival claims to status. Clearly, if such a society was to stand without incessant competition between its members rendering it incapable of acting in concert, there had to be some restraints, some sanctions.

Classical Athens

From honour to dishonour, from shame to revenge

4.8 Fifth-century Athenians valued competition, conspicuous public acclaim and reciprocal obligations as strongly as any Homeric hero. They also introduced sanctions which helped to ensure that the community was not permanently torn apart by open personal rivalries. Although warfare was more or less continuous in fifth-century Athens, and although honour and dishonour awaited success or failure in war, particularly for the generals involved, the main arena for interpersonal rivalries shifted from the battlefield elsewhere. The games associated with religious festivals (3.44) were an influential model, not least because the positive benefits of competition were immediately manifest there and the problems it caused least apparent. The point is that one could compete under the public eye in many different ways – intellectually and socially as well as athletically (cf. 3.44) – at the Greek festivals (e.g. the *Panathēnaia*) and athletic competitions (especially at Olympiā, Delphi, Nemeā and the Isthmus at Corinth) but without threatening life, limb or political revolution. All that counted was beating your opponents on the day (record-breaking was irrelevant). This applied equally to playwrights competing for first prize in the Dionysiac tragedy and comedy competitions. In

4.3 Aiās shows his prowess by carrying the corpse of Akhilleus off the battlefield. This is from the handle of the early sixth-century Athenian *krātēr* known as the François Vase.

his oration over the war dead of 431 (the 'Funeral Speech'), Periklēs even applied the image of athletic victory to the state's treatment of its war-dead heroes and their families:

> If deeds be in question, those who are here interred have received part of their honours already, and for the rest, their children will be brought up till manhood at the People's expense. The state thus offers a valuable prize, as the garland of victory in this race of valour, for the reward of both those who have fallen and their survivors. And where the rewards for excellence are greatest, there are found the best citizens. (Thucydides, *Peloponnesian War* 2.46)

4.4–5 The two sides of this early fifth-century red-figure cup show the Greeks casting ballots as to who should have the armour of the dead Akhilleus, and Aiās' angry response when the armour is not awarded to him.

4.6 Aiās killed himself after, in madness, he killed the sheep of the Greeks at Troy instead of, as he thought, the Greek leaders. Here, on the interior of an early fifth-century red-figure cup, Tekmēssa is shown covering up his corpse.

4.9 In other words, this image was central to civic as well as athletic and social life, and with good reason, since in classical Athens the public life of the citizen, especially in the *ekklēsiā*, offered as much scope for visible success as did the battlefield. Consider how the youthful but extraordinarily talented and wealthy Alkibiadēs explains to the *ekklēsiā* why he should command the expedition to Sicily, despite the fact that Nīkiās, the highly experienced general, has just advised the *ekklēsiā* against him (cf. 1.72.):

> Athenians, since Nīkiās has attacked me on this point, let me begin by saying that I have a better claim to command than others and believe that I am qualified for it. Indeed the very things for which I am criticised in fact bring honour to my ancestors and myself and benefit our country. For, after thinking the war had ruined our city, the Greeks came to overestimate its power because of the magnificent showing I made at the Olympic games. I entered seven chariots for the chariot race (a larger number than any private individual before), took first, second and fourth place, and did everything in suitably grand style. Custom honours such successes, and at the same time they give an impression of power. Again, any display I have made at home by providing choruses and the like, though it may have provoked a natural envy in my fellow citizens, gives an impression of power abroad. It is not mere

4.7 The honour won in athletic victory was made material in the ribbons or branches bestowed upon victors, as here on an early fifth-century red-figure cup.

useless folly when a man benefits not only himself but his city at his own expense, nor is it unfair for the ambitious to expect special treatment; certainly the unsuccessful man does not find others coming to share in his misfortunes. And just as nobody takes any notice of us if we fail, so we should correspondingly be ready to put up with it if the successful look down on us – unless we are prepared for everyone to be treated as equal. What I do know is that men of this kind, and all who have attained to any distinction, are unpopular in their lifetime both with their immediate circle and with their contemporaries more generally. However, later generations are eager to claim relationship with them even if there is none; and further, their own country boasts about them, with no suggestion that they were foreigners or wrongdoers, but as fellow countrymen and heroes. That is my own ambition, and that is why my private life is criticized. But what you must ask yourselves is whether you have anyone who manages your public affairs better than I do. (Thucydides, *Peloponnesian War* 6.16ff.)

Not every political leader in Athens invoked these values, but this passage underlines perfectly how an ambitious, politically motivated Athenian could espouse and manipulate the value put upon public display, public success and public recognition. Yet it is not difficult to perceive the problems that this might cause. In a competitive society, the pain of defeated opponents and the envy of those outstripped were the surest signs of success. But while it was desirable to be envied, those seen to be inferior had a very powerful spur to action.

4.10 For being envied carried its own dangers with it. The most serious was the risk of alienating those who envied you. It is a remarkable fact, but not now one hard to understand, that many of the best-known figures in fifth- and fourth-century Athens faced some sort of trial which usually resulted in heavy fines, or exile or even death (e.g. Aristeidēs, Alkibiadēs, Anaxagorās, Kīmōn, Pheidiās, Dēmosthenēs, Periklēs, Themistoklēs, Xenophōn). So it is not surprising that Greek tragedians saw a pattern in the lives of the great figures of myth who were brought low. *Philotīmiā*, 'love of honour', 'ambition', could always be a double-edged sword, and from time to time those engaged in public life might find it politic to deny that they held any personal ambitions:

> I might indeed recall the money I have spent on trierarchies, on the ransom of prisoners-of-war and on other acts of generosity; but I pass over them in silence. My motives were never personal gain or ambition (*philotīmiā*) and I have steadfastly advocated a course which has made me unpopular, but which would be greatly to your advantage if you were to follow it. (Dēmosthenēs, *On the Kherronēsos* 8.70)

4.11 Nevertheless, for all its dangers, a Greek liked to be envied, and had a strong sense of the public eye upon him. Kroisos' son Atys used an irresistible argument to his father when he asked what people would think of him for staying away from the battlefield and the hunt:

> When Kroisos persisted in his refusal to let his son join the hunting party, the young man said to him: 'My dear father, in the past I have looked for honour and fame in war and hunting. Now you have barred me from both, though you have no evidence against me of cowardice or lack of spirit. What figure do you think I shall cut on my way to and from the assembly? What will people think of me? And what sort of man will my young wife think she is

4.8 This array of *ostraka* cast against Themistoklēs and Hippokratēs includes two (on the right) which seem to have been written by the same hand.

living with? Either let me go on this hunt, or give me good reason why I should obey your wishes.' (Hērodotos, *Histories* 1.38)

4.12 The word for dishonour was *atīmiā* (cf. *atīmos*, 'dishonoured'). It meant that one had not received the *tīmē* one expected. *Atīmiā* had a range of meanings extending from personal slight to exile from the community with loss of all rights (cf. 6.56). The consequences of *atīmiā* in any form were grave. Consider here how the threat of political *atīmiā*, which in fact never materialised, resulted in the most powerful social pressures to take revenge:

> I ask you, gentlemen of the jury, to reckon up what would have been the likely consequences for me, for my wife and my sister if Stephanos had been able to inflict the political damage he intended either in his earlier or later legal actions against me, and how great my shame and misfortune would have been. I was urged, privately, by everyone to avenge myself for the wrongs he had inflicted on us and was told that I should be extremely cowardly if I did not see that justice was done for my sister, my father-in-law, my sister's children and my own wife – all of them my close relatives. ([Dēmosthenēs], *Against Neairā* 11–12; cf. 6.45)

The institution of ostracism (1.31) indicates how sensitive Athenians were to men's feelings of disgrace. The purpose of ostracism was to remove from the city a political figure about whom individual Athenians' personal feelings ran so high that they were liable to cloud their personal judgements when they gathered in the *ekklēsiā*. Ostracism, in other words, allowed citizens to express their fear and envy of one more powerful than them. But while an ostracised Athenian was sent into enforced exile for up to ten years, neither he nor his family suffered any loss of rights. This protected the feelings and honour of the exile and reduced the possibilities of revenge. Again, as we have already noted (4.3), the use of the lot for the purpose of selecting officers of state was a means of choosing a person without in any way degrading or openly judging the others. The candidate was selected without doing damage to anyone else's standing in society.

4.13 If dishonour could be expected to lead to a desire for revenge, an Athenian would often emphasise that more than revenge was at stake. So while those who brought actions in court regularly stressed that they had been *personally* damaged by those they were prosecuting, they might also reinforce their personal motivation by appeal to the public good:

> I regarded the man who had put me in this predicament as an enemy with whom no personal reconciliation was possible. But when I discovered that he had defrauded the city as a whole, I proceeded against him with Euktēmōn's help, thinking it a suitable opportunity to do the city a service and to avenge my own wrongs. (Dēmosthenēs, *Against Tīmokratēs* 24.8)

One of the things that Thucydides observes to have gone wrong in the city of Kerkȳra (Corfu) in 427, where division between supporters of Athens and of democracy on the one side, and of Spartē and of oligarchy on the other, had turned into bitter civil conflict, is that revenge had come to know no bounds:

> Revenge was prized more highly than self-preservation. Solemn agreements, if made, were made to meet an immediate difficulty, and remained valid only until a better weapon presented itself; and the side that, when opportunity offered, was the first to try to take their opponents off their guard enjoyed their revenge all the more for being accomplished by treachery – they reckoned this to be the safer method and one which, because it proceeded by guile, would earn them the reputation of superior intelligence . . . Their acts of reprisal were even more savage, since they paid no regard to ordinary standards of justice or to the common good, but only to the pleasure of their own faction at the moment. And so, to satisfy the passions of the hour, they were ready to pervert justice or to secure power by open violence . . . (Thucydides, *Peloponnesian War* 3.82.7–8)

When it came to dishonour done to the whole city, on the other hand, only reasons of prudence or caution could check the desire of revenge. Thucydides has the Spartan Gylippus urge the Syracusans on to what will be the final great battle against the Athenians in summer 413 (1.74) with the words:

> Let us acknowledge that we are entirely within our rights in dealing with any enemy if in exacting vengeance for his aggression we give free rein to the anger in our hearts, and that there is proverbially nothing sweeter than retaliation upon enemies, which will now be ours. That enemies they are and mortal enemies, you all know. They came here to enslave our country, and if successful intended to do to our men all that is most dreadful, to our wives and children all that is most dishonourable, and to our city what would give it a name conveying the greatest reproach. No one should therefore relent or consider it gain if they go away without further danger to us. This they will do even if they win, while, if we succeed in punishing them, as we may expect, and in handing down to all Sicily her ancient freedom strengthened and confirmed, we shall have achieved no mean triumph. And the rarest of dangers are those in which failure brings little loss and success the greatest advantage. (Thucydides, *Peloponnesian War* 7.68)

Dishonouring your opponent is at the heart of this call to revenge: the Syracusans who were threatened with dishonour must ensure not just that they are rid of the Athenians but that the Athenians are dishonoured by defeat in the process.

Friends and enemies

4.14 A Greek's world could be divided into three groups – those to whom one owed obligations and from whom they were expected (*philoi*, 'friends'); those to whom one was hostile (*ekhthroi*, 'enemies'); and 'outsiders', those to whom one owed nothing and could completely ignore. The basic assumption underlying these categories can be summarised in one word – reciprocity (cf. 3.34).

As you prayed to a god and expected him to be favourable because you had yourself done the god favours (and for no other reason), so you expected your *philoi* to help, your *ekhthroi* to injure. Amongst *philoi* were counted your family, first of all; then friends and others with whom obligations had at one time or other established ties. An *ekhthros* had done some harm in the past, or intended to, or was related to one who had. One who had been a 'friend' and had in some way betrayed you could become your bitterest enemy (cf. the passage from *Against Neairā* quoted in 4.12). In his tragedy *Mēdeia*, Euripidēs explores the most extreme case imaginable of a friend becoming an enemy – the betrayal of a wife by a husband. Mēdeia's violent reaction was hardly to be expected from an Athenian wronged wife, but it builds upon values which the audience could be expected in normal circumstances to sympathise with or even admire. Consider how Mēdeia sets out her decision to kill her own children:

> I will kill my children. No one shall save them. And when I have wiped out all Jasōn's family I will flee from the land, leaving behind the murder of my own dear children and the awful crime I have dared to do. For I will not tolerate the mockery of my enemies. So be it. What is there for me to live for? I have no country, no home, no refuge from trouble. I was wrong to leave my father's house, yielding to the words of a Greek, on whom with god's help I will be avenged. He will not see the children I bore him alive again nor will he beget more children by his newly wedded wife, who must die by my poison, miserable wretch. Let no one think I am a meek, weak woman, of no account. I am another sort, kind to my friends indeed, but bitter to my enemies. That is how fame is won. (Euripidēs, *Mēdeia* 792ff.)

4.15   In warfare it needed to be absolutely clear who was a friend and who an enemy. If ever there was a danger that a military enemy (a *polemios*, 'one hostile to, at war with, you', cf. *polemos*, 'war') was in fact the friend of a leading man in your own city, the situation had to be clarified. So it was that, at the beginning of the Peloponnesian War, Periklēs could imagine himself being taunted with an accusation that he had been closely connected with Arkhidāmos of Spartē, who was leading the attack on Athens. Fearing that Arkhidāmos, either out of friendship or in order to blacken Periklēs' name, would invade Attikē but not ravage Periklēs' possessions, Periklēs felt he had to take action:

> Periklēs son of Xanthippos, one of the *stratēgoi*, knowing that invasion was imminent, suspected that, because Arkhidāmos was a friend (*xenos*, 'guest-friend') of his, Arkhidāmos might spare his estate from the general devastation. This Arkhidāmos might do either as a personal favour or on the instructions of the Spartans who wished to stir up prejudice against him . . . Periklēs therefore gave it out in the *ekklēsiā* that Arkhidāmos was indeed a *xenos* of his, but this friendship would certainly not be detrimental to the city. So, in case the enemy refrained from devastating his land and property like those of other people, he gave them up to be public property, so that no

suspicion should fall on him on their account. (Thucydides, *Peloponnesian War* 2.13)

4.16 But it was when civil conflict occurred in the course of a war that the question of who was a friend and who was an enemy became most confused. Thucydides (*Peloponnesian War* 8.66) attributes the (brief) success of the oligarchic coup in Athens in 411 not least to the inability of people to tell who was and who was not on their side. Earlier, in the discussion of civil war at Kerkȳra, he emphasises how political differences came to divide those who ought to have been *philoi*:

> So savage was the course of the party conflict at Kerkȳra, and it seemed even more savage than it was, because it was one of the first to occur. Later on, one may say, the whole Greek world was torn by domestic conflict in which the democratic leaders tried to bring in the Athenians, the oligarchs the Spartans. In peacetime, there would have been neither justification nor desire for foreign intervention; but in war, a revolutionary faction always had excuses to hand for bringing in the foreigner, assistance from whom would bring advantage to the one faction and destruction to its opponents . . . Further, the ties of blood became less binding than those of faction, because the partisan was less scrupulous: for factions were formed not to work within the existing system, but to overthrow it, and derived their strength not from any religious sanction but from complicity in crime. Reasonable proposals from an adversary were met by the stronger faction with increased precautions and not with generosity. (Thucydides, *Peloponnesian* War 3.82.1–7)

Humiliation

4.17 One experience which Athenians were particularly unlikely to ignore was being humiliated physically in public, i.e. suffering *hubris*. Often translated 'pride', its basic meaning for a Greek was 'aggression', 'violence'; and it came to mean an *unprovoked* assault on someone's person or status, with the express intention of *public humiliation*. Dēmosthenēs (*Against Meidiās* 21.180) claims that the essence of *hubris* was 'treating free men as slaves', and one of the most important distinctions Athenians drew between themselves and slaves was that slaves could be physically punished. Here the prosecutor in a court case, having outlined his previous meetings with a gang of hooligans (whose leader was Konōn), relates the incident which led to the trial:

> As we got to close quarters one of them, I don't know which, fell on my friend Phanostratos and pinioned him, while the defendant Konōn and his son fell on me, stripped me, tripped me up, pushed me into the mud and finally jumped on me and beat me so severely that my lip was split and my eyes closed, and when they left me I could neither stand nor speak. As I lay there I heard a lot of bad language from them, a great deal of it being foul abuse of the kind I should hesitate to repeat to you. But there is one thing I must tell you to show that this was assault (*hubris*) and prove the whole thing was his doing. He began to crow

4.9 The violence which might follow drunkenness is illustrated here on an early fifth-century Athenian red-figure cup.

like a victorious cock, and the rest of the gang told him to flap his arms against his sides like wings. (Dēmosthenēs, *Against Konōn* 54.7ff.)

Being beaten up was bad enough, but what clearly tipped the balance was Konōn's imitation of a triumphant cock over a fallen enemy. Here was an unprovoked assault, accompanied by intentional public degradation, for all to see. The victim had brought a case for assault and battery (*aikeia*), but one of the ways in which he tries to get the court to sympathise and find in his favour is by making it clear that he could have brought a case for *hubris*, which carried a far stiffer penalty.

Moderation

4.18 Athenians could sometimes write as if the only virtues worth displaying were competitive ones. Here Dēmosthenēs gives advice to a young boy:

Even if you are superior to the ordinary run of men, do not give up the effort to excel everyone else; let it be your ambition to be first in everything. To aim at this target brings more credit than respectable mediocrity. (Dēmosthenēs, *On Love* 61.52)

If everyone had followed this advice, then the contest system we have described would clearly offer disastrously self-destructive capacities – of the sort that both Homeric epic and tragedy (8.54) explored. In fact, this competitive capacity was channelled, as we have already seen, into less harmful outlets, such as competitive events at festivals, or the contest of the law-courts. The institution of democracy could itself be effective in diminishing and deflating one man's ambitions where they were perceived to run contrary to people's interests, both by institutional means such as ostracism and the choice of officials by lot, and more informally by people refusing to follow that man's lead. Certainly the various institutions of democracy enabled the envious to take adequate revenge on the envied without (necessarily) violent consequences.

4.19   The destructive side of competitiveness was also kept in check by a range of non-competitive values which could be, and were, urged as virtues. These were used to encourage people to make decisions on grounds other than pure self-interest or blind defence of past practices. The most important of these was the call to be *sōphrōn* (the noun form is *sōphrosunē*). It carried a wide range of meanings – 'prudent', 'discreet', 'sensible', 'chaste', 'law-abiding', 'modest', 'moderate', and 'disciplined'. At heart it implied restraint and acknowledgement of one's own limitations. Its force was perfectly captured by the two famous mottoes inscribed over the entrance to the temple of Apollo at Delphi: *mēden agān* 'nothing in excess' and *gnōthi seauton* 'know yourself'. To know oneself was to know what one could and *could not* do; it was to be constrained by the fact that one was human and not divine (and should not therefore attempt to challenge the gods, cf. 3.23); it was to realise that as a human being one had certain capacities, but *not* others. To do nothing in excess was part of the same picture.

4.20   Such styles of behaviour were as much accepted and praised as that of fierce competitiveness, and acted as a moderating influence upon latent aggression. The choruses of Greek tragedy, usually people of considerably lower status than those whom they advised (and so possibly a body of people with whom the general populace who watched the play could immediately identify) permanently urged this 'sensible' way upon kings and princes tempted, by their status, to push themselves to the limit. The tension between the two patterns of behaviour was a constantly recurring theme of Greek literature.

Whose values?

4.21   We have talked so far in this chapter as if all Athenians – indeed all Greeks – shared the same values. In broad terms, they probably did. But that is not to deny that the values and obligations we have discussed were felt to different degrees by different people. Those we know most about were the wealthy men who had the leisure to participate in all the activities of the city and who had the resources to pursue their disputes in the courts. They could hope to live lives in which they came out on top in contests, and in which they were dishonoured rarely and humiliated never. This was simply not a possibility for the poor. A Greek defined 'wealth' as the condition in which he could live without working, 'poverty' as the condition in which he could live *only* by working. The latter condition removed his independence of action, especially if he was forced into the lowest category of work – working for *someone else*. The rich regularly speak, whether in the *ekklēsiā* or in the courts, as if everyone who listened to them shared their values. We may wonder whether on occasions the poor may not have felt that it did the wealthy good, once in a while, to experience being dishonoured.

4.22   If the poor were less independent than the rich, women and slaves were less independent again. In general, women were seen by the men who wrote about them not only as physically but also as morally, socially (cf. 5.19–20) and intellectually weaker. But there was an inconsistency about men's depiction of women. On the one hand, they were seen as the all-embracing, archetypal source and providers of life; on the other, as she-monsters of outrageous and devilish cunning (cf. the myth of Pandōra at 3.11). When Klytaimēstrā faced her son, the returning Orestēs, knowing full well that he planned to kill her, her first reaction was to call for an axe with which to slaughter him. But a few seconds later, she was appealing to him as his mother:

> *Klytaimēstrā:* What is the matter? What's this shouting in the palace?
> *Servant:* I tell you the dead [i.e. Agamemnōn's spirit] are slaughtering the living.
> *K:* Alas. You speak in riddles, but I understand. We killed him [i.e. Agamemnōn] treacherously, and by treachery shall we die. Quickly, get me an axe. It is the crisis now; will it be death or victory?
> (*Enter Orestēs*)
> *Orestēs:* It is for you I am looking. I have dealt with him. [K.'s lover Aigisthos].
> *K:* Alas. My dearest, strong Aigisthos, dead.
> *O:* You love your man? You shall lie in the same tomb; no chance for you to desert the dead there.
> *K:* Hold your hand, son; see this breast, child, at which you slept and drew the milk that made you grow.
> (Aiskhylos, *Libation Bearers* 885ff.)

4.23   This ambivalent attitude to women perhaps has something to do with men's reaction to female sexuality. Women kept the family line going, and families were of the very highest importance to Greeks. But while women were sexually attractive, they were also felt to be weak-minded, and therefore easily seducible. This threatened the husband's position and the integrity of the household (was this child really *his*?). A wife was also a family outsider, who left one family to be absorbed into another. While her reproductive capacity was vital for the continuation of the family, outsiders could be seen as a dangerous threat to such a tightly knit institution, where the rules were made by men, and the descent of property was through the male line (cf. 5.16).

4.24 One reflection of the fascination which men felt for women's sexuality comes in the story told about the mythical prophet Teiresiās. He had enjoyed the pleasure of being successively both man and woman, and when asked whether men or women found more pleasure in making love, he replied that of the ten units of pleasure involved, the man got one and the woman nine. He was blinded for his pains by the goddess Hērā, on the ground that he had given away woman's great secret. It is not surprising, therefore, that an Athenian felt threatened by male outsiders in his home and would be commended for keeping a close watch on his wife (cf. 5.23). Xenophōn remarked (*Oikonomikos* 3.11) that if one detected a fault in a herd of cattle, one would probably blame the herdsman; but if one detected a fault in a woman, there could be no possible doubt that the husband was to blame (cf. 5.17–24).

Conclusion

4.25 Greeks did not consider that the gods placed an absolute value upon every individual (cf. 5.61). They did not consider that anyone had an inalienable right to life, liberty, happiness or property, simply on the basis of being human. 'Rights' were acquired by virtue of being part of a political community, and were conferred by the laws of that community. So the law of theft established the right to property, and the law about justifiable homicide conferred the right to take another's life in particular circumstances (e.g. if the head of a household caught a man committing adultery with a free woman of his household). In return for such protection, the individual acquired obligations to the state, and the interests of the state took precedence over the interests of the individual. But in a radical democracy the people *were*, in important ways, the state: in the absence of a gigantic governmental apparatus of the sort with which we are acquainted, it was not as if individuals could claim they were being tyrannised by some outside force (cf. 5.1ff.).

4.26 Greeks, then, took the view that rights were not innate and natural, but contextual and the product of one's activity as a citizen. It was what you *achieved* that counted – a view that chimes with the Greek stress on the importance of competitive success, where winning was the only thing that mattered. One of the consequences of this was that Greeks tended to take an uncomplicated view of human responsibility. Results counted rather than intentions, and they were not always willing to consider a man's circumstances to be an extenuating factor. If one had argued in a Greek court, for example, that an individual should be excused for killing his parents on the ground that he had had a disturbed upbringing, a Greek might well have seen that not as an excuse for acquitting him, but as an added *reason* for condemning him. Greeks tended not to confuse reasons with excuses.

4.27 This seems a harsh morality. But in a civilisation in which the opposite of freedom was not imprisonment but slavery, and in which existence was at best precarious, it is understandable. Modern states at war become more totalitarian than in peace. For all that, the most cursory reading of Homer or tragedy makes it clear that Greeks also placed a high value on mercy and pity. If we stress the harsher side of Greek values here, it is to draw attention to them. Christian values were six hundred years away, and Freudian understanding of human motivation some two thousand four hundred.

5 Athenian society

Athens' population

5.1 Athens' population can be analysed in a number of different ways – men and women, adults and children, free and slave, native and immigrant. In this chapter we will explore all these different groupings. But political rights in classical Athens were restricted to adult free native men, that is, males over the age of eighteen who had both an Athenian father and an Athenian mother. It was through these strict and, even by the standards of other Greek states, unusually exclusive laws of citizenship that the Athenians maintained their sense of political community.

5.2 In the United Kingdom today, 'citizenship' means little more than the right to vote in elections, and is automatically bestowed by blood-line or place of birth, and on almost anyone with a residence permit. In Athens, it was very different. Citizenship carried tangible, wide-ranging benefits and responsibilities, and no disgrace could be greater than being stripped of citizen rights (*atīmiā*, discussed at 4.12; 6.56). But first, some facts and figures. The Athenians lived in a state whose citizen body (as opposed to the total population of the state) probably never exceeded 60,000. Athenian citizens aged 18 to 39 could expect to serve in the army or fleet almost every year, at least during parts of the fifth century. Once every 10 days a significant proportion of citizens (always at least 10% and at most periods around 20%) would congregate in the *ekklēsiā* to decide on public policy. A similar proportion were placed on the annual panel of 6,000 from which jurors for the popular courts were drawn at need. 60,000 is a tiny figure by our standards. But in the ancient Greek world, it meant that Athens had a far larger citizen population than any of the other c. 1,035 Greek states scattered from (in modern terms) Spain to South Russia.

5.3 Athens was not only exceptionally populous, it was also exceptionally cosmopolitan. An Athenian could observe thousands of temporary or permanent immigrants from other Greek cities or from non-Greek lands working around him, often doing exactly the same work as he and yet sharing none of his privileges of citizenship (cf. 5.67ff.). The strong sense of the distinctiveness of the Athenian citizen body was something that they reinforced rather than weakened during the classical period. If during the Persian Wars the Athenians stressed what they had in common with other Greeks (1.37), in the years after those wars they increasingly stressed their separateness. One way in which they did this was by their myth that they were 'autochthonous', i.e. originally sprung from the very soil of Attikē. They maintained that while other Greek cities were inhabited by the descendants of immigrants, all Athenians were descended from Iōn (cf. Ionians), son of Apollo and the Athenian queen Kreousa. But the Athenians also took practical steps to see that they remained a restricted descent group: that was seen to by a citizenship law introduced by Periklēs in 451, that insisted that only men who had an Athenian mother as well as an Athenian father should qualify as citizens. The thinking behind this new legal restriction, which was re-enacted in 403, is not entirely clear. But the law does neatly show how jealous Athenians had become of their extensive privileges as citizens of a democracy (cf. 4.2, 5.15).

5.4   Among the free population of Athens all women, whatever their status, and all males lacking the correct parentage, were by definition excluded from full citizenship (though a woman with an Athenian mother and father counted as a 'citizen' for the purpose of producing legitimate Athenian children). It was very exceptional indeed for a resident alien (*metoikos*, hence 'metic') or non-resident foreigner (*xenos*) (cf. 5.67) to be voted Athenian citizenship; it would be a reward for some extraordinary service to the democracy. As for slaves, who were numerous and mainly non-Greek, they were without legally enforceable rights of any kind, private or public (5.63; 4.21). They might be freed (in which case, if they stayed in Athens, they acquired the obligations and legal position of metics); but only in very exceptional cases were they subsequently ever given citizenship. In short, only a fraction of the total population of the Athenian state enjoyed political rights under the democracy.

5.5   What that proportion was depends on our view of the total population resident in the 2,500 sq. km of classical Attikē. It is unfortunately impossible to give precise figures for either the total population or its three main components, the citizens (including women and children), metics and slaves. The reason is that no ancient Greek state took regular overall population censuses. So with one exception, to be noted shortly, our limited sources merely provide figures either in military contexts for (male) land troops or in political contexts for adult male citizens (see the table that follows). As a result modern estimates based on these inadequate sources vary significantly.

5.6   The best evidence for the number of citizens in the fifth century comes from Thucydides. In *Peloponnesian War* 2.13 he made Periklēs tell the Athenians, as they enter the Peloponnesian War, that they had the manpower resources to survive Spartan attack. He numbered their land forces as 13,000 'front line' troops, 16,000 reserves (those citizens too young or too old for regular service, plus metics), and 1,000 cavalry. To convert these numbers into a total of Athenian citizens depends upon making a number of assumptions – about the probable age structure of the Athenian population, about the number of Athenians serving in the navy rather than as land forces, and about the number of metics. It has become regular to adopt a figure of around 50,000 for the total number of Athenian citizens in 431, but that almost certainly understates the number of Athenians in the navy. We should certainly think in terms of 60,000 and perhaps 80,000. This was, however, at the very start of the war. Not only did serious war casualties follow, but so did the plague. Thucydides' statement about the implications of the plague for the Athenian cavalry suggests that perhaps a third of the Athenian population died. We have no figures for the fourth century as good as the figures Thucydides gives for 431; the figures we do have suggest a citizen population of around 30,000, half or less than half of the fifth-century figure.

5.7   The evidence for the number of foreigners in Athens at any one time (temporary or permanent), and for the number of slaves, is very much worse. For metics we must work back from a census carried out (exceptionally) in 317. It is claimed that this counted 10,000 metics. That the number will have been higher in the fifth century there can be no doubt. We should certainly double this figure, but 20,000 may still understate the real number. In the case of slaves the census figure preserved from 317 is corrupt, and the best evidence we have is Thucydides' guess (*Peloponnesian War* 7.27.5) that 'more than two myriads' (i.e. 20,000) of slaves, 'most of them skilled craftsmen', fled during the Dekeleian War (413–404, above 1.75). This guess does not take us very far! All we can do to work out the number of slaves is to guess at (i) the proportion of Athenians who owned slaves; (ii) the average number of slaves owned by a household; and (iii) the number of slaves employed outside the household (e.g. in the mines). The problem is that we end up making far too many assumptions to defend in detail.

5.8   With great caution, therefore, the totals given in the table below may be suggested for the three main groups of population in Attikē in 431 and in the middle of the fourth century:

	431	*c. 350*
Athenian citizens	60,000	30,000
Total number of Athenians, men, women and children	240,000	120,000
Metics (including women and children)	30,000	15,000
Slaves	100,000	50,000
Total	430,000	215,000

The Athenian household

5.9   The typical family unit of the modern Western world is the nuclear family consisting of the parents and a relatively small number of children. The ancient Athenians knew no such thing. In fact the Greeks did not even have a word for 'family' in the sense in which we use it most regularly. Their nearest equivalent, *oikos*, means something more like our 'household' and has a far wider range of reference than our 'family'. It is vital to bear this crucial

5.1 This *ostrakon*, inscribed in the late fifth century in an attempt to remove Kleophōn from the city for a decade, shows the full official nomenclature of an Athenian citizen, personal name, father's name (Kleippidēs), and name of ancestral deme (here, Akharnai).

difference in mind throughout the following discussion, when it will sometimes be impossible to avoid using 'family' simply for convenience.

5.10 The Athenians, particularly when contrasted with the other great Greek power of our period, the Spartans, had a reputation for being compulsive innovators. Yet in their family and kinship organisation they were highly conservative. Except perhaps for the presence of non-Greek slaves, the Athenian *oikos* of the fifth and fourth centuries would have seemed perfectly familiar to the original audiences of Homer. We will understand the Athenian *oikos* best if we realise that it was an instrument to ensure that the property belonging to the kin group of the senior male in the household was passed down the blood-line. Qualified to be a citizen by his parentage, a man demonstrated his suitability for citizenship by his loyalty to his own household and kin. This is nicely illustrated by the questions to which a man had to give satisfactory answers in order to hold office:

> When they are checking qualifications they ask first: 'Who is your father, and what is your *dēmos*? Who was your father's father, and who was your mother, and her father and his *dēmos*?' Then they ask whether the candidate is enrolled in a cult of Apollōn Patrōios ('of our ancestors') and Zeus Herkeios ('of the hearth'), and where the shrines are, then whether he has family tombs and where they are; whether he treats his parents well . . .' ([Aristotle], *Constitution of Athens* 55.3)

Family tombs, built on family land in the countryside, showed that the family had lived in the same place for many years, and implied that it would continue to do so. Preservation of property was as important here as filial piety. The first official act of the chief civil official, the 'eponymous' *arkhōn*, was to proclaim that every Athenian 'shall hold and control until the end of the year such property as he held before [the *arkhōn*] took up his appointment'.

5.11 The property of the family meant, in the first instance, land and the dwellings, storehouses and tombs built on it. But the *oikos* also embraced the instruments needed to work the land and service the property generally. Thus tools, animals and slaves ('animate tools' in Aristotle's unpleasantly accurate phrase) all fell within the definition of the *oikos*. At the head of this composite entity stood the *kūrios*, the male master of the household who had in theory sovereign power over all its constituent elements. Within the *kūrieia* ('protection, tutelage') of the *kūrios*, there fell any sons who had not yet attained the age of majority and all the women of the *oikos*. For women were treated in the eyes of the law as perpetual minors: for at first they were within the *kūrieia* of their father or guardian; then within that of their husband (reverting to their father's on divorce or widowhood); and finally their son's if, as sometimes happened, he should take over the *kūrieia* when he married and the father 'retired'. The *kūrios* therefore had a twofold function. He represented all the females and the male minors of the *oikos* in legal and civic matters, and he was the present holder of ancestral property and estates.

Property and legitimacy

5.12 Real property, that is land and everything built on it, was the basis of an Athenian's social status and political influence (cf. 2.13; 3.35). Land in Attikē, except in the case of a special state exemption, could be held legally only by an Athenian citizen. In almost all cases it passed by bequest from father to son, or by the nearest relationship in the male line through the family. An heir therefore had to be able to prove his legitimacy to secure title to landed property (cf. 3.39). In most cases, we must assume, succession to property passed off fairly smoothly, but several of the surviving fourth-century law-court speeches (especially those of Isaios, the leading probate lawyer of his time) concern disputed parentage and efforts by disgruntled relatives to discredit heirs. Since real property was the basic form of wealth, both sides had much to gain or lose, and it was worth paying for the best legal help. The problem for Athenians was that they had no birth certificates and no state registry of births. Nor were scientific methods of proof available to decide paternity. Instead, legitimacy and citizenship were most easily demonstrated to the satisfaction of a large citizen jury by producing witnesses who would testify to a child's introduction as an infant into a phratry at the *Apatouria* (3.53) and into the deme at the age of majority. It is worth adding here that, where we use first names and surnames, the Athenian citizen would be distinguished by his personal name, his father's name ('patronymic') and deme name, e.g. *Periklēs Xanthippou Kholargeus* ('Periklēs, son of Xanthippos, of the deme Kholargos').

5.13 One of the best examples of what could be involved is provided by a speech ([Dēmosthenēs], *Against Euboulidēs* 57) written for a man who had been voted off the register of his deme in 346/5. In that year, exceptionally, a general scrutiny of all deme registers had been ordered, presumably because there was reason to suspect that large numbers of men had somehow had themselves placed on the registers illegally. In order to prove his legitimacy and citizenship, the speaker has taken his case on appeal to a central Athenian court and seeks to show, first, that both his father and his mother were true Athenians; and, second, that his registration in his father's hereditary deme at the age of eighteen had been legitimate.

5.14 The speaker needed to show not that he had been registered in the deme, for that was not in question – he had even served as its chief official (*dēmarkhos*) – but that he had been *legitimately* so registered. To do so he first cites as witnesses of his father's legitimacy five of his father's male kinsmen by birth and several of his male kinsmen by marriage (his father's female cousins' husbands); then his father's *phrāteres* (fellow phratry members), those with whom he shares his Apollōn Patrōios and Zeus Herkeios and the same family tombs, and his father's fellow deme members. With women, on the other hand, it was much harder to establish legitimacy, since they were not registered in a deme. So to prove his mother's Athenian descent, the speaker cites, apart from a similar range of male kinsmen, only the *phrāteres* and fellow deme members of his mother's male kinsmen. As for his own life history, he first calls witnesses to his mother's (second) marriage and then presents evidence of his induction into phratry and, most important, deme. He stresses that he had later been chosen priest of Hēraklēs for the deme, as well as demarch, without his opponent's objecting to his legitimacy on either occasion. Finally, he sums up his claim to citizenship in terms of the answers required of candidates for public office at Athens (see 5.10). The stakes were appallingly high: if he lost, he would probably have been sold into slavery.

5.15 Except by express decision of the whole city, citizenship could be acquired only by birth. In ideal circumstances property too passed directly to sons, all of whom inherited equally. If any sons were orphaned before they reached the age of eighteen, a guardian would be appointed to protect their interests. Comparative evidence suggests that between 20 and 30 per cent of heads of household are likely to have died with no son over eighteen (or with daughter(s) only, who were under thirteen). The state, in the person of the 'eponymous' *arkhōn*, took the closest interest in the welfare of children in guardianship, but this did not prevent guardians from being or being alleged to be fraudulent. The most celebrated instance of alleged fraud by guardians concerns Dēmosthenēs, who made his debut in the courts to secure the large inheritance of which he claimed to have been unlawfully robbed. But provision had to be made for securing the survival of the household as a property unit, even where there were no surviving sons. Rules of inheritance dictated which other relatives had the first claim to a man's property, but the law also allowed property to be passed on by will. It was almost unheard of for a man to bequeath property when he had sons, but inheritance disputes arose readily between those bequeathed property by will and those other members of a man's kin who would have inherited had there been no will. Very often a man likely to die without a male heir would adopt a relative to whom he would bequeath his property by will. (Adoption in Athens was to prevent a house-hold being 'orphaned', not to prevent a child being orphaned.)

5.16   A daughter could not technically inherit property in her own right, because women could not own and control property under Athenian law. A daughter who had no surviving brothers of the same father did inherit after a fashion, but only as an *epiklēros*, so called because she went with the *klēros* or estate: that is, she acted as a passive instrument in the transfer of the estate to the nearest legitimate heir in the male line. In ideal circumstances this male heir would be her son, and so the law concerned itself with ensuring that she had such a son. The 'eponymous' *arkhōn* had responsibility for seeing to it that an *epiklēros* was properly married to her nearest relative (preferably a relative by birth rather than marriage) and that the property was duly passed on. If the *epiklēros* was already married, she might even be obliged to divorce her husband in order to marry the appropriate relative. This extraordinary inter-vention of law into family life – which seems to have preceded Athens' adop-tion of a democratic constitution – is the most striking illustration of the Athenians' fixed determination to keep property within the family and so pre-serve the number of functioning *oikoi*. There was an important consequence for democracy, when it was invented in 508: since every effort was made to ensure *oikoi* did not die out and their property be taken over by other fam-ilies, it discouraged concentrations of property into a few hands. In this way, the social basis of democracy was maintained and promoted (cf. 5.51, 8.80).

Marriage

5.17   The chief purpose of Athenian marriage, as acknowledged in the words of betrothal, was the procreation of legitimate children. Yet contradictory pres-sures operated on parents in a society without scientific birth control and where almost one child in two died before reaching adulthood. On the one hand, if parents produced too many children, the family property would be fragmented among the male heirs or depleted by the dowries given with daughters in place of landed property. On the other hand, if an Athenian father followed the advice of Hesiod to have only one son, that son might die prematurely and leave the estate without an heir. Infanticide was one response to the first problem, adoption of a son a response to the second problem, but we do not know the scale of either practice. However, there is evidence that some newborn infants were killed or left to die, and that girls were more vulnerable to this fate than boys.

5.18   Both the state and individual *kūrioi* saw betrothal and marriage primarily as matters to do with property and legitimacy. The word for betrothal, *egguē*, also means 'pledge' or 'security', emphasizing that the woman was seen as 'property' in a transaction that moved her from one house to another; and at the marriage ceremony the bride's *kūrios* betrothed the girl to her prospective

5.2–4 (and see over) The procession, here in donkey carts (compare fig. 2.6) formed the central event of the wedding ceremony. The figure holding the wreath on this mid-sixth-century oil flask from the hand of the Amasis Painter (compare figs. 3.4–6) should be identified as the bride.

husband with the formula 'I give you this woman for the ploughing of legitimate children' in the presence of as many witnesses as possible. It was important to have witnesses both to the 'property' transaction itself and legitimacy of subsequent children. Girls seem to have had no say in the matter of their marriage, which was essentially a contract between the *kūrioi* of two *oikoi*. Betrothal regularly occurred when the girl was at, or even before, the age of puberty, but because marriage and property transfer were closely linked it

5.3

was normal for men to marry later, when they came into their inheritance; some ancient sources put the ideal age of men's marriage at thirty.

5.19 Despite the state's interest in the offspring of a marriage, marriage was a private contract and not registered with the state authorities. Legal marriage was not constituted by a wedding ceremony and signing of the register. Instead it was a simple 'living together' (*sunoikein*), embarked upon as a private enterprise and considered valid from the moment the bride entered the house of her lord and master. The new wife brought with her a 'dowry', given her by her father, usually a sum of money. It was so important to provide a respectable dowry that a father might mortgage land to provide it. But, since a woman could not own property, the wife did not technically own her dowry.

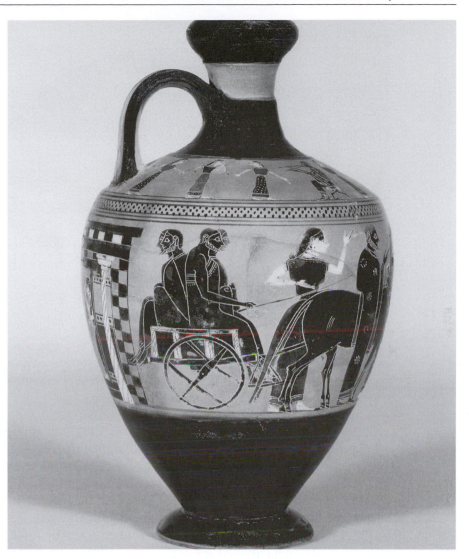

5.4

It was her husband who controlled how it was spent, under two constraints: first, he was (essentially) looking after it to hand it on to the male children of the marriage; second, in the event of divorce, the husband had to see that the dowry was repaid to the wife's father. Divorce proceedings could be initiated by either party, but it was easier for the husband to obtain a divorce, and he was obliged to do so were he to discover that his wife had been unfaithful.

5.20   Different standards of sexual morality were expected of men and of women. Husbands might, with legal impunity, take concubines and mistresses and consort with prostitutes. Any sexual relations between a wife and a man to whom she was not married automatically counted as adultery. A wife convicted of adultery was liable to cruel public humiliation, while an archaic

5.5 The money-bags in the hands of the garlanded men, and the elaborate dress of the women, suggests that we should interpret this scene on a red-figure Athenian cup as referring to the acquisition of sexual favours by men who have been lubricated at the symposium.

law allowed the husband to kill a man whom he caught in adultery with his wife (in a case c. 400, the offended husband argued that the seduction of a woman was a more heinous crime than rape, since seduction implied that the wife's affections had been turned away from her husband, cf. 4.23). The practical reason for all this was that adultery rendered the parentage of children unclear, meaning that inheritance rights could be challenged.

5.21   In the course of relating how his wife's adulterous affair came about, the offended husband mentioned above gives us one of our few descriptions of marital relations and a husband's attitude to his wife:

> When I decided to marry, Athenians, and brought a wife into my house, I was for some time disposed not to harass her, but not to leave her too free to do just as she pleased. So I watched her as far as I could and paid attention to her as far as was reasonable. But when my child was born, thinking this the truest expression of the close tie between us, I began to trust her and I put all my resources at her disposal. At first, gentlemen, she was the best of wives – a clever housekeeper, thrifty and exact in her stewardship. It was my mother's death that was the origin of all my troubles. When she was carried out to burial, my wife went with the cortège, was seen by that man and eventually seduced. He used to wait for the slave-girl who went to market and, making propositions through her, brought about my wife's downfall. (Lysiās, *Against Eratosthenēs* 1.6ff.)

5.22 This passage has another point of interest. It was when she was attending her mother-in-law's funeral, outside the marital home, that the speaker's wife was seen by the alleged adulterer. Thereafter relations between the guilty pair had at first been carried on through an intermediary, the wife's servant-girl. Respectable wives, in other words, or at least the wives of wealthier men, should not, according to the Athenian social code, be as a rule seen in public. Their place was in the home, where we shall meet them again shortly. Only for funerals and festivals might they legitimately and without shame leave the house and play a social role in public (cf. 4.22). The speaker in the disputed citizenship case discussed earlier (5.13) was embarrassed at having to admit in court that his family was so poor his mother had to go to the market to sell ribbons. The respectable woman's contact with the outside world was generally mediated through slaves. The secrets which slaves conveyed are thus indicative both of the close personal relations that could develop between slave and free, and of the degree to which a citizens' behaviour might be constrained by consciousness of their slaves' knowledge of what they were doing.

5.23 As these passages from law-court speeches indicate, the conditions which a woman enjoyed depended on her social status and her position within the household, whether as daughter, sister, wife, or mother, whether rich or poor, free or unfree. So it is difficult anyway to generalise about 'the position of women' in classical Athens – it all depends on which women you are talking about – and on top of that, the evidence available to us is almost entirely produced by and for men. Even this evidence, however, reveals an apparent paradox. In the private, enclosed and often secret world of the Athenian home, relations between men and women who were kindred could be warm, intimate and familiar. It is true that men and women often lived physically separate lives, moving predominantly in different spaces, even during that part of their lives when the men were in the house. But separateness did not necessarily imply inequality, and was a reflection of a desire to protect women from contact with unrelated males. In the world outside the home, however, there was no space for women at all – men alone had the opportunity to shine – except, as we have already seen, when it came to public worship of the gods.

5.24 Women, then, were separate to some extent because of their different functions, not their inferiority. Myths, and particularly the myths that Athenian tragedians chose to stage, backed up this notion. In tragedy, women were strikingly prominent, mainly because tragedians explored myths relating to the family, in which the wife obviously played a major part. But there was no consistency about their functions and roles (cf. 4.22) – at times men feared and even felt revulsion at them, at other times they were total dependent on them (cf. 3.11–12). The reasons for this have already been discussed (4.23): as myth too suggests, women (and women's sexuality) were essential to the functioning and continuity of society, and yet by their sexuality and crossing of

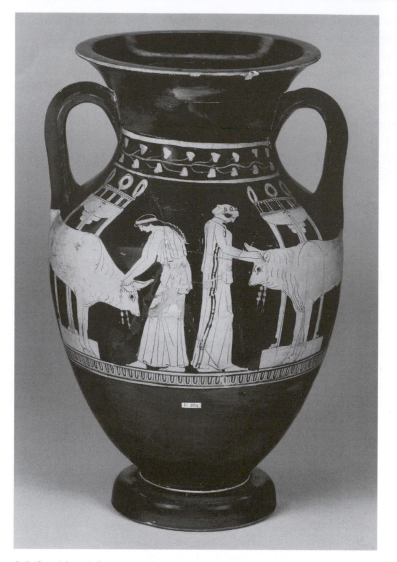

5.6 On this red-figure *amphorā* from the middle of the fifth century women prepare sacrificial animals in a sanctuary.

kinship lines they also constantly threatened the order men would like to impose. In the strictly political arenas of the democracy, however, women were allotted no role whatsoever. They had no political rights and had to be represented at law by their male guardians. But where the public and private spheres overlapped, especially in rituals performed outside the home (like burial, 5.81), women were allowed a role, often indeed an important one. For example, when the chorus in Aristophanēs' *Lȳsistratē* wishes to stress their credentials, the chorus leader goes through a list of the religious roles they have performed:

5.7 This early fifth-century red-figure cup interior shows two well-dressed women working wool.

> When I was seven, I carried the sacred symbols; then at ten I was grinder of Athēnē's barley; then at the Brauronian festival of Artemis I played the bear and shed the saffron robe; and when I was grown up handsome, I carried the sacred basket, wearing a necklace of dried figs. (Aristophanēs, *Lȳsistratē* 641ff.)

That said, the sphere where women depended most, and least, on men was the home. The dysfunctional households that dominate tragedy (e.g. of Oidipous, Agamemnōn, Jasōn) often explore that uncomfortable play between male and female power and dependence.

Home life

5.25 Women and men of wealthy families lived very different lives. The men met together in *ekklēsiā*, law-courts or *agorā* to conduct the business of state, and spent much of their leisure with other men and boys in the wrestling-grounds, *stoai* (s. *stoā*) or cool groves of the Academy or the Lykeion; but their wives

5.8 On this cup interior, painted in the second half of the fifth century, a young mother is shown encouraging an infant sitting in a ceramic high chair.

spent the largest part of their lives inside their homes. From their earliest years, wealthy women were brought up to perform or supervise exclusively domestic tasks (but see 5.38). A passage in Xenophōn's dialogue on household management illustrates the range of a woman's supervisory duties in a well-off household; Iskhomakhos is here addressing the wife whom he married when she was not yet fifteen:

> Your business will be to stay indoors and help to dispatch the servants who work outside, while supervising those who work indoors. You will receive incoming revenue and allocate it to any necessary expenditure, you will be responsible for any surplus and see that the allocation for the year's expenses is not spent in a month. When wool is delivered to you, you will see that garments are made for those that need them, and take care that the dried grain is kept fit for consumption. And there is another of your duties which I'm afraid may seem to you rather thankless – you will have to see that any of the servants who is ill gets proper treatment. (Xenophōn, *Oikonomikos* 7.35ff.)

If a man brought friends home to dine, wives and daughters were not expected to join them. For a woman to dine with an unrelated man could be used in court as evidence that she was not a legitimate Athenian wife. The men's dining-room (*andrōn*) was a world apart, and often accessible without going into the rest of the house; and it was non-Athenian women or slaves, brought in specially from outside the household for sexual or performance purposes, who graced the ritualised male drinking-parties (*sumposia*) held in this room.

5.26 In the case of poorer families, the lives of men and women were less strongly contrasted. Of course, the men could attend political meetings, whether in their deme or in Athens, from which women were excluded. Of course, men would be called upon to fight, whether as lightly armed troops or as rowers (7.18), and women would not. But in both town and country, poor wives must have worked alongside their husbands if they could not afford slaves. A poor wife had to do all the household work herself: the bringing up of children, the provision of food, the combing and spinning of wool, the weaving, and so on. Since all these were time-consuming, she will have enjoyed little or no leisure. Indeed, it was of the essence of women's tasks that they be time-consuming, for to a suspicious male eye they could be seen as ways of keeping the women out of mischief. But poor citizen women also had more of a life outside the household: they went shopping and fetched water from the public fountains – tasks otherwise performed by slaves. Poverty drove some women to act as wet-nurses, midwives or small-time market traders. There is some reason for thinking that the women of rich men were more rigidly secluded than their poor sisters, partly for snobbish reasons. Once more, it was at religious festivals that the distinctions caused by wealth, like the distinctions caused by gender itself, were at least partly eroded. Aristophanēs' *Women at the Thesmophoria* and *Lȳsistratē* (set on the Akropolis) indicated (a man's view, it is true) that women at the public festivals were able to exchange gossip with neighbours and rub shoulders with other women.

5.27 Litigants in the Athenian law-courts took advantage of the convention that respectable men and women kept separate. In [Dēmosthenēs] *Against Euergos* 47.34ff., the speaker, who was a trierarch, had not received the ship's gear from his predecessor (on trierarchy, see 7.43–7). He went round to the house of the previous trierarch, Theophēmos, to demand the gear or its equivalent value. When refused, the speaker prepared to enter the house by force: but, as he was careful to point out to the courts, 'I had already ascertained that Theophēmos was not married.' It was simply not done for a complete stranger to enter a house where a married woman was present. Later on, the speaker contrasts his behaviour with Theophēmos', when Theophēmos and his cronies swooped on the speaker's farm, in the presence of his wife and children and servants, and carried off everything he had. The speaker points out that even a neighbour, on seeing the attack, refused to enter the farm because the *kūrios* was not there.

5.9–10 The scenes on the two sides of this Athenian red-figure *pelikē* (small *amphorā*) seem to show exchange of oil between women in a commercial context on one side, and between young men in a private context (note the mirror on the wall and the wool basket) on the other.

5.28 Both the truth and the fiction of the separation of men and women are revealed by the design of the Athenian house. Athenian houses seem normally to have had just the one entrance, and this gave immediate access to the men's room from which the women were sometimes literally barred. But all the rest of the house was accessed from the central courtyard to which the entrance also led. Greek houses, even those of the very rich, were not elaborate; the rooms had few permanent fixtures, and there was little in the way of furniture or non-essential ornaments. Even the hearth seems to have been moveable. The few rooms had undecorated walls. Much of a woman's life was lived in the courtyard, which was the venue for most domestic tasks and where the women of the household were when Theophēmos made his raid.

5.10

5.29 The activities of the courtyard served subsistence needs. This was the place where food was prepared and wool cleaned and spun, for weaving on a loom which might be set up in one of the rooms off the courtyard. Such activities might make the courtyard a smelly and often unhygienic place. But the activities of the courtyard did not serve merely subsistence needs. Although Greek everyday diet seems to have been remarkably spare, and was mainly vegetarian, with meat-eating confined to occasions when there had been a sacrifice (3.28–32), there were also moments of feasting (for instance at the naming of a child) when more elaborate food was prepared. Among the rich, at least, choice of food, and particularly the expenditure of money on (expensive) fresh, rather than dried, fish, might even be held to indicate political sympathies. Much the same was true of the clothes also prepared in the courtyard. These carried many implications beyond the wealth suggested by the material, and might be elaborate. Vase paintings and the plays of Aristophanēs attest many variations in pattern, colour and design. Religious festivals gave women a chance to show off such finery.

5.11 This late sixth-century terracotta group shows a mother teaching her daughter how to cook.

Prostitution

5.30 So far only citizen women, especially wives, have been under direct consideration. But, as remarked earlier, Athenian custom tolerated temporary or permanent liaisons with other women. These concubines (*pallakai*), courtesans (*hetairai*, literally 'companions') and prostitutes (*pornai*) would normally not be of Athenian birth. Alkibiadēs was notorious for not merely having numerous mistresses but also keeping concubines, slave and free, in addition to his aristocratic wife. Periklēs, who was for a time Alkibiadēs' guardian, divorced his wife and formed a lasting union with Aspasiā. But since she was a native of Mīlētos, it was only as a special mark of respect to Periklēs that the Athenians granted citizenship to their son. (He was one of the generals executed after Arginoussai: see 1.80 and 6.7.)

5.12 On this early fifth-century cup the artist imagines the various delights – music, sexually available women, and wine – which were part of the *sumposion*.

5.31   Concubines had some legal status and offering one's services as a prostitute was legal, and indeed taxed (the *pornikon telos*). Prostitutes seem to have been readily available, although in *Lȳsistratē*, where the plot turns on a sex strike by Athenian wives, Aristophanēs has to suppress that fact. Prostitutes ranged in class and expensiveness from the brothel-girls of the Peiraieus; through the rather more sophisticated *aulos*-girls an Athenian might hire to enliven a male drinking-party (*sumposion*) in the *andrōn* (5.25); to the educated courtesans euphemistically known as *hetairai*. The ways in which some prostitutes verged on respectability is well brought out in Xenophōn's *Memoirs of Sōkratēs*, in the story of Sōkratēs' conversation with a woman named Theodotē. In an artful display of studied innocence Sōkratēs, noting Theodotē's wealth, gradually teases out of her its true source – her rich lovers. The passage incidentally lists the chief sources of wealth in Athens, in order of their importance:

> Sōkratēs asked 'Have you an estate, Theodotē?' 'No.' 'Then perhaps you get your income from house-property.' 'No.' 'Well, does it come from some

5.13 The money-bags and the expressive hand gestures suggest that this scene from an early fifth-century cup shows men negotiating with prostitutes.

manufacturing business?' 'No.' 'Then what *do* you live on?' 'The contributions of kind friends . . .' (Xenophōn, *Memorābilia* 3.11.4)

Homosexual relations

5.32 There was no expectation at Athens that a man's sexual attentions would be exclusively directed at women. Not only did classical authors assume that older men (but not usually beyond the age of 40) would find younger men sexually attractive; but given the separateness of Athenian women's lives, the early age of marriage for girls, and the late age of marriage for men, it tended to be sexual relations with older men that dominated the early years of a young man's life, i.e. while he had (as ancient writers describe it) pubic hair like peach-down and no proper beard. Since puberty was about four years later than today (because of the low-protein diet), such boys (*paides*) would be under 20. In a scene described at the beginning of Plato's *Kharmidēs*, in terms that are clearly meant to be found amusing but not shocking, Sōkratēs describes how, on returning from military service at Poteidaia, he went along to the *palaistrā* and enquired about who was beautiful and who was intelligent among the young men. His question was answered at once by the entry of Kharmidēs, who attracted the attention not only of older men but also of his

5.14–15 The combination of exterior and interior scenes on this late sixth-century red-figure cup suggests that the artist is exploring how athletic success in the gymnasium might attract the sexual attentions of lovers. See also fig. 5.19

5.16 Sixth-century scenes of men courting boys often stress, as here on an Athenian black-figure *amphorā*, the physical contact involved.

contemporaries. Kharmidēs, apparently, had been complaining of morning headaches:

> . . . he entered, and caused much laughter, because each of us who were seated made room for him by pushing hard at his neighbour, in a frantic attempt to have the boy sit next to him, until the man at one end of the bench had to stand up, and we pushed the man at the other end right off it. In the event Kharmidēs came and sat down between me and Kritiās. Well, by then, my friend, I began to feel perplexed, and my former confidence in looking forward to a quite easy time in talking with him had been knocked out of me.

And when Kritiās told him I was the one who knew the cure [for headache],
Kharmidēs gave me such a look with his eyes as passes description, and made
ready to ask me a question. When all the people in the wrestling-school
surged round about us on every side, then, ah then, my noble friend, I saw
inside his cloak (*himation*) and caught fire, and could possess myself no
longer; and I thought none was so wise in love-matters as Kȳdiās, who in
speaking of a beautiful boy recommends someone to 'beware of coming as a
fawn before the lion, and being seized as his portion of flesh'; for I too felt I
had fallen a prey to some such creature. (Plato, *Kharmidēs* 155b–d)

5.33   The nature of the relationship between the older admirer (*erastēs*) and the
younger 'beloved, boy-friend' (*erōmenos* or *paidika*) attracted a good deal of
discussion among Athenian authors. Xenophōn in his *Sumposion* (16–23)
distinguished between men who admired boys for the sake of the boy's character, and those whose attachment was physical, and maintained that boys
did not share a man's enjoyment of sexual intercourse as a woman did.
Elsewhere, in the *Memoirs of Sōkratēs* (1.2.29–30), Xenophōn had Sōkratēs
try to dissuade Kritiās from having sexual intercourse with the young
Euthydēmos by comparing his importuning of Euthydēmos to a beggar
asking for charity. This is consistent with the picture of Sōkratēs painted by
Plato in *Sumposion*, where Alkibiadēs tells how, in a reversal of the conventional roles, he as a young man tried to seduce Sōkratēs, but failed:

As I was saying, Sōkratēs and I were alone together, and I was enjoying the
thought that we should soon plunge into the kind of talk a lover has when he
is alone with his beloved. Not a bit of it; Sōkratēs spent the day with me in
his usual kind of talk, and finally went off and left me. After that I asked him
to come with me and exercise in the gymnasium, which he did, and I hoped
to get somewhere with him then. But though we exercised and wrestled
together, often with no one else present, I need hardly tell you that I got no
further. Finding I made no progress in this way, I decided to make a direct
assault on the man and not give up my efforts, but find out where I stood. So
I invited him to dinner with me, for all the world as if I was the lover and he
the beloved. He did not accept in a hurry, but in the end I persuaded him.
The first time he came, he wanted to leave immediately after the meal, and I
was ashamed and let him go. But I tried again and prolonged the
conversation far into the night, and when he wanted to go I pretended it was
too late and managed to force him to stay. So he lay down on the couch next
to mine, on which he had dined. There was no one else sleeping in the room
except the two of us, and so far the story could be told without impropriety
to anyone . . .

(*Alkibiadēs now offers himself to Sōkratēs, but Sōkratēs points out that
physical beauty and internal goodness are different. Still . . .*)

After this exchange I reckoned that some of my shots had gone home, and
I got up and without allowing him to say another word I wrapped my own
cloak round him (it was winter) and lay down under his shabby garment,
throwing my arms round his extraordinary and wonderful person. I lay there

all night, and you cannot deny it, Sōkratēs. But in spite of my doing so, he defeated me, and despised and scorned and rejected all my youthful charm. And it was just in that charm that I thought I had something, gentlemen of the jury – for you are sitting in judgement on Sōkratēs' disdain for me. For I swear, by all the gods and goddesses, that I got up next day without anything more happening than if I had been sleeping with my father or elder brother. (Plato, *Sumposion* 217a ff.)

In Aristophanēs, too, enjoyment of the sight of naked boys was treated as traditional, and as a feature of the older generation, but Aristophanēs also expected to cause amusement by abuse of those who were the passive sexual partners of other men.

5.34   Sexual relations between men and boys seem primarily to have been judged in terms of honour and shame. Forcible sexual relations with a boy, like forcible sexual relations with a woman, might be treated as *hubris* (4.17), and therefore be dishonourable, but consenting sexual relations between males when an exchange of money was involved were also seen in the same light. The prosecution of Tīmarkhos by Aiskhinēs (fig. 1.17) in the middle of the fourth century was brought under the law banning citizens who had prostituted themselves from speaking in the *ekklēsiā* as active politicians. The assumption behind this law seems to be that a man who was prepared to sell his own body to someone else might also sell his rhetorical skill to someone else, acting in the interests of a third party (who might not be Athenian) rather than offering to the Athenian people his own views. In the course of the speech, Aiskhinēs also mentioned other laws prescribing penalties for a father or other *kūrios* of a boy for hiring him out as a prostitute and for a slave who courted or became the lover of a free boy. This latter law emphasised the way in which sexual relations were linked to social status, precisely because they were a matter of honour and shame.

5.35   Ideals, norms and realities are as difficult to disentangle in the case of homosexual relationships as they are in the case of sexual relationships between men and women. Despite laws against sexual activity with boys under eighteen, it seems likely that older and younger men enjoyed a wide range of relationships from chaste admiration to earthy physicality. The nature of relationships was no doubt affected by wealth and class: only some young men will have had the leisure to spend time in the gymnasium. Nevertheless, speeches in the courts, where the jury may have been largely of older men but cannot have consisted only of the wealthy, suggest that homoerotic relationships were not seen as peculiar to the wealthy élite. Courts seem to have been expected to regard a married man having, or even quarrelling over, a young male lover as no more a source of shame in itself than consorting with or quarrelling over female prostitutes. In his own prosecution of Tīmarkhos, Aiskhinēs had to distinguish his own erotic interest in young men, his reputation for making a nuisance of himself in the gymnasium, and his involvement in brawls over lovers, from the activities for which he criticised Tīmarkhos. One case known from a speech of Lysiās (*Against Simōn*, 3) turned precisely on street fights resulting from a quarrel between two men over a young man named Theodotos, with whom one of them claimed to have made a contract for 300 *drakhmai*. Once more the speaker presented himself as deciding to make Theodotos his 'lover' (*philos*) by doing him good turns, whereas he presented his opponent as compelling Theodotos to do what he wanted by violence and illegality.

5.36 According to Xenophōn in his *Constitution of the Spartans* (2.12–13), the legendary Spartan lawgiver Lykourgos considered it to be the most noble education (*paideia*) if a man, smitten by the charms of a boy, tried to perfect the boy's soul as a blameless 'friend'. Athenian law also seems to have recognised that the relationship formed in the course of education may be sexual. That is probably one of the reasons why the law imposed the minimum, very advanced age, of 40 on those who had charge of young men training for dramatic choruses (5.40) or military service (7.31) – the only areas of education for which provision was made by the state (see 5.32 for the assumption that men over 40 ceased to feel desire for boys).

Education

5.37 In Athens, as in almost all other Greek states with the notable exception of Spartē, education was a private affair, arranged and paid for by parents who were not legally compelled to have their children formally educated. Teachers were often of low status and badly paid: a characteristic of Theophrastos' 'Mean Man' is to make deductions from the teacher's pay if the child is absent through illness. Schools were run from private houses or rooms attached to a public or private training-ground (*palaistrā*) which could be used for physical education.

5.38 Boys began to attend school from about the age of seven, or earlier if the family was rich. Girls' education seems to have been much more informal. They were typically portrayed by our sources as having been educated chiefly for manual and domestic tasks. But this picture was partly ideological, designed to send out a message about the 'proper' upbringing for a girl. It is notable that there were vase paintings showing scenes of girls reading, and references in the orators suggested that women might know a great deal about financial matters and, despite their legal disability, be involved themselves in small-scale financial transactions. Non-Athenian *hetairai* in Athens might be cultivated women, possessing considerable literary or musical skills in addition to their physical charms (Periklēs' mistress Aspasiā from Mīlētos had serious intellectual interests). But the account of Athenian education which follows necessarily concerns only boys and young men (cf. 8.16–17; 8.22ff.).

5.39 There were three main areas of education: basic literacy (and perhaps arithmetic), music, and physical education. Some schools offered training in all three, but parents might choose different teachers for the individual subjects.

5.17 Education in literacy and education in music went together in Athens, where to learn to read poetry is also to learn to sing. So here on an early fifth-century red-figure cup one boy is taken through a piece of epic poetry, while another learns to play the lyre.

Basic literacy, which was greatly facilitated by the Greeks' invention of a fully phonetic alphabet script (1.14, 8.2), was taught by the *grammatistēs*. Despite his low status, his job was fundamentally important, since many aspects of the democracy depended for their efficient functioning on at least a rudimentary knowledge of reading and writing. Once a boy could read he was set Homer and other poets, often to recite from memory. As Plato puts it:

> When a boy knows his letters and is ready to proceed from the spoken to the written word, his teachers set him down at his desk and make him read the works of the great poets and learn them by heart; there he finds plenty of good advice, and many stories and much praise and glorification of great men of the past, which encourage him to admire and imitate them and to model himself on them. (Plato, *Prōtagorās* 325e–326a)

Monotonously repetitive exercises on wax tablets were used to practise writing, and some of the few vase paintings of school scenes showed the teacher wielding a sandal to encourage the others. There were, nevertheless, Athenian illiterates. Plutarch tells the probably apocryphal story of the man who asked Aristeidēs to write 'Aristeidēs' on a potsherd to get him ostracised, because he was sick of hearing Aristeidēs constantly praised for being just (1.31).

5.18 The hand gestures of the older man on this early fifth-century Athenian red-figure cup make the content of his instruction clear.

5.40   The music teacher instructed boys in singing and in playing the *aulos* (a sort of oboe) or lyre. Perhaps not all children had a very extensive musical education, since Aristophanēs represents the ability to play the lyre as a mark of the cultured gentleman. But music was certainly important to people at all levels of Athenian society. Plato, indeed, took its moral significance so seriously that he banned all but one of the musical modes from his utopian state. Music played a large part in many festivals, above all the *Dionȳsia* with its choral lyrics in tragedy and comedy and its contests between choruses of both men and boys in the singing of dithyrambs (songs in honour of Dionȳsos). (Evidence for choruses of girls elsewhere in Greece is one sign that girls' education was not entirely neglected.) These choral contests point to the close connection between music and poetry at Athens; even narrative poetry like Homer's *Iliad* and *Odyssey* was recited to musical accompaniment. Equally close was the link between music and dancing: *khoros* is the Greek for 'a dance' as well as 'a chorus'. For the well-to-do, musical entertainment was an integral part of the private symposium too (cf. 8.1, 45, 49; 5.31).

5.41   Physical training was supervised by a *paidotribēs*, who gave instruction in running, long jump, throwing the javelin and discus, boxing and wrestling. Since Greek *poleis* depended for their survival on their citizen troops, physical skills and fitness were vital (cf. 7.31). For this purpose Athens provided public gymnasia (so called because the Greeks exercised there *gumnoi*,

5.19 In this scene on the late-sixth century cup, already pictured above (figs. 5.14–15), a bearded man provides a text-book illustration of how to throw the javelin.

'naked') in addition to the many *palaistrai* (wrestling schools). These were general meeting-places and used for a variety of purposes besides physical exercise; Plato's Academy, for example, takes its name from its location within the gymnasium of *Akadēmos* (or *Hekadēmo*s) (2.37).

5.42　But physical training did not have only a utilitarian military end in view. Athletic excellence was one of the most important fields in which the Greeks expressed their essentially competitive value-system (see 4.8). The greatest renown was accorded to the victors in the Panhellenic festivals, but not far behind these in prestige came the Panathenaic (All-Athenian) games, which was the greatest of the local festivals (see 3.44, 3.46). During these celebrations, contests in honour of the gods were held, at first in running, but later in other sports, and in music and poetry too. Contestants came from all over the far-flung Greek world, and the victors covered not only themselves but their cities in glory (4.9).

5.43　At Athens the length of a child's formal education varied according to the means and outlook of his parents; there was no school-leaving age. In his pamphlet on the social system of Spartē, Xenophōn assumes that children elsewhere were not normally educated beyond childhood; and though an Athenian by birth and upbringing, Xenophōn praises Spartē for its comprehensive educational curriculum that was obligatory for boys from the age of seven right up to adulthood. What Xenophōn keeps very quiet about is the almost exclusively physical and martial character of Spartan education. There was nothing corresponding to secondary, let alone higher, education in this state, because there was no need for it in a society geared so single-mindedly to fighting wars. But at Athens, especially after the Persian Wars, new social and political needs created the demand for new kinds of education, and the demand was satisfied by men known – often derogatorily – as 'sophists' (see also 8.22–30).

5.44 A *sophistēs* originally meant simply a sage or wise man; Hērodotos refers to Solōn (1.20) as a *sophistēs*, and Solōn became a regular member of the elect 'Seven Sages' of ancient Greece. But already by the end of the fifth century *sophistēs* had acquired the pejorative sense from which we derive our 'sophistical' and 'sophistry'. On this hostile view, a sophist was a charlatan, a clever-clever verbal trickster whose stock-in-trade was to make the worse seem the better argument, thus corrupting the moral sense of those who learned from him and turning them into immoral know-it-alls kicking over the traces of established convention. This is precisely the view that Aristophanēs presented in his comedy *Clouds*, where his stock sophist was Sōkratēs. But whereas the sophist was a professional educator who charged his pupils a fee, Sōkratēs engaged Athenians only in informal conversation and expected no monetary reward.

5.45 In a democracy the use of intellectual and rhetorical skills was not merely a social and economic one, but directly a political one. In an era of rapid political, economic and social change, political success no longer depended simply on a family name and glory won in battle but also, and above all, on the power of persuasive speech (*peithō*) in *ekklēsiā* and law-court. He who by skilful rhetoric could persuade mass audiences of Athenians to his viewpoint could become a leader (*prostatēs*) of the Athenian democracy (cf. 8.16–21, 27–31). Greeks had the highest respect for the power of *peithō*. In his *Praise of Helen*, the Sicilian sophist Gorgiās argued that Helen should be treated as blameless because she was *persuaded* to run away with Paris, and *peithō* could not be resisted, almost amounting to force.

5.46 Our evidence for the sophists and their teaching is unfortunately very one-sided. It comes almost entirely from their opponents, especially Plato. Only a handful of fragments of original sophistic writings have survived verbatim from antiquity. Yet even Plato, for all his intellectual brilliance and verbal dexterity, could not entirely hide the fact that the sophists' teaching filled a serious gap. In two of his dialogues, the question of why the young had failed to match up to their famous fathers was raised explicitly in terms of their defective education. Indeed, Plato's own philosophical achievement is inexplicable unless the contribution of the sophists is taken into account.

5.47 What the sophists provided was in effect a higher education for the sons of the rich. Though the sophists did not form a single school, the issue that lay at the heart of their teaching was *aretē*, 'goodness' or 'excellence'. The sophists claimed both to know what excellence was in any given field, whether politics, religion or private morality, and to be able to teach that excellence to their pupils. Their opponents claimed either, like Plato, that excellence was not teachable or, like Aristophanēs in agreement with Plato, that their versions of excellence were immoral and wrong. It seemed to them and to many ordinary Athenians that the traditional view of morality was threatened by the sophists' ability to present apparently convincing arguments on both sides of any moral question.

5.48 Almost all the sophists who taught in Athens were foreigners, men like Prōtagorās from Abdērā and Hippiās from Ēlis (a sophist of prodigious memory and learning). This was one reason why Aristophanēs in his *Clouds* chose to attack Sōkratēs as the representative of all the sophists, since Sōkratēs was an Athenian citizen and so could be identified as a more immediate threat by an Athenian audience. In the *Apology* (which purports to be the speech Sōkratēs delivered in his defence at his trial in 399), Plato made Sōkratēs say that Aristophanēs' play had influenced many Athenians. The charges against him were that he had corrupted the young and been unorthodox in religion, but the former was clearly the crucial one. Sōkratēs' pupils had included both the opportunistic and apparently amoral Alkibiadēs and the openly traitorous Kritiās (cf. 1.86, 3.36).

5.49 In the fourth century, higher education became a more established matter in Athens, and no longer in the hands of visiting experts. At some time in the 390s Isokratēs set up the first 'university' at Athens, essentially a school of advanced rhetoric, and his example was soon followed by Plato and his more philosophically based Academy. These institutes of higher learning seem not to have attracted the attention which had been given to the sophists during the latter part of the fifth century, but they both had very considerable lasting influence and treated each other extremely seriously and engaged fiercely in debates between themselves. Isokratēs attacked both the sophists, for their verbal quibbling, and Plato, for his 'head-in-the-clouds' attitude to philosophy, and dedicated his own school to the principle of utility in education. The debate is still with us. In the following passage (c. 370), Isokratēs attacks philosophers for their useless speculations:

> There are some who are very proud of their ability to formulate an absurd and paradoxical proposition and then make a tolerable defence of it. There are men who have spent their lives saying that it is impossible to make or to deny a false statement, or to argue on both sides of the same question; there are others who maintain that courage and wisdom and justice are all the same, that we are not born with any of them but that they are all the concern

of a single kind of knowledge; and there are still others who waste time on disputes which are quite useless and liable to get their pupils into trouble . . . They ought to give up this hair-splitting pedantry which pretends to find in verbal argument proof of absurdities which have in practice long been refuted, and turn to the real world and give their pupils instruction in the practicalities of public affairs and some expertise in them. They should remember that it is much better to be able to form a reasonable judgement about practical affairs than to have any amount of precise but useless knowledge, and that it is better to have a marginal superiority in affairs of importance than to excel in detailed knowledge of no consequence.
The truth is that they care for nothing except making money out of the young. This is what their so-called philosophy with its concern with disputation for its own sake can do. For the young, who give little thought to private or public affairs, particularly enjoy completely pointless argument. One can well forgive them for that, for they have always been inclined to extremes and taken in by startling novelties. (Isokratēs, *Helen* 1ff.)

Work and slavery

5.50 When we read about labour in our literary sources we get a very clear picture: trade and manual craftsmanship were despised, being deemed suitable only for slaves, foreigners or the urban proletariat (cf. 1.10). Work meant gentle-manly farming, or the tilling of a peasant plot, and wealth meant agricultural wealth, derived from the land, which guaranteed social stability and status. It would seem that traditional agrarian values, which can be traced back to Homer and Hesiod, were still unchallenged in fifth- and fourth-century Athens. But it is here more than anywhere else that the leisure-class bias of our sources can seriously mislead. Those Athenians and non-Athenians who earned their living from manual crafts, small-scale retail trading and the host of other occupations necessary to the relatively large and complex society of Athens, will not have been in a position to share these values. Even the many Athenians who continued to derive their livelihood mainly from agri-culture could not afford to despise craftsmanship and trade. Xenophōn in *Memorābilia* made Sōkratēs shock previously leisured Athenians who had fallen on hard times as a result of the collapse of Athenian power abroad by telling them to employ female relatives to weave cloth for sale, or themselves to take a job as a farm manager (*Memorābilia* 2.7–8). In fact, many Athenians must have faced such a situation long before this, and as a result of Athenian success rather than Athenian failure.

Farming

5.51 At the outbreak of the Peloponnesian War, so Thucydides records (*Peloponnesian War*, 2.14), the majority of Athenians were still countrymen

5.20 This Athenian black-figure cup from the middle of the sixth century provides one of rather few illustrations of agriculture on Athenian pottery. Here we see both ploughing and sowing (cf. fig. 2.3).

born and bred, and had their homes in the rural districts of Attikē. This observation is reinforced by the comic poet Aristophanēs, who repeatedly alluded to the strength of feeling among Athenians at the disruption of country life during the Peloponnesian War. In other words, the Athenian economy retained a strong agricultural base, and the pattern of widely dispersed landownership does not seem to have altered significantly throughout our period: the ideal of the self-sufficient farmer remained intact. Modern scholars have calculated, indeed, that until the second half of the fifth century, Athens could still feed most of her population from her own agricultural produce, at least in good years (cf. 2.17). This common interest in agriculture and a remarkably equitable distribution of landed property across Attikē (5.16) contributed, along with Athens' military success, to the lack of serious civil discord in fifth-century Athens.

5.52 Farming was not unaffected, however, by Athens' changing fortunes in the Greek world. There can be little doubt that the number of slaves in Athens increased markedly after the Persian Wars, and those slaves were found working in the fields as well as in the city. However, the availability of slaves and the influx of wealth did not lead to the formation of large estates. Even the rich tended to own properties in several different areas of Attikē rather than add field to field in their hereditary deme. To run their estates, they might

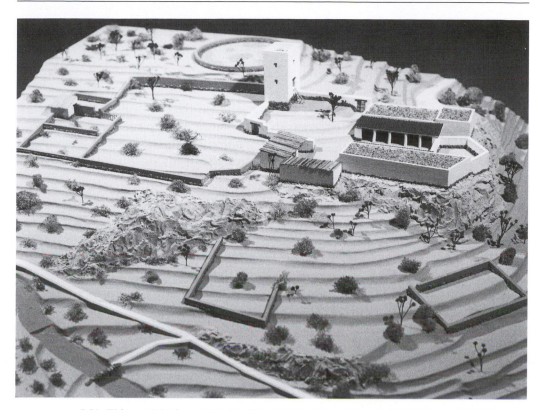

5.21 This model of an Athenian farm is based on archaeological evidence from the classical period discovered in southern Attikē, not far from Cape Sounion.

employ a slave overseer to supervise a slave work-force, but these slaves were not organised in the large chain-gangs familiar from the American South. For the crops grown in Attikē – above all, wheat and barley, the vine and the olive – did not demand large and concentrated labour-forces for their efficient production (see 2.13ff.). Because Mediterranean farming is cyclical, with short bursts of intensive energy at the times of ploughing, planting and harvesting, interspersed with longish stretches of relative inactivity, it was uneconomic to keep a large slave work-force who had to be housed, fed and clothed even when not economically productive. For rich and less rich alike, the slave labour employed in the fields was probably the same slave labour employed in the house. But the access to the markets of the whole Mediterranean enabled Athenians to consume all sorts of exotic products from abroad, and likewise gave them the opportunity to sell goods into that market. Athenians thus diversified their agricultural activities into produce (most famously, olive oil) that was high-value and good for more than mere subsistence. Plutarch is no doubt right to suggest that Periklēs was unusual in selling all the products of his agricultural estate on the market and then buying in what his household needed when it needed it (Plutarch, *Periklēs* 16); but the strategy of exploiting new, far-flung markets will have been one of which Athenians were far from ignorant.

Manufacture

5.53   In many other Greek *poleis*, owning land was the only way one could have a political say in one's country. The fact that at Athens one could be a citizen *without* owning land was treated by some critics as the heart of the problem with Athenian democracy. In the course of his discussion with Prōtagorās, Sōkratēs observed that:

> Whenever advice needs to be given about the running of the city, anyone is allowed to stand up and advise the *ekklēsiā*, smith, cobbler, merchant, ship's captain, rich man, poor man, noble-born or base-born, and no one criticises him. (Plato, *Prōtagorās* 319d, cf. 324c)

When democracy was restored in 403, Athenians faced a proposal to insist in future that only landowners could be citizens, but they rejected it. Most of those who owned no land were no doubt poor, but some rich men chose to invest their wealth in assets that did not include land. Among these was Dēmosthenēs' very wealthy father, also named Dēmosthenēs.

5.54   The scale of the 'manufacturing sector' of the Athenian economy is hard to gauge, either in terms of the size of the labour-force or the amount of money

5.22 This scene on an Athenian red-figure cup of c. 500 shows a cobbler at work, with some of his tools and his products hung up behind him.

invested. Some of Athens' most prominent exports nevertheless involved relatively few men and little investment: it is reliably estimated that no more than 500 potters and painters were active in all over the whole fifth century to provide a very high proportion of all the luxury tableware for the entire Greek world. Small workshops were the order of the day: The two largest establishments of which we hear, which are among the largest known in all antiquity, employed respectively about 120 and about 50 (slave) workers. The typical Athenian craftsman no doubt often worked on his own or with a few slave assistants. The exception to this picture is silver mining, where both the facilities required to refine the ore and the efficient exploitation of the mining concessions meant that economic efficiency demanded larger units (2.9). But Athenian 'manufacturing' bore no comparisons at all with the large-scale industrial enterprises, mass-producing goods for global markets, with which we are familiar today.

Trade

5.55   It was the Athenian silver mines which provided the raw material for what became by far the most widely used Greek coinage, the Athenian silver 'owls', tetradrachms bearing both Athēnē's head and her owl symbol. First minted in the late fifth century, this coinage went on being produced, with only minimal change of type, throughout the classical period. It became known for its reliable purity, and was much imitated. Whatever the prime reason was for a city deciding to mint coinage in the first place, there is no doubt that Athenian coinage, providing a reliable medium for commercial exchange, much facilitated Athenian trade. One sign of the importance of reliable coinage for trade is provided by the law proposed by one Nīkophōn and passed by the Athenians in 375/4 (*RO* 25). This law set up state coin-testers, to whom those engaged in trade could go and have their coin declared up to standard and usable (at the risk that any coinage they had that was not up to standard would be confiscated and rendered unusable). Athens' ability to put large amounts of silver into circulation, and the confidence that merchants could have that they would be paid in Athens with reliable currency, played a significant part in attracting to Athens the trade that she needed – and not least in order to feed herself – as Xenophōn, in his treatise on revenues (*Poroi*), saw:

> In the majority of cities, traders must bring a return cargo with them, as the currency they use is not valid abroad; but at Athens most goods that are of use to anyone can be taken as return cargoes, and if one does not want to do this, one can export silver, an excellent commodity, since wherever one sells it one makes a profit on the original outlay. (Xenophōn, *Poroi* 3.2)

5.56   Feeding the people was important for every ancient state. Athens did this by regularly securing grain through trade. We know of one Greek city which, to secure its food supply, relied, at least in part, on cursing those who prevented the import of grain. The Athenians passed various laws designed to encourage those with grain to bring it to Athens and attempted to penalise those with any link with Athens who did not. Thus if a merchant raised a loan in Athens to purchase a cargo of grain abroad, that merchant had to bring that grain back to Athens. The Athenians also provided for speedy settlement of legal cases in which merchants were involved, as a way of reducing discouragements to trading. Although the Athenians were aware that political measures could be taken to redirect into Athens other kinds of trade also, they did so only for political effect – as when they punished the cities of the island of Keōs for political rebellion by insisting that they export all their valuable ruddle (red ochre for colouring) to Athens.

5.57 Athenians who engaged in trade, therefore, did so without significant state assistance. Nor did Athens offer any significant discouragement to foreigners who wished to trade with Athens. The import and export tax of 2 per cent charged at Athens – and which, even soon after the end of the Peloponnesian War, still brought in 36 talents (Andokidēs 1.133–4, see 6.60) – seems to have been standard to almost all Greek cities. Those who stayed more than a month in Athens became liable to the metic tax (5.67), and Xenophōn thought that they might be discouraged by this because it made them liable to serve with the metic contingents in the Athenian army (*Poroi* 2.2). But beyond that, Athens seems to have been entirely open to non-Athenians engaging in trade. And there was plenty to attract non-Athenians – above all the other traders attracted to Athens and in particular to its port, the Peiraieus, and the goods that they brought.

5.58 At the beginning of the fifth century Athens had no commercial port properly speaking, and her naval harbour was the beach at Phalēron (2.23). But the Peiraieus, with its large natural harbours, was ideally placed and equipped to become the trading centre for the Aegean, and during the fifth century it became the hub of the commerce of the entire eastern Mediterranean world (cf. 1.32). By the middle of the fifth century, Peiraieus had been laid out as a new town on a grid plan by Hippodāmos of Mīlētos, linked to Athens by the Long Walls, and provided with both commercial and naval harbours and dock facilities. In the fourth century, several important boards of officials, in charge of civic order (*astunomoi*), the market (*agorānomoi*), weights and measures (*metronomoi*) and grain supply (*sītophulakes*), were shared equally between Athens and the Peiraieus ([Aristotle], *Constitution of the Athenians* 50–1). To this port came a remarkable variety of goods. Some goods were both required and ensured by Athenian naval dominance, as a late fifth-century *Constitution of the Athenians* preserved among the works of Xenophōn, but not by him, explains:

> If a city is rich in timber for ship-building, where can it dispose of it, unless it persuades the power that rules the sea? And what if a city is rich in iron,

copper, or flax, where can it dispose of them, unless it persuades the power
that rules the sea? Now these are just the materials from which I build my
ships; I get my timber from one place, iron from another, and copper, flax and
wax from yet others. In addition, the Athenians will not allow our
competitors to take their produce elsewhere; if they try to, they will be barred
from the sea. Thus I, doing nothing, get possession of all these products of
the earth through control of the sea. No other city possesses two of these
products. ([Xenophōn], *Constitution of Athens* 2.11–12)

Other goods were attracted by the concentration of wealth among those who
went to the Peiraieus to trade. The comic poet Hermippos salivates over what
can be bought:

From Kūrēnē, stalks of silphium and hides of oxen;
From the Hellespont, mackerel and salted fish of all kinds;
From Thessaly, puddings and ribs of beef . . .
From the Syracusans, pigs and cheese . . .
Those cities, those products. From Egypt, rigging
For sails and papyrus; from Syria, frankincense;
From glorious Crete, cypress for the gods;
From Africa, ivory in plenty at a price;
From Rhodes, raisins and dried figs bringing sweet dreams;
From Euboia, pears and well-fleeced apples;
From Phrygiā, slaves . . .
From Pagasai, slaves with a brand-mark on them;
From the Paphlagonians, Zeus' own acorns and glossy
Almonds, the adornments of a dinner;
From Phoenicia; the fruit of the palm and fine flour;
From Carthage, carpets and bright-coloured cushions.
(Quoted in) Athēnaios, *Deipnosophistai* 1.27–8

5.59   Trade by sea involved considerable risk. Athenian military might have rid the
Aegean of pirates by the 470s, but there remained the commercial risk (not
finding a buyer for the goods), and the risk of shipwreck and loss of cargo.
To enable trade on the scale which is seen at the Peiraieus, traders had to find
a way of minimising the risk. This led to the development of a loan-cum-
insurance scheme, in which the trader borrowed money to the value of cargo
(a 'bottomry loan'). This type of loan – rarely more than 2,000 *drakhmai* –
was made at very high rates of interest (up to 120 per cent!) and was for the
duration of one trip only. The loan was used to buy the cargo. If it arrived
safely at its destination and was sold, the loan was repayable, with interest;
but if for any reason the shipment failed to arrive, the borrower owed
nothing. This type of loan, which is first attested in 421, thus contained an
element of insurance. We do not know how extensively this method of
financing trade was used, but bottomry loans are both mentioned in passing
in a number of law-court speeches and are themselves the subject of legal
arguments. Not surprisingly lenders tended to be suspicious about the

circumstances in which cargoes were lost, and we get vivid descriptions of scuttling a ship to escape repayment of the loan:

> The agreement was, as is usual in such affairs, that the money would be paid back on the ship's safe arrival; but in order to defraud their creditors they laid a plot to sink her. Accordingly Hēgestratos, when they were two or three days on the outward voyage, went down by night into the hold and started to cut through the ship's bottom. Meanwhile Zēnothemis here remained on deck with the other passengers. But the others on board heard the noise Hēgestratos was making and rushed below to prevent the damage being done in the hold. Hēgestratos was caught in the act and anticipating punishment took to his heels, and when the others followed in pursuit jumped overboard, and because it was dark missed the ship's boat and was drowned. He was a bad man and he came to a bad end, very appropriately suffering himself the fate he had planned to inflict on others. His fellow conspirator and accomplice here at first pretended that he knew nothing of the attempted crime and was as alarmed as the rest of them; he tried to persuade the bow-officer and the crew to embark in the ship's boat and abandon the ship forthwith, on the ground that there was no hope of her staying afloat and that she would go down immediately. In this way their object would be achieved, the ship lost, and their creditors defrauded. But he was not successful because our agent on board opposed him and promised a large reward to the crew if the ship was saved, as by god's grace and the courage of the crew she was, and made a safe landfall in Kephallēniā. (Dēmosthenēs, *Against Zēnothemis* 32.5)

5.60   It is a striking feature of these and other speeches concerning Athenian trade that a high proportion of the named long-distance merchants (*emporoi*) are neither Athenian citizens nor even resident alien metics, but foreigners; local retail traders (*kapēloi*), by contrast, were Athenians or metics. The speeches cannot be taken as a representative sample of evidence, but they do support the strong impression given by our sources as a whole that trade overseas was not something that Athenian citizens chose to go in for; it might, indeed, yield handsome profits on occasions, but it did not confer on its practitioners the prestige that Athenians longed for. Similarly banking, which consisted simply of money-lending and exchanging the currencies of different Greek states, was usually conducted by slaves.

Slavery

5.61   Slaves have already been mentioned in several other contexts in this chapter – their numbers and their employment in agriculture, manufacture and banking. Slavery as an institution was very rarely questioned in the ancient world (cf. 4.25). But, characteristically, one of those rare instances occurred at the height of the sophistic movement, when some enlightened spirits held that slavery was contrary to nature and, because it was based on force,

5.23 In this scene on a water jug (*hydriā*) of the second quarter of the fifth century of women fetching water at a fountain, the woman with a water jug on her head is marked as a Thracian slave by the tattoos on her neck and body.

morally wrong. They were very much out on a limb; even the writers of utopias could not imagine a world without slave labour. Aristotle spends the opening chapters of his *Politics* trying to refute those unorthodox sophists and prove that slavery was natural (cf. 3.50).

5.62 Force was the basis of the relationship between master and slave, whose right-less condition represented the extreme version of forced labour (cf. 4.25). In some other Greek states, notably Spartē and Thessaly, there were large subject populations with restricted rights, whose status is best described as that of serfs. The chief difference between these populations and slaves at Athens is that the serfs enjoyed some kind of family life. Slaves, in the sharpest possible contrast, had been uprooted from their family in their native lands and transported forcibly elsewhere. This extract from a document recording the compulsory sale of property belonging to men convicted of sacrilege in 415 (see 1.73) well illustrates the equation of slave and outsider:

> The property of Kēphīsodōros, (*metoikos*) living in the Peiraieus: slaves –
> Thracian female, 165 *drakhmai*; Thracian female, 135; Thracian male, 170;
> Syrian male, 240; Karian male, 105; Illyrian male, 161; Thracian female, 220;
> Thracian male, 115; Scythian male, 144; Illyrian male, 121; Kolkhian male,
> 153; Karian boy, 174; little Karian boy, 72; Syrian male, 301; Maltese (?)
> male, 151; Lydian female, 85. (ML 79A)

This document, which gives the most detailed information we possess on Athenian prices, suggests that by the end of the fifth century, when the slave trade had been firmly established for some two centuries, slaves were relatively cheap to buy in the Athenian slave-market. (A *drakhmē* was then the daily wage of a skilled worker.) This helps to explain the wide distribution of slave ownership in Athenian society. Most slaves came from the north and east – Thrace, the Danubian lands, Asia Minor – but we do not know clearly how Athenians acquired slaves. According to Hērodotos, some Thracians actually sold their own children into slavery because they were so poor. Others had been captured by pirates and sold into slavery, though under the Athenian empire piracy was much reduced in the Aegean. A few slaves at Athens were home-bred, but these were the exceptions. Many may have been made slaves as a result of warfare, with captives sold by their captors to slave-dealers and put on the markets of the Aegean. But there seem to be very few Greeks among Athenian slaves. This suggests that when the Athenians are said to have 'enslaved' a rebel city, that 'enslavement' was short-lived and that the victims, one way and another, soon had their freedom bought for them.

5.63 As a general principle, a slave was a man or a woman without enforceable legal rights. Slaves were chattels, mere property, of which their masters could dispose as they wished (cf. 5.11). Slaves therefore stood near or at the bottom of the social scale. Nevertheless, within the broad category of slaves, it is not surprising that distinctions of status existed. These distinctions in part reflected that fact that slaves were people who had had the misfortune to be captured, but who might well have acquired various skills in their former lives – they could have been e.g. traders, teachers, financiers, craftsmen, builders, farmers. Whether a man ended up as a public slave, like the *dokimastēs* (the tester of coinage), or a private slave, such as the Laureion miners, would be influenced by his previously acquired skills, and had marked consequences for the conditions in which he worked. Public slaves, a group which also included the state police force of Scythian archers and a number of state secretaries, were something of an élite: the city even paid for public slaves to be initiated into the Eleusinian Mysteries. Some private slaves were also relatively privileged. The most striking of 'rags to riches' stories at Athens involve slaves employed in banking who end up not only being freed but acquiring Athenian citizenship. Some slaves who were skilled craftsmen were set up by their masters in independent workshops: the master seems often to have taken a percentage of their earnings (and the risk if the business failed), while the slave took the rest. These skilled men were among those with the greatest hope of eventually buying their freedom, though in general manumission does not seem to have been nearly as likely a prospect in Athens as it was to be for Roman slaves. Large numbers of slaves were employed within the household, with many doubling as domestic or agricultural labour depending on the demands of the agricultural year (above 5.52). Such slaves might strike up something of a personal relationship with their master or mistress. Many caring roles fell to slaves, who looked after the children, or the elderly (e.g. the blind Teiresiās in Greek tragedy was traditionally accompanied by an adult male slave). Lowest of the low were the slaves employed in the mines, for whom death from their appalling conditions of work probably came as a blessed release (cf. 6.31).

5.64 There were formally no specifically slave occupations, apart from that of policeman. Athenians and slaves often performed exactly the same tasks, sometimes side by side, as when dressing vines in rural Attikē or fluting the columns of the Erekhtheion on the Athenian Akropolis. For Athenians, like other Greeks, the status of an occupation was determined less by the nature of the work than by whether the worker was self-employed or working for another (cf. 4.21). It was the mark of the truly free man, according to Aristotle, not to live for the sake of someone else. This meant that the more visible the dependence upon another, the more likely the job would be to be largely performed by slaves. Dependence was highly visible in the case of the silver mines, where the conditions were such that no free man would willingly subject himself to them – Xenophōn (*Memorābilia* 3.6.12) even has Sōkratēs jest that a free man might reckon the pollution so bad as to justify not even visiting the mining works! And although the word for a household slave, which was also used as a general word for slave (*oiketēs*), was sometimes applied to a free domestic servant too, domestic service was also a position which advertised dependence and which no citizen would willingly undertake.

5.65 The availability of cheap slaves enabled Athenians, rich and poor, to avoid (by and large) taking on tasks which would have rendered them visibly dependent upon the whims of fellow citizens. This, along with the fact that slaves provided Athenians with the free time in which actively to pursue politics, made slavery one of the factors that enabled Athenian democracy to work. Slaves were an essential feature of Athenian democracy, but the

5.24 This late fifth-century tombstone of a metic who had come to Athens from the Ionian city of Erythrai is in its iconography indistinguishable from the tombstones of Athenians.

Athenians did not enslave people in order to be democrats – slavery was endemic the world over till the nineteenth century AD. Whether the Athenians would have invented radical, citizen democracy if they had not had slaves is a question which we cannot answer.

5.66   The strictly economic significance of slavery is harder to fathom in the absence of the kind of statistical data a modern economist takes for granted. We can only guess what proportion of the total population of Athens was slave – perhaps around one-quarter of the total (5.7–8). Essential economic activities, such as getting the harvest in, depended upon slave as well as free labour, and the vital resource of the silver mines was exploited exclusively by slave labour. It has been suggested that the level of production and the productivity of labour might have been higher if the Athenians had relied less on slaves, but it is not clear that slavery was the sole or even the main cause of the stagnation of Greek technology. It is not irrelevant that many of the major technological advances were applied not to peacetime industry but to warfare, which the Greeks regarded as a major means of production because of the booty and ransom from prisoners that it brought in. Slavery is to us (and was to a tiny number of ancient Greeks) a great evil. But if one wants to make moral judgements, the fact that Athenians (like everyone else in the ancient world) kept slaves should not take away from them the credit for, uniquely, developing the idea of citizen freedom and democracy, two key aspects of 'the glory that was Greece'. It is worth reflecting that, in the UK, males and females did not *all* automatically get a vote till 1918 (and not till 1928 on the same terms as each other).

Metics and foreigners (*xenoi*)

5.67   Athenian citizenship laws were unusually strict. Slaves were property and belonged to whoever had bought them. But any freeborn non-Athenian, whether Greek or non-Greek (*barbaros*), who took up residence in Athens came under special conditions. After residence of one month, an alien was compelled to register as a metic (*metoikos*) and pay the poll-tax of one *drakhmē* a month (*metoikion*), or half that for a woman. He or she had to have an Athenian patron (*prostatēs*), and though metics had access to the courts, were admitted to theatres and festivals (and might be required to help fund them), served with the Athenian armed forces, and could make a handsome living, there was never any doubt of the inferiority of metic status as such. Above all, metics were not allowed to own real property in Attikē, unless individually awarded permission to do so (*egktēsis*).

5.68   What kind of people chose to live long-term in Athens under these conditions? Some metics were not freeborn but freed. Slaves who were manumitted and remained in Athens became not citizens but metics. Among freeborn metics, many were probably quite humble people to whom for one reason or another the Athenian grass had seemed greener. A large and cosmopolitan state like Athens offered opportunities, not available in many other cities. In 401–400 the Athenians voted rewards to those metics who had helped in the overthrow two years earlier of the vicious Spartan-backed junta of the Thirty Tyrants (1.84). An official document listed the honorands, in all probability metics, together with their often lowly occupations:

> Khairedēmos, farm-worker; Leptinēs, butcher/cook; Dēmētrios, carpenter; Euphoriōn, muleteer; Kēphīsodōros, builder; Hēgēsiās, gardener; Epameinōn,

> ass-herder; [. . .]opos, olive-seller; Glaukiās, farm-worker; [. . .]n, nut-[seller]; Dionÿsios, a farm-worker; Bendīphanēs, (?); Emporiōn, farm-worker; Paidikos, bread-[seller]; Sōsiās, fuller; Psammis, farm-worker; Egersis, [. . .]; Eukoliōn, hired labourer; Kalliās, sculptor. (RO 4.col.6, 1–11, col.7.1–9)

Those on this list with common Greek names were presumably immigrants from other cities, but Psammis is an Egyptian name and Bendīphanēs is named from the Thracian goddess Bendīs (2.24, 5.71), and they, together with Paidikos and perhaps Eukoliōn, seem likely to be ex-slaves.

5.69 By far the most famous of the metics who was opposed to the Thirty is known to have moved in the circles of the Athenian élite. This is Lysiās, speech-writer extraordinary, who with his brother (murdered by the Thirty (1.82)) owned the shield factory with some 120 slave workers mentioned above (5.54). His father was from Syracuse and is said to have been a friend of none other than Periklēs, who invited him to take up residence in Athens. At the beginning of the *Republic*, Plato portrayed this distinguished and surely exceptional family of metics at home in the Peiraieus (see 2.24). Evidently they had settled easily into Athenian society. Men like these were required to perform expensive public services (the *leitourgiai* discussed in 6.62–3) or, if less well-off, to serve as hoplites in the Athenian army (7.18).

5.70 One ex-slave metic has been alluded to above, and deserves further discussion. This is Pāsiōn, who died about 370. He had begun his career in Athens as a banker's slave. By his master's will he was not only manumitted but he acquired the bank and his master's widow as well. Thereafter as a metic he grew inordinately rich, and came to own not only the bank but a shield factory (staffed no doubt by slave workers). He knew where his interests lay, so disbursed large amounts of his wealth for the benefit of the Athenian people – so large that in return he was rewarded with a public grant of Athenian citizenship. On his death, he bequeathed to his son landed estates worth 20 talents, scattered in three demes. His son Apollodōros, the speaker of the *Against Neairā* speech, presents himself as more Athenian than the Athenians in his moral and political outlook (6.45). Pāsiōn's career was exceptional; but there was no shortage of wealthy metics who threw in their lot with the Athenians.

5.71 But those who came to reside in Athens brought more than just their money with them. The annual festival of the Thracian cult of Bendīs was adopted as part of Athenian public cult following a consultation of the oracle at Dōdōnā. This festival was particularly grand, with two processions, one of Thracians and one of Athenians, starting out from the symbolic centre of the city, the hearth of the Prytaneum, and an unprecedented torch race on horseback. The opening of Plato's *Republic* sees Sōkratēs returning from the festival and indicates the degree of public interest which it excited at Athens (2.24). No other foreign cult made quite such an impact, but during the fourth century both Egyptians and merchants from Kition on Cyprus were given permission, on the proposal of the prominent Athenian politician

5.25 In this unique scene from a red-figure pot of the second quarter of the fifth century a doctor is seen treating a patient.

Lykourgos, to acquire land on which to build shrines to their own gods, as we learn from a decree of 333:

> Concerning the resolution that the Kitian merchants were making a lawful supplication in asking the people for the right to acquire a plot of land on which to found the sanctuary of Aphrodītē, be it resolved by the people: grant to the merchants of Kition the right to acquire land on which to found the sanctuary of Aphrodītē, just as the Egyptians have founded the sanctuary of Īsis. (RO 91.33–45)

Preserving life and coping with death

Health-care

5.72 Doctors appear in Greek literature from the *Iliad* on, where Asklēpios is described as the 'blameless physician' and pupil of the centaur Kheirōn, and his sons Machaōn and Podaleiros lead a contingent from Thessaly. They are both involved in fighting the Trojans and in healing the wounded. Machaōn

5.26 This scene on the same vase seems to show two men and a dwarf waiting to see the doctor. The dwarf carries a hare over his shoulder – perhaps his payment for the doctor?

tends Menelāos in *Iliad* 4 after he has been struck by an arrow, and we are given a detailed description of his sucking the blood from the wound and applying healing ointment. Such practical treatment of the wounded co-exists in the *Iliad* with a notion that sickness is sent by the gods and to be dealt with by propitiation. The plot of the whole *Iliad* turns on Apollo sending a plague on the Greek camp because Agamemnōn refused to return the daughter of Apollo's priest Khrȳsēs.

5.73 We know little about medicine in archaic Greece, though Hērodotos does mention the international celebrity doctor, Dēmokēdēs from Krotōn, who worked successively (and for ever greater rewards) for the Aiginetans, the Athenians, Polykratēs from Samos, and the Persian king Dareios (Hērodotos, *Histories* 3.125, 129–37). But in the classical Greek world, we still find practical healing co-existing with treatment by divine intervention. Indeed it is striking that our evidence suggests that healing cults expanded at the same

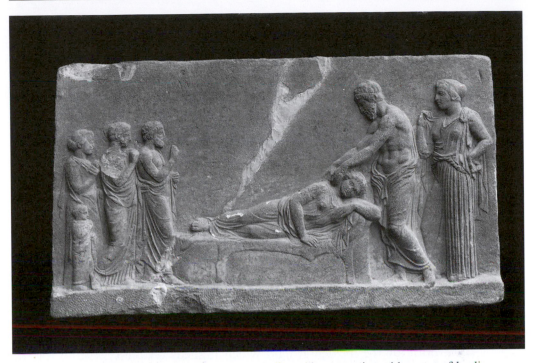

5.27 This fourth-century relief was dedicated in connection with an act of healing. Asklēpios is here shown laying his hands on the sleeping patient.

time as medicine developed along increasingly rational lines. The cult of Asklēpios, whom some identified as a son of Apollo, was introduced to Athens and to a sanctuary on the south slope of the Akropolis only in 420, and Asklēpios' great sanctuary at Epidauros in the Argolid underwent massive expansion in the fourth century (3.16). But it is also from the late fifth century that the earliest texts of the 'Hippokratic corpus' date, that is, texts identified with the medical tradition centred on the island of Kōs and associated with Hippokratēs.

5.74   The writings of the Hippokratic corpus are important evidence for the nature and development of scientific thinking in classical Greece, and this aspect will be discussed below (8.12, 37–9). But they also afford vivid indications of what life was like for both doctors and patients. Standards were very variable. Some appear to have maintained very high standards in both practice and ethics, and treatises were written on how the good doctor should behave at all times, as the following extract shows:

> The physician ought to have a certain flexibility; inflexibility repels both the sick and the healthy. He must keep a close watch on himself and not give himself away; he must not gossip to laymen, but say no more than is necessary; to say too much is to expose his treatment to criticism. Look out for your patients' misbehaviour. They often lie about taking the medicine you have prescribed. They won't take medicine they don't like, whether purges or tonics,

and they sometimes die in consequence. They never confess what they have done, and the doctor gets the blame. Carry out your treatment in a calm and orderly way, concealing most things from the patient, while you are treating him. If you have to give orders give them cheerfully and calmly, turning a deaf ear to any comments. Reproach your patient sharply and emphatically at times, and at others encourage him with concern and careful attention; but do not reveal anything about his present or future condition. Statements on the subject often cause a setback . . . When you have made these arrangements and the necessary preparations for what is to be done, decide before you enter the sick man's room what treatment is needed. For what is needed is often not reasoned diagnosis, but practical help. So you must predict the outcome from your previous experience; it makes a good impression and is pretty easy. When you do go in, be careful how you sit and maintain your reserve. Be careful of your dress, be authoritative in what you say, but be brief, be reassuring and sympathetic, show care and reply to objections, meet any difficulties with calm assurance, forbid noise and disturbance, be ready to do what has to be done. ([Hippokratēs], *Decōrum* 7–13, excerpts)

5.75   The work known as *Epidemics* gives case histories of a large number of patients, many of whom die. The work is not concerned to chart the treatment given, but the way in which the illness progressed. It is of great interest both for the incidental light which it sheds on lifestyles, and for the symptoms which the doctors chose to observe. We meet a number of men who fell ill after drinking, including one young man 'who had been running a temperature for a long time as the result of drinking and much sexual activity' (3.17.16), and one man whose condition developed after he ate beef and drank cow's milk, and got worse 'through taking a large amount of milk, both boiled and cold, both goat's and sheep's' (3.17.13). A youth of twenty died after developing 'a fever as a result of exhaustion, having exerted himself by running more than he was accustomed' (3.1.8). In all cases the description of the illness focused on the presence or absence of fever, and on the nature of the urine and faeces; delirium and insomnia also featured regularly, with other symptoms being observed in relation to particular patients. A more or less typical day in the life of one of these patients reads like this:

> Eighth day: about noon she became warm, thirsty and comatose; nausea, vomited a small quantity of yellowish bile-stained material. An uneasy night without sleep. Frequently unconsciously incontinent of large quantities of urine. (*Epidemics* 3.1.12)

5.76   The material in *Epidemics* is drawn from various cities of Greece, but particularly from the north Aegean (and especially the island of Thasos). What little information we have specifically about doctors at Athens comes from one very unusual Athenian pot which shows two scenes from a doctor's consulting-room, the waiting patients and the doctor actually treating someone, and from occasional mentions of doctors in law-court speeches. One of our most vivid sketches comes in a description by one Aristōn of what happened after he was beaten up:

> It so happened, gentlemen of the jury, that Euxitheos of Kholleidai, a relation of mine who is here in court, and Meidiās, who were on their way home after a dinner-party, came up with me when I was nearly home, followed me as I was carried to the bath and were present when the doctor arrived. I was so weak that they decided, in order to avoid carrying me the long distance from the bath to my house, that it would be best to take me to Meidiās' house for the night. And they did so.
>
> The immediate result of the blows and maltreatment to which I had been subjected was that I was reduced to the condition I have described to you and to which all the eye-witnesses whose evidence you have heard have testified. Subsequently, though my doctor said that the swellings on my face and my bruises did not give him any great anxiety, I suffered from continuous fever and severe body pains, particularly in the ribs and abdomen, and was unable to take food. And indeed my doctor said that, if I had not had a spontaneous haemorrhage when the pain was at its worst and my attendants in despair, I should have died of internal suppuration; it was the haemorrhage that saved me. (Dēmosthenēs, *Against Konōn* 54. 9–10)

5.77 Medicine was largely a private matter, but some cities paid doctors with public money. In Delphi a health tax was levied to pay a doctor's salary. Those who went to a sanctuary of Asklēpios, or some other healing deity, to be healed there while they slept were also expected to pay the god for his services by making offerings. Many people treated themselves on the basis of traditional, widespread beliefs about the curative properties of certain plants. Some 'root-cutters' and drug-sellers became famous for their special knowledge of obscure plants and their effects. In his *Inquiry into Plants* Theophrastos, the pupil of Aristotle, details the medicinal uses of various plants:

> The root of the 'wild vine' is also heating and pungent: for this reason it is useful as a depilatory and to remove freckles: and the fruit is used for smoothing hides. It is cut at any season, but especially in autumn. The root of edderwort given in milk is useful for stopping a cough. It has a variegated snake-like stem; the seed is not used. The root of thapsia has emetic properties, and if one retains it, it purges both upwards and downwards. It is also able to remove bruises, and it restores other contusions to a pale colour. Its juice is stronger and purges both upwards and downwards; the seed is not used. It grows especially in Attikē, but also in other places; the cattle of the country do not touch it, but imported cattle feed on it and perish of diarrhoea.' (*Inquiry into Plants* 9.20.3, trans. Hort)

Such knowledge of the effects of plants on health could be used for other purposes, both to poison oneself or others, and to avoid work:

> They say that slaves often take meadow saffron when greatly provoked, and then themselves have recourse to the antidote and effect a cure . . . (*Inquiry into Plants* 9.16.6)

Death

5.78   At one point, Theophrastos reported on the best way to prepare hemlock to ensure an easy death. But for most Greeks in the classical period, death came of its own accord, and too soon rather than too late. The cases recorded in *Epidemics* made plain the ever-present threat of death to men and women of all ages. But though death was an everyday occurrence, death and the dead were not treated with indifference. For all but the very young, death rituals were elaborate, and the attitude a person took towards the dead was an important index of their moral status. The desire for proper burial at the hands of relatives and in one's native land was extremely strong. The plot of Sophoklēs' *Antigonē*, where Antigonē was forbidden by state decree to give due burial to a brother, would have struck a deep chord with the Athenian audience. A prospective office-holder had to satisfy the state concerning his family tombs (see 5.10). Powerful too was the concern to leave a good name among the living, to live on after death in vivid memory. Hence the conventional stress on honour (*tīmē*) and glory (*doxa*) in the funeral speeches (*epitaphioi*) delivered annually when the bones of those who had died fighting for Athens were accorded a public burial at Athens.

5.79   In the funeral speech of Periklēs, delivered in the first year of the Peloponnesian War and recorded by Thucydides (9.9), Periklēs began by speaking about the Athenians' ancestors, both their dim and distant ones and the immediately preceding generation who had created the radical democracy and the empire. He then eulogised the Athenians' present way of life and in particular their democratic ideals. Only after that did he come to those who had died in that particular year of war, declaring that they had the whole earth for their tomb. Finally, Periklēs addressed the relatives of the dead. Their parents should not be downcast, he said, but rather uplifted by their good fortune in having had sons who died gloriously in the service of their country; their sons and brothers should strive to equal their fathers' and brothers' achievements, though this would be a near-impossible task.

5.80   Memory of the dead was preserved by the performance of annual rites at the family tomb (cf. 2.31, 5.10). Some of these rites were poignantly rendered on Athenian vases, especially those designed to hold the special oil used. If a family could afford it, a gravestone or other grave-marker (*stēlē*; see 8.98 and figs. 1.15, 2.7, 5.24, 29 and 8.32) might be erected, and a suitable laudatory epitaph cut. The tomb itself also depended for its elaboration on the family's wealth. Funerals of the rich were liable to become the occasion of ostentatious expenditure, and attempts were made as early as the time of Solōn to limit by law the amount that could be spent, the number of mourners in attendance and the extent of public demonstration of grief. The formal lament was restricted to the house and the graveside, and the funeral procession had to be held before dawn (cf. 4.3).

5.81   On the day of the death, the corpse was formally laid out (the *prothesis*), usually in the house of the next of kin, by the close female relatives. The body

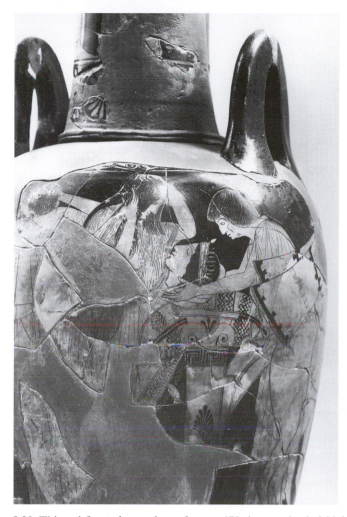

5.28 This red-figure *loutrophoros* from c. 470 shows a dead girl laid to rest on a bier by a slave woman while a female relative tears her hair in mourning (cf. fig. 2.6).

was ritually bathed, anointed, dressed and garlanded, and laid on a bier. Friends and relatives came to pay their last respects, and women, dressed in black with their hair shorn, beat their breasts and sang a ritual lament; from antiquity to today this lament has been the prerogative of women in Greece. Since death was considered to pollute both house and mourners, a vessel containing spring water was placed outside the entrance to warn others of the pollution, and to enable visitors to purify themselves on departure (cf. 3.33).

5.82   The funeral took place on the third day, before sunrise. The corpse, wrapped in a shroud and covered by a cloak, was carried to the graveyard in procession (*ekphorā*). At different periods, the Athenians practised predominantly cremation or inhumation. In the classical period, inhumation was normal, but the war dead were cremated on the battlefield before their bones were

5.29 This late fifth-century Athenian grave *stēlē* puts on public display a domestic scene, as the deceased Hēgēsō, a particularly elaborately dressed lady attended by a simply dressed slave, looks through her jewellery box.

gathered and brought back to Athens for burial in the annual ceremony. The bodies of plague victims were also cremated (the invading Spartans withdrew from Attikē when they saw the smoke rising from the pyres during the plague of Athens in 430: they realized the reason why). Thucydides comments on the breakdown of customary practice involved in relatives disposing of dead bodies by throwing them onto the already burning pyres of others:

> The funeral rites which had customarily been observed were disrupted and they buried their dead as best they could. Many had resort to the most shameless methods of burial, for lack of the necessary means and because so many deaths had already occurred in their households. They would anticipate the builders of a pyre, put their own dead on it and set it alight, or throw the corpse they were carrying on top of an already lighted pyre and leave it. (Thucydides, *Peloponnesian War* 2.52)

Burial, of the body or of cremated bones, took place either in the city cemeteries of Athens, which were sited outside the walls (2.31), in village cemeteries, or on the family estates of the deceased in the countryside. Offerings were made at the grave, and libations of wine and oil poured. Then followed the funeral banquet.

5.83 After the funeral, further rites were performed on the ninth day, and annually thereafter. Maintenance of the family tombs and the annual rites of the dead were the most solemn duties. This was partly because claims to the property of those who had died could be undermined, if those who inherited did not show suitable respect. But it was also that, although there was no 'orthodox' Athenian view on the afterlife, there was a widespread feeling that, unless the dead were properly disposed of and their graves properly tended, their aggrieved spirits might somehow escape to haunt the living like spectres (cf. 3.47). The power of the dead could even have significant political force. The great patriotic rallying cry to the Athenians at Salamīs in 480 was to fight to free their land, the tombs of their ancestors and the shrines of the gods. It was these too which the country people of Attikē were so loath to abandon in the face of the Spartan invasions during the Peloponnesian War (2.21). In the tombs of their ancestors the Athenians saw tangible witnesses of what bound them together as Athenians. So we return at the finish to the sense of community with which this chapter began (cf. 3.41).

6   Athenian democracy and imperialism

The theory of democracy

6.1   If democracy is 'government of the people, by the people, for the people', everything depends on what counts as 'government' and what counts as 'the people'. In what pass for democracies in the modern world, 'the people' generally means men and women over the age of 18 who have qualified by birth and/or residence in the particular country, and 'government' means 'casting a vote in an election'. But making the actual decisions about how the country is to be run is done by those who have been elected by this process, usually without consulting the people who elected them. Aristotle might well have called the system not 'democracy', but 'elective oligarchy'. In classical Athens, however, 'the people' took all the decisions, 'people' being defined as males over the age of 18, born of parents both of whom were Athenian. The 'people' did this by attending meetings – the Assembly, *ekklēsiā* – where they voted on what was to be done; by allowing their names to go forward for the various offices of state which were selected by lot; and by casting votes to elect the limited number of officials (military and financial officers) who were chosen in that way. Whether 'the people' for whom government acted were this same group of all adult male Athenians, or were just the poor majority, 'the people' in the sense of the lower classes, was debated by Greek observers.

6.2   Athens moved in stages from rule by a basically self-appointed élite (1.17–18) to rule by the people. The powers of the people were crucially extended by Solōn at the beginning of the sixth century, and some scholars would say that Athens was essentially a democracy from the 590s (1.20–1). But power struggles between groups of élite families and Peisistratos' political coup made the weakness of the people more apparent than their power. Only at the end of the sixth century, after Peisistratos' son Hippiās was thrown out and Kleisthenēs had carried out his reforms, can we talk of the real origins of 'democracy' familiar from the fifth and fourth centuries (1.25).

6.3   If we, like Hērodotos, are inclined to give the title 'democracy' to Kleisthenēs' constitution, the Athenians were not. The word *dēmokratiā* seems not to have been invented until more than a generation after Kleisthenēs' reforms. The earliest shadow of the term 'democracy' comes in Aiskhylos' phrase *dēmou kratousa kheir*, 'the sovereign hand of the *dēmos*', which occurs in his

6.1 On the top of a law against tyranny passed in 337/6 BC, the Athenians had a relief sculpted in which a personification of Democracy places a wreath on the head of a personification of Dēmos (the People).

Suppliants of 463. It seems that the contemporary description of Kleisthenēs' constitution was *isonomiā*, 'equality under the law'. This was an ideal that had obvious appeal after the overthrow of tyranny. Like the term *isēgoriā* ('equal rights to speak'), also used by Hērodotos to describe Kleisthenēs' constitution, it puts the stress on equality of opportunity rather than on popular power.

6.4 It is *isonomiā* too that Hērodotos uses in the debate over the theoretical benefits and drawbacks of different constitutional arrangements which he claims occurred in Persia in 522. This debate is wholly Greek in its inspiration, and some of the ideas expressed are unlikely to have been current until well into the fifth century. But even if it does not accurately reflect sixth-century thought, the passage remains the earliest example of political theory in history. In this 'Persian Debate', the speakers argue respectively for democracy (*isonomiā*), oligarchy (rule by some, in this case the few rich and well-born), and monarchy (rule by one, here hereditary kingship):

> Otanēs recommended that the Persians should bring their political affairs into the open. 'I think', he said, 'we should no longer have a single monarch; this is neither an agreeable nor a good form of government. How can it admit of proper adjustment when it allows one man to do what he likes without being answerable for it? Even the best of men put in that position is bound to overstep the bounds of normality. The advantages he enjoys breed pride, and envy is deeply engrained in human nature [cf. 4.9–10]. A man with these two faults is wholly evil . . . The worst feature of all is that he breaks down traditional law and custom, puts men to death without trial and subjects women to sexual violence. The rule of the people on the other hand has the most attractive of descriptions, equality under the law (*isonomiā*), and moreover does none of the things a monarch does. Offices are filled by lot, officials are answerable for what they do, and all questions are publicly debated. I propose therefore that we do away with monarchy and raise the people to power. For in the people everything is comprised.'
>
> This was the opinion of Otanēs. He was followed by Megabyzos, who recommended oligarchy: 'To be rid of the violence of a tyrant only to fall under the violence of an uncontrollable mob would be intolerable. A tyrant at least knows what he is doing. The people have no knowledge at all. How can they have, being uneducated and without sense of what is right and proper? They rush mindlessly into public affairs like a river in flood. So leave democracy to the enemies of Persia, and let us give power to a chosen few of the best among us.'
>
> This was the opinion of Megabyzos, and Dareios finally gave his in the following words: 'We have three alternatives before us, democracy, oligarchy and monarchy. The last of the three seems to me to be far the best. There can be nothing better than government by the best man. Because of his abilities, his control of the people will be above criticism, and the measures he takes against wrongdoers will have maximum secrecy. In conclusion, I ask, where did we get our present freedom from, and who gave it to us? Was it from democracy or oligarchy or monarchy? My view is that, as we were given our freedom by one man, we should preserve that kind of constitution; and quite apart from this, it is never an improvement to change our ancestral laws and customs so long as they work well.' (Hērodotos, *Histories* 3.80ff.)

6.5 Otanēs' single sentence of praise is elaborated by Periklēs in the Funeral Oration:

> Our constitution does not copy the laws of neighbouring states; we are rather a pattern to others than imitators ourselves. Its administration favours the many instead of the few; this is why it is called a *dēmokratiā*. If we look to the laws, they afford equal justice to all in their private differences; if to social standing, advancement in public life falls to reputation for capacity, class

considerations not being allowed to interfere with *aretē*; nor again does poverty bar the way. If a man is able to serve the state, he is not hindered by the obscurity of his condition. The freedom which we enjoy in our government extends also to our ordinary life. There, far from spying jealously on each other, we do not feel called upon to be angry with our neighbour for doing what he likes, or even to indulge in those hard looks which cannot fail to be offensive, although they inflict no positive penalty. But all this ease in our private relations does not make us lawless as citizens. Against this, fear is our chief safeguard, teaching us to obey those in office and the laws, particularly such as regard the protection of the injured, whether they are actually on public display, or belong to that code which, although unwritten, yet cannot be broken without acknowledged disgrace. (Thucydides, *Peloponnesian War* 2.37, trans. Crawley)

Outside these two texts, little praise and much criticism of democracy are to be found in classical texts. Almost without exception, our sources are out of sympathy with, or actively hostile towards, the Athenian democracy. Ancient critics sometimes claimed to prefer the moderate constitution of Kleisthenēs to the radical democracy ushered in by the reforms of Ephialtēs in 462, or even called for a return to the 'democracy' of Solōn. What they knew or understood of these earlier constitutions is unclear, and the suspicion that they were prepared to foist their own ideals onto past figures cannot always be suppressed. There were indeed some champions of democracy, but democratic theory has to be reconstructed in reverse from the attacks of its critics, above all from various works of Plato and from Aristotle's *Politics* (cf. 8.29). But its chief elements are clear: these were the beliefs that there were some matters on which collective judgement was better and more reliable than the judgement of any individual, and that democracy alone guaranteed true freedom and equality (cf. 8.15).

Democracy in action

6.6 If we are poorly informed about democratic theory, we are abundantly informed about democratic practice. But even for the way democracy worked, our best evidence comes not from the fifth but from the fourth century. This is because so much more fourth-century information survives: many speeches given in the *ekklēsiā* and in law-courts from cases arising from action in the *ekklēsiā*; the inscribed records of Athenian decision-making; and the systematic discussion of the constitution in the *Constitution of the Athenians* written as part of a research project under Aristotle's direction. As a result, we know a great deal in detail about fourth-century democracy. Since Athenian democracy was not static, but continually revised its own rules, we need to be extremely careful not to assume that what we find to be the case in the fourth century was in every respect identical in the fifth.

The *ekklēsiā* and the Council

6.7 Two accounts of debates in the *ekklēsiā*, though neither of them is from an unbiased source, give a good impression of the immediacy of political proceedings in Athens and introduce some of the most important features of the democracy. The first relates to events of 406 towards the close of the Peloponnesian War, when against the run of events Athens won the sea-battle of Arginoussai (1.80). Victory, however, was marred by the fact that Athenian survivors had not been picked up. This prompted Therāmenēs, a man of oligarchic sympathies and himself liable to blame for not picking up the survivors, to institute proceedings against the overall commanders (the *stratēgoi*) for dereliction of duty. An *ekklēsiā* was held at which the commanders were permitted to speak, though more briefly than the law allowed, in their own defence. They claimed that rescue had been made impossible by a violent storm, and they offered to produce witnesses to that effect:

> With such arguments they were on the point of convincing the *ekklēsiā*; many citizens were standing up and offering to go bail for them. However, it was decided that the matter should be adjourned to another meeting of the *ekklēsiā* – for by then it was late and it would have been impossible to count votes – and that the *boulē* should draft a motion as to what sort of trial the men should have . . .
>
> Then came the meeting of the *ekklēsiā*, at which the Council (*boulē*) presented its motion on the proposals of Kallixenos [a supporter of Therāmenēs]: 'Resolved that, since speeches in accusation of the *stratēgoi* and speeches of the *stratēgoi* in their own defence have been heard at the previous *ekklēsiā*, all the Athenians do now proceed to hold a ballot by tribes; that for each tribe there be two urns; that in each tribe a herald proclaim that whoever thinks the *stratēgoi* did wrong in failing to rescue those who won the victory in the naval battle shall cast his vote in the first urn; whoever thinks contrary, in the second urn; and that, if it be decided that they did wrong, they be punished with death and handed over to the Eleven, and their property be confiscated, and a tithe thereof belong to the Goddess [Athēnē].'
>
> . . . Next a summons was served on Kallixenos for having made an unconstitutional proposal; Euryptolemos . . . and a few others were the sponsors. Some of the people showed their approval, but the great mass shouted out that it was monstrous if the people were not allowed to do whatever they pleased . . . Then some of the *prutaneis* [the standing committee] declared that they would not put the motion to the vote, since it was illegal. At this Kallixenos again mounted the rostrum and made the same complaint against them as had been made against Euryptolemos, and the crowd shouted that if they refused to put the motion to the vote they should be prosecuted. This terrified the *prutaneis*, and all agreed to put the motion except Sōkratēs . . . who said he would do nothing contrary to law.
>
> Euryptolemos then rose and spoke in defence of the *stratēgoi* . . . After making this speech, he moved that the men should be tried in accordance with the decree of Kannōnos, each of them separately. The *boulē*'s motion,

however, was that judgment should be passed on all of them together by a single vote. When there was a show of hands to decide between the rival motions, they decided at first in favour of Euryptolemos' proposal; but when Meneklēs (under oath) alleged the proposal was illegal, there was a fresh vote, and the *boulē*'s motion was approved. They then voted on the eight *stratēgoi* who had taken part in the battle. The vote went against them, and the six who were in Athens were executed. Not long afterwards, however, the Athenians repented and voted that preliminary plaints be lodged against those who had deceived the people. (Xenophōn, *Hellēnika* 1.7.7–35)

6.8 Sixty-seven years later, Athens was at war with King Philip II of Makedōn (1.101–6). Athens had once been an ally of Philip, by the terms of a peace which had been concluded between them in 346. But under the influence of Dēmosthenēs, above all, the Athenians had been persuaded that Philip meant Athens harm and they had declared war on him again. One evening in November 339, news reached Athens that Philip had seized the town of Elateia in central Greece and so was menacing Athens. This is how Dēmosthenēs nine years later described the scene:

> It was evening when the messenger arrived for the *prutaneis* with the news that Elateia had fallen. They were in the middle of supper but rose at once, cleared the stalls in the market-place and burnt the wicker screens, while others sent for the *stratēgoi* and summoned the trumpeter. The whole city was soon in an uproar. At dawn next day the *prutaneis* summoned the *boulē* to the *bouleutērion* while you all made your way to the *ekklēsiā*; the whole body of citizens had taken their places before the *boulē* could proceed to business or propose a motion. Subsequently, when the *boulē* had arrived and the *prutaneis* had reported the news they had received, the messenger was introduced and told his tale; the herald then put the question 'Who wishes to speak?' No one came forward. He put the question again a number of times, but there was still no response, though all the *stratēgoi* were there and all the active politicians, and though our native land was crying aloud for someone to speak for her salvation. It was I who answered her call on that day, and came forward to address you. (Dēmosthenēs, *On the Crown* 18.169)

6.9 As these two passages indicate, the body responsible for managing decision-taking was the *boulē* (Council of 500) and its standing committee (the *prutaneis*). But the *ekklēsiā* (Assembly) was the body which expected, and was expected, to take all major decisions. The *ekklēsiā* when summoned (*ekklēsiā* means a body that is 'called out') gathered on the Pnyx hill to the south-west of the *agorā*, the civic centre of Athens (2.26–7, 29). The meeting-place on the Pnyx was remodelled twice in the classical period, with a change in the direction of the speaker at the end of the fifth century, and a significant enlargement in the second half of the fourth century. Until that enlargement, the Pnyx held about 6,000 people. A remark reported in Thucydides (*Peloponnesian War* 8.72.1) by a speaker arguing in favour of restricting the franchise has sometimes been taken to indicate that the *ekklēsiā* was poorly

6.2 The Pnyx hill, west of the Akropolis and *agorā*, where the Athenian Assembly met.

attended in the fifth century; but at least in the fourth century (see below 6.13) it seems generally to have been full – votes on significant matters involving individuals required a quorum of 6,000. In the fifth century, the *ekklēsiā* made laws as well as decisions of policy (decrees, *psēphismata*); but after the restoration of democracy in 403, the function of passing general laws (*nomoi*) was delegated to a smaller body of Lawmakers (*nomothetai*) drawn from the panel of 6,000 jurors (see below 6.40).

6.10   By the 320s, the *ekklēsiā* held four stated meetings in each of the ten civil months. It is not known whether this prescribed number was already laid down in the fifth century. The first meeting of the four was called the 'sovereign' (*kūria*) *ekklēsiā*, at which the grain supply, national defence and the continuation of officials in office had always to be discussed. Emergency meetings could be called at need. The *ekklēsiā* always met early in the day, emergency or not. Aristophanēs in *Acharnians* (425) describes how loiterers in the *agorā* were herded in with a red-dyed rope by the state police force of 300 Scythian slaves who were in charge of public order. The credentials of the participants were checked, order was kept by the Scythians, purification

6.3 A model of the west side of the *agorā*. The round *tholos*, where the *prutaneis* stayed, on the left was built in the fifth century, the old and new Council chambers immediately to its right date to either end of the fifth century, and to the fifth century also belong the two winged *stoai,* right of centre, and the Hephaisteion on the hill above. But the buildings in the foreground were added to the *agorā*, filling up the open space in its centre, during the reign of Augustus (30 BC–AD 14).

offerings were made (3.33), a curse on traitors was pronounced, and business began:

> There's a sovereign *ekklēsiā* this morning and the Pnyx here is deserted. They're chattering in the *agorā*, edging this way and that to avoid the red rope. Even the *prutaneis* aren't here yet either. They'll be late and then they'll come jostling each other for the front row like nobody's business, flooding down in throngs. But as for peace they don't care a damn for that. O my city, my city! And I'm always the first to come to the *ekklēsiā* and take my place; and then when I'm alone, I groan and yawn and stretch, fart and don't know what to do, longing for peace, looking out over my *dēmos*. So now I have come quite prepared to shout and interrupt and slang the speakers if any of them says a single word other than on the subject of peace. But here are the *prutaneis* arriving – now that it's noon. (Aristophanēs, *Acharnians* 17ff.).

6.11 In the fifth century, the chairman (*epistatēs*) of the *boulē*'s standing committee of *prutaneis* was also chairman of the *ekklēsiā*. The herald read out the agenda, and the people voted whether to discuss the items. If they wished to do so, the herald proclaimed, 'Who wishes to speak?' Speakers mounted the rostrum (*bēma*), and after the speeches a vote was taken by show of hands (hence Aiskhylos' *dēmou kratousa kheir* (see 6.3)). Once a matter reached the *ekklēsiā*, any citizen present could speak, but it was the *boulē* which determined the matters to be discussed and voted on at the *ekklēsiā*. But the *ekklēsiā* could ask the *boulē* to put a particular matter on its next agenda.

6.12   The prior deliberation (*probouleusis*) of matters on the *ekklēsiā*'s agenda was the *boulē*'s most basic function. The *boulē* normally made a proposal about the matter for discussion (*probouleuma*), as in the Xenophōn passage (6.7), although sometimes it simply forwarded an issue without suggesting an answer. The *ekklēsiā* was free to amend any proposal made by the *boulē*, or to replace the *boulē*'s suggested answer with a quite different one. Many decrees survive on stone record amendments, which usually add minor details to a *probouleuma* approved by the *ekklēsiā*, but occasionally quite alter the implications of the decree. There was never any question of the *boulē*'s being able to dictate to the *ekklēsiā*: here, as elsewhere, the *ekklēsiā* was sovereign. Part of the decision was always whether to inscribe the decree – and it is from surviving inscriptions on flat stone slabs (*stēlai*) that we can trace in detail the way in which the relationship between *boulē* and *ekklēsiā* worked out in practice, and can identify at least some of those who took part in the debates.

6.13   Patterns of participation in Athenian politics seem to have changed in various ways between the fifth and the fourth century. These changes were partly a matter of wealthy men based in Athens itself becoming less dominant among those who were politically active (holders of offices, etc.). But there was also a change in the approach to attracting citizens to the *ekklēsiā*: in place of the 'stick' represented by the red rope, the Athenians tried the 'carrot'. Around 400, pay for attendance at the *ekklēsiā* was first introduced to compensate, partially, for loss of working time; by 392, it had been raised twice, to three obols; and by the 320s, it was up to a *drakhmē*, with a *drakhmē* and a half for a sovereign *ekklēsiā* (see 6.10), which was more or less the average day's wage.

6.14   The task of addressing the *ekklēsiā* of 6,000 people in the open air was clearly both daunting and physically demanding. It would not be surprising if many ordinary Athenians considered themselves not to be up to such a task. But the evidence from fifth-century decree amendments suggests that men who were not otherwise much involved in affairs (that is, men of whom we otherwise know nothing) did get up, address the *ekklēsiā*, and persuade it to adopt minor or even significant changes to the policy suggested by the *boulē*. Occasionally, those who proposed amendments did so with a claim to be experts in the matter in question. For example, when the Athenians attempted to institute the giving of first-fruits to the Eleusinian deities (6.80; cf. 3.50) by Greek communities in general, Lampōn, a seer, attempted to

6.4 *Ostraka* cast against Kīmōn and Themistoklēs in the 470s can be seen to have been inscribed on joining sherds of the same pot.

amend this in various technical ways (ML 73). Significantly, the people decided to refer his suggestions back to the *boulē* to be further discussed at the next *ekklēsiā*.

6.15 Displays of expertise in fact seem to have had little place in the *ekklēsiā*. Xenophōn, in *Memorābilia* 3.6, reports a conversation in which Sōkratēs scares one Glaukōn off a career in politics by pointing out to him everything that anyone ought to know who set himself up as an adviser to the Athenian people. But here, as elsewhere in *Memorābilia*, the view which Sōkratēs expresses is rational, but at odds with prevailing practice. It is striking that few of the speeches delivered to the *ekklēsiā* which are recorded in historians or survive in the works of orators deploy detailed, expert knowledge. The major speeches in the *ekklēsiā* attempted to persuade the people either that what was being proposed was in the interests of the city or that it was not. The arguments about the city's interests did not rest on technical details, but on a view of how a city of Athens' power, wealth, and self-image ought to act. The debate which Thucydides recorded over whether to launch an expedition against Sicily in 415 is highly revealing here. The Athenians made use of the expertise of Nīkiās to help them decide the appropriate scale for the expedition; but they rejected Nīkiās' conclusion that they should not undertake the enterprise in the first place. Nīkiās also wanted to settle the details of the expedition not in the *ekklēsiā* but in discussion with fellow officers. This suggests that it was normal for the people to leave to the military or other appropriate officials the details of how to execute a policy which had been decided upon by the *ekklēsiā*.

6.16 Persuasiveness in the *ekklēsiā* no doubt demanded rhetorical skill, as well as a stentorian voice (cf. 8.17–20), but this did not limit participation to a few. For example, the policy of Kleōn over what to do with the citizens of

Mytilēnē was overturned by the *ekklēsiā* after a speech by Diodotus, a man otherwise unknown. That is unlikely to have been by chance: even on big occasions, the previously unheard voice could turn a debate. Those Athenians who spoke regularly became known as the *rhētores* (orators) or *hoi politeuomenoi* (the politicians), and it was not always an advantage to be part of this definable group within the citizen body. But a man who spoke too often could find his audience bored and resistant. At best they might come to ignore him, at worst they would write his name on an *ostrakon* (potsherd) the next time there was an ostracism (1.31; 4.12; cf. 5.39). Periklēs is said deliberately to have limited his appearances in the *ekklēsiā*, reserving himself for the big occasions. In the fifth century, there are some signs that the Athenians were inclined to listen most intently to men who had proved themselves outside the *ekklēsiā*. Alkibiadēs claimed the right to be heard on the basis of his Olympic chariot victories; more logically the *stratēgoi* were frequently also *rhētores* as well as military and naval commanders. This was, for example, part of the basis for Periklēs' influence with the *ekklēsiā*. But in the fourth century, the age of the specialist, a division of function hardened between *rhētores* like Dēmosthenēs (see fig. 1.16), who was never a *stratēgos*, and semi-professional commanders (cf. 6.25; 7.29).

6.17   *Rhētores* spoke in the *ekklēsiā* as individuals or leaders of small groups of like-minded politicians. In the direct democracy of Athens, there were no political parties, with stated policies, as we understand them. The practice of some ancient writers of referring to political groups as 'those around so-and-so' reflects the way in which, within the informal groupings, certain men will have been the most persuasive speakers and hence their spokesmen. Since most of the leaders prominent up to the 420s came from families with a distinguished ancestry, it seems that in the fifth century aristocratic traditions still counted for something in leadership, but these became increasingly weakened. The career of Kleōn, a non-aristocrat whose inherited fortune came from slave-run manufacture rather than landowning, marked something of a turning-point (1.58). A new vocabulary seems to have been formed to refer to the phenomenon of popular leaders: both the phrase 'champion [*prostatēs*] of the people' and the term 'demagogue' (*dēmagōgos*) are first deployed in late fifth-century texts. Thucydides reserved 'demagogue' for Kleōn, but used 'champion of the people' more widely in discussions of politics both at Athens and in other cities. *Dēmagōgos* means literally 'leader of the *dēmos*', and in as far as the Athenian democracy was government by mass meeting, leaders were an indispensable part of the democratic structure. But when he called Kleōn and others like him 'demagogues', Aristophanēs intended to imply that they were mis-leaders of the People, who pandered to the *ekklēsiā*'s baser whims. Thucydides explicitly identified competition over who would be 'champion of the people' as the source of the policy errors which led to Athens' defeat in the Peloponnesian War.

6.18   When we read Thucydides' account of the great debates in the Athenian *ekklēsiā*, we might well wonder how many hours meetings lasted. But most of the business of the *ekklēsiā* did not concern major military expeditions, or the fate of a rebellious ally. Even in the fifth century, most of the business concerned relatively uncritical issues: decisions about alliances which had no immediate military implications; the honouring of individuals who had been and could be expected to continue to be useful to Athens in one way or another; or decisions to go ahead with religious initiatives (e.g. building projects in sanctuaries, or alterations to the regulations concerning a cult or its festivals). In the fourth century, when the making of general rules (and setting up a new priesthood, for example, would count as a general rule) was assigned to the *nomothetai*, decisions about honouring individuals became even more dominant. No doubt the relative triviality of the matter under discussion was not always reflected in the brevity of the proceedings, but it seems that normal meetings usually occupied less than a full day. Rain could interrupt proceedings; and because travel by sea was so difficult during the winter, the amount of business brought to Athens at that time must have been fairly small. Meetings between November and February will probably have been shorter than those at other times of the year. Comparative evidence from the Cantons of Switzerland today suggests that it is perfectly possible for 6,000 people, all with the right to speak, to discuss and to vote, by a show of hands, on a dozen motions in the space of two to four hours.

6.19   The efficiency of meetings of the *ekklēsiā* depended crucially on how well business had been prepared by the *boulē*. In view of this, it is striking that the *boulē* was made up in such a way as to prevent its members becoming real experts; presumably the Athenians did not want it to acquire political power independent of the *ekklēsiā*'s control. *Bouleutai* ('councillors') (s. *bouleutēs*) had to be Athenian citizens and aged thirty or over. They were elected by lot (according to a quota system which gave a fixed number of places to each deme), served for one year at a time, and could not serve more than twice in all. They met in the Council House (*bouleutērion*) in the *agorā* every day except for festival days, and the public could observe their proceedings. Some time before 411, when the *boulē* was temporarily abolished by the oligarchic counter-revolution, pay was introduced for *bouleutai* in accordance with the democratic principle that no citizen should be debarred from participating in government by poverty. We do not know how much the pay was then, but it was probably not less than the three obols paid to jurymen (6.41).

6.20   The deme quotas for *bouleutai* were organised in such a way as to ensure that the 500 *boulē* members consisted of fifty men from each of the ten 'tribes' (*phūlai*), artificial divisions of the citizen body. This tribal system was a democratic innovation by Kleisthenēs and replaced the four ancient kinship tribes, which had been dominated by leading aristocratic families (see 1.25). The number of *bouleutai* from each deme varied with the size of the deme: the lowest number was one, the highest twenty-two. From the way in which prominent politicians are found on the *boulē* in what are particularly crucial years, it seems likely that the number of men who put their names into the hat in a deme often did not much exceed the number of places that had to be filled. It has been calculated that more than half of Athenians must have ended up serving on the *boulē* at some point in their lives. Certainly Sōkratēs, who claims to have kept out of public life, still served on the *boulē*, as we have seen (6.7)

6.21 The civil calendar was divided up into ten 'months' or prytanies (as opposed to the twelve of the sacred calendar according to which the dates of festivals, and the deadlines of ordinary life (such as paying off debts), were calculated). So each 'prytany' lasted 35 or 36 days. The fifty councillors from each of the ten tribes took it in turns to be the *boulē*'s standing committee of *prutaneis* for the 'prytany', and the prytany was known from the name of the tribe which provided the *prutaneis* (see 6.7–8). In the fifth century, the *epistatēs* ('chairman') of the *prutaneis* was selected daily, again by lot, and could serve as such only once. Given that there were fifty *prutaneis* and 36 days to a prytany, there was therefore a better than 70 per cent chance of each member of the *boulē* having to serve as *epistatēs*. In the fourth century, an additional sub-division of the *boulē* was created known as the *proedroi*, made up of one man from each tribe chosen by lot. It was the *proedroi* who then took charge when the *ekklēsiā* met, so that the conduct of *ekklēsiā* business did not fall into the hands of members of a single tribe.

6.22 So far as our evidence goes, the *boulē*'s chief function was to be the steering committee of the *ekklēsiā*. It could not decide policy, but the steer which it gave to the *ekklēsiā* determined the course of the debate, even if it could not determine its outcome. Apart from preparing the *ekklēsiā*'s agenda, the *boulē* was essentially an administrative body, seeing to it that the decisions of the *ekklēsiā* were duly carried out. The *boulē*, or rather its various boards and sub-committees (we know of about ten in Aristotle's day) therefore oversaw (often literally) the necessary financial and other transactions and, together with the courts, exercised a general supervision of the responsible officials. Two examples will illustrate. Here are two parts of Aristotle's description of the *boulē*'s responsibilities. The first deals with responsibility for Athens' major military arm, the navy (cf. 7.42), the second with its administration of the disability allowance:

> The *boulē* is in charge of the completed triremes, the tackle stores and the shipsheds, and builds new triremes . . . The triremes are constructed under the supervision of a board of ten members of the *boulē*. The *boulē* inspects all public buildings, and if it decides that someone has committed an offence, it reports him to the people, and hands him over to the jury court if they find him guilty. ([Aristotle], *Constitution of Athens* 46.1–2)

> The *boulē* also examines the disabled. There is a law which orders that the *boulē* must examine men who have less than 300 *drakhmai*'s worth of

property and have some bodily impairment such that they can do no work, and give them two obols a day. A treasurer for them is chosen by lot.
([Aristotle], *Constitution of Athens* 49.2)

Officials (*arkhai*)

6.23 The Athenians reckoned that they had had elected annual officials, known simply as archons (*arkhontes*), since the seventh century (1.17). Repeatedly during the sixth century, the moment of election of the nine archons, chosen from Solōn's top two property groups (*pentakosiomedimnoi* and *hippeis*), had been a moment of tension and political conflict. From Kleisthenēs' reforms on, the power and prestige of the archons were progressively diminished. The chief *arkhōn* continued to give his name to the civil year (for example, the year we call 403/2 was referred to by Athenians as 'the archonship of Eukleidēs'). But in 501 the new office of *stratēgos* began to take over some of the archon's functions; in 487 archons ceased to be elected but were chosen instead by the democratic device of the lot; finally, in 458/7, the archonship was thrown open officially to the third of Solōn's property groupings, the *zeugītai*; and, at least in the fourth century, even the *thētes*, the lowest property grouping, could in practice hold the office.

6.24 From 501, ten *stratēgoi* were elected (one from each of the ten new tribes) to serve various military functions (though they soon became important politically too). This made relations with the old office of the war *arkhōn* (*polemarkhos*) difficult. The ambiguity was neatly exposed, and cleverly manipulated, after the battle of Marathōn in 490. Miltiadēs, the prime mover of Athens' famous victory, was a *stratēgos*, but the war *arkhōn* Kallimakhos played a crucial role in taking the decision to attack, and it was he who had an expensive memorial set up to him as if he had been in undisputed overall command of the army (1.29–30). Kallimakhos is the last polemarch we know to have made any impact on Athenian military history: it was as *stratēgoi* that Themistoklēs, Kīmōn and Periklēs exercised military and political influence.

6.25 The combination of political and military leadership roles in the figure of the *stratēgos* lasted from Marathōn to the Peloponnesian War, but with that war came a further change. Athens' leading general Dēmosthenēs (not to be confused with the orator, his fourth-century namesake) is not known to have exercised any political leadership, and many of the political leaders made little or no direct contribution to military affairs. Kleōn did act as *stratēgos*, but at first almost by accident. Further, although he was capable of selecting his own military advisers well (as at Pylos), his own military leadership capacities seem to have been rather limited (1.63–7). Nīkiās was almost the last to achieve success both as *stratēgos* and as politician, but he failed to persuade the Athenians in the most famous *ekklēsiā* debate in which he took part (above 6.15). In the fourth century, the distinction between the *stratēgoi* and the politicians became absolute, e.g. Dēmosthenēs the fourth-century *rhētōr* was never a *stratēgos*, and yet his authority over the *ekklēsiā* and law-courts was unparalleled, whereas Phokiōn was *stratēgos* forty-five times but had little influence in the *ekklēsiā*.

6.26　Unlike almost all Athenian *arkhai* under the democracy, the *stratēgoi* were appointed by election (by the *ekklēsiā*) and not by lot. The Athenians had the sense not to sacrifice efficiency to democratic principle in an era when they were at war three years in every four. Similarly, unlike all other *arkhai*, the *stratēgoi* could hold office as often as the electorate wished, and in successive years as well. Periklēs, for example, was *stratēgos* continuously between 443 and 429. The number of *stratēgoi* who served for anything like that length of time was very small, however, and turnover among the ten *stratēgoi* was high. Being *stratēgos* could be a risky business, too, since the Athenians held their generals responsible for military failure. Thucydides the historian was exiled for arriving at Amphipolis too late to save it from Brasidas' assault (1.66); the generals put on trial after the successful sea-battle at Arginoussai were executed (6.7); and even the great Periklēs was fined (and perhaps deposed from office) in 430 (cf. 4.9–10).

6.27　The fining of Periklēs illustrates another cardinal principle of the democracy, that all officials should be responsible to the people. From highest to lowest, all Athenian *arkhai* had to hand in accounts (*euthūnai*) for scrutiny at the end of their usually annual term of office. This check ('audit' is the technical term) was held in two stages. First, any financial accounts were examined by thirty Reckoners (*logistai*, a subcommittee of the *boulē*); then it was open to anyone who wished to bring a charge of misconduct. In this way the Athenian people kept control of the executive and administrative branches of government.

6.28　With the exception of the *stratēgoi*, other high-ranking military officials, and the *Hellēnotamiai* (treasurers overseeing imperial expenditure in the fifth century), all officials were selected by lot (cf. 4.3). Only the archonship and the office of the Ten Treasurers of Athēnē had a property qualification attached to them, and even here in the fourth century the poorest Athenians could stand for the archonship (cf. 6.23, 38). Otherwise the qualifications were only that one should be thirty or over and a citizen of good standing. A candidate had to undergo a preliminary scrutiny (*dokimasiā*) that tested his standing in the community. The beginning of the passage where Aristotle lists the questions put in the *dokimasiā* has been quoted in 5.10; the remainder runs as follows:

> . . . then [they ask] whether he treats his parents well, pays his taxes, and has performed the required military service. When these questions have been put, the candidate is required to call witnesses. When he has produced his witnesses, the question is put: 'Does anyone wish to bring a charge against this man?' If an accuser appears, the accusation and defence are heard, and then the matter is decided by show of hands in the *boulē* or (if the *boulē's* decision is appealed against) by a ballot in the jury-court. If no accuser appears, the vote is held immediately. ([Aristotle], *Constitution of Athens* 55.3–4)

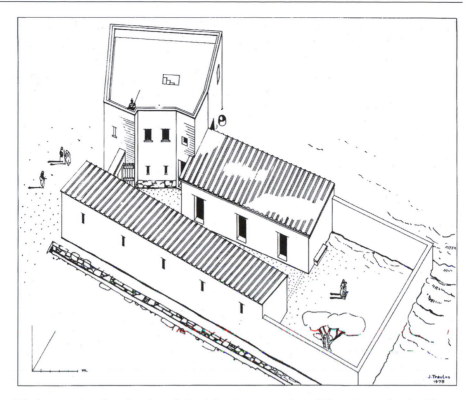

6.5 A reconstruction drawing of the Athenian state prison. Sōkratēs was detained here before his execution and it is here that Plato's *Kritōn* and *Phaidōn* are set.

Candidates who survived this ordeal proceeded to take their oath of office standing on a particular block of stone in the *agorā* (see 2.33).

6.29   Athens lacked a bureaucracy in the modern sense, in that she had no permanent civil servants beyond a very small number of public slaves (5.63). But
she did have a relatively huge number of officials in post every year. In the
second half of the fifth century, according to [Aristotle's] *Constitution of
Athens*, there were 700 officials with domestic responsibilities, and up to the
same number whose duties lay outside Attikē in the Athenian empire. This
figure for fifth-century domestic officials has been thought too high, because
Athens apparently had more in the fourth century, and yet Aristotle lists only
some 350 for his day. However, when the (incomplete) evidence of contemporary official inscriptions is taken into account, Aristotle's listing is seen to
be only partial, and there may well have been 600 to 700 officials in his day.
If we add in both those officials who were not technically described as *arkhai*
(because they were not appointed directly by or responsible directly to the
People) and the 500 *bouleutai*, then out of a citizen population of some
30,000 in the 320s no fewer than 5 per cent of those of the required minimum
age will have been involved in government in some way each year. The per-
centages would have been similar in 431 (almost twice as many officials out

6.6 Official Athenian weight, inscribed with a symbol (this one has a knucklebone, other weights have a tortoise or a shield) to indicate the weight involved.

of a citizen population around twice as large), but even greater in the last years of the Peloponnesian War. So Athens easily satisfied Aristotle's criterion of citizenship in a democracy, that all citizens should have the chance of filling official posts in turn.

6.30 The titles and duties of all Athenian officials cannot be listed here; in any case, most were relatively minor and indeed part-time. But some were individually important. Next to the *stratēgoi* in importance were the nine archons. The 'eponymous' *arkhōn* dealt with state festivals and family matters, and gave his name to the year. The king *arkhōn* supervised the religious life of the city. After Ephialtēs' reforms the polemarch, despite his name, was a civilian official in charge of lawsuits involving metics and foreigners (6.38). The other six archons, known as *thesmothetai*, organised the state's administration of justice and themselves presided over the various jury-courts.

6.31 Below the archons came 'the Eleven', officials responsible for executing legal punishments and maintaining the state prison (*desmōtērion*) (cf. 3.36). To keep order in the city, they were assisted by the 300 Scythian archers, but the apprehension of criminals was largely left to private individuals (6.42). Then there were the various treasurers, most notably the *Hellēnotamiai* and the Ten Treasurers of Athēnē already mentioned. Religious treasurers also included such important men as the *epistatai Eleusīnothen*, who were the financial administrators of the Eleusinian Mysteries. Among the other treasurers we know, for example, of the Treasurers of the People, who managed the annual allowance made for public expenses like the publication of decrees. Especially important in the fourth century was the manager of the 'theoric' ('spectating') fund, which enabled poor Athenians to attend festivals.

6.32 Of the minor officials, we may mention the *astunomoi*, whose job was to see that streets and highways were kept clear and clean; the ten *agorānomoi*, who

6.7 A range of official Athenian measures of capacity, with the first letters of 'dēmosion', 'public' visible in three cases.

supervised markets, collecting fees from stallholders and checking for adulterated goods; the *metronomoi*, who checked weights and measures by the official standards in the Mint and the *tholos*; and finally the *grammateis*, who acted as secretaries to the *boulē*, the *ekklēsiā*, and the *thesmothetai*. In the absence of anything like a foreign office, diplomatic relations were conducted through heralds (*kērukes*) and envoys (*presbeis*). These important figures need a little further discussion.

Heralds (*kērux*, pl. *kērukes*)

6.33 The *kērux* in Homeric times was an arm of the king, maintaining order at meetings, making proclamations, carrying messages, even serving wine at meals. He was felt to be under Hērmēs' protection. In classical Athens, the *kērux* continued to possess special status and was considered to be under divine protection. *Kērukes* were appointed by the *ekklēsiā*, paid for out of the public funds and kept at the public expense. In general the presence of a *kērux* indicated that the state was acting in an official capacity. Their duties were wide-ranging. At home, they summoned and controlled meetings of both the *boulē* and *ekklēsiā*, and were empowered to accompany official deputations (e.g. when the Eleven went to arrest someone). *Kērukes* could also be sent abroad on the authority of the *boulē* or the *ekklēsiā*. In the following decree, dating from 425/4, they were being sent to ensure that Athens received its proper tribute:

> The *boulē* is to appoint eight *kērukes* to summon representatives from the cities, and ten *taktai* (managers, literally 'arrangers') to list and assess the

cities liable to tribute . . . The *kērukes* work under the orders of the *taktai* [for their route] and the *ekklēsiā* [for what they are to say]. (ML 69)

But note that they had power only to send a message, never to negotiate.

6.34 Abroad, the *kērux* had a vital role to play in the declaration and cessation of combat. He declared war, he asked for a truce, he opened peace negotiations. In such situations, the *kērux* had to be able to rely upon the immunity which his office gave him. In general a *kērux* was regarded as under the protection of the gods, and his immunity was respected.

Envoys (*presbeis*, s. *presbeutēs*, lit. 'elders')

6.35 *Presbeis*, by contrast, enjoyed no *specific* immunity. Chosen in general from the wealthy and well-connected citizens, they would frequently enjoy private ties as *xenoi* with citizens of the *polis* to which they were sent. The word *presbeis* implies that they were originally the elders of the state (in Athens the minimum age was normally 50). Between states at war, *kērukes* would normally go first to secure agreement for *presbeis* to be sent – which would impose a moral obligation on the receiving state – or an envoy might be led by a *kērux*, whose task would be to secure safe passage. The *presbeis* would then carry out the negotiations, having been entrusted with powers to make agreements within certain limits.

6.36 Spartē regularly sent three *presbeis*, but the number sent by other states might vary. It all depended either on the importance attached to the mission, or on the need for a variety of political views to be represented. Serving on a diplomatic mission was a matter of prestige, and a service to the state in which one could take pride. *Presbeis* were selected by the state and given token public funds (one *drakhmē* per day) for the journey, but considerable private expense was likely to be incurred, and even more likely to be recouped one way or another, e.g. by accepting gifts (bribes). Aristophanēs in *Acharnians* mocked the luxurious life of an envoy to Persia.

6.37 It was a serious matter to mistreat *presbeis* and normally, even if their arrival was unwelcome or they were dismissed, they would expect simply to be given an ultimatum to leave. But if the diplomatic situation changed rapidly, *presbeis* could be put into considerable danger. In 378 a sudden attack on the Peiraieus by Sphodriās (1.95), a Spartan commander in Boiōtiā, embarrassed the three Spartan *presbeis* who happened to be present in Athens:

> Now it happened that there were ambassadors of the Spartans in Athens at the house of Kalliās, the Spartan *proxenos* ('honorary consul', cf. 6.87), Etymoklēs, Aristolokhos, and Okyllos; and when the invasion was reported, the Athenians seized them and kept them under guard, believing that they too were concerned in the plot. But they were completely bewildered over the affair and said in their defence that if they had known that an attempt was being made to seize the Peiraieus, they would never have been so foolish as to

put themselves in the power of the Athenians in the city, and, still less, at the house of their *proxenos*, where they would most quickly be found. They said, further, that it would become clear to the Athenians also that the Spartan authorities did not know of this attempt, either. As for Sphodrias, they said they were certain they would hear that he had been executed by the state. So they were judged to be ignorant of the affair and were released. (Xenophōn, *Hellēnika* 5.4.22)

Law-courts

The Areopagus (*Areios Pagos*, Hill of Arēs)

6.38 The Areopagus council, so named from the crag of Arēs where it met (between the Akropolis and the Pnyx), was the oldest permanent organ of the Athenian *polis*. It was made up of all those who had served as *arkhōn* (6.23), and had once had significant political responsibilities. But the loss of prestige of the archons (in favour of *stratēgoi*) affected the Areopagus, and by the reforms of Ephialtēs in 462/1 (1.45) it was reduced to being merely a law-court. Although conservative thinkers in the fourth century proposed a larger role for the Areopagus, and its powers were slightly increased, the strictly political power of the Areopagus was ended in 462/1. Aiskhylos provides a mythical justification for the Areopagus as a homicide court in his *Eumenides* of 458, and that has made some think that he was among those who approved the reforms of Ephialtēs. Aiskhylos has Athēnē at the trial of Orestēs speak as follows:

> Hear now my ordinance, men of Attikē, who pronounce judgement at this first trial ever held for bloodshed. Henceforth, even as now, this court of judges shall abide unto the people of Aigeus for ever. And . . . on this Crag of Arēs Reverence, in the hearts of my citizens, and Fear, her kinsman, shall withhold them from doing wrong . . . And I counsel my citizens to maintain and hold in reverence neither anarchy nor tyranny, nor to banish fear completely from the city. For who among men is righteous that fears nothing? Stand then in just reverence of such majesty . . . This tribunal I do now establish, inviolable by lust of gain, august, quick to avenge, a guardian of the land, vigilant in defence of them that sleep. (Aiskhylos, *Eumenides* 681ff.)

After 462/1, the Areopagus functioned as a court trying cases of deliberate homicide (other forms of homicide were treated by the *ephetai*), of arson and of some forms of sacrilege. For example, it investigated the status of Phanō, illicitly married to the democracy's chief religious official; and it tried men accused of offences related to the sacred olive trees, from whose fruit was pressed the special oil given in magnificent *amphorā*s as prizes at the *Panathēnaia* (3.46). In 403 the Areopagus was entrusted with the supervision of Athens' newly revised law-code in deference to the judicial experience of its members (see above for the judicial functions of the *arkhontes* after 462/1).

The jury-courts (*dikastēria*)

6.39   Aristotle in his *Politics* defined the citizen of a democracy as the man with a share in *krisis* and *arkhai*. The *arkhai* we have already discussed (see 6.23ff.). By *krisis*, Aristotle meant the power to deliver judgement in a court of law. In Athens, as in ancient Greece generally, there was neither in theory nor in practice any separation of powers between 'political' bodies (the *ekklēsiā* and *boulē*) and judicial bodies. When the Athenian People became master of the courts, as [Aristotle] puts it, they became master of the constitution.

6.40   In one sense the Athenians became master of the courts with the reforms of Solōn in the early sixth century (1.20). Solōn established a popular court of appeal against the decisions of officials, which was called the Ēliaiā. After the reforms of Ephialtēs in 462/1, all the various jury-courts were known collectively as the Ēliaiā, but now they were courts of first instance as well as appeal courts, and they were often referred to as *dikastēria*. This is because they were jury-courts staffed by jurors (*dikastai*) who numbered from 201 to 2,501 depending on the case. In the fifth century the juries were selected at need from an annual roll of 6,000 jurors, in the fourth century from those who put themselves forward. Although the *dikastai* were indeed 'jurors' in as far as they had to swear an oath – the so-called 'heliastic oath' – that they would pass fair judgements, they were quite different from a modern jury in that they received no direction from any judge (effectively there were no judges) and they had no opportunity to confer as a group before casting their vote.

6.41   From the middle of the fifth century on, jurors were paid a small allowance (two and later three obols, about half a day's wage) for every day they sat. It has been estimated that, when allowance is made for festivals, *ekklēsiai* and so on, they might sit on between 150 and 200 days in the year (3.41). In principle, such a payment made it possible for any Athenian to serve as a juror, but in practice men based in Athens and men with few other calls on their time seem to have dominated. If we are to believe Aristophanēs' extended satire on the courts, the *Wasps* of 422, some elderly Athenians had a passion to serve in the Ēliaiā (and were very grateful to Kleōn for raising jury pay to 3 obols by 425). Here a slave describes his master's mania:

> He loves it, this juror business; and he groans if he can't sit on the front bench. He doesn't get even a wink of sleep at night, but if in fact he does doze off just for a moment, his mind still flies through the night to the water-clock . . . And by god, if he saw any graffito by the doorway saying 'Dēmos, son of Pyrilampēs, is beautiful', he would go and write beside it, '*kēmos* (the ballot-box) is beautiful' . . .
>
>   Straight after supper he shouts for his shoes, and then off he goes to the court in the early hours and sleeps there, clinging to the court-pillar like a

6.8 Reconstructed model of Athenian official water-clock (*klepsydra*), as used in the law-court to control the time each speaker was given.

limpet. And through bad temper he awards the long line to all the defendants, and then comes home like a bee . . . with wax plastered under his fingernails [because, when the jurors had to decide between penalties, they were given a wax tablet on which to mark a longer or shorter line, the former indicating the heavier penalty, cf. 6.45, 52]. And because he's afraid that some day he may run short of voting-pebbles, he keeps a whole beach in his house. That's how mad he is . . .' (Aristophanēs, *Wasps* 87–112)

6.42 In modern legal systems, the agents of the state are the state prosecutors; but in Athens, there was no Criminal Prosecution Service or Justice Department

6.9 A scene of Athenian citizens casting votes, on a red-figure cup of the second quarter of the fifth century.

of Public Prosecutions, no 'case for the Crown', and no investigatory police force. If the state was wronged, or the community or gods were attacked, there was no state body to initiate proceedings for reparation or punishment in the courts. That was left to private initiative, and the state depended on 'anyone willing' (*ho boulomenos*) to bring a case. In other words, if there were agents of the state, they were actually the jurors, and speakers in the courts often appeal to the jurors as judges as much as citizens in any case. The Athenians distinguished between offences where a prosecution could be brought by any volunteer (*graphē*, 'writ', cf. *graphō* 'I write') and offences where the injured party was in a position to seek redress in court himself, and where he alone had the right so to seek redress (*dikē*, 'suit'). *Graphai* (pl.) included such offences as desertion (injuring the state), impiety and temple robbery (injuring the gods), *hubris* and wrongful imprisonment (preventing the victim from seeking redress himself). *Dikai* included not only suits for damages, breaches of various sorts of agreement, cases of wounding with malice aforethought, slander and false witness, but also, rather surprisingly, murder. This was because murder was regarded as injuring not just the person who lost their life but the whole kin group. Some offences might be prosecuted either by a *graphē* or a *dikē*: so a victim of violent attack might prosecute in a *dikē* for battery or wounding with malice aforethought, or in a *graphē* for *hubris*. *Graphai* attracted more public attention, and a prosecutor in a *graphē* who did not obtain one fifth of the votes was liable to a fine of 1,000 *drakhmai*. Some particular varieties of *graphē*, however, notably the procedure known as *phasis* ('denunciation'), which was used in particular to prosecute breaches of commercial laws, rewarded the prosecutor with a share of the fine.

6.43   One particular *graphē* illustrates the logic of the system well. The *graphē paranomōn*, ('writ concerning illegal proposals') could be issued against any speaker in the *ekklēsiā* who had introduced a proposal held to be in conflict with the law (cf. 6.7). It could be brought by 'anyone who wished', and seems to have been intended as a constitutional safeguard against attacks on the democracy. It is notable that its first attested use is in 415, a time of crisis and rumours of subversion (1.73). But it could also be employed as a weapon to attack a rival politician. In both these uses, it went some way to replacing ostracism, which was used for the last time to banish the populist politician Hyperbolos (on whom see 1.58) in 416. Once the writ had been issued, the motion, law or decree at issue was suspended, and its proposer brought before a jury-court. If the proposer was found guilty of proposing an unconstitutional law or decree, the law or decree was automatically cancelled, and the proposer fined.

6.44   In a modern state, a second chamber (such as the British House of Lords) generally reviews the decisions of the first chamber, and the Head of State may have ultimate veto on acts of parliament. In Athens, it was the People-as-jurors who sat in judgement on the People-in-*ekklēsiā* in their role as decision-makers; but it was only the proposer of the illegal decree, as well as the decision, that stood to be condemned – not the People-in-*ekklēsiā* who passed the decree in the first place (!). For the People was sovereign: it could, by definition, do no wrong. Here again we see the cardinal democratic principle of accountability in operation, not for e.g. failing in the performance of public office, but for the single public act of putting a proposal to the *ekklēsiā*. But this also meant that the *graphē paranomōn* became ammunition in the raging competition for political success (cf. 4.2, 12).

6.45   Consider the case of Apollodōros, son of Pāsiōn (cf. 5.70). Apollodōros had been selected by lot as a *bouleutēs* for 349/8, and in 348, at a moment of crisis in the war against Philip, he (in the words of Theomnēstos):

> brought forward in the *boulē* a bill and carried it as a *probouleuma* to the *ekklēsiā*: it proposed that the People should decide whether the funds remaining over from the state's expenditure should be used for military purposes, or for public spectacles. For the laws prescribed that, in time of war, funds remaining over from state expenditures should be devoted to military purposes; and when the voting took place, there was no one who opposed such use. Even now [late 340s], when the matter is mentioned anywhere, it is universally acknowledged that Apollodōros gave the best advice, and was unjustly treated. Your anger should therefore be directed against the man whose arguments deceived the jurors, and not against those he deceived.
>
> This fellow Stephanos indicted the decree as illegal and took the matter to court. He produced false witnesses to slander Apollodōros, saying that he had been a state debtor for twenty-five years, and by making all sorts of

accusations that were irrelevant to the incident he won a verdict against the decree. ([Dēmosthenēs], *Against Neairā* 59.4–6)

The *graphē paranomōn* was one of a number of cases where there was no fixed penalty. Instead, once the jury had found a man guilty, first the prosecution and then the defendant proposed alternative fines. Theomnēstos goes on to explain what happened in this particular case:

> When the jurors were voting to fix the penalty, we begged Stephanos to compromise but he refused; he fixed the amount at fifteen talents with the object of depriving Apollodōros and his children of their civic rights, and causing my sister and all of us the extremest distress and deprivation. For the property of Apollodōros was worth no more than three talents, which made the payment of such a fine quite impossible. Yet failure to pay by the ninth prytany would have doubled the fine; Apollodōros would have been registered as owing thirty talents to the Treasury; his property would have been confiscated by the state and sold; and Apollodōros himself, his wife and children, and all of us would have been reduced to extreme destitution. What is more, his other daughter would have been unable to marry; for who would ever have married a girl without a dowry with a father in debt to the Treasury and without resources? . . . I remain therefore deeply grateful to the jurors in the case for refusing to let Apollodōros be ruined and fixing the fine at a talent, a sum he was able to pay, albeit with difficulty. ([Dēmosthenēs], *Against Neairā* 59.6–8)

6.46 Aristophanēs' juror desperate for a conviction, Apollodōros threatened with economic and social ruin, the courts as an instrument for confounding political enemies – all this suggests colourful courtroom dramas. The presence of bystanders contributed to the drama, and at times there were clearly scenes in court that would be regarded as unseemly in a modern courtroom. Sōkratēs, in Plato's version of the defence speech he gave at his capital trial in 399, is made to appeal to the jurors not to shout him down. Not only was there no judge to direct the jury, but there were no lawyers to represent the litigants. They had to represent themselves, though the richer ones might commission a Lysiās or a Dēmosthenēs to write their speech for them, and they could call upon friends (*synēgoroi*, 'co-speakers') to make further speeches on their behalf (Theomnēstos speaks on behalf of Apollodōros, above). Rules of evidence existed but were not sharply enforced. Witnesses were not cross-examined. Any direction of the jury on points of law had to come from the litigants, and what a litigant claimed about the law stood to be corrected only by the opposing litigant. Jurors no doubt responded to appeals to their emotions and moral prejudices, as well as to hard fact (which anyway was difficult to establish). Finally, trials had to be over the same day; speeches were time-limited (the same for both sides, measured by a water-clock, stopped only when documents were being read out); and having heard them both, the jurors voted on the issue at once.

6.47 As in modern judicial systems, so in Athenian courts, witnesses were important; but as the absence of cross-questioning suggests, they played a rather different role. In the great majority of cases, Athenian witnesses corroborated claims already made by the litigant; they did not provide the material from which the litigant subsequently built his case. While we might think that impartial witnesses would carry more weight than partial ones, the Greeks were well aware of the importance of friends, and knew there was danger in trying to get evidence from someone you did not know, let alone from an enemy (4.13). Much of the evidence given was a matter of support rather than of information. The orator Isaios, who wrote cases particularly for those involved in inheritance disputes, makes the point nicely:

> You all know that when we are acting without concealment and need witnesses, we normally make use of our close relatives and intimate friends as witnesses of such actions; but for the unforeseen and unexpected, we call on anyone who happens to be present. When evidence is needed in court, we have to bring as witnesses persons who were actually present, whoever they are. (Isaios, *On the Estate of Pyrrhos*, 3.19)

6.48 Some classes of people were simply not allowed to give evidence. These included women, children and slaves. In the case of slaves, evidence could be accepted only if it had been extracted under torture. Slaves were rightly thought to be in a peculiarly difficult position when it came to giving evidence, and torture was the institutional way to counter undue partiality or hostility towards an owner. Athenian speakers recognise the problems with this convention, and in fact few instances of slave testimony are known. Since slaves were valuable, few masters would willingly submit to torture and possibly serious maiming a slave with whom they had good relations, while they were unlikely to risk what a slave might say with whom their relations were bad. The rule about torture may thus have had the effect of restricting evidence from such an 'unreliable' source.

6.49 This attitude to witnesses and evidence is best understood in the light of other features of Athenian procedure which seem odd to us – in particular, their extraordinary care over the proceedings before a case came to trial and over the selection of jurors. Before a case ever came to court, the aggrieved party could first present his opponent with his claim in front of witnesses. Misunderstandings might be smoothed out at this stage. If not, private arbitrators could be called in. Both parties agreed on a panel of arbitrators and their terms of reference, and contracted to stand by their decision, which had judicial force. If both these methods failed, a summons was served. The aggrieved party visited the *agorā*, confirmed (to his satisfaction at least) that the law displayed there supported his case, and found out when his type of case was due to be heard. The summons was served orally, and the defendant was told before witnesses to present himself to the appropriate *arkhōn* or judicial board on a stated day. On that day, the *arkhōn* decided whether the case

6.10 Fourth-century Athenian bronze ballots, with a hollow hub for condemnation and a solid one for acquittal. Some of them are inscribed *psēphos dēmosiā* ('public ballot') and have a letter to indicate the court.

6.11 A fourth-century bronze *pinakion* (identity ticket) for one Dēmophanēs of Kēphisiā.

was actionable (that is, whether the offence complained of came under the law in question); if it was, the charge was formally deposed in writing, though the accused could lodge an official objection. A down-payment was made by both parties against costs, which the loser paid in full after the trial. A day was fixed for the preliminary hearing by the *arkhōn*, and a copy of the plaint was displayed publicly in the *agorā*.

6.50 The preliminary hearing seems to have involved some cross-questioning by the prosecution to establish the basis of the case, and it seems to have been possible at this stage for the precise nature of the claim to be modified. Immediately after the preliminary hearing, the case was considered by the public arbitrators. These were drawn by lot from men in their sixtieth year, who had just been released from military obligations. Both sides swore an oath that their case was correct and presented their supporting evidence. A decision might be reached at this stage. If not, all the evidence was sealed up in a box (it would be read out in court) and could not be added to later. The box was deposited with the *arkhōn*, and the matter submitted to public jurisdiction in a jury-court.

6.51 The Athenians seems to have revised the system for selecting jurors on a number of occasions. By the later fourth century, jurors for a particular trial were chosen at the last minute by an allotment machine (*klērōtērion*), which selected jurors at random and distributed them to courts at random. They were drawn from the 6,000 on the jurymen's roll for the year who had taken the oath to abide by the laws (6.40). Each received a ticket with his name on entitling him to serve (the *pinakion*); there was, of course, no guarantee that a juror would be selected to serve. Once selected, and now armed with a lettered ball drawn from an urn, the juror proceeded to the court marked with the corresponding letter. There he handed in his *pinakion*, which he would get back, together with his pay, at the end of the session. In exchange he was given a short rod (*baktērion*) with paint of a certain colour on it, another device for making sure he went to the right court. At the end of the litigants' speeches, jurors were handed their voting tokens; only if they voted did they receive another token, which they exchanged for their three-obol pay.

6.52 How do we explain the Athenian decision to take so much care over pre-trial procedures and over jury selection? Answering that question requires asking another: what did the Athenians think that laws were for? It is easy to assume that the role of the courts was to punish. The Athenian law on damages apparently maintained that there should be simple restitution when the damage had been done accidentally, but double restitution when it had been done deliberately, and the additional fine in this case would seem to be punishment for malevolence. But in the absence of a judge and of jury discussion, Athenian law was not well suited to making the punishment fit the crime in any more subtle manner. In some cases, there was no single statutory penalty, because such a wide variety of offences were covered by a single law (e.g. impiety). As a result, the jury had to choose between the penalty suggested by the prosecutor and that suggested by the defendant. The passage of *Wasps* quoted in 6.41 alludes to this. It was this procedure which led to the execution of Sōkratēs after his own suggested penalty (free meals at public expense!) mocked the court's decision to find him guilty. The simple choice between two alternatives was not well designed to produce sensitivity to the magnitude of the offence. On the other hand, if court actions were seen not as providing appropriate punishment for moral turpitude, but as settling disputes between individuals, most of the peculiarity of these procedures becomes explicable. Limiting witnesses to fellow citizens; giving ample opportunity for arriving at a mutual settlement; ensuring that the case made in court is the one that the other party is expecting; preventing the packing of juries by the friends of one party; making it possible for the party found guilty nevertheless to be offered the penalty they regard as appropriate – all these features make sense where it is settlement of disputes and the social consequences of actions, rather than punishment as such, that are the focus of concern.

6.53 This focus on restoring reasonable relations between disputing parties is reflected in the fact that, in a *dikē*, enforcement of the verdict was left to the individual concerned. Repeated refusal to settle could lead to further suits and eventual loss of full citizen rights (*atīmiā*, see 6.56, 4.12). If the convicted man refused to pay a fine, the successful litigant was allowed to seize property to the stated amount of the fine (cf. 5.27). The *arkhōn* who presided at the trial was bound to see that the jury's decision was enforced if he could, since he was accountable to the People at the end of his term of office. Even so, enforcement was often difficult in practice. Judgement in a *graphē* and sentences of death were attended to by officers of the state (6.31).

6.54   It is a problem in any legal system that making justice available to those with little money or education often allows those who have money to spare and skill in speaking to exploit the courts. Athenians worried about this, and both comedies and law-court speeches are riddled with references to *sukophantai* ('vexatious litigants'). We get a telling caricature of the *sukophantēs* in Aristophanēs' final play, *Wealth* (*Ploutos*) (388):

> *Just Man:* How do you live then, and what on, if you don't *do* anything?
> *Sukophantēs:* I am a supervisor of public affairs; private affairs too. Everything.
> *J.M.:* You? Who put you on to that game?
> *S.:* I do it because I enjoy it.
> *J.M.:* And you call yourself a good citizen, you who break into people's homes and get yourself loathed for meddling with things that are none of your business?
> *S.:* So serving my country to the best of my ability is none of my business, you moron?
> *J.M.:* Then serving one's country means playing the busybody?
> *S.:* Giving one's support to the established laws and stepping in to prevent offences being committed: that's service to one's country.
> *J.M.:* But hasn't the state put jurors on the job precisely for that purpose?
> *S.:* But who is to bring the charges?
> *J.M.:* Anyone who is willing.
> *S.:* Well it's I who am willing. So the government of the country falls to me.
> (Aristophanēs, *Ploutos* 906ff.)

It is very hard to tell how great the problem of vexatious litigation was at Athens. To judge from Aristophanēs' portrayal, the problem was with those who brought prosecutions open to whoever was willing. But in the orators, the term *sukophantēs* is repeatedly applied to prosecutors who were themselves (claiming to be) the injured party. This use of the term as a term of abuse should warn us against measuring the seriousness of the problem from the frequency of the accusation.

6.55   The Athenians were inordinately proud of their respect for law and justice. In Sophoklēs' *Oidipous at Kolōnos* the Athenian founder-hero Thēseus announces to the Theban Kreōn: 'You have come into a *polis* that cultivates justice, and sanctions nothing without law,' and Athenians in the fourth century frequently identified democracy with the rule of law. The Athenians were, in fact, continually developing both their judicial procedures and indeed the content of their laws. In the late fifth century, they undertook a complete revision of the laws, and in the fourth century special procedures

6.12 A fragment of one of the inscriptions recording property (here including various items of furniture) confiscated from those found guilty over the profanation of the Mysteries and mutilation of the Hermai in 415 (see 1.73).

were devised in order to ensure that new laws did not accidentally contradict old ones. Although the Athenians were always claiming that their laws were all 'laws of Solōn', in various particular areas of law we are able to get a measure of how far the Athenian legal system had developed from its origins in the laws of Drakōn and Solōn to the laws of the later fifth and fourth centuries. The law concerned with *atīmiā* brings this out particularly sharply.

6.56   *Atīmiā* means literally deprivation of *tīmē* or acclaim (cf. 4.12). In the sixth and early fifth centuries, to be in a state of *atīmiā* (to be *atīmos*) was equivalent to being an outlaw: the *atīmos* man could be killed or robbed of his property without the possibility of legal redress. Prudence therefore dictated that he exile himself from Attikē. By the end of the fifth century, outlawry had become distinguished from *atīmiā*, and the latter was the less severe penalty of the two. Thus those citizens who were found guilty of sacrilege in 415 (1.73) were sentenced to outlawry, not *atīmiā;* they were executed unless they fled abroad in time, their property was confiscated by the state and sold at public auction.

6.57   *Atīmiā*, on the other hand, did not necessarily entail loss of property or the need to go into exile. All the same, it was the stiffest penalty handed out by the courts short of exile or death, and in its extreme form amounted to political death. For the totally disenfranchised man could not speak in *ekklēsiā* or law-court, hold any public office, act as *bouleutēs* or juror, or enter either temples or the *agorā*. Anyone who saw an *atīmos* man in a prohibited place could arrest him on the spot and present him to the Eleven or the *thesmo-thetai*. Disenfranchisement, moreover, was normally for life, and in particularly grave cases could be applied to the offender's descendants too.

6.58   In 415, Andokidēs suffered partial disenfranchisement for being implicated in the profanation of the Eleusinian Mysteries. This sentence was revoked under the extraordinary general amnesty of 403, the first recorded in human history, but in 399 Andokidēs found himself in the courts again. Here he lists some of the offences for which *atīmiā* was the specified punishment:

> Those who owed money to the treasury; all those who had failed to pass their *euthūnai*; or were guilty of disobeying court orders; or had lost public lawsuits; or had summary fines imposed on them; or after buying tax-collecting privileges had failed to pay the agreed sum; or after acting as guarantors for the treasury had failed to pay – all these had to pay during the ninth prytany, or their debts were doubled and their possessions sold. This was one form of *atīmiā*. But another consisted of those whose persons were disenfranchised, but who retained and enjoyed possession of their property. In this second group were those convicted of embezzlement or bribery. These and their descendants were to be disenfranchised. All those who deserted their post; or were convicted of evading military service or cowardice in the field or avoiding a naval battle or throwing away their shield; or were convicted three times of giving false testimony or claiming falsely to have witnessed a summons, or who misused their parents – all these had their persons disenfranchised, but kept their property. Others again were disenfranchised . . . not totally but partially: for example, soldiers who . . . had stayed in the city at the time of the Four Hundred (411) . . . were not permitted to speak in the *ekklēsiā* of the *dēmos* or be *bouleutai* . . . Others did not have the right to prosecute publicly, others to lay information before an official. For others the specification was not to sail to the Hellespont or to Iōniā, for others [like Andokidēs himself] not to enter the *agorā*. (Andokidēs, *On the Mysteries* 1.73–6)

The *atīmiā* legislation neatly illustrates the inextricable connection between politics and the law with which we began this section.

The public economy

Income and expenditure

6.59   The Athenian state derived its regular income primarily from taxes, fees and fines of various sorts. There was no state budget in the modern sense, but from the middle of the fourth century the Athenians did appoint an official to oversee financial administration. The evidence is scrappy, but we can at least gauge something of the scale of annual income and expenditure.

Thucydides (*Peloponnesian War* 2.13) made Periklēs tell the Athenians in 431 that they had an annual income of 600 talents from the allies. To judge from the extant fragments of the inscribed tribute quota lists, this was too much for the tribute paid by the allies alone, but not impossible for total revenue from the whole empire. Modern scholars have reckoned 400 talents to be a reasonable estimate for revenue internal to Athens at the same date, giving a total annual revenue of about 1,000 talents. But at the end of the Peloponnesian War, Athens lost her empire and all imperial revenues. Although some contributions came to be made by the members of the Second Athenian Confederacy, formed in 378/7, Athens' *external* revenues never again became of major significance in her economy. *Internal* revenue, too, seems to have dropped: it appears that, in 355, internal revenue had plummeted to 130 talents per annum, about a third of the 431 figure. This was derived from harbour and market dues; taxes on metics; occasional taxes on citizen property (*eisphorā*); rents from mining concessions and other leases controlled by the *pōlētai* (sellers); and a host of lesser sources.

The chief elements of state expenditure were pay and maintenance for various officials; for a relatively small number of public slaves; for the cost of maintaining and deploying army and navy; and for the cost of public festivals. Expenditure on pay and maintenance increased markedly after it was first introduced in about 460 to pay jurors. By 411, when it was temporarily abolished, there was also pay for service as *bouleutēs*. In the fourth century, there was pay for attendance at the *ekklēsiā* and certain festivals. The amount of money spent by the state on the fleet and on festivals is hard to judge, since many expenses were imposed directly on the richest Athenians as 'liturgies' (*leitourgiai*).

6.60 Two examples will illustrate the processes whereby the state derived its internal income. The Peiraieus, as we saw (5.58), became the most important commercial centre of the eastern Mediterranean. It acted not only as the import–export centre for Athens but also as a clearing-house for goods passing to and from other states. Not unnaturally, Athens sought to tap this commerce for her own benefit, and one of the chief ways she did so was to levy a 2 per cent tax on the value of goods imported to, or exported from, Attikē. As with all Athenian taxes, the collection of this tax was sold off to the highest bidder. Bidders estimated what 2 per cent of the exports and imports amounted to, reckoned how efficiently they could manage to collect ('farm') the tax, and sought to buy the tax for something under the figure that resulted. The lower their bid, the greater the difference between what they collected and what they paid over to the state. Andokidēs, in his speech *On the Mysteries*, manages to turn his own bid for the tax into an act of public service:

> Agyrrhios, that honest man you know well, had been for two years the chief farmer of the 2 per cent tax. He had won the right to collect it for thirty

> talents . . . [He and his associates], having made a profit of six talents and
> seeing what a profitable business they were on to, formed a syndicate, bought
> off rivals by giving them a share in the profits and again offered thirty talents
> for the tax. As no one was putting in a rival bid, I came forward before the
> *boulē* and outbid them, purchasing the right to collect the tax for thirty-six
> talents . . . So, thanks to me, these men were prevented from sharing out
> among themselves six talents of money that was rightfully yours. (Andokidēs,
> *On the Mysteries* 1.133–4)

6.61 For our second example we look to the leasing of the silver mines in the
Laureion district of south-east Attikē. There had been mining here since as
far back as the bronze age, but production first acquired major economic
significance for Athens with the invention of the Athenian 'owl' coinage in
the late sixth century. The mines were certainly in some sense state-owned, as
is clear from the story of Themistoklēs diverting windfall revenue from the
mines into building the Athenian navy (1.32); but evidence for the way the
mines were managed in the fifth century is scanty. The labour was certainly
provided overwhelmingly by slaves, and some of the richest Athenians had
mining interests. They included the general Nīkiās, who was held to have
1,000 slaves leased out as labour in the mines. For the fourth century, we have
the evidence of inscriptions as well as literary sources. Aristotle specifies that
the *pōlētai* leased out the mines and ratified concessions granted by the *boulē*.
Here are the first half-dozen entries from the only completely surviving
annual record, for 367/6. The lessees are all citizens, and it is worth noting
both the range and the size of the rents paid (scholars dispute the period
which the rent mentioned covered):

> Mines sold during the first prytany, of Hippothontis: (1) *Dexiakon* at Skopiai
> in Napē, the neighbour of which on all sides is Nīkiās of Kydantidai,
> purchaser Kalliās of Sphettos, 20 dr.; (2) *Diakon* at Laureion, the neighbour
> of which, to the east, is the land of Exōpios, to the west, the mountain,
> purchaser Epitelēs from Kerameis, 20 dr.; (3) at *Sounion* on the property of
> the sons of Charmylos, the neighbour of which, on the north, is Kleocritos
> of Aigiliā, on the south, Leukios of Sounion, purchaser Pheidippos of
> Pithos, 20 dr.; (4) *Poseidōniakon* in Napē, one of those on the *stēlē*, on the
> property of Alypetos, the neighbours of which are Kalliās of Sphettos and
> Dioklēs of Pithos, purchaser Thrasylochos of Anagyrous, 1,550 dr.; (5)
> *Hagnosiakon*, one of those on the *stēlē*, purchaser Telesarchos of Aixōnē,
> 1,550 dr.; (6) *Artemisiakon*, one of those on the *stēlē*, purchaser Thrasylochos
> of Anagyrous 150 dr. (RO 36.40–51)

Leitourgiai (liturgies) and *eisphorai* (property tax)

6.62 Like all other ancient states, Athens had no tax on income. The rich were
made to use their wealth for state purposes by means of property tax (*eisphorā*) and liturgies (*leitourgiai*).

A *leitourgiā* meant originally a service performed voluntarily for the community, but under the Athenian democracy, liturgies were effectively compulsory for those who owned a certain amount of property. They fell into two main categories: the trierarchy and festival liturgies. A trierarch was assigned to a state trireme (see 7.43–6), which for one year he had to keep in good order, man with a crew (paid in theory by the state, but times were hard in the fourth century) and command. A festival liturgy involved the selection, financing and training of teams competing in the athletic, dramatic or musical contests at Athens' many religious festivals (8.45). There seem to have been nearly a hundred festival *leitourgiai* to be performed each year. Both in the frequency with which they took on liturgies and in the way they executed them, there was scope for rich men to skimp or to make conspicuous displays of generosity. For some rich men, in particular, conspicuously fine public service as a liturgist was a way of building up credit with the Athenian People. Here is a part of a law-court speech delivered in about 400 which clearly illustrates the wide range and potential expense of *leitourgiai:*

> I passed my *dokimasiā* to become a citizen in the archonship of Theopompos (411/10). I was then appointed a producer (*khorēgos*) for tragedy and spent thirty *mnā*s. Two months later I won first prize at the *Thargēlia* with a men's dithyrambic chorus, having spent 2,000 *drakhmai*. In the archonship of Glaukippos (410/9) I spent 8,000 *drakhmai* on Pyrrhic dancers at the Great *Panathēnaia*, and I won first prize as *khorēgos* with a men's dithyrambic chorus at the Dionȳsia, spending 5,000 *drakhmai* including the cost of dedicating the tripod. In the archonship of Dioklēs (409/8) I spent 300 *drakhmai* on a cyclic chorus at the Little *Panathēnaia*.
>
> Meanwhile I was trierarch for seven years and spent six talents, and . . . twice paid *eisphorai*, on one occasion thirty *mnā*s, on the other 4,000 *drakhmai*.
>
> Directly after sailing back to Athens, in the archonship of Alexiās (405/4), I served as producer of a gymnastic display (*gumnasiarkhos*) at the *Promētheia* and won first prize, having spent twelve *mnā*s. Afterwards I was appointed *khorēgos* for a boys' chorus and spent over fifteen *mnā*s. Next, in the archonship of Eukleidēs (403/2) I won first prize as *khorēgos* for a comedy by Kēphīsodōros and spent sixteen *mnā*s including the cost of dedicating the equipment. Then at the Little *Panathēnaia* I was a producer for boy Pyrrhic dancers and spent seven *mnā*s.
>
> I have won first prize in a trireme race off Sounion, at a cost of fifteen *mnā*s; not to mention leading delegations to festivals and paying for the *Arrhēphoria* and other such items, which together have cost me more than thirty *mnā*s. (Lysiās, *On a Bribery Charge*, 21.1ff.)

6.63   This speaker, who is defending himself on a charge which seems to involve possessing public property, and perhaps embezzling sacred funds, cannot have been a typical liturgist. The 10½ talents he has spent in ten years represent more than four times the legally required minimum, and, as he expressly tells the jury, he has overspent to build up credit with the People. He must have possessed exceptional wealth (perhaps 20 to 30 talents), but his family may also have had a dubious political record of involvement with the oligarchic coup of 411 which left him open to accusation in the courts. For the average liturgist, it seems, *leitourgiai* became an increasing burden in the fourth century, especially the trierarchy. This was reformed in 357 to spread the load more equitably (see 7.47), but without notable success.

If a man was asked to perform a liturgy, he could avoid it only by finding another man richer than himself who was doing less than his share of *leitourgiai*; he would then challenge him in the courts either to perform the *leitourgiā* in his place, or exchange property with him. It is very hard indeed to see how this would work in fact, since individuals had all sorts of sentimental ties to their estates. But the theory seems to have been that if the property of the man who was challenged really was of less value, he would not mind exchanging it for a property of greater value.

6.64 *Eisphorai*, emergency war-taxes, were first certainly levied in the early part of the Peloponnesian War. The principle was that a man's property was valued and he was expected to pay a small percentage (a quarter or a half per cent) of the value. In the fourth century, when there was no imperial tribute and Athenian state finances grew steadily more precarious, *eisphorai* became increasingly frequent. In 378/7 the whole system was overhauled, with a re-evaluation of property, and citizens liable to pay seem to have been grouped into tax syndicates (*summoriai*) (7.47) to make payment more regular and efficient. The speeches of Dēmosthenēs feature repeated calls to the citizens to do their patriotic duty in the struggle against Philip by paying the *eisphorai* they owed, so the system seems in practice to have been far less successful than hoped.

The grain supply

6.65 From at least the middle of the fifth century, Athens' population could not be fed from the wheat and barley grown in Attikē (cf. 2.17). Modern estimates of the area of Attikē that was cultivable, the yield of the land, and of the proportion of food requirements met by cereal consumption all vary significantly, but a realistic guess might be that between 150,000 and 200,000 people could normally be fed from Attic grain. This is less than half the total number of residents of Attikē in 431 which we suggested in 5.8, and not enough to feed even the reduced fourth-century population. It is unsurprising in these circumstances that, once every prytany, the grain supply was a regular item for the *ekklēsiā*.

6.66 How did the Athenians secure their food supply? Grain was grown all round the Mediterranean, but the patterns of rainfall meant that almost anywhere was liable to significant variations in yield from year to year. Thus a region which in one season had plenty of grain to export might in the following year itself need to import grain. References in literature suggest that at different times the Athenians and other Greek cities drew on grain from northern Greece, the Black Sea, Sicily, and North Africa. The one place from which grain could invariably be acquired was Egypt, where fertility depended not on rainfall but the regular flooding of the Nile. If a state could establish a regular link with Egypt, it could reckon to meet all its needs regularly that way, but if it could not, it was necessary to maintain as many links as possible. For example, Athens extended the Delian League into areas like the Black Sea and intervened, diplomatically and then militarily, in Sicily. But scholars are divided whether these links were formed for political reasons which subsequently turned out to be rather convenient for Athenian grain supply, or whether the need for grain actually drove the policy.

6.67   It is certainly the case that, in the fifth century, Athenian naval power masks from us the extent of Athens' reliance on grain from abroad. At no point in the fifth century, until Athens is actually blockaded by the Spartans at the end of the Peloponnesian War, do we know of any Athenian grain crisis, and the Athenian grain supply goes virtually unmentioned in Thucydides' account of the Peloponnesian War. The closest Athens comes in the fifth century to showing how important imported grain was for her was in 445 when the Athenians received with gratitude a gift of 30,000 *medimnoi* of Egyptian grain (not a vast quantity) from an Egyptian king – an act which suggests that grain may have figured among the motives for their prolonged intervention in Egypt in the previous decade (1.48). We can only speculate about how many Athenian foreign policy decisions were at least partly motivated by Athenian need for grain. But it is likely that, when the Athenians established a 'cleruchy' by confiscating land from an ally and sending out Athenians to look after it, securing grain from the land taken over was one advantage that the Athenians had in mind.

6.68   In the fourth century, Athenian dependence on imported grain is repeatedly apparent. Since naval power was at first a thing of the past and later exercised only fitfully at best, other devices for influencing the grain trade had to be employed. One of these was the force of law. One Athenian law, passed in 374/3, required that the tax revenue from the three Aegean islands over which the Athenians retained control, Lēmnos, Imbros, and Skȳros, should be paid in grain, rather than in money. Other laws stipulated that any resident of Athens who made a bottomry loan (5.59) for purchasing a cargo of grain had to require that grain to be brought back to Athens; a similar requirement was imposed upon all residents in Athens who were themselves involved in the grain trade. Two-thirds of the grain which was imported into the Peiraieus had to be transported to Athens itself (i.e. not re-exported). Supervision of the grain trade was entrusted, not to the *agorānomoi*, but to a special board of grain inspectors (*sītophulakes*). This board oversaw prices, making sure that millers and bakers did not make undue profits. Strikingly, the grain trade was the only branch of foreign commerce which was normally treated as a strictly political matter.

6.69   These legal measures alone were not sufficient to ensure that the Athenians received all the grain that they needed. The Athenians were reliant on foreigners making gifts or otherwise ensuring that their grain went to Athens rather than elsewhere. This affected Athenian foreign policy. Individuals, including non-Athenians, got honoured for their part in supplying grain, and the Athenians took particular care to cultivate the ruling family of the Kimmerian Bosporos (the Crimea) in order to secure grain from there. The *ekklēsiā* voted Leukōn, ruler of the Kimmerian Bosporos, honorary citizenship, together with freedom from the taxation to which Athenian citizens were liable. Here in 355/4 Dēmosthenēs refers to Leukōn's reciprocal benefaction to Athens:

> You know that we are more dependent than anyone else on imported grain. Our imports from the Black Sea are equal to those from all other sources. There is nothing surprising in this. Not only is it the area of highest production but Leukōn, who controls it, has granted exemption from dues to shippers bound for Athens and announced that they are to have priority of lading . . .
>
>   Consider what this amounts to. He exacts dues of a thirtieth on all grain exports. We import from him about 400,000 *medimnoi* – the figure can be checked from the records of the grain commissioners. So for each 300,000 *medimnoi* he makes us a free gift of 10,000 *medimnoi*, and on the balance of 100,000 one of roughly 3,000 . . .
>
>   Two years ago when there was a general shortage of grain, he supplied your needs so generously that you were left with a surplus worth fifteen talents. (Dēmosthenēs, *Against Leptinēs* 20.30–3)

Following the death of Leukōn in 349/8, Athens in 346 confirmed the privileges for his three sons, and the handsome decree recording this grant survives.

Athenian imperialism

The creation of the Athenian empire

6.70   The city for which Solōn and Kleisthenēs had devised laws and constitutional rules was relatively small and far from being militarily dominant, even within the mainland Greek world. Solōn's Athens had an unusually large territory, but no especial wealth. Kleisthenēs' city had begun to exploit the Laureion silver resources in a big way, but their profits had not made any significant impact on the Athenian state. In the fifth century, Athens turned itself into a city unlike any other. It acquired a population far larger than any other city; allies numbered not even in tens of cities but in hundreds; a navy outnumbering all other navies and outclassing them in experience; an army numerically outstanding as the army of a single city; and an economic life that was both on a scale and of a kind never previously seen within the Greek world.

These changes were directly a product of, or closely linked to, Athens' acquisition of an empire. For this reason, Athenian imperialism needs to be examined in the context of the workings of Athenian democracy. (For what follows compare 1.40ff.)

6.71 After the victory over the Persians at Plataia in 479, the Spartans had been reluctant to carry the war against Persia into Asia Minor. When they did so, the arrogant behaviour of their leader Pausaniās worried the Ionian Greeks. So Athens was prevailed upon to take on the leadership and formed a new anti-Persian league, known to us as the Delian League because it had been on the island of Dēlos, in the centre of the Aegean, that the representatives of Greek states in 478/7 took their oaths of alliance (see 1.40). They swore to have the same friends and enemies, that is, they concluded an offensive and defensive alliance; and they dropped lumps of iron into the sea and swore not to desert the alliance before they rose again to the surface. The alliance, in other words, was to be eternal. Formally all allies were of equal status, but in fact the predominance of Athens was clear-cut from the start. In the first place, the allies did not all swear oaths of alliance to each other. Instead, each ally swore individually to have the same friends and enemies as Athens, and Aristeidēs reciprocated the oaths on Athens' behalf. Second, the league officials (military commanders and treasurers (*Hellēnotamiai*)) were from the beginning all Athenian. Athens was to be recognised as *hēgemōn* ('leader').

6.72 The aims of the alliance are variously described in ancient sources. As allies became less happy with Athens' leadership, so they became keen to draw attention to the difference between Athens' promises and actions. But there is little doubt that the alliance was primarily anti-Persian, seeking revenge for damage done, freedom from the remaining vestiges of Persian rule, and security from future Persian attack. Given the geography of the area, the alliance was inevitably going to rely on naval force, unlike the land-based Peloponnesian League of which Spartē was *hēgemōn*. But naval warfare was incomparably more expensive than hoplite warfare (7.42ff.), and from the beginning arrangements had to be made to cover the cost. The agreement was that the Delian League allies would have to pay towards the cost of the alliance, either by contributing ships or by making a cash payment. It is in this arrangement that we see the third sign of Athenian dominance: it was Athens (initially in the person of Aristeidēs) who decided which allied states were to contribute ships and which money, and what amount of each.

6.73 At first, so far as we know, no complaint was voiced against Athens' dominance of the alliance: the Aegean and Ionian Greeks knew that they needed powerful leadership, and Athens alone could provide it. The tribute in ships was only what the allies would have had to provide had they been acting on their own behalf, and the cash tribute was not unduly burdensome. Athens contributed by far the largest number of ships of any ally, and almost certainly suffered the largest number of casualties. Nevertheless, within fifteen years important ship-contributing island states had tried to secede from the

Delian League, and relations between Athens and her allies had become tense. We do not know the motives for the large island of Naxos attempting to leave the Delian League; but when the even wealthier north Aegean island of Thasos revolted in the middle of the 460s, our sources tell us that this was not over foreign policy objectives but over Athenian interference in what Thasos saw as *her* mineral resources on the mainland opposite. Athens reacted to these revolts by 'enslaving' Naxos (Thucydides, *Peloponnesian War* 1.98), and besieging Thasos, demolishing its walls, imposing a fine and confiscating its mainland interests. In this way, she made it clear that she intended to allow no limits to be set to her control of the League's resources.

6.74 Thucydides' narrative of the growth of Athenian power details a number of further later revolts, all successfully suppressed. In the lists of that quota of tribute paid to Athēnē (once the League treasury had been moved from Dēlos to Athens), there are patterns of non-payment and late payment which cannot be accounted for merely by gaps in the surviving records. There is little doubt that, all over the empire, there were people discontented with Athenian leadership. But to speak of the transformation of the Delian League into an Athenian empire around the middle of the fifth century is to obscure the crucial point made above in describing the foundation of the alliance: Athens was from the start unquestionably the *hēgemōn*, the dominant partner. Since Greek competitive values were as firmly entrenched in inter-state relations as elsewhere in Greek life (4.1, 15), the predominantly powerful tended to take control. The earliest League offensives were of more benefit to Athens than to the alliance as a whole, and they set the pattern for the future. What changed in the relationship was not so much Athenian behaviour as the priorities of the allies. When the Delian League was formed, the allies' priority was freedom from the Persian threat. As soon as individual allies felt themselves no longer threatened by Persia, their priorities became dominated by economics or by internal politics. Athenian control put a limit on the independent economic activities of the wealthy men among the allies, and much reduced the opportunities for those wealthy men to dominate the less wealthy majority within their own city. Athens was bound to be unpopular with such men; and when the wealthy could persuade their cities that the city's interest was the interest of its wealthy men, action against Athens, on a small or large scale, was frequently the result. But where those outside the wealthy élite saw the wealthy as a bigger threat to their own political power than Athens, Athenian rule was viewed much more positively.

The economics of empire

6.75 The changing priorities of the allies are seen in the way in which an increasing number of Athenian allies opted to pay their dues in money rather than ships. The obligation to contribute ships was apparently found burdensome mainly because of the cost of manning, equipping and running them. Pay alone for the crew of one trireme cost one talent a month in 431; even if it was only half that fifty years earlier, it was still far more expensive to contribute in this way than to make a straight cash payment to Athens. By comparison, the cash tribute (*phoros*, literally 'burden') seems at first to have been recognised to be a mild imposition. But as time went on, even this tribute was found irksome, partly because the very word *phoros* acquired unpleasant overtones of subservience, and partly because the relationship between the money contributed and Athenian activity on behalf of the allies was obscure.

6.76 In 460, Athens had launched a large expedition to Egypt to aid a native ruler in rebellion from the Persian empire (1.48–9). The expedition proved a major disaster, and it was following that disaster that the League treasury was moved to the security of Athens. If this failed Athenian initiative worried the allies, their feelings will not have been calmed by Athens' subsequent inability to dislodge the Phoenicians (who provided the Persians' chief naval arm in the Mediterranean) from Cyprus. But the majority of scholars have believed that the allies were most disturbed by an event which Thucydides does not even mention – a peace with Persia concluded by the Athenian ambassador Kalliās (1.50). Hērodotos attests an embassy by Kalliās to Sousa, but the earliest direct mention of a formal peace comes in a fourth-century text. Whether there was a formal peace is to some extent unimportant. Although there are various occasions in the following decades when the Persians gave assistance to those opposing Athens, or when the Athenians assisted those opposing Persia, the campaign around 450 was the last Athenian campaign in which the Athenians directly attacked the Persians.

6.77 It is not difficult to imagine how the Athenians would justify what might seem to be a radical change of policy. True, they had given up their attempt to remove Persian influence from Cyprus, but Cyprus had never been other than the most marginal of Greek-speaking areas. But Persia had been made to pay for her invasion of Greece, and giving up the fight over Cyprus improved, rather than endangered, the security of Ionia and the Aegean. Continuing to annoy the Persians only invited them to contemplate further reprisals once other problems within the Persian empire had been solved. Agreeing to leave the Persians alone gave hope that positive relations between Greeks and Persians would follow, to everyone's advantage. What was now important was to keep close control of the allies, to make sure that for reasons of their own they did not attempt to bring in the Persians to settle internal disputes or disputes with their neighbours.

6.78 Equally, it is not difficult to imagine the questions Athens' allies would raise. If Persia had agreed to undertake no further hostilities, what was the Delian League for? What need could there be for either allied ships or allied money when there were no campaigns to be fought? On what grounds now were allies to accept Athenian interference in the way they governed themselves, like Erythrai (apparently) in the late 450s? But if the allies did ask such questions, they seem not to have pressed for an answer. Although there are patterns of non-payment in the tribute quota lists, and although one whole year's list is (and always was) mysteriously missing from the inscribed record, the alliance did not break up. Scholars once thought that a range of Athenian measures tightening up on tribute payment, imposing new obligations on the allies, and changing the language by which the allies were referred to dated to the 440s. But many of the key inscriptions involved have now been redated, and it has been realised that the language changes with context, not with date. The Athenians referred to the allies as 'the cities over which the Athenians rule' not to emphasise the absence of allied autonomy, but to indicate their ability to deliver the sorts of protection that they promised to favoured individuals.

6.79 This is not to deny that Athens' actions in the 440s and 430s were likely to have gone on raising questions with the allies. When, from 447 onwards, the Athenians initiated a programme of building on the Akropolis to replace the temples destroyed by the Persians and build a new monumental gateway, she seems to have been careful not to take the money from funds belonging to the League. But allies would not find it hard to see that, without their tribute, the Athenians would have had distinctly less spare cash to spend in this con-spicuous way. When the Athenians increasingly encouraged the allies to con-tribute to her own major festivals, the City *Dionȳsia* and the *Panathēnaia*, the allies may well have asked why they were expected to contribute, when the fes-tivals were festivals for Athenian citizens. And when, in the 430s, the Athenians punished border offences by the Megarians by requiring Megarians to be excluded from all the ports of the empire (1.55), the allies might have wondered why a league against Persia should be involved in trivial Athenian territorial squabbles. Likewise, in the early 430s, Athens extended the empire into the Black Sea (1.54), and established, at least by the end of the 430s, a checkpoint at the Hellespont to determine the destination of shipping passing through. Allies might well have questioned what this had got to do with maintaining a strong anti-Persian position.

6.80 Thucy dides made Periklēs declare in 431 that Athens' reserve fund stood at the gigantic figure of 6,000 talents – and this despite the expenditure on the Akropolis building programme and the heavy cost of putting down the revolt of Samos in 440/39 (1.53); further, that the annual external income from tribute, fines such as that imposed on Samos and other sources, amounted to 600 talents (see above, 6.68). With reason did Periklēs stress Athens' financial preparedness for the coming war. Five years later, however, the demands of the war were proving unmanageable, and in these circumstances the Athenian attitude to their allies seems to have changed markedly. First of all they tight-ened up on tribute collection. From 430 onwards we hear of the Athenians sending out ships to collect the tribute, and in 426 the Athenians passed a decree making it a treasonable offence to impede the collection of tribute. Second, they put up the amounts of tribute they demanded. Tribute levels seem to have been steady over the previous three decades, adjusted only in the light of local circumstances, but in 425 the amount of tribute demanded from cities was increased by anything up to a factor of five, bringing the total demanded to perhaps as much as 1,460 talents per annum. Third, they imposed new gratuitous obligations on their allies, most notoriously the 'Standards Decree' demanding that allies use the same weights, measures and silver coinage as the Athenians. This measure brought little advantage to the Athenians (exchange was straightforward and cost little when coins were literally worth their weight in silver), but deprived allies of one of the most tangible signs that they were independent. The Athenians seem to have had some success in enforcing this rule, but when shortly afterwards they attempted to oblige all Greeks to pay a tithe to Dēmētēr, goddess of agriculture, at her sanctuary at Eleusīs there is no sign that they met with any success at all.

6.81 It is hard to know what effect these changes had upon Athens' allies. Athens had been so ruthless in putting down revolts, famously executing more than 1,000 Mytilenians after the revolt there in 428/7 (after initially voting to execute the whole citizen body), that the absence of revolt following the tribute increases should not surprise. But it is in any case true that the burden of tribute payment is likely to have fallen, directly at least, upon the rich who probably had little love for the Athenian democracy anyway. The pressure on the wealthy among the allies may be seen indirectly in the landed estates which rich Athenians acquired abroad. The richest Athenian of whom we happen to know (he was convicted of sacrilege in 415 and his property sold at public auction) owned tracts of property in Euboia and elsewhere outside Attikē. How did rich Athenians come by these estates abroad? It is most likely that they bought them from men who needed to raise cash quickly, or demanded them as security for loans they offered, which they promptly seized when the borrower could not repay. In either instance, these lands illustrate how much more advantageous the empire was for the Athenian élite than for the wealthy allies. Poor allies, on the other hand, might continue to welcome the Athenian empire on economic grounds, since it provided employment as rowers, dockers and so on, and opportunities for booty. When the Athenians launched their expedition against Syracuse in 415, they seem to have had no difficulty attracting a large contingent of allies.

6.82 The financial costs of Athenian military activity did not leave the Athenian élite unscathed, however. The property tax (*eisphorā*, 6.64) may have been initiated, and was certainly raised, in 428, when no fewer than 200 talents were collected. The case can indeed be made that the real beneficiaries of the empire were the Athenian poor, especially the lowest property class, with little or no land, the *thētes*. Athenian power ensured a reliable supply of grain, protecting the poor from seasonal shortage and high prices. The growth of the empire created jobs – in the fleet, in the dockyards, in the manufacture of arms and other necessities, in public works and in the administration of the empire. Aristotle says that up to 700 officials were employed abroad in the second half of the fifth century, more for its size than in the Roman empire, and although some of these will have been filled by the wealthy, many must have been filled by those with fewer resources. Some Athenians too – perhaps as many as 10,000 in all – benefited from the land they received abroad, whether as cleruchs (*klēroukhoi*) or colonists (*apoikoi*). Colonists gave up their Athenian citizen rights, but cleruchs retained them: some cleruchs indeed seem to have simply set up tenants to work the land that they had acquired and themselves returned to Athens and waited for the rent to come in. That there was some degree of social engineering involved in these settlements emerges from the decree establishing a colony at Breā in Thrace, probably in the 440s:

> Land-distributors (*geōnomoi*) shall be elected, ten in number, one from each tribe. These are to distribute the land. Dēmokleidēs shall establish the colony at his discretion as best he can. The sacred precincts which have been reserved for the gods shall be left as they are, and others shall not be consecrated. A cow and a panoply shall be brought to the Great *Panathēnaia* and to the *Dionȳsia* a phallos. If anyone wages a campaign against the territory of the settlers, aid shall be dispatched by the cities as swiftly as possible as prescribed by the agreements . . . Phantoklēs proposed: as to the settlement at Brea. Dēmokleidēs' proposal should stand, but the Erekhtheid prytany is to summon Phantoklēs before the Council at its first sitting. And the settlers to be drawn from the *thētes* and the *zeugītai* [i.e. the two lowest property classes]. (ML 49 = LACTOR 1⁴ 232)

We are not certain that Breā was ever in fact established, but Phantoklēs' amendment indicates Athenian willingness to use their military power and military needs to enrich their poor citizens.

The politics of empire

6.83   We hear little of any opposition in Athens to the policies she adopted towards her allies, but we should not assume that there was no criticism. Not only is it clear from Thucydides and from the evidence of inscriptions that there was often discussion of both the principles and the details of proposed actions, but Aristophanēs' comedies draw attention in a variety of ways to abuses of Athenian power. This is most particularly true of *Birds*, which won second prize at the City *Dionȳsia* of 414. The plot of this play involves two Athenians seeking to escape from the lawsuits and bustle of Athens and, with the help of the birds, to establish a new city, Cloudcuckooland, in the sky. Much of the play is devoted to their attempt to fend off the various menaces who visit them from the earth. These include not only a *sukophantēs* (above, 6.54) but figures who are representative of Athenian imperialist officialdom – an oracle-monger, a decree-seller (selling something very like the Standards Decree, above 6.80), and an Inspector. The chilling picture painted was of corrupt officials keener to make money than to serve either the allies' or Athens' interests. Given that Aristophanēs elsewhere pointed the finger at corrupt Athenian political leaders at home, there was, in some sense, no surprise that he pointed the finger also at corrupt Athenian officials abroad. However, revealing corruption within the society to which the audience belonged, and revealing corruption inflicted by that society on others, were two very different things.

6.84 How typical Aristophanēs' Inspector is it is difficult to tell. Although corruption may have undermined the moral authority of Athens, it is unlikely significantly to have altered the material and political consequences for the allies. Poor allies, who may well have welcomed the empire for its economic advantages, also stood to benefit politically. Democracy was the rule of the majority, and the majority in Greek terms was poor. Athens, being a democracy, naturally had an interest in promoting democracy within the empire, if only for the practical reason that a democratic ally was likely to be more loyal than an oligarchic ally. On the other hand, the rich men who traditionally formed the governing class of oligarchic states were the men who paid the tribute, and we should not suppose that Athens deliberately went out of her way on principle to create democracy throughout the alliance. Rather, Athens tolerated oligarchy, at least in the larger allied states like Mīlētos and Samos, unless and until civil conflict arose in the allied state or the state tried to defect from the alliance. Then Athens would intervene on the side of the democrats and of democracy. However, even a democratic ally would not have wished in an ideal world to be subject to Athens. It was a case of setting off this loss of the political freedom that was so dear to a Greek against the even less desirable alternative of Persian and/or oligarchic control.

6.85 The Athenians were, at least to judge from Thucydides and Aristophanēs, capable of a very realistic assessment of their power over their allies. They were aware that both the autonomy (*autonomiā*) and the liberty (*eleutheriā*) of the allies were infringed by Athenian actions. But for the Athenians, the infringement was necessary and justified in order to make the alliance an effective anti-Persian instrument. Two surviving decrees illustrate Athenian thinking and the forms imperial interference might take. First, here is an extract from the regulations Athens prescribed for the Asiatic Greek city of Erythrai, probably in 453/2:

> Among the Erythraians lots shall be drawn for a *boulē* of 120 men. The men allotted the office shall undergo scrutiny in the Erythraian Council. No one shall be allowed to serve as a member of the *boulē* who is less than thirty years old. Prosecution shall lie against those found guilty, and they shall not be *bouleutai* for the space of four years. The allotment shall be carried out and the establishment of the *boulē* effected for the present by the Inspectors (*episkopoi*) and the Garrison Commander (*phrourarkhos*), in future by the *boulē* and the Garrison Commander . . .' (ML 40 = LACTOR 1⁴ 216)

There follows the *boulē*'s oath of allegiance, in which there is a reference to 'those who fled to the Medes'; presumably it was these Persian sympathisers whose collusion had occasioned Athens' intervention and the establishment of a democratic *boulē*. The garrison was not necessarily forced on Erythrai. It could have been welcomed as a temporary safeguard of the new democracy against any Persian-backed attempt to subvert it.

6.86 In 446 Athens was faced with a crisis at the tail end of the so-called First Peloponnesian War. The cities of the island of Euboia revolted (1.52). Athenian reaction was severe. One city, Histiaiā, was utterly depopulated and settled with Athenian colonists. Eretriā and Khalkis, the two principal cities, were treated more leniently – but not much more, as this part of the decree recording regulations for Khalkis in 446/5 reveals:

> The Khalkidians shall take the following oath: 'I shall not rebel against the *dēmos* of the Athenians either by artifice or by device of any kind either by word or by deed. Nor shall I follow anyone in rebellion and if anyone does rebel, I shall denounce him to the Athenians. I shall pay the tribute to the Athenians which I persuade them to assess, and as an ally I shall be the best and truest possible. And I shall assist the *dēmos* of the Athenians and defend them if anyone does injury to the *dēmos* of the Athenians, and I shall obey the *dēmos* of the Athenians.' This oath shall be taken by the Khalkidian adults, all without exception. Whoever does not take the oath is to be deprived of his citizen rights and his property shall be confiscated, and Olympian Zeus [in Khalkis] shall receive the tithe consecrated from his property.

There follows a record of Athens' chilly response to the Khalkidians' pleas for concessions. The decree as preserved concludes with the following amendment:

> The legal processes of punishment shall be in the hands of the Khalkidians, as regards their own citizens in Khalkis, just as they are in Athens for the Athenians, except when the penalty involved is exile, death or loss of citizen rights. In regard to these, appeal shall lie in Athens, in the Ēliaiā of the *thesmothetai*, in accordance with the decree of the *dēmos*. (ML 52 = LACTOR 1⁴ 78)

The imperialistic tone of this document is unmistakable and wholly in keeping with the fact that at just this time Athens concluded the Thirty Years' Peace by which Spartē in effect formally recognised the Athenian empire. Particularly important in the document is the extension of Athens' control of Khalkis' internal affairs to the sphere of jurisdiction; law and politics, as stressed earlier, went hand-in-hand. Not all trials, however, were to be transferred from Khalkis to the Athenian jury-courts, but only those carrying the penalty of death, exile or *atīmiā*. The aim of this transfer was to prevent the unjust condemnation of Khalkidian friends of Athens and the unjust acquittal of Athens' enemies. The penalties, and not the offences, are specified in order to prevent evasion in Khalkis – for example, the prosecution of a friend of Athens on a trumped-up charge of homicide that carried the death penalty.

6.87 This was not all Athens did to encourage its friends. Apart from installing democratic constitutions and garrisons and instituting legal safeguards,

Athens took steps to protect and honour the democratic leaders upon whom the duty of representing Athens' interests in the allied cities chiefly fell. Here is a good example of a proxeny decree, whereby the Athenians in about 450 made one Akheloion a *proxenos* or a kind of honorary consul of the Athenians:

> Akheloion is to be proxenos and benefactor of the Athenians: and if Akheloion is wronged by anyone, he can prosecute them at Athens in the court of the *polemarkhos*, and he is not to pay court fees except for five *drakhmai* . . . If anyone kills Akheloion or one of his sons in one of the cities which the Athenians rule, the city is to owe a fine of five talents, as if one of the Athenians were to die, and vengeance is to be taken against this person as if an Athenian had died. (*IG* i³ 19 = LACTOR 1⁴ 235)

6.88 One final example of the politics of imperialism illustrates both the way the Athenians expanded their range of intervention over time (particularly in the Peloponnesian War), and the continuing role of Athens in protecting the interests of their allies. In 424/3 the Athenians passed a decree concerning the Makedonian city of Methōnē, quoting within it a decree which had been passed two years earlier concerning the same city:

> Three ambassadors aged over 50 are to be sent to [the Makedonian king] Perdikkās and say to Perdikkās that fairness dictates that the people of Methōnē be allowed to use the sea, and their movement not be limited, and allow them to import goods to the land just as before, and neither doing nor suffering injury, and that he should not lead an army through the territory of Methōnē without permission from Methōnē . . .
>
> The Council and People decided . . . on the proposal of Kleōnymos that the people of Methōnē be allowed to import from Byzantion up to . . . thousand *medimnoi* of grain each year, and that the Athenian officials at the Hellespont should neither themselves prevent this import nor allow any other to prevent it, on pain of a fine of 10,000 *drakhmai* each on their scrutiny. After the officials at the Hellespont have been informed in writing they may import that stated amount. (ML 65 = LACTOR 1⁴ 121)

Athenian military might continued to be deployed to protect her allies against all-comers, but in return Athens imposed demands and controls on those allies. Those impositions stored up significant anti-Athenian resentment, and made the Spartan rhetoric of liberation increasingly attractive.

Athenian imperialism in the fourth century

6.89 The Peloponnesian War proved enormously expensive for the Athenians. Not even the desperate resort to the reserve of 1,000 talents, set aside in 431, was able to counteract the combination of Athenian mistakes, allied defections and Persian aid that eventually won the war for the Spartans. By 404 Athens no longer ruled any other cities, and her own was ruled by a pro-Spartan oligarchic junta backed up by a Spartan garrison (1.82). Spartē had deprived Athens of her last shreds of empire by levelling her walls to the ground and reducing her fleet to a token twelve ships. The desire for empire, however, remained strong at Athens, and within a remarkably short space of time the democracy (restored in 403) showed signs of ambitions to control the Aegean once again.

6.90 The refortification of the Peiraieus was begun in 395/4, and more or less completed a few years later thanks, ironically, to a gift of Persian money. Despite this gift, Athens allied herself in 390 to a revolted Persian vassal, and over the next couple of years the rejuvenated Athenian fleet began to act in a manner noticeably reminiscent of the fifth-century empire; for example, a toll-station was established at Byzantion (1.92). Persia was naturally alarmed, and it was once more with Persian money that the Spartans were again able to cut off Athens' corn supply at the Hellēspont in 387. By the King's Peace of 386 (1.93), to which all Greeks were formally party, Spartē was in effect recognised as *hēgemōn* of the Greek world outside Asia. When Spartē grossly abused her position, Athens had the chance to reassert herself as leader of an alliance ostensibly designed for mutual protection against Spartē's infringements of the King's Peace.

6.91 The alliance, which was founded in 378/7, is generally known today as the Second Athenian League (or Confederacy) (1.95). The text of the prospectus by which Athens sought to attract allies is preserved on a magnificent monument. Since most members of the League had also been subjects of Athens' fifth-century empire, the promises made by the Athenians in the prospectus are the best possible clues to what they and the allies thought had gone wrong there:

> If any of the Greeks or of the barbarians living in Europe or of the islanders who are not subject to the Great King wishes to be an ally of the Athenians and their allies, he may be – remaining free and independent, being governed under whatever constitution he wishes, without receiving a garrison or submitting to a governor or paying tribute . . . For those who make alliance with the Athenians and their allies, the People shall renounce whatever Athenian possessions, whether public or private, there may be in the territory of those who make the alliance, and shall give them guarantee of this. If there are in Athens *stēlai* [inscribed pillars] unfavourable to any of the cities which makes alliance with Athens, the *boulē* in office shall have authority to demolish them.
>
> From the archonship of Nausinikos, it shall be illegal for any Athenian to own either publicly or privately, by purchase or by mortgage or in any other way whatever, any house or land in the territory of the allies. If anyone does buy, acquire or take out a mortgage on such property in any way, any of the allies who wishes may report him to the *sunedroi* [delegates] of the allies: the delegates shall sell the property and give half the proceeds to the informer, while the other half shall be the common property of the allies. (RO 22, lines 15–45 = LACTOR 1⁴ 246)

6.92 These good intentions only paved a road back to imperialism. The Athenians did not collect tribute (*phoros*), but by 373 they were levying 'contributions' (*suntaxeis*), distinct in name but not in substance. No Athenians were settled on the territory of those allies whose names are listed on the monument after the text of the prospectus, but after 373 Athens did once more establish cleruchies, for example on the island of Samos, and by the 350s governors and garrisons were to be found in some member states of the alliance. Although the allies' delegates had their own permanent and separate congress (*sunedrion*) at Athens, this had no independent power over Athens' decisions.

6.93 The nature of Athens' fourth-century empire is best illustrated by the history of her relations with the island of Keōs. Keōs had four cities, and the Athenians seem consistently to have resisted moves by these cities to unite together, preferring to deal with each separately. In the mid-360s two of the four cities, at least, revolted, killing the Athenian *proxenos*. The Athenians intervened militarily and imposed an agreement. Some of those from the city of Ioulis, forced into exile in consequence of the revolt, returned and set about killing and confiscating the property of the friends of the Athenians. The Athenians intervened again, offering those they held responsible the choice between exile and property confiscation and standing trial. They also agreed to an amnesty for all who kept the agreement, and insisted on an oath of alliance and loyalty to Athens from the Keans. More or less at the same time, however, they seem to have imposed upon the cities of Keōs an agreement that all the ruddle (red ochre) produced in the island would be exported to Athens. Ruddle had a variety of uses but was hardly a strategic necessity. Athenian intervention in the ruddle trade is perhaps the closest Athens comes in the fourth century to the gratuitous demands she placed upon allies in the fifth.

6.94 Athenian imperialist behaviour led to allied revolt. The so-called Social War (= war of the allies) in 357–5 emptied Athenian coffers and effectively spelt the end of Athens as an imperial power. The Confederacy remained notionally in existence until 338, and Athens remained the leading naval power in the Aegean, but she was quite incapable of turning the remnant alliance into an effective weapon against Philip of Makedōn. Within little more than a decade after the end of the Second Athenian League, the Makedonian army under Alexander the Great had conquered Persia to establish an empire on a scale that put all Athens' fifth- and fourth-century efforts into the shade.

7 Athens at war

Introduction

7.1 For fifth-century Athenians, war was a permanent condition of life, fought almost annually. But warfare in classical Greece was in many ways distinct from warfare in the modern, or even the early modern, world. Although the Trojan wars dominated mythological battles, and the Persian Wars became the key reference point for subsequent Greek history, most battles in the classical period were fought between Greeks. Wars were fought neither for primarily economic reasons, nor to take over the territory of others, but rather to assert and maintain political dominance. Wars were fought by arming (some of) the citizen body. Standing armies and standing navies were neither economically feasible for most cities (Spartē being the great exception), nor regarded as desirable, since it was widely recognised that there was a close link between military and political power. Conflicts in which a city staked its whole armed force of citizens were fairly rare occurrences; far more common, and perhaps more to be feared, was ravaging – the more or less systematic destruction of food supplies. Civil war within a city was regarded as the worst of fates, but we find no expression of principled objection to war against others.

7.2 Like the rest of public life (3.33, 39), the whole life of the army – before the march, on the march, before and after conflict – was accompanied by religious rituals. Each army had its own seers (*manteis* – see 3.20). They divined the will of the gods by, for instance, examining the livers of sacrificed animals, and, to judge by the number of times they prevented military commanders from engaging when they wanted to, they were no mere yes-men. Divination before battle (*ta hiera*), and blood-sacrifice (*ta sphagia*) as the army marched to fight were standard practice (7.17), and often stopped proceedings (cf. Hērodotos, *Histories* 9.37–61 and see 3.20). Nīkiās' belief in his *manteis* at Syracuse, which held up the retreat for 27 days (Thucydides, *Peloponnesian War* 7.50), may well have caused the destruction of the Athenian army there. When armies marched to battle, they sang paeans (hymns to avert evils); if they won, they erected a *tropaion* ('trophy', literally the place where the rout started, the 'turning-point') as a thank-offering to the god as well as the tangible, visible proof of victory.

7.3 Athens' power in the fifth and fourth centuries depended on her fleet. It is important to appreciate what a radical change Athens' construction of a

7.1 The goddess Victory before a trophy on a mid-fifth-century Athenian red-figure *pelikē* (small *amphorā*).

major fleet in the early fifth century meant (1.32). With a navy of 200 to 400 ships and about 200 people on board each ship, where did classical Athens get the men to serve in them? Not from her own citizens alone, clearly. And getting the men was only the beginning. They needed to be supplied with food – no significant supplies could be carried on the ships themselves. Getting the wood to build such a huge fleet was already a major task, for Attikē itself could make little contribution. With 170 rowers, a fleet of 200 ships requires 34,000 oars even without the wood to build the ship itself, the canvas for sails, the ropes, the bronze fitments for the rams. The late fifth-century pamphlet *The Constitution of the Athenians*, whose author is some-times rather misleadingly referred to as 'the Old Oligarch', shrewdly observed in the passage quoted at 5.58 that getting the material for a fleet and having a fleet that dominated the sea went together.

It was in fact from Makedōn and the north that Athens got most of its wood, and this compelled Athens to take a close interest in the politics of Makedōn and Thrace and in the kings there (cf. 5.58; 2.10). Nor was it a matter simply of building the ships; maintaining the fleet (hulls rot if kept in the water too long, split if left on land too long) was a major headache. Our literary sources give us little insight into the serious logistical questions involved in Athenian maintenance of the fleet. The inscriptions with their lists of trierarchs and what they owed to the city give only a little more, but if we are to understand the Greeks at war we must always keep logistical issues in mind (5.58; 7.42–50).

7.4 From 497 to 338, Athens was at war for three years out of four, and Greek states in general regarded periods of peace more as respite from inevitable war than as the normal state of affairs. In the fifth century, 'truces' were made for limited periods only. Spartē and Athens, for instance, made a thirty-year peace in 446, and more than a generation was not to be thought of. In the fourth century, dreams of a more abiding state of peace found expression in talk of 'peace', something more positive than the mere cessation of war implied by 'truces', and the so-called Common Peaces (1.93), made to ensure peace and goodwill amongst all the Greeks, had no time limits. But the dreams were vain. In 375, to express jubilation over the end of hostilities with Spartē, the Athenians erected an altar to peace, and every year from then on sacrifices were made to this abstract deity; but by 373 they were at war again. War was central to Greek life (1.112).

Land warfare

7.5 Most Athenian wars were in large degree naval, and it was in naval warfare that Athens excelled. On land her record was far from glorious. If one excepts the battle of Marathōn (1.30), Athens on her own won few major land battles; the real warriors on land were (until the rise of the Makedonians under Philip) the Spartans and the Boiotians, and it is to their battles that we must look for enlightenment.

7.6 The rarity of major battles in a period of constant warfare is striking. Between 479 and 404, Spartē, the dominant power on land in that period, fought only four major land battles, and in the course of the Peloponnesian

War Thucydides had only two, the battles of Dēlion (424, 1.65) and (First) Mantineia (418, 1.70), to describe. In the fourth century, Boiotian supremacy was established by a mere two major engagements, Leuktrā (371, 1.97) and (Second) Mantineia (362, 1.98). For the rest, warfare was a matter of skirmishing and ravaging, which sounds to our ears somewhat trivial. It was not so to the Greeks.

Ravaging

7.7   Greece was a poor country. Most states lived off home-grown produce (unlike Athens), so that hostile ravaging was very much to be feared, and invasions took place when the corn was ripe. The Greek word for ravaging was 'cutting'. Cereal crops were cut (and presumably consumed by the invading army or burned), vines likewise, and trees ring-barked (i.e. a strip of bark cut off right round the trunk), to look like whipped slaves (Aristophanēs, *Peace* 747). Cutting cereals was no less hard work when done by soldiers than when done in the normal course of events, however, and cutting vines or other trees could be extremely laborious. Further, olive trees, in particular, are extremely hardy and very difficult to kill off. While the economic effects of prolonged ravaging could be severe, few armies could devote sufficient time to achieve such an impact. It is notable that, in the later years of the Peloponnesian War, the ravaging by the Peloponnesian troops during their month-long invasions came to seem minor compared to the systematic plundering of the Athenian countryside, involving buildings as well as crops, which was possible once the Spartans were permanently resident at the fortress of Dekeleia (Thucydides, *Peloponnesian War* 7.27–8). Athens, however, did not depend on Attikē alone and could endure (cf. 1.20, 5.58). Other states must have suffered greatly, and the impact could be particularly severe if the enemy were able to round up flocks, which were much easier to remove than standing crops.

Major battles

7.8   What we know of how land battles were fought depends ultimately upon literary descriptions. This is something of a problem. In the first place, the descriptions of battle in Homeric epic, which are shaped by literary considerations rather than by experience or observation, cast their shadow over all subsequent descriptions. Many historians' descriptions are manifestly works of fiction, often constructed from particular stereotypes of how battles worked. Second, no participant in an ancient battle was in a position to know all that was happening in that battle, so that the stories told by those who fought stood a high chance of being misleading. Much scholarly ink has been spilt trying to make sense of some of Alexander the Great's battles against Dareios, for instance, when in the end there is little chance that the features preserved in accounts written long after the battles they describe are accurate reflections of what actually happened. Our best chance of accurate literary descriptions comes from the major battles at Dēlion, in 424, and Mantineia, in 418, recorded by Thucydides. Thucydides was a participant in neither of these battles, but he was himself an Athenian general, and is highly likely to have asked the right questions as he went about his scholarly researches.

7.9 Thucydides' description of the battle of Mantineia runs as follows:

(66) The next day the Argives and their allies formed up in battle order, ready for the enemy. The Spartans, returning from the water to their old camp by the temple of Hēraklēs, found themselves at close quarters with the enemy already drawn up for battle and advancing from the hill. This caused them greater alarm than any other occasion on record. There was little time for preparation, and they formed ranks in haste, under the orders of Agis. For it is their rule that when a king is in command all orders are given by him. He instructs the *polemarkhoi*, they give the word to the *lokhāgoi*, they to the *pentekontēres*, they in turn to the *enōmotia*. All necessary orders are passed on through the same channels and quickly reach the ranks. For almost the whole Spartan army with a few exceptions consists of officers serving under officers and responsibility for seeing that orders are carried out is widely delegated . . .[*Thucydides now describes the formation and estimates sizes.*]

(69) Before they actually engaged, the generals on either side spoke a few words of encouragement . . . The Spartans meanwhile sang war-songs and exchanged words of individual encouragement, reminding each other of their proven courage and well aware that long training in action is more effective than a few words of encouragement, however well delivered.

(70) After this they joined battle, the Argives and their allies advancing with vigour and fury, the Spartans slowly to the sound of pipes, a standing institution in their army, not for religious reasons but to make them advance evenly, keeping time, without breaking ranks as large armies are apt to do at the moment of impact. (71) As they were approaching each other, Agis decided on the following manoeuvre. All armies have a common tendency as they go into action; they get pushed out towards the right, and overlap the enemy left with their own right wing, because each man seeks protection for his own uncovered right-hand side from the shield of his right-hand neighbour, thinking that the more closely the shields are locked the safer he will be. The man primarily responsible is the man on the extreme right of the front line, who keeps trying to keep his own unarmed side away from the enemy; the rest follow him with the same motive. On the present occasion the Mantineians far outflanked the Skirītai, and the Spartans and Tegeans outflanked the Athenians still further, their force being correspondingly larger. Agis was afraid that his left would be surrounded, and that the Mantineians were outflanking it too far; he therefore ordered the Skirītai and the Brasideioi to move out of their position in the line and level up the front with the Mantineians, while he passed word to the two generals Hipponoīdās and Aristoklēs to move two companies from the right wing to fill the gap, thinking he had men to spare on his right and that he would strengthen the line facing the Mantineians. (72) But because the order was given at the very

moment of the attack and with little notice, Aristoklēs and Hipponoïdās were not willing to change position – and for that very reason they were later considered to have acted in a cowardly fashion and went into exile from Spartē. When he perceived that the two companies did not come Agis ordered the Skirītai to engage, but the enemy anticipated them and they could not close the gap. It was pretty well universally the case that the Spartans were outdone in skill, but they showed that they were not inferior in bravery. For when it came to hand-to-hand fighting with the enemy, the right wing of the Mantineians turned the Brasideioi and Skirītai, and the Mantineians and their allies and the thousand picked troops from Argos fell upon the gap which had not been closed up and destroyed the Spartans, surrounding and routing them and forcing them back to the waggons and killing some of the older men drawn up there. So in this quarter the Spartans were defeated. But in the rest of the line, and particularly in the middle where king Agis was and the three hundred so-called 'knights', an attack was made upon the older Argives and the so-called 'five companies' and the Kleōnaioi, Orneātai and Athenians drew up with them, and they turned men who mostly did not even wait to face hand-to-hand fighting but gave in as soon as the Spartans attacked, and some of them were trampled down attempting to avoid being captured. (73) When the army of the Argives and their allies had given way at this point, they were simultaneously broken off from both wings. At the same time, the right wing of the Spartans and Tegeans was encircling the Athenians with the remainder of their force, and danger surrounded them from both sides, since they were encircled on one side and already defeated on the other. The Athenians would have been liable to serious losses had not their cavalry who were present proved useful to them, and had not Agis, when he realised that his left wing, facing the Mantineians and the thousand Argives, was in trouble, told the whole army to go to help those being beaten. When this occurred, and the Spartan army marched past and away from them, the Athenians were quietly saved along with the defeated force of Argives with them. The Mantineians and their allies and the select Argives did not have the resolution to continue the pressure on the enemy, but when they saw their own side being beaten and the Spartans bearing down upon them they turned to flight. Of the Mantineians the majority were killed, but most of the select Argives were saved. The flight and retreat, however, were pressed neither hard nor long. The Spartans fight long and stubbornly until they have routed the enemy, but that once done their pursuit is short and brief.

(74) That, or something very much like it, was the course of the battle, which was the greatest that had occurred for a long time among the Greeks and involved the most famous of their cities. The Spartans took up a position in front of the enemy dead, and proceeded at once to set up a trophy and strip the bodies of the fallen. Their own dead they took up and carried to Tegeā, where they buried them; the enemy dead they gave back under truce. The Argives, Orneātai and Kleōnaioi lost seven hundred killed, the Mantineians two hundred, the Athenians and men of Aigīna two hundred with both generals. On the Spartan side the allies suffered no losses worth

mentioning; of the Spartans themselves it was reported that three hundred were killed, but the true figure was difficult to find out. (Thucydides, *Peloponnesian War* 5.66–74)

7.10   This passage draws attention to a number of fundamental features of Greek land battles. First, the size and organisation of the armies. In ch. 66, Thucydides describes the Spartan army as consisting of 'officers serving under officers' (*arkhontes*). Because Spartē had effectively a standing army, these positions in the hierarchy were more deeply embedded in Spartan society, but in the Athenian army too there were a whole array of officers, the highest ranking of whom were elected. Plato at one point describes the ambition of those seeking lowly offices in the army. It was an essential feature of Greek, as of Roman, armies that they were not an amorphous mass of men but were made up of discrete units. This both facilitated communication, as here, and made manifest the degree to which the soldiers were reliant upon each other. For these units were not large. In a passage omitted from what is quoted above, Thucydides calculated the size of the Spartan army on the basis of the size of the smallest unit, which was of 32 men, and the Spartan front line was 448 men across (and generally 8 deep). The problem is that Thucydides' description of the Spartan army and that given by Xenophōn for the fourth century do not square, and Thucydides seems to be describing only the Spartans in one part of the battle line. As a result, scholars have debated exactly what the figures given by Thucydides indicate for total army size; it seems likely that this was something between 5,000 and 6,000. As this makes clear, even the most major Greek battles involved armies that were, by modern standards, tiny: at most only 17,000–20,000 in all engaged that day at Mantineia. Yet Thucydides spoke of it as 'the greatest . . . for a long time'. Only when the Greeks united, as against the Persians at Plataia, for example, or against Philip at Khairōneia, were significantly greater numbers of men involved.

7.11   Second, army training. Apart from the Spartans, and small 'crack' units in other cities, Greek land armies were essentially amateur. As the numerous units to which special names are given in the account of this battle indicate, cities did distinguish some soldiers as more skilful than others, but in some cases, as apparently here with the Argives, this was simply because they were the troops still in the prime of life (7.26). Only in the 330s does Athens seem to have instituted systematic military training (7.31) for young men when they came of age, and even then after their two years of training they practised only on campaign. Thucydides sees fit to describe the Spartans' method of transmitting orders, as something worth reporting to the Greeks. The Spartans were better trained in every way. Others received and needed harangues to excite valour; the Spartans, with professionals' confidence in their well-practised powers, needed no reminding, but sang their familiar martial songs. Their opponents advanced to battle in unrestrained fashion; the Spartans advanced with slow and measured tread to the sound of the *aulos*, thus keeping their distances and their alignment. Nothing better demonstrates the superiority of their military training than the difficult tactical manoeuvre that King Agis ordered during the very advance. Only for a highly practised army was such a move to be conceived. In crimson raiment and with flowing locks, bearing polished shields with L (Greek Λ) for Lakedaimonioi, the Spartans' official name, plain to see, they were the terror of Greece. No wonder that many did not dare to close with them. Nevertheless on this occasion Thucydides goes out of his way to say that it was the Spartans who were deficient in skill, and that their success was due to their bravery.

7.12   Third, decisions had to be taken not simply by generals but by officers and individual soldiers. Agis can contemplate a late manoeuvre because of the training of the Spartan soldiers; his order can be conveyed rapidly because of the command structure; but the decision as to whether obeying the order makes sense rests upon two individual officers. And in this case they disobey. Ironically Thucydides identifies fear as the motive for Agis' order, only for Aristoklēs and Hipponoīdās to be accused of disobeying through cowardice. Responsibility may be diffused through the command structure, but power rests with the Spartan king.

7.13   Fourth, the actual fighting is relatively brief, fortunes on the battlefield are quickly decided, and the whole run of events is extremely fluid. Both where the Mantineians break into the Spartan line and where the Spartans around Agis push back those opposed to them, troops who recognise that they are at a disadvantage rapidly fall back. We can only understand what happens in this battle if we envisage the soldiers being quite widely spaced rather than shoulder to shoulder. It is this that enables Agis to send his troops across the battlefield to relieve the beleaguered Brasideioi and Skirītai, and it is this that enables the Athenian troops, surrounded at one moment, to escape at the next with the aid of their cavalry.

7.14   Fifth, armies do not travel alone. In the course of the battle, the Mantineians push the Spartans who face them back onto their waggons and some of the older men drawn up there are killed. All armies need to be kept supplied, and there need to be men in charge of the supplies, and of protecting the supplies, who are not involved in the fighting. Greek battles were not without their spectators, and, as here, those 'spectators' could face danger and death.

7.15   Finally, casualties. On the Spartan side there were alleged to have been 'about 300', on the other side 1,100 in all, a discrepancy at first surprising. But it is typical. The main strength of Greek armies, the hoplite, was generally well protected (see 7.19) and in direct conflict only a few were killed (e.g. at Plataia (1.38), according to Hērodotos, '91 Spartans, 16 Tegeans, 52 Athenians' – and according to another source, all the Athenians came from a single Athenian tribe). It was in the rout that most of the fatal casualties occurred: here this explains the large numbers of dead on the Argive side. Of course there must have been many a man lamed or maimed, although historians rarely allude to them, but in general fatal casualties were not numerically enormous. Nevertheless total casualties here of 1,400 men amount to 7 per cent of the combatants, or slightly more. A few years earlier the prospect of losing 292 men who had been captured alive on Sphaktēriā was enough to make the Spartans suspend invasions of Attikē and engage seriously in peace negotiations.

7.16   Although the Athenian cavalry play a role in helping to save the Athenian hoplites in this battle, the battle itself is decided primarily by the hoplites. This was indeed the normal pattern of Greek battles, and when they came across enemies who fought differently, Athenian armies sometimes found themselves in serious difficulties. This was what happened when the Athenians were persuaded to make an expedition into Aitōliā in 426 and found themselves not facing a line of hoplites, but being harried by light-armed spear-throwers:

> The Aitōlians attacked the Athenians and their allies. They ran down from the hills in all directions and threw their spears. When the Athenian army attacked, the Aitōlians retreated, only to attack the Athenians as they withdrew. That was how the battle mostly went on, with pursuits and retreats, and in both, the Athenians came off second best. While the Athenian archers had arrows and were able to use them, they resisted, for the Aitōlians were lightly armed men and fell back when shot at. But when, on the death of the commander of the archers, the archers were scattered and the soldiers had become tired by the continual repetition of the same manoeuvres, the Aitōlians attacked and threw their spears, the Athenians were routed, fled and were destroyed, having fallen into ravines from which there was no exit and locations of which they had no knowledge. (Thucydides, *Peloponnesian War* 3.97.3–98.1)

7.17   There were some battles in which both sides used light troops, hoplites, and cavalry, but generally at different stages of the battle. This is well illustrated from a clash between the Athenians and the Syracusans in the winter of 415– 14 during the Athenian invasion of Syracusan territory (1.72–4):

> (69) The engagement started with a preliminary skirmish between the stone-throwers, slingers and archers, in which, as usually happens with light-armed troops, fortunes varied. Then the priests brought out the usual victims for sacrifice and the trumpeters sounded the charge for the hoplites, who advanced . . .
>
> (70) When battle was joined, for a long time neither side gave way. Meanwhile a thunderstorm broke, with thunder, lightning and heavy rain, which added to the fears of the Syracusans, who were in battle for the first time and had little experience of war, though the more experienced Athenians put it down to the time of year and were more alarmed by the continued resistance of the army. The Argives were the first to push back the Syracusan left, the Athenians followed up on their part of the front, and Syracusan resistance elsewhere was then broken and flight ensued. The Athenians did not press the pursuit far. They were prevented from doing so by the numerous and still undefeated Syracusan cavalry who attacked the Athenian hoplites and

7.2 Much of the Parthenōn frieze represents a procession of Athenian cavalry, shown in tribal formation.

> drove off any they saw pursuing in advance of the rest. But the Athenians did follow up the fugitives so far as it was safe to do so in close formation. They then withdrew and set up a trophy. (Thucydides, *Peloponnesian War* 6.69–70)

First, the light-armed troops skirmished before the battle but had no real part in it, and Thucydides dismisses them somewhat contemptuously. Then in the battle proper there was a long hand-to-hand combat, and at a later stage, when the Syracusans had begun to fare less well it came to 'shoving', i.e. with overlapping shields, the Athenians and their allies pushed back the Syracusans. These latter then fled and the Syracusan cavalry came into play for the first time (although the Athenians had none) in preventing the Athenian pursuit. In this battle the three elements of the fifth-century army show themselves distinctly enough, viz. cavalry, hoplites, and light-armed, and it is time to describe them and their armament.

Economics of service

7.18 Since the state did not fully provide arms and armour, wealth determined whether a man fought in the cavalry, as a hoplite, or in light armour. Keeping horses was an expensive business, and the cavalry (*hippeis*) were the richest

7.3 Various stages of arming as a hoplite are shown on this Athenian red-figure wine-mixing bowl (*krātēr*) from the end of the sixth century.

men in the state. The Athenian cavalry never numbered more than 1,200 and by the middle of the fourth century considerably fewer. Hoplite equipment too was not cheap, though elements of it are likely to have been passed down from father to son, and the hoplite class at Athens was drawn from the third of Solōn's property classes (1.20, 6.23), the so-called *zeugītai*, in origin men rich enough to own a yoke of oxen. Finally, the poorest citizens, the so-called *thētes*, were liable for service as the light-armed troops, the *psīloi* (literally, 'bare') (7.22–4), as well as rowers in the fleet. All citizens were liable for military service of some sort from the ages of 18 to 60 (5.2, 6; 6.50). Initially in the sixth century, and even in the early years of democracy, political as well as military responsibilities had been restricted according to one's wealth. But after the middle of the fifth century, there is no sign that the landless were in any way formally restricted in the political role they could play, although in the oligarchic coup of 411 ability to bear arms (as a hoplite) was made a criterion for active citizenship. Conversely, the politically powerless metics were also expected to serve in the Athenian army, though they seem in general not to have formed the 'front-line' troops.

Hoplites

7.19   Throughout the archaic and classical period, the hoplite was the main strength of Greek armies. He was well protected, principally by a round shield a metre in diameter, a helmet, a breastplate or a corslet, and greaves (see figs. 1.10, 2.7, 3.1, 8, 14, 4.5, 7.1). His principal weapon was the spear; hence Aiskhylos in his tragedy *Persians* 147ff. (and cf. 239–40) represented warfare between Greeks and Persians as the conflict of spear and bow. But the hoplite also carried a short, single-edged, curving sword used, as we see represented on vases, in a downward hack. Hoplite equipment was arduous to carry, and in ideal circumstances hoplites would often be accompanied by slaves to carry their equipment for them. Thucydides says that at the battle of Dēlion a great number of Athenian baggage-carriers were killed (*Peloponnesian War* 4.101.2).

7.20   But what actually happened in hoplite warfare? This question has been sharply debated by modern scholars. From vase paintings, we can see how the spear was used. It was either raised above the shoulder and aimed at the hoplite's most vulnerable point, the gap between helmet and breastplate, or it was used underarm, aiming again at the vulnerable point at the bottom of the breastplate. Part of the skill of the hoplite in attack was in being able to spot what sort of spear thrust would be most effective, and to change from one approach to the other efficiently. Part of the skill of the hoplite in defence was being able to deploy the shield effectively to ward off a spear thrust, whether it came from above or below. From literary sources, it is clear that there was regularly in battles a phase of concerted shoving (*ōthismos*) at some stage of the battle; and there must be some point in the measured advance to battle, controlled by an *aulos*-player (see 7.11). Xenophōn describes how Agēsilāos fought the battle of Korōneia in 394 in these terms:

> He crashed into the Theban army head-on. As they threw shield against shield they pushed, they fought, they killed, they died. (Xenophōn, *Hellēnika* 4.3.19)

Here the pushing comes immediately after the engagement, and it is this sequence that has encouraged some scholars to see hoplite battle as pitching the weight of the massed ranks on one side against the weight of the massed ranks on the other. But at Plataia, according to Hērodotos (*Histories* 9.67), there was a 'fierce battle for a long time until they came to shoving'. So too, in the hand-to-hand battle outside Syracuse in 415, the two sides long resisted each other and the shoving came later (see 7.17). This possible variation in the timing of the push does not suggest that we are dealing with one interlocked line engaging with another; it looks more like a battle where each hoplite has his eye primarily on the hoplite opposite to him, and that pushing was one tactic used in the attempt to get the opponent to let down his defences.

7.21   If it is correct that much hoplite warfare was made up of successive engagements between individuals, rather than of the concerted thrust of massed ranks, then the best description of warfare may come from Euripidēs' description in *Phoenician Women* of the clash between Polyneikēs and Eteoklēs:

> When the torch was hurled, like the echo of the Etruscan trumpet as sign of bloody battle, they rushed against each other in a dreadful run. Like wild boars who had whetted their savage tusks they came together, their beards foaming with sweat. They darted with their spears, but crouched behind their round shields so that the iron would slip aside in vain. If one saw the other's eye above the shield he wielded his spear to strike the mouth first, but well did they direct the eye at the shields' studs so that there was nothing for the spear to do . . . Eteoklēs brushing aside a rock that was in the way of his tread placed his leg outside the spear. Polyneikēs saw that it was offered to the steel and met it with a blow of his spear; the Argive spear pierced the greave, and the whole army of the Danaids raised a cry. In this struggle the man wounded first saw a bare shoulder, aimed the spear with force at Polyneikēs' chest, and gave pleasure to the citizens of Kadmos. But the tip of the spear broke . . . Then both took the handles of their swords and came together, clashing their shields and producing a great din of battle as they engaged. Eteoklēs had come to know a Thessalian device by familiarity with that land: he released himself from his current labour, brought his left foot round to the back while taking care for his belly's hollow in front. Then moving his right leg forward, he sent his sword down through the navel and brought it to the backbone. Doubled over with chest against belly, wretched Polyneikēs fell in pools of blood. (*Phoenician Women* 1377–87, 1390–9, 1404–15)

Euripidēs' description here captures the initial rushing into battle – more to frighten the enemy than actually to engage him on the run – the desperate search for ways through the defence of shield and armour, the resort to the sword when spear fails, and the use of a turning trick to catch the opponent off balance and render him vulnerable. In hoplite battle, all of these would have been familiar; but the hoplite had also to pay attention to what else was happening in the battle line, because even an individual holding his own, or getting the better of an opponent, would have to beat a retreat if all around him also retreated.

Light-armed troops

7.22   Light-armed troops are little discussed in our literary sources. They came to play a very important part in warfare, and this development is often thought to have begun in the 420s. This is in part because ancient sources tend simply to ignore light-armed troops: only when we have an account as detailed as Thucydides' of the Peloponnesian War do light troops begin regularly to get mentioned. On several occasions, Thucydides includes no light-armed troops when he describes how many ships and soldiers the Athenians dispatched on a campaign; but when the fighting subsequently occurs, it turns

7.4 A light-armed peltast crouches in the tondo of this late sixth-century Athenian red-figure cup.

out that the Athenian force did indeed include light-armed troops (drawn, scholars presume, from the rowers). Such light troops are familiar in the images painted on Athenian pottery in the late sixth and early fifth century, and play a crucial role in a famous Athenian massacre of Corinthians in 458 (Thucydides, *Peloponnesian War* 1.106). We should probably assume some light troops to have been regularly present with the rest of the Athenian army, though they may have been used in a wide range of capacities.

7.23   A Greek army might regard it as worthwhile to include large numbers of light-armed troops. Hērodotos records that, at Plataia in 479, the 5,000 Spartan hoplites were attended by no fewer than 35,000 light-armed helots. In his account of the battle of Dēlion (424), Thucydides tells us that the Boiotians mustered more than 10,000 light-armed troops, outnumbering their hoplites by 3:2; the Athenians, by contrast, Thucydides says, had no 'regularly constituted light-armed units', although a very large number of Athenians and non-Athenians without proper arms had joined the Athenian invasion of Boiōtiā. Here as elsewhere Thucydides distinguishes between light-armed troops (*psīloi*) and troops armed not with the heavy round hoplite shield but with the crescent-shaped shield (*peltā*) which gave them the name 'peltasts'. But the function of all light-armed troops was much the same. Like the Aitolians (7.16), they exploited their higher

7.5 A rare representation of a slinger on an Athenian red-figure *amphorā* of the second quarter of the fifth century.

mobility to get close to the hoplites, discharge missiles (stones, javelins, arrows) from a certain distance, and withdraw. Where there were light troops on both sides, as in the Athenian clash at Syracuse, an attempt would be made to use one's own force of light troops to neutralise the enemy's force. In general, light troops were more of a nuisance to the enemy than a serious danger, but on occasion they could cause significant disruption.

7.24 From the Peloponnesian War on, there are signs of increasing interest in organising light troops more effectively to take advantage of their mobility. Dēmosthenēs, arguably Athens' greatest general in the fifth century (6.25),

7.6 Just how 'other' the Athenians thought light-armed troops to be is revealed by this early fifth-century '*negro alabastron*' showing a peltast as a black wearing a Thracian cloak. Compare figs. 8.3–4 below.

was alerted to the importance of the light-armed by the rough handling his own hoplites had received in Aitōliā the previous year (7.16). So he assembled a huge force of light-armed for his attack on the Spartan hoplites, unwisely placed on the adjacent island of Sphaktēriā (Thucydides, *Peloponnesian War* 4.32ff.; cf.1.62–3). The circumstances were indeed unique, but it remained the case that Dēmosthenēs killed or captured every Spartan on the island. In the early fourth century, the general Iphikratēs made this pay off particularly impressively when, using light-armed mercenary troops, he massacred a Spartan detachment at Lekhaion in 390 (1.92). This was one of the most celebrated of military victories, not least because it was unexpected. Here is Xenophōn's account:

> (13) The generals in Corinth, Kalliās the son of Hipponikos who commanded the Athenian hoplites, and Iphikratēs who commanded the peltasts, when they saw that the Spartans were few in number and unescorted by peltasts or cavalry, decided that it was safe enough to attack them with their own peltasts. If they marched along the road, they could be attacked on their unprotected side with javelins and destroyed; and if they turned in pursuit it would be easy enough for the peltasts with their light equipment to get away from hoplites. (14) Kalliās drew up his hoplites close to the city and Iphikratēs with his peltasts attacked the Spartan regiment. Under this assault by javelin some of the Spartans were wounded and some killed, and the shield-bearers were ordered to pick them up and carry them to Lekhaion; and they were the only men in the regiment to get away safely. The general then ordered the first ten year-groups to drive off their assailants. (15) They went after them, but failed to catch any of them. They were hoplites chasing peltasts who had a javelin throw's start, and Iphikratēs had given orders that they were to retire before the hoplites got to grips with them. Besides, the hoplites became scattered in their efforts at pursuit, and when they turned to retire Iphikratēs' men wheeled round and attacked them again, some from the front and some from the flank, running along to expose their unprotected side. In the first pursuit nine or ten of the peltasts' javelins struck home, which encouraged them to attack still more boldly. (16) As the Spartans continued to suffer casualties, their general ordered the first fifteen year-groups to the attack and pursuit. But when they turned to retire they suffered more casualties than before. They had already lost all their best men, when the cavalry appeared and they attempted a joint pursuit. The peltasts turned to run, but the cavalry mismanaged their attack. Instead of pressing their pursuit till they had inflicted casualties they kept a continuous front with the hoplites both in advance and retreat. The Spartans continued to pursue the same tactics with the same result, becoming fewer and less resolute while their assailants became bolder and more numerous. (17) At last in desperation they formed up on a small hill, about half a mile from the sea and two miles from Lekhaion. The men of Lekhaion, when they saw them, embarked in small boats and sailed along till they were opposite the hill. The Spartans were already desperate; they were suffering acutely and being killed without being able to retaliate, and when they finally saw the hoplites coming up they broke and ran. Some plunged into the sea and a few managed to escape to Lekhaion with the cavalry; but in the whole engagement and in the subsequent flight about two hundred and fifty of them were killed. (Xenophōn, *Hellēnika* 4.5.13–17)

In itself this engagement had no important influence on the course of the war. But two hundred and fifty Spartans in all were killed, and only three hundred and fifty survived. The disaster was the clearest demonstration that the long dominance of the hoplite could be effectively challenged.

7.7 The relief from the public funerary monument to Athenian cavalrymen who died in combat in Corinth and in Boiōtiā in 394. Their names would have been listed below (see also fig. 1.15).

Cavalry

7.25 Cavalry proper, i.e., men who fought on horseback, were a late development in the Greek world. Earlier, the richest citizens had ridden to battle, but dismounted to fight. Use of the name 'knights' (*hippeis*) for the Spartan cavalry that fought as the king's bodyguard at Mantineia (see 7.9; Thucydides, *Peloponnesian War* 5.72), was a survival of what had once been general. In the fifth century, the use of cavalry was, and had to be, limited to very subsidiary roles (as in the battle at Syracuse, 7.17). The horses of southern Greece seem to have been rather a puny breed (cf. 2.16). The cavalryman might be armed like a hoplite with helmet and cuirass, and carrying a spear and a sword as offensive weapons. But the stirrup had not been invented, and the cavalryman was equally likely to fall off if he missed, or be pushed off it he hit too firmly, or if struck himself. So fighting like a hoplite on horseback was not really an option. A frontal assault on a line of hoplites would have been worse than useless. Instead, cavalry generally operated more like light-armed troops, riding in, throwing spears, and riding away again, and for this light armour seems to have been preferred.

7.26 The success of the light-armed foot-soldiers signalled the beginning of the end for hoplite dominance, but in the long run the rise of the cavalry was more important. At the battle of Khairōneia in 338, it was the Makedonian cavalry, under the command of the youthful Alexander the Great, that delivered the fatal blow to the Greek army (1.105 and fig. 1.18). The full development was largely due to Alexander's father King Philip, who had at his disposal a people long habituated to fighting on horseback. He developed new weapons (the four- or five-metre-long spear known as the *sarīs(s)a* and the slashing sword) and new tactics (charging obliquely with a narrow front). But notable landmarks in the development of cavalry were the two great battles of the Theban military genius, Epameinōndās. At the battle of Leuktrā in 371, the Boiotian cavalry were used to play an integral part in his plan for the battle; while they fought the Spartan cavalry, the Boiotians advanced, under cover as it were, and began the attack on one flank (1.97, 7.30). At the battle of (Second) Mantineia in 362, Epameinōndās used his cavalry in conjunction with infantry to 'ram' part of the opposing line (1.98). The cavalry were, in short, already coming into their own, and in cavalry use as well as in infantry tactics it is clear that Philip learnt from the Thebans.

Fourth-century revolutions in warfare

7.27 In the fifth century, the Spartans were the only full-time state army in a world where most soldiers were part-time. But as early as (First) Mantineia, other cities had begun to form full-time units. The 1,000 picked Argive troops, who were stationed separately from the regular Argive companies, and who fought with considerable effect against the Spartan left wing when most of their countrymen did not dare even to endure combat, were, as the historian Diodōros later commented, 'admirably trained in the business of war'. In the fourth century the Spartans were equalled or outdone by the Theban 'Sacred Band' of three hundred, who fought heroically on the battlefield of Leuktrā and died to a man, it is said, at Khairōneia. Here again, however, the supreme professionals were the Makedonian army, and despite the attempts of Greeks to adjust to the new age they were surpassed by Philip, his 'Companion Foot' and his 'Companion Cavalry'.

7.28 From well back into archaic history, there had been professional soldiers available for hire to Greek states as to foreign rulers. Inscriptional evidence reveals their presence in Egypt at the end of the seventh century and 'helpers' (*epikouroi*), as they were known, figure both in Homeric epic and in archaic lyric poetry. In the fifth century, mercenaries play a relatively small part in events because both Athens and Spartē had large pools of allies to call upon (although many Athenian rowers were effectively mercenaries, see 7.38); but it was mercenaries whom the Corinthians sent to defend Poteidaia in 432 (Thucydides, *Peloponnesian War* 1.60.1). At the end of the Peloponnesian War, the Persian Cȳrus had no difficulty recruiting

10,000 Greek mercenaries to fight for the throne against his brother Artaxerxēs (1.88, 3.19). It was with a mercenary force that Iphikratēs wiped out the Spartan divisions at Lekhaion (7.24), and in the fourth century no city could do without them to cope with wars that could be continuous through summers and winters and that were increasingly complex. However, the claims found in the speeches of Isokratēs and Dēmosthenēs that mercenaries were waging wars 'by themselves' while citizens were sitting idle, like the claims that all mercenaries were exiles and runaways, were clearly exaggerations made to sting citizens into action.

7.29   Along with mercenary troops went professional generals. The illustrious mercenary generals of the age, Iphikratēs, Tīmotheos, Khabriās, Kharēs, to name a few, unlike Periklēs, Nīkiās and Alkibiadēs in the preceding century, confined themselves to war and left politics to specialist politicians (6.25). Such generals could make money from their skill and might hire themselves out to other cities when not needed by their own. Even the Spartan king Agēsilāos did service as a mercenary commander. Military theory too developed, and professional teachers of the military art are to be found, men like Dionȳsodōros, an Athenian whom we meet in Xenophōn's *Memorābilia* 3.1.1, professing 'to teach how to be a general', or that curious figure the Boiotian Phalīnos, the 'expert on tactics and arms-drill' who turns up in the service of the King of Persia in 401 (Xenophōn, *Anabasis* 2.1.7). Indeed a military literature began to be in vogue (cf. 8.24), and Xenophōn himself was a significant contributor to the genre, writing, in particular, works about cavalry and cavalry commanders.

7.30   New theories of how to fight got played out on the battlefield, in particular by the Thebans with their professional 'Sacred Band'. The man attributed with many innovations is Epameinōndās who, at the battle of Leuktrā in 371, concentrated his forces on his left flank, whereas one normally sought to win on the right. The Thebans were drawn up fifty deep, a startling fact, but only the further development of an earlier idea: at Dēlion, the Thebans had been twenty-five deep, so someone in Thebes in the fifth century was already conceiving of new ways of war. Further, when the Spartans sought to outflank the Thebans, the 'Sacred Band' was sent in to prevent them. Thus the general Epameinōndās continued to control the battle after it had been joined. He had thought out new methods of war and trained his men for them.

7.31   From this picture of military development the Athenians are largely absent. Their professional generals in the fourth century, in so far as they fought on land, made considerable use of mercenary troops, and the Athenians never developed any specialist hoplite unit. Xenophōn declared (*Memorābilia* 3.12) that the Athenians had 'no public training in military matters'. But there must always have been some initial training for Athenians who came of age. The conversation in Plato's dialogue, *Lakhēs*, which discussed the nature of courage (cf. 8.34), was occasioned by the sight of a famous teacher of hoplite fighting; and from the 330s a more serious two-year programme of military training was put in place. Now, upon being enrolled as citizens, those of the zeugite census, at least, took an oath to defend their fatherland and were put through a two-year training programme as ephebes (*ephēboi*). Special officials, known as *kosmētai* and *sōphronistai* (i.e. men to maintain order (*kosmos*) and instil self-control (*sōphrosunē*)) were appointed to see to the training. Here, the ephebes learnt a whole range of military skills and spent considerable time as garrison forces in the forts on Athens' northern border (Eleusīs, Phȳlē, Rhamnous). After that it was left to individuals to keep themselves ready for war. After their own fashion, which may not have been all that different from the general practice, Athenians did train (cf. 5.41).

Siegecraft

7.32 There was one form of land warfare, not yet discussed, in which Athens had a particularly strong reputation in the fifth century, though again she was to be outshone by Makedōn in the fourth. This was siege warfare. It was Athens' reputation in this that meant that in the late 460s the Spartans called on the city for help in the siege of the Messenian stronghold, Ithōmē (1.97). Generally, in the fifth century the only really effective way of taking a city was by circumvallation, i.e. putting a wall around it and starving it into submission. This could be both a very long and a very expensive business, and cities built themselves increasingly long walls, encompassing very much more than the built-up area, to make such sieges more difficult. There was some development of artillery: we hear of Periklēs using a battering-ram and 'tortoise-shell' of shields (which acted as a platform from which to scale walls) in the siege of Samos in 440 (1.53), and of Spartans using siege-engines against Plataia (1.56; Thucydides, *Peloponnesian War* 2.71ff.). But it was all rather ineffective. It took Periklēs nine months to reduce Samos, and the Spartans two years to reduce Plataia – manned in the earlier stages of the siege by 480 men, in the later by fewer than 240! The operations round Syracuse in 414 and 413 typified the age (1.74). The best the Athenians could think of was to try and wall the city off from harbour to sea, and let time and hunger do their worst.

7.33 It was in Sicily that crucial developments in siege warfare occurred, but not at the hands of the Athenians. The Carthaginians fighting against the Greeks in Sicily in the last decade of the fifth century succeeded in taking various cities by assault. We hear of rams and mounds, of wheeled towers and mines, and we shortly encounter for the first time in the service of Dionȳsios of Syracuse the 'catapult', a weapon rather like a cross-bow that discharged arrows at defenders of walls. The best indication of the new state of affairs is provided by what survives of the military handbook of the Arkadian Aineiās, the so-called Tactician, published in the early 350s. In it is much advice about how to defend cities against rams and mines and the like, but not a word about cir-

7.8 Two triremes with boar-shaped prows sail round this Athenian black-figure cup of c. 530.

cumvallation. And city defences built after the middle of the fourth century concentrate not on length but on strength. In this development Athens played her part. The general Tīmotheos took Samos by assault in 366/5 and a string of Thracian cities thereafter. But the real master of the art was Philip of Makedōn. Eleven cities are recorded as falling to him, and what is particularly striking is his speed. He could take a city in double-quick time before the Athenians could get help to it. Cities were no longer secure. But powerful artillery was not the only reason for this. Aineiās spends much time on ways of preventing treachery, and Philip was as famous for what he achieved with bags of gold as for what he achieved by battery.

Naval warfare

Triremes and their crews

7.34   Throughout the classical period, one sort of warship was almost universal, the trireme (the *trirēs* in Greek (cf. 2.19)). It was a long, slender ship (the dimensions attested by the fourth-century remains of the ship-sheds at the

7.9 The reconstructed trireme, *Olympias*, during sea trials.

Peiraieus were 35–7 m. by 3.5 m.) with a low draught. Its chief armament was the bronze ram which was an extension of the keel. There were 170 rowers, in three superimposed banks: 27 on each side in the lowest bank, the so-called *thalamītai*; likewise 27 in the middle bank, the *zugioi*; and 31 on each side in the top bank, the *thrānītai*, who sat on benches above the gunwale and rowed by means of an out-rigger (and since their oars were rowed at the sharpest angle to the water, their task was the most strenuous, and was rewarded with a higher rate of pay). Above the level of the *thrānītai* a deck ran from stem to stern on which the marines travelled and fought. The ship was commanded by a trierarch who had under him a steersman (*kubernētēs*), a rowing officer (*keleustēs*), a bow officer (*prōrātēs*) (whose function was mainly to keep watch), a quartermaster, and others including a ship's carpenter, an *aulos*-player to pipe the time for the rowers, ten hoplite marines and four archers. In all there were two hundred men.

7.35   The trireme carried masts, and on a long voyage it was possible to exploit a favourable wind. Nor did all the rowers row all the time, except in battle. There was no room on board for eating or sleeping, and little room for supplies (a crew would need about 300 kg of grain and 500 litres of water a day). The trireme, generally speaking, had to be beached at night for crews to acquire provisions, eat and sleep (cf. 2.19). The account given by Xenophōn of the voyage of Iphikratēs round the Peloponnese illuminates normal practice;

Iphikratēs was in a hurry and wanted to train his crews at the same time, but one can infer what was normal from Xenophōn's account:

> When Iphikratēs began his voyage round the Peloponnese, he took with him all the equipment he needed for a naval battle. He left his large sails at home, as if he was sailing to battle, and made very little use of his small sails even when the wind was favourable. By proceeding under oars in this way he made his crews fitter and his ships faster. And when the expedition was due for its morning or evening meal at any particular place, he would order the leading ships back, turn the line round again to face the land and make them race at a signal for the shore . . . Again, if they were taking a meal on hostile territory, he set the usual sentries on land but he also raised his ships' masts and had men keeping watch from the top of them. They had a far wider view from their point of vantage than they would have had from ground level . . . On daylight voyages he trained them to form line ahead or line abreast at a signal, so that in the course of their voyage they had practised and become skilled at the manoeuvres needed in a naval battle before they reached the area of sea which they supposed to be in enemy control. (Xenophōn, *Hellēnika* 6.2.27–30)

One point, which does not emerge from this account, was of great importance: the trireme was so light that it could not be used in really rough weather. This meant that naval operations were, generally speaking, not possible in winter, nor in the bad weather caused by the Etesian winds (see 2.4–5). Weather was a constant limiting factor in naval strategy.

Manning the Athenian navy

7.36 Maintaining a successful fleet of any significant size demanded both access to large reserves of manpower and an ability to train those men. Training was essential simply to ensure that crews could cope with moderately rough weather, quite apart from that required to manoeuvre effectively against the enemy. Athenian success depended not least on their having the best-trained crews – best-trained not least because they were so constantly involved in naval operations.

7.37 The favourite tactical manoeuvre, the *diekplous*, was particularly demanding. In it a ship would pass through the enemy line, swing round and attack the enemy, either by ramming it broadside or by shearing off its oars. Speed of movement, speed in turning, and accuracy in attack were essential and not easily acquired. Steering was particularly a matter for skill, which is partly why the steersman, the *kubernētēs*, was in many ways the key man. (When Alkibiadēs went off on a small mission in 407 he left the whole Athenian fleet at Samos under the command of his steersman – albeit with unfortunate consequences.) But all the crew needed to be skilled at their tasks, as we will see from the account below (7.39–41)

7.38 It was not, of course, the case that all Athenians could row well. There was a celebrated moment in 411 when the whole Athenian people rushed down to the Peiraieus, manned the ships, and presented a spectacle of far from well-trained seamanship (Thucydides, *Peloponnesian War* 8.95). But many lived by rowing. In the *Akharnians* Aristophanēs refers to 'the *thrānītai* folk (key rowers, see 7.34), the city savers', and Aristotle in the *Politics* attributed the rise of democracy to 'the naval throng'. But to a large extent the Athenian navy was mercenary. 'The Athenian naval power is hired rather than their own,' the Corinthians asserted in 432, and Periklēs' reply, while declaring that Athens could man the fleet herself if necessary, conceded the point (Thucydides, *Peloponnesian War* 1.121–40). A fleet of sixty ships required over 10,000 rowers. If Athens had had to rely solely on her citizens and resident aliens, the *metoikoi*, she would never have been able to man the large fleets she constantly did. But rowing was not a pleasant experience, especially on the lower benches (note how Athenian rowers are assumed by Aristophanēs in that passage to row on the top bench). The unpleasantness of the conditions could make crews liable to rebel at any further imposition, and attempts to discipline crews or their commanders often backfired (Thucydides, *Peloponnesian War* 8.84). Only those unable to gain a living by other means would choose to sign up for naval service, but those who rowed for money might worry more about how much they were being paid than about who paid them, and would desert to a better paymaster. A significant proportion of the Athenian navy was in fact manned by slaves (who had, of course, motives of their own for absconding; see Thucydides, *Peloponnesian War* 7.13). It is notable that historians never recorded numbers of casualties after naval battles.

The development of naval warfare

7.39 The discussion of land warfare above emphasised the constant development of the art of war. In the case of naval warfare, we are confronted by the apparent contrary. Naval tactics remained virtually unchanged, as far as we know, from the start of the Peloponnesian War to the bitter defeat of the Athenian navy, and the end of Athens as a naval power, at the battle of Amorgos in 322 (7.50). What development there was had come earlier. The Persian fleet which fought the Greeks at Artemision and Salamīs in 480 (1.35–6) consisted of ships rather unlike triremes, being decked all over, higher, lighter and carrying more than thirty marines. At that stage the Phoenicians, fighting on the Persian side, excelled the Greeks in seamanship. Their aim, amply fulfilled at Artemision, was to sail through the Greek line, turn, come alongside and send their marines aboard. In the confined waters of the bay of Salamīs, however, their seamanship was frustrated, and the heavier Greek ships won the battle *by ramming*. This was to be the method of the future, yet in 480 the Greeks could see the battle only as a freak bit of luck. For when in the early 460s Kīmōn sailed out to confront a grand Persian naval and land force at the battle of the Eurymedōn (1.44), he fully

7.10 This aerial view of the Peiraieus shows the two southern harbours used by the Athenian navy. The Great Harbour (Kantharos), the commercial harbour, is at the top left of the picture (see fig. 2.9).

decked his ships and loaded them with marines in the Phoenician manner. As late as 433, many Greeks, though not the Athenians, were still fighting in the same old-fashioned way. Thucydides' account of the battle of Sybota makes this plain:

> As soon as the signals were given, the ships on both sides came to close quarters and fighting began. Both sides had many hoplites on deck, as well as a number of archers and javelineers, for owing to their inexperience they were still using old-fashioned tactics. The battle was obstinately fought, but without corresponding skill, being more like a land engagement fought at sea. Once they had grappled with each other, they found it difficult to disengage because of the number of vessels involved and their crowding together; they relied for victory mainly on the hoplites on deck, who stood and fought while the ships remained stationary. There was no attempt at the manoeuvre of breaking the line; courage and brute force played a greater part than skill. Confusion reigned throughout the battle, and there was tumult everywhere. (Thucydides, *Peloponnesian War* 1.49)

7.40 But in the naval operations of the Athenian Phormiōn at the mouth of the Gulf of Corinth in 429, the Corinthians came up against the new naval tactics of the Athenians, and were clearly terrified (1.60):

(83) Phormiōn watched the Corinthian fleet as they coasted along out of the gulf, intending to attack them in the open sea. But the Corinthians and their allies had to put to sea with no thought of fighting, their object being the transport of troops to Akarnāniā; and they assumed that the Athenians with their twenty ships would not venture to attack their own forty-seven. However, as they sailed along their own coast, they saw the Athenians sailing parallel to them, and when they tried to cross from Patrai in Akhaia to the opposite mainland they noticed them again sailing from Khalkis and the Euēnos river to meet them. They failed to give them the slip by putting out at night, and so were compelled to fight in mid-passage . . . The Peloponnesians drew their ships up in a circle, as large as they could make it without allowing the enemy passage between the vessels, whose prows faced outwards and sterns inwards. The lighter craft of the expedition were placed inside the circle together with five of their fastest ships ready to sally out at short notice to meet any enemy attack.

(84) The Athenians drew up in line ahead and sailed round and round them, gradually forcing the circle to contract by sailing very close and pretending to attack, though Phormiōn had given orders that no attack was to be made till he gave the signal. He expected that they would not be able to keep formation, as they would on land, and that the warships and the lighter craft would foul each other and fall into confusion, while the wind which usually got up towards evening and for which he was waiting during the manoeuvre, would complete their disorder in no time. He judged that he could pick his own time for the attack, as his ships were the more manoeuvrable, and that the best moment was when the wind rose. When the wind did rise the Peloponnesian ships were already crowded together, and what with the wind and their own light craft were soon in confusion. The warships fouled each other and the crews tried to push them free with poles, shouting and swearing and struggling with each other; the noise made it impossible to hear the orders of the ships' captains and the helmsmen, and the rough water prevented the inexperienced crews from clearing their oars and made it more difficult for the helmsmen to control their vessels. At this moment Phormiōn gave the signal, and the Athenians attacked. They first sank the ship of one of the enemy commanders, and then went on to disable any ship they came across; in the confusion the enemy's resistance was completely broken and they fled to Patrai and Dymē in Akhaiā. (Thucydides, *Peloponnesian War* 2.83–4)

7.41 In this first engagement, the forty-seven Peloponnesian ships were still equipped in the old-fashioned way seen at Sybota. Forming up in a circle for fear of the Athenian *diekplous*, they were driven together in confusion by the Athenians circling round them. For the second engagement, the Spartans called for new ships to be built, better fitted to the new ways of war, and a fleet of seventy-seven was assembled. The Athenians still had only twenty, but the Peloponnesian fleet was afraid to face them in open sea. Before the battle, the Peloponnesian commander tried to minimise the importance of Athenian experience and skill; but, although some of the Athenian ships were

7.11 On this red-figure oil flask (*lekythos*) from the end of the first quarter of the fifth century, Athēnē is shown holding a ship's stern (*aphlaston*), a token of naval victory.

caught within the narrow waters of the gulf and suffered, in the end it was Athenian experience and skill that took the real credit. And on this occasion, rather than take prisoners as they had after the first engagement, the Athenians killed some of the crews of the ships they captured, just as the Peloponnesians killed the crews of the disabled ships who failed to swim ashore:

> (90) When the Peloponnesians saw Phormiōn sailing along inside the gulf, in line ahead and close inshore, which was just what they wanted, at a given signal they all turned to port and bore down with all speed in line abreast on the Athenians, hoping to cut the whole squadron off. The eleven leading ships evaded the Peloponnesian wing and its turning movement and escaped into open water, but the rest were caught, driven ashore as they tried to escape, and disabled; any of the crews who failed to swim ashore were killed . . .
>
> (91) Meanwhile their twenty ships from the right wing were chasing the eleven Athenian ships which had evaded the turning movement and reached the open sea. The Athenians, with the exception of one ship, outdistanced them and made good their escape to Naupaktos, and drawing up by the temple of Apollo, with prows seaward, prepared to defend themselves against a Peloponnesian attack. The Peloponnesians came up later, singing a paean of victory as they advanced. A long way ahead of the rest was a Leukadian ship pursuing the one Athenian straggler. There happened to be a merchant ship anchored off shore, and the Athenian ship outwitted the pursuit by sailing round this merchantman, ramming its pursuer amidships and sinking it. This unlikely and unexpected exploit caused panic among the Peloponnesians, who had fallen out of formation in the excitement of victory, and some of them stopped rowing so as to lose way till the others came up (a very dangerous thing to do with the Athenians so close), while others, not knowing the coast, ran aground in the shallows. (92) When they saw what had happened, the Athenians plucked up courage, and at a single word of command fell on the enemy with a cheer. They, because of their mistakes and the disorder into which they had fallen, after a brief resistance made off for Panormos, from where they had originally put out. The Athenians pursued them and captured six of the ships nearest to them, and recovered those of their own which had been disabled close inshore when the action began and taken in tow. Of the crews they killed some and took others prisoner. (Thucydides, *Peloponnesian War* 2.90–2)

In short, after the battle of Sybota the Peloponnesians slowly saw the light. For Athens the perfection of the use of the trireme had come before the Peloponnesian War. No serious challenge to Athenian naval supremacy was mounted in the course of the war, although at Syracuse the particular conditions of the Great Harbour enabled the Syracusans, by modifying their ships, to defeat the Athenians. After the war, neither the Athenians, their navy initially reduced to twelve ships, nor anyone else had the resources to devote to naval developments, and for over a century there was no significant advance in the art of naval warfare.

The Athenian naval system

7.42   We are given a particularly vivid picture of how the Athenians put a fleet together by Thucydides' account of the formation of the expedition to Sicily in 415:

> The fleet had been equipped at great expense both by the trierarchs and from public funds. Public funds paid each member of the crews at the rate of a *drakhmē* a day besides providing sixty warships and forty troopships with picked petty officers; the trierarchs added a bonus to the public payment for the *thrānītai* and petty officers and spared no expense on figureheads and other gear, rivalling each other in the provision of vessels which would be outstanding in both appearance and speed. The land forces were picked from the best muster-rolls and individuals competed keenly in the quality of their arms and other equipment . . . Indeed the total outlay found by the city amounted to an enormous sum, if you reckon up the private expenses of individuals serving in the forces as well as public expenditure by the state. Public expenditure included funds already expended as well as moneys in the hands of the generals for the expenses of the expedition, private expenditure both what individuals had laid out on their equipment and what the trierarchs had already incurred on their ships and were likely to incur in the future; to this should be added the provision individuals were likely to have made by way of journey money for a long campaign quite apart from its cost to the state, and what soldiers and merchants took with them with a view to trade . . .
>
>   When the ships were manned and everything they meant to take was on board, the trumpet gave the signal for silence and the prayers customary before putting to sea were offered, not ship by ship but all together, conducted by a herald, and officers and crew throughout the whole force mixed and poured libations from gold and silver cups. The crowds on shore joined in the prayers, both citizens and those who wished them well. And when the paean had been sung and the libations poured, they put to sea, sailing out first in line ahead and then racing to Aigīna. (Thucydides, *Peloponnesian War* 6.31)

For the fourth century, our knowledge of how the Athenians organised their navy depends partly on long inscriptions listing trierarchs and their obligations, and partly from a speech delivered by Apollodōros in [Dēmosthenēs], *Against Polyklēs* 50. In it we see the Athenian navy at a time of particular stress in the late 360s. The supply of rowing labour in the Peiraieus roughly matched the regular demand, and when in autumn 362 the call came for yet more ships, exceptional measures had to be taken. Moreover Apollodōros was an extravagant young man (cf. 6.45) and spent more on his ship and his crew than he could reasonably expect his successor to take over lightly, but the dynamics of trierarchic service had not essentially changed since the fifth century.

(a) Trierarchy

7.43 Trierarchy was a form of military service (a *leitourgiā*, see 6.62) which all men of the necessary minimum wealth were obliged to undertake. Its functions were primarily financial, for although the trierarch shared the danger of service, the knowledge and experience necessary for naval operations lay, as has already been remarked, with the *kubernētēs* (7.37). Since a trierarchy lasted for a full twelve months from the day it commenced, it certainly was costly. Although the city provided the ship, paid the crew, and made the naval equipment in the dockyards available for trierarchs to draw on, a trierarch often found it expedient to have his own equipment, especially things as vital as ropes, and to hire as expert a set of officers as he could. The threat made by a general in Aristophanēs' *Knights* (912–18), to see that a trierarch got an old leaky ship and a rotten sail, showed what a trierarch might face. Because trierarchy was so costly in the later years of the Peloponnesian War, when Athens was much impoverished, there were not enough sufficiently rich men of military age to take the duty on, and the 'syntrierarchy' was introduced. Here the cost was shared by two men, each of whom served in person for six months.

7.44 Equipping a trireme involved providing two classes of gear, wooden and hanging. The wooden gear, a set of oars, a mast, steering-oars, ladders, sail-yards and poles, was kept in the ship-shed, where the ship was docked when not at sea. The hanging gear, sails, sail-tackle, ropes, anchors and some other items, was kept in the gear-store. Many of the ship-sheds were situated in the Peiraeus harbour of Zeā, while the gear-stores were probably mainly in the main Peiraeus harbour, Kantharos. So, to prepare an expedition, someone would bring the ship, with the wooden gear, round from Zeā to the quay in Kantharos, where the ship's hanging gear would be loaded (not all of it, as ordinary sails were not taken into battle) (6.22).

7.45 The ship would then be manned. The crews would know which ship they belonged to as they would have practised together (manoeuvring the ship in battle required timing and experience, which could be gained only by regular sessions). They would come with their *tropōtēr* (a leather thong for tying the oar to the pin against which it worked) and *hupēresion* (a cushion, perhaps tallowed underneath for sliding back and forth at the oar). It seems that the oars were placed on a rack on board while the ship was being manned, and that the amount of pay due to the trierarch for distribution to the sailors was calculated on a count of hands (the lower banks of rowers would have to stick their hands through the oar-ports, giving an opportunity for cheating if one of the crew was absent).

7.46 Trierarchs competed with one another for the quality of their ships, equipment, and crew (5.27). This was variously encouraged by the Athenians. One decree sending out a fleet expressly offers gold crowns to the trierarchs of the ships ready first, second and third (RO 100.190–204). Some members of the *boulē* would be on the quay to see that preparations went smoothly (cf. 6.22). Their task would, of course, have been doubly difficult at night, when the Peiraicus would have to be lighted by torches, unless there was a moon. When the ships were ready, the trierarchs would offer libations to the gods, and then the *keleustēs* on a signal from the trierarch or *kubernētēs* would give the order to get under way. At the end of service, the trierarch had to ensure that all state equipment was handed on in good order (cf. the incident at 5.27).

(b) Summoriai

7.47 Syntrierarchy was a satisfactory enough system in a city so lacking in a bureaucracy, and in principle it served Athens perfectly well. But in the fourth century the city was much poorer than in the fifth, and pay for the sailors became irregular and was rarely complete. As the city approached the nadir of its financial condition in the mid-350s, a law, at first sight revolutionary, was passed – the law of Periandros of 357. This stated that the person ordered to pay for the trireme did not have also to serve on it. So from now on, even elderly Athenians like Isokratēs, long past the age of military service, were obliged to pay a share. Boards (*summoriai*) were formed, consisting of up to sixteen persons, to which the duty was assigned not simply of financing a certain group of triremes but of looking after their equipment. The system did not long satisfy. In 340 Dēmosthenēs succeeded in passing a law, whereby financial liability was more equitably shared by sub-dividing the *summoriai* into smaller groups. In the following decade there was significant investment in new ship-sheds and a new naval arsenal in the Peiraeus.

(c) The success of the system

7.48 In various ways, as we have seen, land warfare in the fourth century was increasingly professional. Was the same true in naval matters? The law of Periandros did seem to open the door to the professional, making it possible for a man devoted to the sea to be hired by a *summoriā*, but since the law was primarily financial, it might be thought to have let in the professional by accident by a back door. This is illusion. The separation of payment and service had already begun, and Periandros merely gave legal approval to what was increasingly fact. At the battle of Peparēthos in 361, there were quite a number of trierarchs who had hired out their trierarchies. Characteristically the Athenians rounded on them and blamed them for the defeat. But the practice went on, as Dēmosthenēs' speech (*On the Crown of the Trierarchy* 51) shows. Where there was room for it, professionalism asserted itself, but the real advances had been made back in the days of Periklēs. The perfection of the navy was one of his greatest achievements.

7.49 In theory, the system was not perfect. It took time to get a fleet out to sea, precious time in which the city's cause might be lost. But what was the alternative? A standing navy with rowers and trierarchs ready to leave within the hour would have cost more than the city-state of Athens probably in the fifth century and certainly in the fourth could have afforded. Again, a standing navy in the Peiraieus would have been no use in the north once the Etesian winds had begun to blow, and a standing navy would have brought the city's fortunes to a standstill. It was better to devote resources as they did, to keeping up the supply of new ships. Ships that were waterlogged and leaked did not, as Nīkiās found at Syracuse (Thucydides, *Peloponnesian War* 7.12), move as fast as new ships. In the navy lists of the fourth century, which are a prime source of information about the Athenian navy, we are at first astonished to find how many hulls the city possessed; between 357/6 and 353/2, a period when Athens was financially at her lowest, the number of triremes increased from 283 to 349. But such expenditure was inevitable if Athens was to maintain her naval primacy, and far more important than a standing navy (cf. 7.1).

7.50 The system worked. There was no competition. But once the Makedonian Alexander had captured the naval bases of the Persian empire in Phoenicia in 332, the writing was on the wall, for Alexander now had control of the mighty Phoenician fleet. At the battle of Amorgos in 322, the largest Athenian fleet ever to take part in a battle after the Persian Wars, 170 ships, faced the Makedonian, Kleitos, with 240. At the end of the day Athens' naval glory became a matter of history. Kleitos, 'trident in hand, had himself proclaimed Poseidōn'.

8   The culture of Athens

Background to the classical achievement

The production of Greek literature

8.1 We do not know when the inhabitants of the Greek peninsula began telling each other stories, but they had surely done so for millennia before our first written records of such stories. Those earliest records, the hexameter poetry of the Boiotian poet Hesiod and the Homeric epics, *Iliad* and *Odyssey*, attained more or less the form in which we have them around or shortly after 700 BC, and simply assume that those who hear them will already be familiar with a wide range of stories. Much the same is true of the songs surviving (words only, not music) from the seventh century – the songs written by Arkhilokhos or Sēmōnidēs for solo performance at the formalised drinking parties known as *sumposia*, or the songs written by Alkman for choral performance in the context of religious festivals in Spartē. We know these works, and not what was told and sung c. 800 BC, simply because in the eighth century the Greeks learned the art of writing.

8.2 The Greeks developed their own, unique system of writing in the years 800–750 from the Phoenicians (1.13). Phoenicians, in common with other literate cultures of the Near East at the time, used symbols to represent consonantal sounds (as in Hebrew). The Greeks invented the first fully phonetic alphabet, i.e. one with symbols representing vowels as well as consonants, taking over some of the Phoenician letter forms and names, e.g.:

ℵ aleph   A alpha
ℶ beth   B beta
ℷ gimel   Γ gamma
ℸ daleth   Δ delta

8.3 The earliest traces of Greek writing date to the second quarter of the eighth century, and by the end of the century snatches of quite sophisticated verse compositions survive, scratched onto pottery. This evidence, along with the development of distinct local forms of the Greek alphabet, suggests that writing was in fairly widespread use in Greece by the beginning of the seventh century. By comparison to the Greek which we are used to reading, the main feature of all writing that survives on inscriptions and poetry from the archaic period is that it was in capital letters, most frequently with no gaps between words and no punctuation, and sometimes written backwards, right to left, sometimes alternately right–left, left–right (*boustrophēdon*, like an 'ox turning' up and down a field). The range of letters used varied from place to place. For example, fifth-century Athenians largely used the Attic alphabet, which lacked the letters ω, ζ, χ, υ, used H not for long e but for the aspirate, and used o for o (short o), ω (long o), or ου (ou); and ε for e (short e), η (long e), or ει (ei). In 403, Athens agreed to adopt an Ionic alphabet which gradually became standard throughout the Greek world, and it is from this agreed alphabet (through its Roman adaptation) that our system of writing has developed (though punctuation, gaps between words and minuscule writing did not become standard till the ninth century AD).

8.4   In our world, prose is the main medium of written communication, but the earliest Greek writing was in verse, not prose, and, apart from records of state decisions (and even then some laws were said to have been in verse), the first prose in Greece was not written till the sixth century. Virtually all the earliest philosopher-scientists wrote in verse. Verse had the advantage of being more easily memorable, and poets were seen rather as teachers, practical men of business, wise men and scientists, than as inspired and unworldly visionaries.

8.5   The story of how the literature of the Greeks has survived to this day is a fascinating one. All we can do here is to offer the barest outline. Nearly all the Greek literature that has survived has done so because it was copied and recopied down the ages. But recopying texts by hand (and excerpting them for e.g. school use) had soon left many texts in a state of chaos. In the third century the Greek scholars gathered at the Museum of Alexandria in Egypt (which the Ptolemies turned into the intellectual centre of the world) decided to produce a 'best text' of all surviving Greek literature. It is from these texts that our texts all ultimately derive; it is, for example, the Alexandrian editors' text of the Homeric epics that we have, and that text is inevitably rather different from the text that had been performed in the seventh century. What the Alexandrians did not edit does not survive. The Romans, soon to be masters of the Mediterranean, were captivated by Greek culture and ensured that its products continued to be copied (selectively) for individuals, schools and libraries. The collapse of the Roman Empire in the fifth century AD, in the West, and the stagnation of monasteries and anti-pagan feeling in the East, left the Greek heritage hanging by a thread, but in the ninth century AD there was a revival of learning, when Greek literature was 'rediscovered' and began to be copied again, and virtually everything that survived through till then is with us today. Our most tantalising loss from this time is that of early Greek lyric poetry. The Church did not look kindly on it, because of its frequently risqué nature, and it was simply not recopied. The Greek lyric poetry that we have has survived as quotations, in anthologies, or has been recovered from the desert sands. This loss is all the more infuriating when we know that virtually the sole female voice of the ancient Greek world, the sixth-century poetess from Lesbos, Sapphō, had had her works gathered into some nine books. All we have of Sapphō is one complete 28 line poem; four incomplete poems of over 20 lines; five incomplete poems of over 10 lines; 120 other complete lines, some in runs of two, three or four; and hundreds of bits and pieces, half lines, single words, half-words. Major discoveries continue to be made on papyri recovered from Egyptian mummies and rubbish dumps: in the last thirty years our knowledge of both Arkhilokhos and Simōnidēs has been significantly supplemented from these sources.

Discounting the gods: myth, philosophy and medicine

8.6   Scholars have sometimes suggested that when people acquire the ability to write this changes the way in which people think. Whatever the truth of that, there is little doubt that the writing down of the Homeric epics corresponded with an important development in the way in which the Greeks envisaged the mythical past. The scraps that have been preserved of other archaic epic poems – the poems which, with the Homeric epics, have come to be known as the 'epic cycle' – reveal a world which is rather little on display in the *Iliad* or *Odyssey*. The poem known as the *Cūpria*, for instance, featured the Greek at Troy being fed by the three daughters of Anios who could produce at will wine, olive oil, and grain. It also featured one Lynkeus, whose eyesight was so acute that he could survey the whole Peloponnese at a glance and see Kastōr and Polydeukēs when they were hiding in the hollow of a tree. Poems of the cycle feature grants of immortality (e.g. to Memnōn after he has been 'killed' by Akhilleus) and acts of rejuvenation (of Aisōn by Mēdeia). Hesiod too tells of monsters like Ekhidna 'who is half a nymph with fair cheeks and glancing eyes, and half a monstrous snake, terrible, large and speckled, eating raw flesh in the secret parts of the holy earth'. She was the mother of Kerberos, the Hydrā and the Khimairā, with three heads, one of a lion, one of a snake, and one of a goat. Although such monsters attracted some attention from Greek artists in the archaic period and make occasional appearances in later literature, that literature very largely takes its lead from the *Iliad*'s inclination to distance the monstrous and the miraculous and to engage directly in its narrative only with situations that can be understood in the terms of the natural world with which its audience was familiar. As we meet them in classical literature, Greek myths are largely populated by human heroes behaving in humanly intelligible ways, and (in general) there is little or nothing of the grotesque, the absurd and the fantastic. This insistence that the world should make sense in human terms, and that it could be explained without recourse to the supernatural, is the hallmark of Greek literature and philosophy.

8.7   Greeks invented philosophy, but the first Greek philosophers were more what we should call 'natural scientists'. They asked much the same question that

Hesiod asked in the *Theogony* – 'Where does the world come from?' – but whereas Hesiod assumed that the story of the creation of earth, rivers and sea was also a story of the gods and their actions, those whom the Greeks came to regard as the first philosophers asked not who was responsible but what the world was made of. Behind this lies the remarkable assumption that it must be possible to get behind the observed diversity of the world and find some straightforward rationalisation. The first philosopher, Thalēs of Mīlētos (c. 580), pronounced that the guiding principle (*arkhē*) behind everything was water, a most subtle guess (consider how it can be readily observed to take liquid, solid and gaseous forms). He explained earthquakes by saying that since the world rested on water, earthquakes occurred when the water was disturbed by the wind. He was wrong, but the important observation to make is that he did not say they were caused by the god of earthquakes, Poseidōn. Other early thinkers proposed other *arkhai*.

8.8   Speculations about there being a single original substance raised issues about what constituted sameness and difference and about what counted as evidence for sameness and difference. Two particular thinkers stand out in this debate, Hērakleitos from Ephesos and Parmenidēs (c. 480), an eastern Greek who moved to Eleā in Italy, both active in the early fifth century. Hērakleitos is famous for pointing out the unity of opposites ('the way up and the way down are one and the same') and that the world is in constant flux ('you cannot step into the same river twice'). Parmenidēs, by contrast, maintained that change was impossible – since how could 'water' change to 'not-water'? It either *was* or *was not* water: it could not be both. So change (and all its associations, e.g. movement) was not possible. To the natural objection that one was moving every waking moment of one's life, Parmenidēs devastatingly replied that this simply proved that the senses were unreliable guides to the real nature of the world, and should not be trusted. This was much the same conclusion as Hērakleitos had also reached: 'Eyes and ears are bad witnesses for men if they have barbarian souls [i.e. souls which do not understand their language]'. Thoughts such as these put an end to speculation that identified one particular substance as the *arkhē*, and led to models which posited multiple original substances which formed the world as perceived by mixture (so Empedoklēs' four elements, earth, air, fire and water, or Anaxagorās' mixture of particles of infinite number and smallness). Most intriguing to modern thought, because of the parallels with more recent speculation, is the 'atomic' theory of the universe proposed by Dēmokritos. According to this, matter consisted of minute indivisible particles *below* the level of perception, which did not of themselves change, but merely regrouped themselves to make the different shapes, sizes, textures and tastes of the world we experience. An atomic theory was at the basis of the Epicurean philosophical school of the Hellenistic and Roman period, but it was the four-element theory which had the greatest influence in antiquity, not least because it was embraced by Aristotle.

8.9   This simplified account of one of a number of running debates amongst early thinkers reveals their strengths and weaknesses. On the credit side, there was no dogma. Everything was open to question. There was no authority, religious or political, determining what was thought. On the debit side, much Greek thought tended to be, on the model of mathematics, axiomatic. That is, on the basis of a number of assumptions, Greek thinkers constructed a model of the universe without recourse to anything other than unsystematic observations and pure logic. When Greeks did experiments, it was generally to demonstrate, rather than to prove, a hypothesis. But Greek medical writing shows some understanding of the importance of the principle of verification, and if we are surprised by the lack of experimentation amongst the early philosophers, we should take into account the nature of the questions they were asking and the means of observation open to them: what sort of experiment could they possibly do to prove a theory of the origin of the universe? All the same, while the Greeks started a process which in time would make empirical research the basis of Western intellectual enquiry, they were only in a limited sense 'scientific' themselves and tended generally towards large-scale, abstract speculation throughout the classical and Hellenistic period.

8.10 We see two powerful analytical tools repeatedly used by these early (and later) thinkers to help them get a grip on their problems. These were arguments from analogy and from polarity. Argument from analogy is an argument in which the phenomenon to be explained is likened to a similar phenomenon already understood, and the one is used to cast light on the other (the frequent use of similes by Homer, a comparable literary device, suggests the technique was particularly congenial to Greek thought). Analogy is necessarily the basis for any understanding of the world – it is at the root of the interest in history, for example. What marks early Greek philosophers out are the leaps of thought involved in some of their analogies. For example, Anaximandros describes the order of the cosmos in terms of an equilibrium caused by opposed substances which make up the cosmos 'paying the penalty and recompensing one another for their injustice', an image taken from the rule of law in the human world.

8.11 The principle of polarity is seen at work when early thinkers got a grip on problems by presenting the world and its constituent parts in terms of opposites: hot and cold, wet and dry, light and dark, and so on. Aristotle attributes to the fifth-century thinker Alkmaiōn the view that 'most human things go in pairs', and we can see in later Greek thought a tendency to look for oppositions (two of the most common particles in the Greek language are *men* and *de* – meaning 'on the one hand . . . on the other hand').

8.12 The Greeks invented the discipline of medicine, removing it from the realm of quackery, charlatanism and magic and making its foundation empirical observation. One treatise famously (*On the Sacred Disease*) insists that it is not right to single out one disease (epilepsy) as 'the sacred disease' since no disease is more sacred than another. Another treatise insists that the menstrual problems of young girls are to be solved not by making dedications to Artemis but by having sexual intercourse. In the early fifth century Alkmaiōn of Krotōn (in South Italy), head of a famous medical school, was said to have dissected the eye. This is almost certainly not the case, but he may have drawn his important conclusions about the path of the optic nerve into the brain, and located the brain as the centre of thought, through experimental dissection of animals and the treatment of war wounds. This empirical trend was to develop from then on. Both analogy and polarity are also seen at work in medical thought (see further 5.72–7; 8.37–9): 'If sudden changes in various diets are found to make a great difference to healthy people, it is only to be expected that they will have a great effect in disease, and the greatest in the acute diseases' (*Regimen in Acute Diseases* 28) offers an example of analogy; that men are 'dry', women 'wet', of polarity.

8.13   If medical writings tend to stress how much can be understood about the human body without invoking the gods, philosophers were also interested in what the gods were like. Some of the most independent and original observations made by early thinkers were about the gods, many of them striking at the heart of the conventional, 'Homeric' view (cf. 3.53). Xenophanēs, an Ionian (c. 570–470), quite explicitly attacked Homer and satirised the way in which he represented gods as men (anthropomorphism):

> Homer and Hesiod have attributed to the gods everything that among men earns shame and abuse – theft, adultery and mutual deceit. (fr. 11)

> Men think the gods are born and have clothes and voices and bodies like their own. (fr. 14)

> If oxen and lions and horses had hands like men and could draw and make works of art, horses would make gods like horses and oxen like oxen and each would draw pictures of the gods as if they had bodies like their own. (fr. 15)

Hērakleitos draws attention to the curious logic involved in both ritual purification after murder (cf. 3.26) and praying to statues:

> They purify themselves vainly with blood when they are suffering from blood-pollution, as if someone who had stepped into mud were to try and wash it off with mud. Anyone who noticed him do this would think him mad. And they pray to the images of the gods, which is like trying to have a conversation with a house; for they do not know the true nature of gods and heroes. (fr. 5)

8.14   It is a striking and important feature of early Greek thinkers that none of them were Athenians. Most of them came from the Ionian coast and its adjacent islands. If we look for a reason why speculation of the sort discussed above should have originated there, it is difficult to resist the conclusion that the contact between Greek and Near Eastern culture was an important stimulus. (Cf. the Near Eastern impact on Greek art at 8.84–5). It is also important to acknowledge that those who engaged in such speculative thought were often, but not always aristocrats, whose wealth gave them the leisure and therefore the time to devote to intellectual pursuits. (Greek *skholē* 'leisure' is the origin of our 'school, scholar', cf. 5.25, 50. Leisure was a luxury available only occasionally to the vast majority of ancients, scraping a living from the land.) Such intellectuals were in no way representative of the 'average' Greek, and their views made relatively little impact. Healing sanctuaries actually grew more important at exactly the same time as medical speculation argued most strongly against seeing illness or healing as emanating from the gods. As in modern societies, the gap between new academic thought and common opinion could be extremely wide.

Classical Athens

8.15   The cultural and intellectual achievements of classical Greece were built on the extraordinary work of the preceding centuries. In mathematics, rhetoric, history, ethics, politics, linguistics, logic, and then in the more scientific disciplines (medicine, biology and physics), thinkers of the stature of Prōtagorās, Hippokratēs, Sōkratēs, Plato and Aristotle constructed systematic disciplines which have been the basis of Western understanding for most of the two and a half millennia since their time. In the arts, the tragedians, sculptors and architects created works of such excellence that they continue to shape what drama, statues and buildings look like in the Western world today. What fuelled this intense creativity is far from clear. Many of the crucial developments were made by men born and active in cities other than Athens, and we often know little of their social and political background. Many of those men visited or spent time in Athens. But while we can be reasonably confident of the importance of the particular Athenian situation on a long-term resident such as Aristotle, born in the north Aegean town of Stageirā, it is less clear that Prōtagorās from Abdērā, for example, gained a great deal from his brief visit to Athens, closely related though Prōtagorās' ideas are to the theory of democracy (8.29). Some cultural and intellectual developments, however, such as tragedy and comedy, Socratic philosophy, and forensic rhetoric, seem more closely related to specifically Athenian institutions, while it is hard to divorce developments in sculpture from the unprecedented investment in architectural sculpture which Athenian imperial wealth made possible (8.91, 95). The absence of a ruling class of priests imposing 'truth' from on high and a strong sense of independence may also have something to do with it.

Literacy and the spoken word

8.16   In the fifth century, literacy would seem to have been fairly widespread amongst male Athenians living in Athens. The Athenians simply assumed

8.1 A young man writes with a stylus on a wax writing tablet on this early fifth-century Athenian red-figure cup. Another writing tablet is to be seen tied up on the wall to the left of the lyre.

that the effective way of conveying information was to display a notice, and notices of lawsuits, lists for military service, and so on were displayed beside the statues of the eponymous heroes in the *agorā* (cf. 2.35, 5.39, figs. 1.9, 4.8). In the fourth century, all witness statements in court had to be written down at an early stage in the proceedings, and were then read out in court. Writing was, indeed, sufficiently common for something of a backlash to develop. A pamphlet survives by one Alkidamas, active in the first half of the fourth century, which argues that oral communication is much better than writing. Literacy may have been less common in country areas, although some Attic demes made much use of inscriptions to record their business. Whether the same levels of literacy could be found among women is hard to tell – but pot painters certainly show women reading (5.38). Literacy rates were no doubt higher among the wealthy than among the poor, and it may be that the wealth-threshold for female literacy was higher than for male. There was certainly a book trade in fifth-century Athens – Sōkratēs in his defence speech claims one could buy a copy of Anaxagorās' work in the *agorā* for about a *drakhmē* – but we know nothing of the size of the book market.

8.17 The ability to speak (and understand the spoken word) was vital on far more occasions than the ability to write and read. Where we read books, Athenians would more normally listen to live recitations, when a poet or historian or scientist would stand up and address an audience (in public or private). Where we read news or see it, through newspapers or television, the Athenians heard it passed on by word of mouth at the barber shop or other social meeting-place. The information on which government decisions are made is conveyed today by way of written reports, and legislation is proposed by way of government papers; the Athenian *ekklēsiā* heard largely oral reports (though generals might in some circumstances send letters to be read out; see Thucydides, *Peloponnesian War* 7.8, 10–11), and arguments for a particular course of action were laid out in the *ekklēsiā* as part of a debate (cf. 6.114–19). Athenians probably heard the *Iliad* and *Odyssey* performed by rhapsodes at the *Panathēnaia* much more often than they actually sat down and *read* Homer, although scrolls shown on painted pottery where Homeric lines are visible suggest that boys learnt Homer at school from a written text (3.44). The works of other poets became familiar in similar ways – again a painted pot shows a singer at a symposium performing a line of the sixth-century poet from Megara, Theognis. No living poet 'published' his work in our sense of the word. A tragedian like Sophoklēs had his plays performed, and it is unlikely that most Athenians would have read again a play they had seen. But in the fourth century, the Athenians were keen to have archive copies of the works of Aiskhylos, Sophoklēs and Euripidēs, and it must have been on the basis of written texts that the frequent revivals and productions elsewhere in Attikē of plays by the great tragedians were put on (cf. 8.46).

8.18 Active political life and the power to influence decisions depended on joining in debates in massed gatherings (*ekklēsiā, boulē* and law-courts, deme assemblies), where the ability to speak persuasively was of paramount importance (cf. 6.16). Just as in Homer the leaders argued over matters amongst themselves, so in classical Athens much political discussion took place among small groups (the generals amongst themselves; like-minded friends at symposia; the 'clubs' (*hetaireiai*) which played an important part in overthrowing democracy in 411; and so on). But just as Homer's chieftains had to address and persuade the assembled army as a whole, so fifth- and fourth-century Athenians who wished to determine public opinion had finally to persuade an audience of several thousand. That audience was by no means bound even to listen to, let alone accept, what was said to them (cf. the debate at 6.7). Consequently, a successful speaker had not only to propose policies in a way that would be understood and acceptable, he had to know how to catch his audience's attention in the first place and hold it.

8.19 It was in the democratic *polis* of Syracuse that, according to tradition, the very first handbooks of rhetorical technique were produced, by Teisiās and Korax, in the 460s. These handbooks soon reached Athens, so that by the end of the fifth century anyone could have got hold of the basic principles of public speaking. The advice was written with an eye to speeches in the law-courts, but must have had relevance to speaking in the *ekklēsiā* too. Plato in his *Phaidros* gives us some idea what the handbooks must have contained:

> *Sōkratēs:* 'In the first place a speech must begin with an 'Introduction'. That's the sort of technical term you mean, isn't it?
> *Phaidros:* Yes.
> *Sōkratēs:* That is followed by a 'statement of the facts' and 'evidence from witnesses'; thirdly there is 'indirect evidence' and fourthly 'arguments from probability'; and I think our expert friend from Byzantion would want to add the further niceties of 'confirmation' and 'additional confirmation'.
> *Phaidros:* You mean the good Theodōros?
> *Sōkratēs:* Of course. (Plato, *Phaidros* 266d)

8.20 *Peithō* 'persuasion', the ability to make someone acquiesce peacefully, became something of a watchword of the late fifth century, and its influence was felt not only in the *ekklēsiā* and courts but on the stage and in higher education too. But questions were still asked about the ends and means of *peithō*. On the one hand it was felt to be typical of a lawful, civilised, as against a barbarian, society, and so was contrasted with *dolos* (treachery, deceit) and *biā* (force, violence), but on the other hand it was recognised that it was not always the better counsel that persuaded, and that persuasive words might virtually amount to force. In a famous pamphlet, the sophist Gorgiās argued that Helen should not be blamed for allowing herself to be seduced since persuasion amounted effectively to force:

> If, then, the eye of Helen, charmed by Paris's beauty, gave to her soul excitement and amorous incitement, what wonder? How could one who was weaker, repel and expel him who, being divine, had power divine? If it was physical diversion and psychical perversion, we should not execrate it as reprehensible, but deprecate it as indefensible. For it came to whom it came by fortuitous insinuations, not by judicious resolutions; by erotic compulsions, not by despotic machinations. How then is it fair to blame Helen who, whether by love captivated or by word persuaded, or by violence dominated, or by divine necessity subjugated, did what she did, and is completely absolved from blame?
>
> By this discourse I have freed a woman from evil reputation; I have kept the promise which I made in the beginning; I have essayed to dispose of the injustice of defamation and the folly of allegation; I have prayed to compose a lucubration for Helen's adulation and my own delectation. (Gorgiās, *Helen* 19)

This may seem a playful argument, but in a speech delivered around 400 Lysiās relied on Athenians taking a similar view of persuasion when he claimed in an Athenian court that it was right to take a harsher attitude to adulterers who employed the persuasion of seduction than to rapists (5.20).

8.21 Gorgiās, who was from Leontīnoi in Sicily, had visited Athens as an ambassador in 427, and Athenians were given the first taste of his extraordinary prose style – rhythmical, rhyming, obsessed with antithesis and parallelism, even down to equalising the number of syllables in parallel clauses. He seems to have seen rhetoric as a form of enchantment. It gave the speakers the means to stir the passions, to work on the emotions and convince the mind.

Gorgiās' style seems not to have been imitated in its pure form (3.45), but there can be little doubt that the later fifth century did see a rise in self-consciousness about persuasive techniques. A previously unconscious skill now became available for anyone to learn. But to be effective, rhetoric had to teach what to say as well as how to say it. The rise of rhetoric and the sharpening of the skills of argumentation went hand in hand. The clearest sign of recognition that such skills could be dangerous is that the teaching of rhetoric was outlawed during the oligarchic coup of 404.

The Sophists and intellectual concerns (cf. 5.43–9)

8.22 Gorgiās came to Athens on a political mission, but many other leading intellectuals came to Athens because of the opportunities which its large and wealthy community offered for earning money from teaching. These teachers are generally lumped together under the title of 'sophists', but though Plato (who hated them, and drew a strong distinction between them and Sōkratēs, who never taught formally and never charged) has given the word a bad name, many of them were men of the highest intellectual distinction. They developed and taught their own specialities and grappled in their own way with many major philosophical questions. It is their questions, along with those of Sōkratēs, which provide the background and basis for the dialogues of Plato and so for the whole development of Western philosophy.

8.23 The sophists both helped to create a demand for education, and also came when there was an unfulfilled need for it. They taught a vast variety of subjects – from astronomy and law through to mathematics and rhetoric. It is in large measure due to the sophists that subjects such as grammar, logic, ethics, politics, physics and metaphysics first emerged as separate entities. The sophists were at the head of a movement to make man, not the physical world, the centre of intellectual debate. If their main preoccupation was to describe how man could be most successful in life, rather than with questions of right and wrong of the sort that Sōkratēs and Plato insisted upon, this does not undermine their intellectual importance.

8.24 Much work was going on in other fields at this time too. If our sources can be trusted, technical manuals were written by Sophoklēs on tragedy, by Iktīnos on the Parthenōn, by Polykleitos on the symmetry of the human body, and by Hippodāmos (who designed the layout of the Peiraeus) on town planning and social engineering. Rudimentary experimental work in sciences may also have been going on, if we wish so to interpret the evidence of Aristophanēs' *Clouds*. When the rustic Strepsiadēs is introduced into Sōkratēs' private school (*phrontistērion* or 'think tank'), he finds all sorts of extraordinary devices cluttering up the place:

> *Strepsiadēs:* [*examining some of the objects in the* phrontistērion] Tell me, what on earth are these?

Student: This is astronomy.
Streps.: And this?
Student: Geometry.
Streps.: And what is the use of it?
Student: It is for land measurement.
Streps.: For a new settlement?
Student: For any land whatever.
Streps.: That's a smart dodge. What a useful democratic device.
Student: And here we have a map of the world. This is Athens . . .
Streps.: Come off it. I don't believe you. Where are the juries?' (Aristophanēs, *Clouds* 200ff.)

These cosmic models (celestial globes? star maps? compasses? maps?) are an important feature of the play, where the association between the new thought and its various trappings is constantly being made. It suggests that the use of models and apparatus, generally seen as a later, post-Aristotelian device, was understood well enough in fifth-century Athens to be made the subject of comic humour.

8.25 Pythagorās of Samos (c. 525), who, to escape the tyranny of Polykratēs, tyrant of Samos, fled to Krotōn in South Italy and there set up a school which taught a whole way of life, made an important series of observations about the relationship between the natural world and numbers. The most famous of these is the way in which musical intervals can be expressed in terms of numerical ratios. This led Pythagoreans to suggest that 'number' might lie at the heart of reality, and so began the movement which was to give understanding of nature a mathematical foundation. This idea proved widely attractive. Plato for one saw in mathematics a perfection which did not exist elsewhere in this imperfect world: it worked through expressible but unchanging and apparently eternal laws. The Greeks desired to categorise the problems of existence with the precision of mathematics. But the Greeks were well aware that even mathematics posed some insoluble problems. For example, they knew that the hypotenuse of a right-angled triangle whose base and perpendicular $=1$ was $\sqrt{2}$ and that $\sqrt{2}$ *could not be mathematically expressed*. Yet it was real, tangible and apparently measurable.

8.26 Such puzzles were particularly associated with Zēnōn of Eleā in southern Italy (who flourished in the middle of the fifth century), who in particular devised ways of revealing the problem of infinities. Zēnōn pointed out that if you kept on cutting a line in half, you would continue to do so infinitely. How therefore could a line have finite length? He expressed this in another way – the paradox of Akhilleus and the tortoise. If Akhilleus gave a tortoise a 20 metres' start, Akhilleus could never catch it. For while Akhilleus ran the 20m, the tortoise would run 1m; while Akhilleus ran the 1m, the tortoise would run 1cm; while Akhilleus ran 1cm, the tortoise would run 1mm; while Akhilleus . . . and so on. So even in the 'pure' world of mathematics, there were irrationalities.

8.27   Verbal paradoxes intrigued Greeks just as much as mathematical ones. The mere use of words seemed able entirely to distort perceptions of reality in the most bewildering way (cf. Zēnōn's paradox above). One particular problem was that of negative statements, e.g. if falsehood consists of saying something that *is not so*, does not that imply *saying nothing*? Hence the notorious sophistic paradox that it is impossible to *speak falsely*. Plato parodies some of the arguments used when he has the sophist Euthydēmos 'prove' to Sōkratēs ('I') that his father is not his father (the 'Patroklos' referred to in the first line is Sōkratēs' half-brother):

> *Euthudēmos:* 'And Patroklos is your brother?
> *Sōkratēs:* He is; we have the same mother but not the same father.
> *E:* Then he is both your brother and not your brother.
> *S:* Our fathers are different as I've said. His father is Khairedēmos, mine Sōphroniskos.
> *E:* But Sōphroniskos and Khairedēmos are both fathers.
> *S:* Of course, one mine and one his.
> *E:* Then Khairedēmos isn't the same as 'father'.
> *S:* He's not the same as *my* father.
> *E:* So he is 'father' and not the same as 'father'. Or are you the same as 'stone'?
> *S:* I don't think I am, but I expect you will prove I am.
> *E:* Then are you different from 'stone'?
> *S:* Yes, different.
> *E:* And if you are different from 'stone' you aren't a stone, any more than if you are different from gold you are golden.
> *S:* That's so.
> *E:* So Khairedēmos not being the same as 'father', isn't a father.
> (Plato, *Euthydēmos* 297e)

Another problem concerned the relationship between a word and its meaning. In what sense does a word 'tell' us about the object it applies to? Plato's *Kratulos* is concerned with this fundamental question, though many of Plato's arguments are etymologically nonsense (as the one here is):

> The name Zeus is like a sentence: we divide it in half and some use one half, some the other, some calling him [in the accusative case] *Zēna* and some *Dia*. The two forms, when put together, express the nature of the god which is just what we say a name should be able to do. For Zeus is the chief author of life [*zēn* = 'to live'] to all the rest of us, being lord and king of all. So this god is rightly named, *through* [*dia* = 'through'] whom all things have life. (Plato, *Kratylos* 396a)

8.28   Interest in patterns of human behaviour is apparent in Greek tragedy and in Greek history. Belief in the regularity of human responses underlay, indeed, work in rhetoric also. The argument from probability, which may have been invented by Teisiās and Korax (see 8.19), used common experience to suggest how people would behave or had in fact behaved, e.g. 'The defendant was drunk: is it likely or probable that a drunk man would be so foolish as to try to negotiate a difficult gangplank from a rocking ship to the shore?' Alternatively, examples of past behaviour might be quoted to offer a model for the present, either to understand present behaviour or to prescribe it ('X behaved like this: so should you'). This was a form of argument already much used in Homer. Here the historian Thucydides puts into the mouths of some Athenian ambassadors a justification for their demand that the people of the island of Mēlos should become subject to Athens:

> Our claims and our actions are entirely consistent with men's beliefs about the gods and with the principles which govern their own conduct to each other. Of the gods we believe and of men we know that by a universal and necessary natural law they rule wherever they have the power. We did not make this law nor were we the first to take advantage of it. We found it already in force and we shall leave it to operate in perpetuity for our successors; all we are doing is to make use of it in the full knowledge that you yourselves, and anyone else who enjoyed the same power as we have, would act in precisely the same way. (Thucydides, *Peloponnesian War* 5.105)

Thucydides himself believed that human nature was such that, given similar conditions, humans would behave in largely the same way (*Peloponnesian War* 1.22; quoted at 8.31).

8.29 Considerable interest was taken in the origins of human society. A sort of evolutionary theory was developed: early man, Plato makes Prōtagorās suggest, found survival difficult because of wild animals, illness, and lack of food, and so on pragmatic grounds was spurred to invent *tekhnai* ('skills, the results of applied intelligence') like hunting, medicine and agriculture in order to survive. But men were still at risk from other men. So social compacts were formed, giving rise to *philiā* ('making common cause with another', cf. *philos*), for example, and *peithō* ('getting someone to acquiesce peacefully' cf. 8.18). These utilitarian practices became enshrined in time into a moral code, giving rise to constraints such as *aidōs* ('shame' or 'respect for others') and *dikē* ('justice'). From these beginnings fully civilised societies, characterised by laws, religious observances and democratic practices, were able to develop. The basis of this view of man's development was ultimately utilitarian, and this fact reflects the enlightened self-interest and ethically relativistic view of many sophists, against which Plato and Sōkratēs reacted strongly (8.33–6).

8.30 Prōtagorās is also the thinker credited with first making the claim that there were two sides to every question, and that to be successful, one should be able to argue both cases. The following extraordinary extract from a sophistic pamphlet of unknown authorship will give some idea of the extremes to which this could be taken. It may well be typical of the sort of manual of argumentation which was available in late fifth-century Athens:

> So sickness is bad for the sick, but good for the doctor: death is bad for the dead, but good for the undertakers and monumental masons; a good

> harvest is good for the farmers, but bad for the grain-traders; shipwrecks
> are bad for the ship-owners, but good for the ship-builder; when iron is
> blunted and worn away it is bad for others but good for the blacksmith;
> when pottery is broken it is bad for others but good for the potter; when
> shoes wear out and fall to pieces it is bad for others but good for the
> cobbler; in athletics victory in the quarter mile is good for the victor but bad
> for the losers. (*Dissoi Logoi* 1.3)

The importance of this method of argument lies in its inherent implication
that all cases have two sides, i.e. nothing is absolute; it all depends on the circumstances. When extended to the sphere of moral values, it was a short step
to Prōtagorās' famous dictum, 'Man is the measure of all things,' and thence
to the assertion that there were no higher authorities to whom one could
appeal to determine what was right and wrong.

8.31   In general, there was an increasing interest among Greeks in what sort of evidence was acceptable to prove or disprove a case. Giving a rational account
of an illness, and assessing the value of evidence adduced, formed an important part, for example, of medical casework, and this principle was easily
extended to other spheres of human life (political and moral, for example).
Here Thucydides discusses how he gathered the evidence for his history:

> But on the whole I think that anyone who accepts the narrative which I have
> based on the proofs cited can do so with confidence. The poets are not to be
> trusted because they elaborate and exaggerate, and the prose writers prefer
> the entertainment of their readers to the truth; their facts cannot be checked
> because of the passage of time and are legend rather than reliable history. My
> own narrative is based on the clearest evidence that can be expected
> considering the antiquity of the events . . . not on a casual enquiry nor on my
> personal opinion, but partly on my own experience and partly by following
> up as closely as I could the accounts of eyewitnesses. This last process was a
> difficult one because the accounts of eyewitnesses differed according to
> memory and partiality. (Thucydides, *Peloponnesian War* 1.22)

8.32   One of the reasons why collecting reliable evidence for historical events is so
difficult is that those who write about the events also pass judgement on them,
e.g. that individuals or groups should have acted differently. That judgement
affects writers' decisions about what information it is relevant to give, and so
an interpretation is frequently built into the very account of events. This
means that it is often difficult to disentangle what happened from the reasons
why it happened, the assessment of the events and the questions about right
and wrong that they raised. Narrating historical events and discussing political action alike required for Greeks a debate over the nature of justice and the
relationship between it and written law; the nature of right and wrong, and
where expediency fitted in; the nature of power and the rights that the stronger
held over the weaker; and, most famous of all, the relationship between *nomos*
('custom', 'law', 'culture') and *phusis* ('nature') and the question, 'Is there
an absolute right and wrong in any situation, or does it depend on the

circumstances?' History frequently ends up raising issues which we would regard as philosophical. Consider the following comment by Hērodotos:

> If anyone were to offer men the opportunity to make from all the customs in the world what seemed to them the best selection, everyone would after careful consideration choose his own; for everyone considers his own customs far the best. So no one except a madman would make fun of such things. There is ample evidence that this is the common opinion of mankind about their customs. A particular piece of evidence is this: when Dareios was King of Persia he summoned certain Greeks who were at his court and asked them how much he would have to pay them to eat the bodies of their dead fathers. They replied that there was no sum for which they would do such a thing. Later he summoned certain Indians of a tribe called Callatians, who do eat their parents' bodies, and asked them in the presence of the Greeks, through an interpreter so that the Greeks understood what was being said, how much they would have to be paid to burn their fathers' dead bodies. They cried aloud and told him not to utter such blasphemy. Such is custom and Pindar was in my opinion right when he wrote that 'Custom is King of all.'
> (Hērodotos, *Histories* 3.38)

The argument was easily extended. Did the gods exist in reality, or only by convention? Did states exist in reality or only by convention? Were human races naturally, or only conventionally, divided? Should one man control another, or one nation control another nation, because it was natural, or only because it was convention? These questions can easily seem, and seemed to many Athenians, to strike at the very heart of morality, and set the stage for the long and at times bitter intellectual debate which rages still today. It is in the context of this particular debate that Sōkratēs can be seen to have made a particularly notable contribution.

8.33 Sōkratēs never wrote a word, but he was the key figure in changing the direction of Greek philosophy away from cosmology to man's position in the world. We have to reconstruct what Sōkratēs said from the testimony of three main witnesses, none of them impartial and all with tendencies to reinterpret Sōkratēs according to their own interests. These are Plato, Xenophōn, and Aristophanēs. Sōkratēs was part of the same intellectual movement which produced the sophists, and Aristophanēs' treatment of him in *Clouds* suggests that many Athenians thought of him as a sophist. The Sōkratēs of *Clouds* is a composite figure – all 'modern' movements rolled into one – but one element is the sophist. Plato, who draws a sharp contrast between Sōkratēs and the sophists, nevertheless represents him in discussion with them. As far as Plato is concerned, the sophists were interested in success, in giving their pupils techniques, especially in the art of speaking (see 8.19ff.; 5.46) that would enable them to get on in the world, whereas Sōkratēs was interested in morals, in what I must do to be good. Xenophōn confirms this moral preoccupation, and Aristotle characterises Sōkratēs as 'concerned with the moral virtues'.

8.34   Sōkratēs emerges from all the descriptions as a great arguer, concerned with both clarity and precision of thought. Aristotle attributes to him the systematic use of 'inductive argument and general definition'. One must beware of the modern associations of the word 'induction', and 'argument from example' is a better translation. The following passage from the *Lakhēs* is an excellent illustration. The argument 'leads you on' (the literal meaning of the Greek word for 'induction') by observation of particular instances to understand the general characteristics of the class of actions or objects being considered. And so of course to a 'general definition'. Sōkratēs was looking for precision and definite standards. If you want to be good or brave you must first know what goodness or bravery is; so, in a sense, goodness is knowledge and it should be possible to be as *precise* about moral virtue as a carpenter is about what makes a good chair. Sōkratēs pursued his general definition in *dialogue* with others, and the word 'dialectic' (which Plato was to use as a term for philosophy) is derived from the Greek word for dialogue. Here is how Plato presents Sōkratēs and the famous general Lakhēs discussing the definition of bravery:

> *Sōkratēs:* Very well: let us take as an example the brave man you have mentioned, the man who keeps his position in the line and fights the enemy.
> *Lakhēs:* Yes, he is a brave man.
> *Sōkratēs:* I agree. But what about a man who fights the enemy not by keeping position but by retreating?
> *Lakhēs:* What do you mean, retreating?
> *Sōkratēs:* I'm thinking of the Scythians who are said to fight by withdrawing as much as by pursuing . . . For I wanted to get your opinion not only of bravery in the hoplite line, but also in cavalry engagements and in all forms of fighting; and indeed of bravery not only in fighting but also at sea, and in the face of illness and poverty and public affairs. And there is bravery not only in face of pain and fear, but also of desire and pleasure, both fearsome to fight against whether by attack or retreat – for some men are brave in these encounters, aren't they, Lakhēs?
> *Lakhēs:* Yes, certainly.
> *Sōkratēs:* Then all these are examples of bravery, only some men show it in pleasure, some in pain, some in desire, some in danger. And there are others who show cowardice in the same circumstances.
> *Lakhēs:* Yes.
> *Sōkratēs:* Now what I want to know was just *what* each of these two qualities *is*. So try again and tell me first, what is this common characteristic of courage which they all share? Do you understand now what I mean?
> *Lakhēs:* I'm afraid I don't. (Plato, *Lakhēs* 191a)

8.35   Plato portrays Sōkratēs arguing against the relativism and scepticism which characterised much of sophistic thought and looking for a precision about definitions of moral virtues of the sort that existed in the technical world. Plato's Sōkratēs is looking for some kind of stable reality and standard behind the confusion of perceptions and standards in the world of common experience. In a dialogue written at a period when scholars suspect that Plato was increasingly using the character 'Sōkratēs' as his own mouthpiece, Sōkratēs describes his methods to one *Theaitētos*:

> My art of midwifery is concerned with men and not women, and I am concerned with minds in labour, not bodies. And the most important thing about my art is its ability to test fully whether the mind of the young man is giving birth to a mere image and a falsehood or to a legitimate truth. For there is another point which I have in common with the midwives – I cannot myself give birth to wisdom, and the criticism which has so often been made of me, that though I ask questions of others I have no contribution to make myself because I have no wisdom in me, is quite true. The reason is that the god compels me to be midwife but forbids me to give birth. So I am myself quite without wisdom nor has my mind produced any original thought; but those who keep my company, though at first some of them may appear quite ignorant, if the god wills, in due course make what both they and others think is marvellous progress. This is clearly not because of anything they have learned from me, but because they have made many marvellous discoveries of themselves and given birth to them. But the delivery of them is my work and the god's . . .
>
> Now the reason why I have rehearsed all this at length to you, my dear Theaitētos, is that I suspect that – as you think yourself – you are in labour with some thought you have conceived. So put yourself in my hands, remembering I am a midwife's son and practised in her craft, and answer my questions as best you can. (Plato, *Theaitētos* 150b)

8.36 Plato's picture of Sōkratēs as the epitome of the goodness (*aretē*) he so ardently sought to define has been of enormous influence on the history of Western philosophy. Plato portrayed Sōkratēs as the uncompromising searcher after truth, who would allow no consideration of person or position of influence to stand in the way (but cf. Aristophanēs' very different picture in *Clouds*). It cost Sōkratēs his life (1.86). Put on trial on a charge of corrupting the young (cf. Alkibiadēs' attraction to him at 5.33) and introducing new gods, he was found guilty and, refusing the chance of escaping from Athens, was executed with hemlock (cf. 1.83; 5.48). Nevertheless, it is arguable that the sophists' achievement was as important as Sōkratēs', and Plato's engagement with their ideas reveals their importance for his, and therefore also Aristotle's, work.

Medicine and history

8.37 The Greeks were the first people we know of to turn medicine into something approaching a scientific discipline (cf. on Alkmaiōn 8.12). The leading advocate of 'rational' medicine was Hippokratēs from the island of Kōs. He established a medical 'school' there, and his very success means that we know very little about him, since virtually *all* medical treatises of the fifth and fourth centuries were ascribed to him. That attribution does, however, accord with a general similarity in approach to be seen in the works. The passage taken from *On the Sacred Disease* (epilepsy) at 3.22 illustrates the stand Hippokratic doctors took against magical cures. It continued:

> The so-called sacred disease is due to the same causes as all other diseases, to bodily intake and waste, to cold and sun and constant atmosphere and weather changes. These are all 'divine' and there is no need to put this disease in a class by itself and regard it as more 'divine' than all others; all are equally divine and human. But each disease has its own particular nature and characteristics, and none is hopeless or insusceptible to treatment. ([Hippokratēs], *On the Sacred Disease* 2ff.)

8.38 If the strength of Greek medicine was its assumption that the body worked, or failed to work, in rational rather than random ways, the weakness of Greek medicine was (as one can see from the above) in diagnosis. Conviction *that* the body worked according to rules, without a real understanding of *how* the body worked, led Hippokratic doctors to resort to cures calculated to restore an imagined 'balance' to the (Empedoclean) four elements of which the body was composed (cf. 8.8, 8.11), by such means as dieting, exercising, blood-letting, surgery and purgative drugs. But the assumption that there should be a pattern to what happened to the body led to an emphasis on careful observation of the course a disease took, so that if similar symptoms arose, doctors could predict what would ensue ('prognosis'). This gave confidence to patients (an important consideration for doctors, who on the whole acted privately and had to win patients), and alerted them to the periods when their help would be most needed. Their understanding of anatomy came from surgical work (especially dealing with war wounds) and by analogy from animal dissection. Dissection of humans was taboo (cf. Greek reverence for the dead, 5.78; 8.32), although such dissection, and probably even vivisection too, were practised briefly in the very different cultural atmosphere of the Alexandrian Museum in Egypt in the third century.

8.39 In all this, the Hippokratic doctors were in tension with what went on at, for example, the shrine of Asklēpios at Epidauros, where cures depended upon divine intervention through dreams and so on (cf. 3.16; 5.73). Hippokratic doctors did not displace temple doctors, and different medical conditions responded better to one or the other approach, but both sides were conscious of the threat posed by the other not merely to their business but to their whole rational or supernatural way of looking at the world (cf. 8.20 on *peithō* in public life, and 4.2 on Greek competitiveness). The importance of the Hippokratic argument for the future of medicine lay in its studied lack of interest in divine or mystical reasons/cures for illness, and in its realisation of a distinction between genuine cause and merely associated side-effects of illnesses.

8.40 The development of an interest in what happened to individuals and why (their medical history), went very much hand in hand with the development

8.2 Athenian potters made 'head vases' but only of heads of women, satyrs, the god Dionȳsos, and blacks, never of Athenian males (9.7). This pot dates to around 500.

of an interest in what happened to societies and why. This was tackled by some thinkers in an essentially abstract fashion, but it also led to the invention of what we know as history, as an attempt was made to recover and understand past and indeed current events. And so it was that the Greeks invented history (*historiā* means 'research', 'enquiry'). Before this happened, Greeks had been interested in the past primarily in order to situate themselves in the present. Myths, epics, family stories and trees, and lists of 'eponymous' officials (it was common to express the year as 'in the archonship of X'), settled questions of why the observed world was as it was e.g. with regard to cult practices, territorial disputes and the right to exercise power. As the Greeks came into contact with other peoples and places, both through trade activities and through

8.3–4 (and see over) The so-called '*negro alabastra*' produced in Athens in the early fifth century show a variety of non-Athenians – here a Scythian archer and a black are juxtaposed. Compare fig.7.6, above.

settlement abroad, there was a need for information about the wider world, a need fulfilled by writers called *logographoi*, who described places geographically, intimated local customs and filled in with a little 'background'. As such descriptions raised questions of how different customs were to be explained, history began. Perhaps the first historical statement we possess is that of Hekataios from Mīlētos, a late sixth-century *logographos* who constructed a map of the world and wrote a commentary to accompany it, who at one stage comments, 'What I write here is the account I believe to be true. The Greeks tell many stories on the topic which are (in my opinion) absurd.'

8.4

8.41   The key figure in the development of history, however, the man referred to as 'father of *historiā*' by Cicero, was Hērodotos from Halikarnassos (c. 470–410). His *Histories* (of the period 490–479; see 1.2–4) was an extremely daring venture. In the first place, he took it upon himself to ask the questions 'Why?' and 'How?' in relation to events some two hundred years earlier. In the second place, he integrated into his work the history, culture and customs of peoples from all over the Mediterranean (e.g. Egyptians, Scythians, Babylonians) who had come into contact with the two great powers, Greece and Persia, involved in the final conflict. In the process he developed an important historical attitude: that evidence should, as far as possible, be ascertained by personal enquiry and research. Here was the start of a scientific approach to the past. The result goes beyond the *logographoi* to the extent that, while there is still much fascinating local detail and description of place and custom, Hērodotos perceives an overall pattern to human affairs beyond the individual and the particular – the permanent rise and fall of the powerful. In the last analysis, Hērodotos does see this as the consequence of supernatural intervention in human affairs, but there is nonetheless much discounting of the gods *en route*, and the influence of Ionian thinkers is strong (8.6–14).

8.42 Thucydides (c. 460–400), an Athenian writing about Athenian history in which he himself was a (minor) actor (1.2–4; 66), took Hērodotos' concept and narrowed it. He cut out from his account of the Peloponnesian War (1.56–81) ethnography, 'romance', conversations and local colour of the sort very evident in Hērodotos. Thucydides focused on the public military and political aspects of the war (though showing theoretical awareness of the importance of domestic and economic factors). Thucydides divided his account by summers and winters because the military activities were largely seasonally determined; and started the annalistic tradition of historical writing by analysing the war year by year. He applied extremely rigorous standards for testing evidence (see 8.31) and, in contrast to Hērodotos, he 'ministered to man's knowledge of man' in his history by excluding the gods entirely from his own exposition. He acknowledged, of course, that men's belief in the gods affected the way they behaved, but he did not himself believe that the gods were actually responsible for history: man was. In one vitally important point Thucydides agreed with Hērodotos, that the historian was in a unique position to see the patterns to history. For Thucydides, the pattern was what we might call 'behavioural': men behaved in certain ways under certain pressures, so that if similar events occurred again, the intelligent man would be able to foresee them (cf. his recipe for how people behaved during revolution at 4.13, and cf. 8.28 on Greek interest in human behaviour). For all that, Thucydides acknowledged that *tukhē*, chance, was the great unknowable factor, although he insisted it was not a divine visitation. Even Periklēs, Thucydides' prime example of the man who could read the future, could not have foreseen the plague which devastated Athens in 430 and carried him off as well (see 1.57–8). Thucydides brings this point about the importance of the unforeseen by placing his description of the plague *immediately* after Periklēs' famous statement about the greatness of Athens – the Funeral Speech.

8.43 Thucydides had an immediate influence on the way history was written. Several authors wrote accounts of Greek history starting where Thucydides' account breaks off (in 410, although we know that Thucydides lived through to after the end of the Peloponnesian War in 404). One of those histories, recovered on papyrus from the rubbish dumps of Oxyrhynchus in Egypt and known as the 'Greek history from Oxyrhynchus' (*Hellēnika Oxyrhygkhia*), follows Thucydides carefully in the structure of his work, but goes into internal Athenian politics more deeply than Thucydides. Xenophōn's continuation of Thucydides (the *Hellēnika*) becomes rather less Thucydidean as it proceeds (it seems to have been written in two instalments). Scholars have often been critical of Xenophōn for his bias (he gives the Spartans a better press than many think they deserve) and for his moralising judgements, but among his positive achievements are an interest in the whole range of Greek *poleis* and their politics, not simply in Athens and Spartē, and the skill of his story-telling technique has often been overlooked.

8.44   In the course of the fourth century, the writing of history developed in two contrary directions. On the one hand local history, the attempt to tell the history of a single place over a long timescale, became popular, with these historians finding more and more to say about early history (cf. 1.3). On the other hand, there were attempts to write 'universal history'. The most important such attempt was by Ephoros from Kȳmē. He gave an account of both Greek and Near Eastern history from the return of the Hērakleidai to Philip of Makedōn's siege of Perinthos in 340, dividing his account by topic rather than working annalistically (year by year). Ephoros' thirty books are themselves lost, but they form a very important source for Diodōros of Sicily's extant history, written in the last century BC.

Drama: tragedy and comedy

8.45   Comedies and tragedies were put on in Athens at specific times of the year, as part of festivals celebrating Dionȳsos (cf. 3.40). The festivals known as the *Lēnaia* took place in January and featured only comedy; the *Dionȳsia*, in March, featured both comedy and tragedy, along with the elaborate choral song known as dithyramb. As well as being elements of a religious occasion (cf. 3.44), the plays were intensely competitive since the best work of tragedy and comedy was awarded a much coveted prize (judged by 10 judges, one from each of ten tribes (*phūlai*)). The plays were staged at the theatre of Dionȳsos in Athens, just below the Akropolis (for the theatre, which survives but not in its fifth-century state, see below 8.64), and could seat c. 14,000 people (cf. 2.29). It is uncertain whether women and children were present at them.

8.46   Although the plays were put on only once in Athens, they might also be performed in deme theatres at the 'Rural *Dionȳsia*', and thus 'revived'. Although the absence of a 'run' might seem to give little scope for actors, there were already professional actors in the fifth century, and the services of the best actors were much sought after by playwrights. As drama spread from Athens to other parts of the Greek world, it became more and more common for actors to move in an itinerant lifestyle from festival to festival, and in the Hellenistic period many cities essentially contracted out drama festivals to the 'actors of Dionȳsos' (*Dionūsou technītai*). The playwrights directed, choreographed and wrote the music for their work, and at first acted in them.

8.5 On this Athenian red-figure *hydriā* (water jar) dating to the second quarter of the fifth century, actors dressed up as satyrs appear to be assembling some complex throne to the music of an elaborately dressed pipe player (right).

Sophoklēs and Euripidēs may have written especially for actors of their choice, but by the fourth century, playwrights probably had no choice in their selection of a lead actor. The 'eponymous' *arkhōn* assigned a wealthy citizen to bear the expense of the play, as part of a state liturgy (the *khorēgiā*). He (the *khorēgos*) paid for the musicians and the chorus (and its training in singing and dancing), stage sets, costumes and so on (cf. on *leitourgiai*, 6.62).

8.47 For the comic competition at the *Dionȳsia*, five single plays by five different playwrights were featured. For the tragic competition, three playwrights entered four plays each: three tragedies followed by a 'satyr' play in which a familiar myth was burlesqued by setting it in a world of satyrs. In the early days, the three tragedies were often fairly tightly connected in subject matter and formed a 'trilogy'. Aiskhylos' *Oresteia*, the story of the death of Agamemnōn at the hands of his wife Klytaimēstrā (*Agamemnōn*), the return of their son Orestēs to take revenge on her (*Libation Bearers*), and Orestēs' trial on a murder charge and acquittal at Athens (*Eumenides*), is a trilogy of this sort and is the only trilogy we have. We know that Euripidēs' plays of 415 all centred on Troy, but examined the war from radically different angles and moods: in *Alexandros*, it was revealed that Paris, exposed as an infant and assumed dead, was in fact living as a shepherd in the mountains; in *Palamēdēs* was told a story of treachery and intrigue in the Greek camp outside Troy; and in *Trojan Women* (the only play of the 'trilogy' we possess in full), Euripidēs explored the sack of Troy and departure of its womenfolk into slavery. Many later fifth-century trilogies seem to have been formed from plays which were connected, by continuity or contrast of *mood* rather than subject matter (e.g. Euripidēs' *Iphigeneia at Aulis* and *Bacchae* were written for production together). It is a very great loss that we have no more groups of plays, since our understanding of the single plays we do possess would be much enhanced if we could see them in their original programme setting.

8.48 Six plays of Aiskhylos (525–456) are extant (*Promētheus* is probably not by him), seven by Sophoklēs (496–406) and nineteen of Euripidēs (485–406). But we have records of the titles of c. 80 plays by Aiskhylos, 123 by Sophoklēs and 92 by Euripidēs. We also have records of who was victorious when, and so know that Sophoklēs was victorious on 24 occasions, but Euripidēs on just 6 occasions.

(a) Tragedy

8.49 The earliest tragedy that we possess in full is Aiskhylos' *Persians*, produced in 472, and the development of tragedy as a form is as obscure to us as it was to the fourth-century Greeks. Whereas many other cultural developments discussed in this chapter were pioneered in other Greek cities, tragedy seems to have been an Athenian invention. What the term 'tragedy' (*tragōidiā*) meant is disputed. It could mean 'song of goats' (i.e. of men dressed up as goats), suggesting that the proto-tragedy was a form of satyr play (except that satyrs are not goats . . .). But the word most commonly used for 'tragedy' in the fifth century was not *tragōidiā*, but *tragōidoi* (pl.), a word which referred to the human participants in tragedy, probably the chorus. This word cannot mean 'goats who sing'; it can only mean 'singers who have something to do with a goat'. This meaning fits better with a second explanation offered in antiquity, that *tragōidiā* meant 'song for the prize of a goat', or 'song at the sacrifice of a goat' (goats were sacrificed to Dionȳsos, as to other gods).

8.50 Sacrifice was the climax of the festival (cf. 3.28–30). The pleasure of the festival and the death of an animal, returned back to the gods in a complicated ritual to ensure that animals would continue to be available as food (cf. 3.42), were part of the same ceremony: life was affirmed through death. This made sense in the context of the worship of Dionȳsos (cf. 3.48); and the image of sacrifice as slaughter, not only of animals but also of humans, runs through tragedy (e.g. Aiskhylos' *Agamemnōn*, and cf. Euripidēs' *Bacchae*, especially the scene in which the god Dionȳsos dresses Pentheus up in woman's clothes and leads him off to the mountains where the Bacchic woman will 'sacrifice' him; the whole scene is chillingly close to the ceremony of preparing an animal for slaughter).

8.51   Another explanation ignores goat songs and suggests that choral songs and dances in honour of Dionȳsos formed the original core (cf. dithyramb). On this evolutionary view, drama developed when the chorus leader (*koruphaios*, called *exarkhos* when applied to early non-dramatic choral song) took a more dynamic role by singing against the chorus. This enabled conflict to develop, and when, in time, other individual chorus members joined in, they formed the nucleus of a dramatic performance. This explanation would, at any rate, help to account for the very special form of the tragedy: a chorus (of 12 or 15 members), and no more than three individual actors (who had to divide amongst themselves all the speaking parts of the play). It also fits with the presence at the heart of the plays of a contest, a conflict between opposing forces (cf. 4.2). The chorus (and increasingly during the fifth century the actors also) sang and danced those parts of tragedy written in lyric metres, but the details of the music and movement which were so vital a part of the spectacle are lost to us. All we have are the words. Originally Greek tragedy was perhaps rather more like an opera than what we would call a play (5.40).

8.52   Given the Dionysiac origins of tragedy, it may seem odd that very few extant plays are about Dionȳsos. Although Dionysiac themes are represented among the titles of the earliest tragedies known, tragedy seems never to have been exclusively Dionysiac in theme. Nevertheless, tragedies nearly always take their themes from mythology (Aiskhylos' *Persians*, our very first extant tragedy, is a unique exception among plays that survive in that its subject is a historical one, the defeat of the Persians at Salamīs in 480 and the reception of the news at the Persian court). But we know of two 'historical' plays by Phrȳnikhos (*Fall of Mīlētos* ?492, and *Phoinissai* (about Salamīs) ?476), so perhaps such 'historical' plays were more common in the early fifth century. Drawing on myth relieved the playwright, faced with the problem of writing three tragedies and a satyr play each year if he wished to compete annually, of the problem of inventing plots.

8.53   Use of mythology did little to make tragedy predictable. Myths were highly unstable, changing in every telling. And the point of tragic use of myth was precisely to give a particular retelling: reinterpretation was (almost) all. For example, Aiskhylos, Sophoklēs and Euripidēs all wrote a tragedy about the return of Orestēs to take revenge upon Klytaimēstrā (Aiskhylos' *Libation Bearers*, and Sophoklēs' and Euripidēs' *Elektra*). The audience doubtless knew that Klytaimēstrā would be killed by Orestēs, but the handling, perspective and point of view of each are differentiated extremely sharply. In Aiskhylos' *Libation Bearers*, the whole of the first half of the play is taken up with the rather perfunctory meeting between Orestēs and his sister Ēlektrā and the lament at Agamemnōn's tomb. Ēlektrā then disappears entirely. The deed is done and Orestēs is pursued off-stage by Klytaimēstrā's avenging Furies. In Sophoklēs, Ēlektrā is the focal point of the whole play, the encounter with Orestēs is postponed and enormously elaborated, and Orestēs is almost a tool of personal revenge in her hands. For Euripidēs, Ēlektrā has been married off to a peasant farmer, and the scene is set not in the palace but in the farmer's hut, to which Klytaimēstrā has to come in order to be dispatched. No Furies appear at the end of Sophoklēs' play; in Euripidēs', the twin gods Kastōr and Pollux tie the ends up neatly. In other words, the playwright's imaginations were so rich and subtle that each of their plays represented to the audience a wholly fresh experience.

8.54 Myth to a Greek was, at one level, his history: Agamemnōn, Oidipous, Hekabē *were* his past. But myth was not merely 'history'. As we have seen (3.10–12), one of the functions of myth was to make sense of the way the world was, and that is why Greek myth dealt almost exclusively with issues of the highest importance to Greeks and made of them a generally coherent ethical structure. We see this particularly in the relationship of gods with men (cf. 3.22–7), in the emphasis on the preservation of human decency (manslaughter, guest–host relationships, trust and betrayal) and most of all in the concern with the stability of the household and family, particularly when this was threatened by sexual crimes, mistreatment of parents, murder, revenge.

Consider, for example, the themes explored through the myth of the House of Atreus, subject of many Greek tragedies (of which Aiskhylos' *Oresteia* is our most important surviving example): Tantalos is punished for testing to see if the gods would eat human flesh by serving his son Pelops to them at a feast. Pelops is restored to life and decides to win the hand of Hippodameia, daughter of King Oinomaos. To do that, he must defeat Oinomaos in a chariot race (punishment for failure is death). He enlists the help of Oinomaos' charioteer Myrtilos, promising him as a reward the first night with Hippodameia. Myrtilos replaces the wooden lynch-pins of Oinomaos' chariot with wax, and Oinomaos is killed. Pelops wins the race but does not fulfil his promise to Myrtilos, flinging him over a cliff instead. Pelops has two sons, Atreus and Thyestēs. Thyestēs commits adultery with Atreus' wife and to punish him, Atreus serves up all but one of Thyestēs' children to him in a pie (Aigisthos survives). Atreus' son Agamemnōn has to sacrifice his own child Iphigeneia in order to get a favourable wind for the expedition to sail to Troy to win back Helen for his brother Menelāos and restore the family honour. When Agamemnōn returns, his wife Klytaimēstrā has married Aigisthos and slaughters Agamemnōn in revenge for his sacrifice of Iphigeneia. But Agamemnōn's surviving son Orestēs returns to take his due revenge on Klytaimēstrā.

8.55 The most obvious point to make is that myth gave Greeks their sense of what it was to be *Greek*, since in myth they were confronted with the basis for their

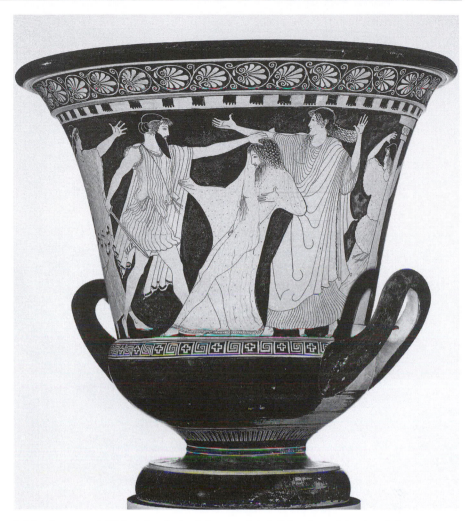

8.6 (and see over) This Athenian red-figure calyx *krātēr* wine-mixing bowl shows Agamemnōn caught in a net and about to be killed by Aigisthos.

moral and ethical understanding (cf. 3.10). The authority of tragedy stems from the conviction of the tragedian that he is handling topics which lie at the very heart of his own understanding of the human condition (cf. 8.89). The power of tragedy lies in the way in which the tragedians, wielding an astonishingly sophisticated dramatic skill, subjected this powerful and emotional material to a questioning examination which at times threatened to destroy that understanding (cf. 3.24). If we ask what lay behind this insistently questioning examination, we cannot divorce the answer from the social and intellectual climate of fifth-century Athens. It was a consequence of democracy that the citizen population had control of events put into their own hands. The possibility of acting wisely in those circumstances depended upon the assumption that the world was humanly intelligible (cf. 8.6). It is significant

8.7 On the other side of the same vessel Aigisthos is about to be killed by Orestēs. The figure behind Orestēs, with the axe, is his mother Klytaimēstrā, whom Orestēs will go on to kill.

that, of all the titles of Greek tragedy to have come down to us (nearly 1,000), only a couple feature the names of gods, and in only a few of the plays did the gods appear on stage in anything other than a very restricted role. The gods were extremely important in Greek tragedy in all sorts of ways, but man was always there at the centre.

8.56   Greek tragedy was, then, a highly contemporary art form. It is even possible to find in it references to democracy and contemporary constitutional and political problems (cf. 6.38). Some find overt criticism of Athenian imperialism in Euripidēs' *Trojan Women* (see 8.47), produced a year after the Athenian subjugation of Mēlos (see 1.71). Others have seen a connection between the plague in *Oidipous Turannos* and the great plague of Athens (see 1.57). But its true contemporaneity is not to be found here. The plays were not political or social commentaries. They were up-to-date in the way the tragedians brought to bear on myths the whole intellectual armoury of Athens: the new techniques of argument, the understanding of human psychology, the debates about the nature of the gods, the *nomos–phusis* controversy outlined above. Here are two examples, both from Euripidēs, which exploit the possibilities presented by the interaction of myth with contemporary understanding of the world. Hekabē, queen of Troy, whose city has been captured by the Greeks and is about to be destroyed, argues that Helen should not be spared by her husband Menelāos now that he has her back in his grip again. Helen has just pleaded her case and, like a skilful advocate, Hekabē answers her point by point. Paris, who took Helen back to Troy, is Hekabē's son:

> But, you say, the goddess of Love herself went with my son to Menelāos' palace. What an absurd suggestion. Couldn't she have stayed quietly in heaven and transported you and your home town Amyklai to Troy without having to stir herself?
>
> The fact is that my son Paris is extremely good-looking; one look at him and your mind was all Love. Men call all their silly infatuations Love, and Love and mad Lust begin the same way. You saw him gorgeously dressed, glittering with foreign gold, quite unlike anything you were used to in poor provincial Argos, and you went mad about him. Once rid of Spartē, so you thought, and in a Troy flowing with gold, expense could flow freely, and away from the constrictions of Menelāos' palace luxury and insolence would be unrestrained.
>
> So much for that. And you say my son brought you here by force. Did any Spartan notice it? Did you cry rape? And when you came to Troy with the Greeks in hot pursuit, and battle was joined, if you heard the Greeks were winning then you were full of Menelāos' praise – a great lover and rival who would bring my son to grief; but if fortune favoured the Trojans, no more was heard of Menelāos. You kept your eye on the main chance; loyalty counted for nothing, your concern was to be on the winning side.
>
> Then there's that tale of ropes let down from the battlements and you an unwilling prisoner. Who found you in a suicide noose or sharpening a sword as any honest woman would have done, pining for her lost husband? What is more I often urged you to go. 'Daughter,' I would say, 'leave us. There are other women for my sons to marry. I will help you to escape to the Greek ships and stop this war between them and us.' But not a bit of it. You were queening it in Paris' house and liked the homage of us barbarians which flattered your pride. And to crown it all you have dolled yourself up for your husband and dare to face him openly, you abominable bitch. You ought to crawl in rags to him, trembling with fear, with shaven head, ashamed at last of your evil doing. (Euripidēs, *Trojan Women* 983ff.)

8.57 In the following passage, Euripidēs uses his knowledge of psychology to depict how the maddened Agauē, queen of Thebes, who holds in her hands, unknown to herself, the head of her son Pentheus whom she has killed (she

8.8 This *hydriā* (water jar) of c. 500 shows three well-dressed women with the dismembered parts of Pentheus' body. There is no pictorial allusion here to the theatre.

believes it to be a lion, caught in a hunt), is brought to her senses by her father Kadmos (cf. 3.48):

> *Kadmos:* Oh grief immeasurable, sight that eyes cannot bear to see, death inflicted by your unhappy hands. A fair sacrifice it is you lay before the gods, and call Thebes and me to join the feast. I weep for your suffering first, and then my own . . .
>
> *Agauē:* How old men complain and scowl! I wish my son was as good a hunter as his mother, and went hunting wild beasts with the young men of Thebes. All he can do is to fight the gods. You must correct him, father. Call him here, someone, to see his mother's happy triumph.
>
> *Kadmos:* Alas, alas. How terrible your grief will be when you know what you have done. And if you remain unknowing, as you are, happy you will hardly be but at least you will not know your wretchedness.
>
> *Agauē:* But what is wrong? What reason is there for wretchedness?
>
> *Kadmos:* Look child, turn your eye skyward.
>
> *Agauē:* I see the sky. But why do you want me to look at it?
>
> *Kadmos:* Has it its usual look, or do you see a change?
>
> *Agauē:* It seems brighter and clearer than before.
>
> *Kadmos:* And is your mind still in its former confusion?

8.9 The pipe player on this Athenian red-figure *pelikē* of the second quarter of the fifth century certainly alludes to ritual, but is this dramatic ritual or an imaginative reconstruction of contemporary Dionysiac worship?

Agauē: I don't know what you mean. But my mind is somehow clearing, and
   my former mood is changing.
Kadmos: Could you listen now and give a clear reply?
Agauē: Yes: but I have forgotten what you last said to me.
Kadmos: To whose house did you go when you married?
Agauē: You gave me to Ekhiōn, one of the Sown Warriors, so they said.
Kadmos: And who was the son born to him?
Agauē: Pentheus, born of our union.
Kadmos: And whose head is it that you hold in your arms?
Agauē: It is a lion's, as my fellow huntresses told me.
Kadmos: Look straight at it – that's easy enough to do.
[Agauē screams in horror]
Agauē: What is it I see? What have I in my hands?
Kadmos: Look closely at it and make sure.

> *Agauē:* Oh deadly sight, oh misery.
> *Kadmos:* Does it look like a lion's head?
> *Agauē:* No, no. It's Pentheus' head in these unhappy hands.
> *Kadmos:* Tears have been shed for him before you knew.
> *Agauē:* Who killed him? How did he come into my hands?
> *Kadmos:* The bitter truth dawns at an ill moment. (Euripidēs, *Bacchae*
>   1244ff.)

8.58   The very nature of the material with which the tragedians dealt, and the skill with which they worked it, ensured that tragedy was an emotional as well as an intellectual experience. Tragedy confronted the deepest questions of human existence and challenged the spectators to make sense of the human suffering not of any ordinary man but of the greatest figures of Greek myth, heroes who (by any normal standards, cf. 4.9–10) should have had the world at their feet (and perhaps for a while did) but who now found themselves utterly destroyed. It is their human greatness which makes their predicament so agonising; were their roots not so deep, their uprooting would not be so tragic (cf. 3.23).

8.59   The emotional impact of the plays was considerably increased by the distance created between play and spectators not only by the myths themselves, but also by the formal appearance of the actors (with their masks and stylised clothing: see 8.65) and the strict maintenance of the dramatic illusion. In contrast with comedy, which continually involves the audience, it is arguable that nowhere in Greek tragedy was the audience directly addressed. The tragedians refer neither to themselves, nor to the actors, nor to the theatre. The audience was not 'there' as far as the tragedy itself was concerned. Aloof, dignified, distanced, Greek tragedy engaged the emotions of the community in its probing of the deepest human questions.

8.60   Greek tragedy as we have it spans the period from 472 (Aiskhylos' *Persians*) to 402 (Sophoklēs' *Oidipous at Kolōnos*, posthumously produced). In that time, profound changes had come over the form. In early tragedy, the role of the chorus was very pronounced; there were only two actors; and the action could be at times highly formalised. There was sometimes little sense of personal interaction between actors and chorus. Consider the following rather distant and ritualised exchange between the Persian queen Atossa and the chorus. She enquires about Athens' whereabouts and power:

> *Atossa:* But tell me, friends, where is this Athens reported to be?
> *Chorus:* In the far west, where the Sun-god's rays grow dim and set.
> *Atossa:* But why should my son be so anxious to make it his prey?
> *Chorus:* Athens won, all Greece would be subject to him.
> *Atossa:* Has it so plentiful a supply of fighting men?
> *Chorus:* It has, and has inflicted much damage on the Persians.
> *Atossa:* What else has it? Are its people wealthy?
> *Chorus:* There is a spring of silver which the earth treasures for them.
> *Atossa:* Have they the bow-stretching arrow in their hands?

> *Chorus:* They have not. They carry spears for close fighting and are equipped with shields.
> *Atossa:* What leader and commander have they?
> *Chorus:* They are no man's slave and take no man's orders.
> *Atossa:* How then can they withstand invading enemies?
> *Chorus:* So well that they destroyed Dareios' great and splendid army.
> *Atossa:* Dread words to those whose sons are with the army now.
> *Chorus:* Soon, I think, you will know the full truth. This man is surely a Persian courier bringing news, good or bad. (Aiskhylos, *Persians* 230ff.)

8.61 The form of this dialogue – exchanges known as 'stichomythia' in which each speaker speaks just one line (*stykhos*) at a time – is traditional. Other playwrights turned it to quite different use and gave it a quite different tone, especially when a third actor was added. Compare the famous scene in Sophoklēs' *Oidipous Tyrannos* where Oidipous questions the old shepherd. This old shepherd knows the whole truth – that Oidipous killed his father King Lāios and married his mother, but clearly does not want Oidipous to know. The interview is carried out in the presence of a messenger with news from Corinth. The shepherd had long ago given the baby Oidipous to this same Corinthian, though the shepherd had been instructed to expose the baby, so it would die. The Corinthian does not know the significance of Oidipous' questions and cannot understand the shepherd's reluctance to agree with him:

> *Oidipous:* Though I have never met him, I guess, my friends, that I see the shepherd whom we have been looking for all this time. He is an old man, like our friend here, and I recognise those who are bringing him as my servants. But you may have seen him before and so have the advantage of me.
> *Chorus:* Yes, I know him. He was one of Lāios' most trusty shepherds.
> *[Enter shepherd, attended]*
> *Oidipous:* My first question is for you, my Corinthian friend. Is this the man you mean?
> *Corinthian:* Yes, he is the man before you.
> *Oidipous:* Come then, old man, look at me and answer my questions. Were you in Lāios' service?
> *Shepherd:* I was a slave of his, born and bred in his household.
> *Oidipous:* What was your occupation and way of life?
> *Shepherd:* For most of my life I was a shepherd.
> *Oidipous:* In what part of the country did you mostly spend your time?
> *Shepherd:* In Kithairōn – or its neighbourhood.
> *Oidipous:* Do you remember having seen this man in those parts?
> *Shepherd:* Doing what? What man do you mean?
> *Oidipous:* This man here; have you ever met him?
> *Shepherd:* I can't say I remember him at first sight.
> *Corinthian:* That's not surprising. But I will revive the memory of what he has forgotten. I am sure he remembers the days when we were neighbours in

Kithairōn, he with two flocks, I with one, for three grazing seasons, spring to autumn; when winter came I would drive my flocks home to Corinth and he to Lāios' folds. Is that what happened? Am I right?

Shepherd: True enough, though it's long ago.

Corinthian: Come then, tell me, do you remember giving me a baby to bring up as my own child?

Shepherd: What do you mean? Why this question?

Corinthian: Because, my friend, here stands that one-time child.

Shepherd: Damnation take you – hold your tongue.

Oidipous: Don't abuse him, old man; your words call for more abuse than his.

Shepherd: But best of masters, how have I offended?

Oidipous: By not telling me of the child about whom he is asking.

Shepherd: He does not know what he is talking about; his words are vain.

Oidipous: If you will not answer a request, torture will make you speak.

Shepherd: No, no, for God's sake; don't hurt an old man.

Oidipous: Pinion his arms, someone, at once.

Shepherd: Oh misery, why? What do you want to know?

Oidipous: That child he asks about – did you give it to him?

Shepherd: I did – and I wish I had died that day.

Oidipous: And die you will unless you tell me the truth.

Shepherd: And if I do, ruin is still more certain.

Oidipous: The fellow still evades my questions.

Shepherd: No, no. I said before that I gave it to him.

Oidipous: Where did it come from? Was it yours or someone else's?

Shepherd: Not mine; I had it from another.

Oidipous: From whom? What was its home?

Shepherd: For god's love, master, question me no more.

Oidipous: If I have to ask again, you die.

Shepherd: Very well – it was a child from Lāios' house.

Oidipous: A slave, or one of his own family?

Shepherd: Oh misery: I am on the brink of telling the awful truth.

Oidipous: And I of hearing it – yet it must be heard.

Shepherd: It was said to be his own child. But your wife within can best tell you that.

Oidipous: Did she give it you?

Shepherd: Yes, my lord.

Oidipous: And what were you to do?

Shepherd: To kill it.

Oidipous: Wretched woman – her own child.

Shepherd: She did it in fear of evil prophecies.

Oidipous: What prophecies?

Shepherd: Prophecies which said it would kill its own father.

Oidipous: Then why did you give it to this old man here?

Shepherd: In pity, master, thinking he would take it away to his own country. And he rescued it indeed, but for what a terrible fate. For if you are that child, you were born to misfortune.

> *Oidipous:* Ah God, ah God: all come true and known! Let this be the last
> time I see the light of day. Cursed in my parents, cursed in my marriage,
> cursed in the blood I have shed! (Sophoklēs, *Oidipous Tyrannos* 1110ff.)

This almost intimate exchange conveys a sense of the engagement of the total
personality of all three characters, as they respond emotionally to the twists
and turns of the gradual revelation of the truth. This shows the same dramatic form could be used for different purposes in different hands (it is not a
matter of 'early incompetence' vs. 'later sophistication', but of dramatic
intention). The exchanges between Pentheus and the god Dionȳsos in
Euripidēs' *Bacchae* 810ff. illustrate another use again: the god formal and
correct, the man a tool in his hands, the whole highly emotionally charged.

8.62   Human character too was handled differently. In Aiskhylos, the major characters tended to be distanced, powerful, archetypal figures. In Sophoklēs, the
action characteristically moved around great individual heroes faced with the
contradictions of a past of glory and a present of shame. With Euripidēs,
generalisation is more difficult. His range seems greater, and he has the dis-
concerting habit of exploring 'realistic' situations in highly stylised forms. For
example, the earthy nurse of Euripidēs' *Hippolutos* inhabits the same world
as the austere and rhetorical Hippolytos himself. To point up extremes, the
great hero Menelāos in *Helen* verges on the comic (on his return from Troy,
he has been swept ashore on a hostile Egyptian coast):

> *Menelāos:* Hi there! Come to the door: this is a cry for help.
> *Old Woman:* Who's that knocking? Don't stand there disturbing the bosses.
>   Go away; you'll get killed if you don't – you're a Greek and we have no
>   dealings with Greeks.
> *Menelāos:* Come off it, old girl. Keep a civil tongue in your head. I'll do what
>   you say, but do unbolt the door.
> *[She opens the door]*
> *Old Woman:* Be off. My orders are to admit no Greeks.
> *Menelāos:* Here, hands off, no shoving.
> *Old Woman:* You've only yourself to blame if you won't listen to what I say.
> *Menelāos:* Take a message to your master —
> *Old Woman:* He won't be pleased to hear it.
> *Menelāos:* I've been shipwrecked, and you have to be kind to shipwrecked
>   sailors.
> *Old Woman:* Be off, and knock on someone else's door.
> *Menelāos:* I won't. I'm coming in. Do what I tell you.
> *Old Woman:* You're a nuisance. You'll be thrown out soon.
> *Menelāos:* Hell! I wish I had my army here.
> *Old Woman:* You may impress them, but you don't impress me.
> *Menelāos:* God, what humiliating treatment!
> *Old Woman:* Tears in the eyes? What are you crying for?
> *Menelāos:* At the thought of my past happiness.
> *Old Woman:* Well, run away and weep on some friendly shoulder.
> *Menelāos:* Where am I anyway? Whose palace is this?

> *Old Woman:* It's Proteus' palace, and you're in Egypt.
> *Menelāos:* Egypt! What a wretched place to have got to. (Euripidēs,
>   *Helen* 435–61)

Contrast this with Mēdeia in Euripidēs' *Mēdeia* 1021ff., where she wrestles with her heart whether to kill her children or not. The writing is highly stylised, yet she is in the grip of the most primitive feelings which reduce her almost to emotional paralysis.

8.63   Finally, while the role of the chorus did change considerably between Aiskhylos and late Euripidēs, it is important to stress that the element of singing and dancing, for which the chorus was largely responsible, did not disappear. This element became transferred, especially in Euripidēs' hands, from the chorus to the individual. In Euripidēs, there were far more solo arias than in previous tragedy. Euripidēs, in other words, continued to experiment with different ways of creating emotional impact through music and dance on the stage.

8.64   There is much dispute about what the theatre looked like in the fifth century. Certainly there was the large circular dancing area (18m across in the fourth-century theatre at the sanctuary of Asklēpios at Epidauros), the *orkhēstrā*, where the chorus moved and danced and sang; and almost certainly there was a low raised stage at the back, on which the actors moved (they also used the *orkhēstrā*) and behind which was a long, flat-roofed building (*skēnē*, which could stand for a palace or hut or tent, and be used as the actors' dressing-rooms). This building probably had a single door in the middle of it. There were also entrances along the sides, called *eisodoi* or *parodoi*. Sophoklēs is said to have introduced 'scene painting' (perspective sets along the front of the *skēnē*, which could be replaced as needed).

8.65   Actors and chorus wore all-over face masks (including hair) and dramatic, highly coloured costumes. Roles could be identified by the masks and costumes worn (a Greek audience would know at once who was 'king', who 'messenger'), but clearly the onus on actors was very great. Wearing a mask, the actor could not express emotions by facial expression. The audience stretched back up the theatre a very long way (and in the open air), so that the small intimate gesture and the subtle whisper (especially behind a mask) would be entirely lost on them. For all the excellence of the acoustics of the theatres, acting had to be 'big', using expansive gestures – especially since it is often difficult to tell *which* of a number of masked actors is speaking – with clear and audible enunciation. Likewise, the words had to carry much of the weight of a play. New characters were usually introduced by what others said about them ('Look! Here comes Menelāos'). Emotions were verbally expressed ('I weep' etc.). Extraordinary versatility was also demanded of actors. Given that the playwright was only allowed three, any one actor could be called upon to play a great number of roles. For example, in Sophoklēs' *Antigonē*, one of the actors had to play Antigonē's young sister Ismēnē, a guard, Antigonē's lover Haimōn, an old prophet Teiresiās, and Haimōn's mother Eurydikē.

8.66   The main stumbling-block to our appreciation of the plays is that all we have are words on the page. We have no stage instructions, except what the characters themselves tell us. We have almost no idea at all what the singing and dancing sounded or looked like. (There are even doubts about the assignation of parts to characters, since manuscripts give us lists of *dramatis personae* but do not actually say who is speaking at any one time, merely marking a *change* of speaker by a dash.) Consequently, we have lost entirely any sense of the spectacle – the colour, dash, movement, music – of tragedy. But at least we have the words, and these can tell us a great deal. We can appreciate the agony of the predicaments with which characters are faced, and enjoy the power of the rhetoric in which the great debates (*agōnes*) are expressed. Production can bring out clearly the Greek playwright's suggestive use of stage implements and stage actions to carry significance and reinforce the spoken word. Oidipous, for example, at the start of *Oidipous Tyrannos* comes out of the palace to be supplicated by the people of Thebes as the only man to whom the city can turn in its hour of need: he is king of Thebes, honoured by all, almost a god. At the end he is *led* back into the palace, against his will and express plea, blinded, accursed, almost an object, having found out who he really is – that he had married his own mother and killed his own father. Visually, the contrast between the two states at the beginning and end of the play could not be more clearly indicated, but it is difficult to appreciate it unless you actually go to a production, or develop the capacity to 'see' a play as you read it. Stage implements could be used to equally moving effect: in Sophoklēs' *Philoktētēs* the possession of Philoktētēs' magic bow (which is what Odysseus and Neoptolemos are out to get) expresses visually the dramatic struggle for mastery with which the play is concerned.

(b) Comedy

8.67   It may be that at the *Dionӯsia*, a day's tragic fare (i.e. trilogy plus a satyr play) was followed by one of the comedies which was being judged in the comic competition. If so, the audience underwent a most extraordinary experience. From the distant world of myth, and a performance which did not acknowledge their presence, the audience was thrown headlong into a fantastic and wholly contemporary comic world, where actors and chorus handled any issue of the day – literary, intellectual, political, personal, social – and where the audience itself would be the butt of the jokes as much as the characters and issues on stage, in language as extreme (and as obscene) as the action. As in tragedy actors were all-male, there was a three-actor rule (though four speaking parts are needed in some places); and there was a chorus; but quite contrasting were the grotesque costumes (padded stomachs and rumps, leather *phallos*, exaggerated but life-like masks: it is likely that the actor playing Sōkratēs in *Clouds* wore a recognisable mask).

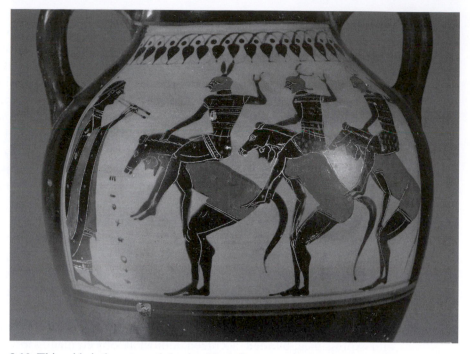

8.10 This mid-sixth-century Athenian black-figure *amphorā* presents us with something of a puzzle. The pipe player and the troupe of men dressed as animals correspond to the animal choruses of Old Comedy, but comedy is said to have been invented only in the fifth century. This and other similar vases may indicate that there were masquerades of some sort that were part of religious festivals before the formal rules of comedy were devised.

8.68 The Alexandrians (see 8.5) divided Attic comedy into three types: Old, Middle, and New, broadly corresponding with plays written between 450 and 380, between 380 and 320, and after 320. We know the names of about fifty writers of Old Comedy, but the only complete plays we possess are those of Aristophanēs (c. 445–c. 385). We have eleven complete plays by him, which span the length of his career (from *Akharnians*, produced in 425, to *Ploutos* (*Wealth*), produced in 388). They were preserved not necessarily because later readers saw anything especially fine in them as comedy, but because of their pure Attic language.

8.69 The origins of comedy (*kōmōidiā*, 'song to do with a *kōmos*' ('group revel')) are obscure, but are probably to be found in choral revels in Dionȳsos' honour, perhaps in a phallic ritual, to which episodes became attached. Some scholars have suggested origins in Dorian or Sicilian farce, but all elements of Attic comedy can be shown to have perfectly feasible origins in Attikē.

8.70 Comedy became a state-financed feature of festivals in Athens in 486 at the *Dionȳsia*, and was added to the *Lēnaia* c. 445. In *Knights* (517ff.), Aristophanēs talks scathingly about early comic writers. He cites Magnēs who won eleven victories in all (a record), but lacked satirical power; then Kratīnos (*fl.* 450–420), who had become a pathetic drunkard falling apart at the seams; and finally, Kratēs, renowned for his refinement. From surviving fragments of the work of Kratīnos and Kratēs, we can see the major influences upon Attic comedy and Aristophanēs. Magnēs, we may guess, developed the comic element of the *kōmos* of men dressed as animals; Kratīnos may have been the key figure in the development of comedy as drama in which politics and social grievances could be publicly aired. He was renowned for his ferocious obscenity, and his plays often burlesqued mythology (he would take a common myth and use it to criticise contemporary politicians e.g. his *Dionūsalexandros*, in which an analogy is drawn between Helen and Paris and Periklēs and his mistress Aspasiā). He also criticised and parodied current literary fashions, as Aristophanēs was to do in, for example, *Frogs* and *Thesmophoriazousai*. Kratēs (who won his first victory probably in 450) was said to have given up invective and to have developed a better plot structure.

8.71 Common to all Old Comedy seems to have been the general structure (see 8.73) and a number of traditions and subjects of attack. There were two main features: first, Old Comedy was relentlessly political, i.e. it existed and flourished within the framework of the radically democratic *polis* self-confidently ruling its own empire; second, whatever its forms and themes and characters, it always began with a contemporary human predicament. As for technique, literary parody and burlesque of mythology were common. Dionȳsos, Odysseus and the Kyklōps were characters in the comedies of more than one playwright, and Euripidēs and Sōkratēs were depicted as typical 'intellectuals'. Amongst politicians, Periklēs (with his mistress Aspasiā) was frequently attacked, and of the intellectuals, Periklēs' associates Anaxagorās and Lampōn came under repeated fire. Nostalgic looking back to the 'golden age' of the past seems to have been a common theme.

8.72 Aristophanēs, though in some ways his plays seem typical, seems to have taken all the traditions and techniques that his precursors offered (though some he rejected, e.g. mythological burlesque) and, combining them with his own sensitivity to contemporary issues (e.g. the war, the sophists, literary fashions, politicians) and sharp eye for the absurd, to have produced a brand new confection whose sheer range and variety (from the downright obscene to the elegant lyrical) make it almost undefinable. He must have been born c. 445, and his first play *Banqueters* (lost) was produced in 427 in his teens. Normally, the playwright produced it, but because of his youth Aristophanēs gave his first three plays to one Kallistratos to produce. *Banqueters* came second. There then followed an extraordinary run, for a young playwright: *Babylonians* (lost) 426 (probably 1st), *Akharnians* 425 (1st), *Knights* 424 (1st). The sequence was broken by *Clouds* 423 (3rd), a result which so shocked Aristophanēs that he rewrote it, though it was never reproduced (it is the rewritten version that we possess). Then came *Wasps* 422 (2nd) and *Peace* 421 (2nd). These early plays show off many of Aristophanēs' abiding interests. The theme of *Banqueters* was the new education. A father brought up two sons differently, one in the new, one in the old, education, and the results were observed. *Clouds* picked up this theme (cf. 5.48). *Babylonians'* main theme was the relationship between a central power and her subject allies, and this led Kleōn to prosecute Aristophanēs (unsuccessfully) for bringing Athens into disrepute with this play. Aristophanēs' next four plays proceeded to pour a torrent of vicious abuse on Kleōn's head, the most violent of all being *Knights*, in which Kleōn was the central figure. Rivalries with other comic dramatists were also played out on stage: in *Clouds*, Aristophanēs claimed that the contemporary comic playwright Eupolis (449–412) had cribbed material from *Knights* for his play *Marikās;* Eupolis replied that he had helped Aristophanēs write *Knights* – and for free. In *Knights* Aristophanēs accused Kratīnos of being a drunken has-been (see 8.70). Kratīnos responded with *Flask* in 423, with himself as the main character (a drunken has-been) in conflict with his wife Kōmōidiā. Kōmōidiā was shown complaining about his relations with the slut Methē ('drink') and the pretty little boy Oiniskos ('little wine'). Kratīnos excused himself on the grounds that only the drunkard could produce anything worthwhile. The audience agreed, and he won first prize – sweet revenge, since Aristophanēs came last with *Clouds*!

8.73 Old Comedy, like pantomime, features recurring dramatic moments which the audience have come to expect (e.g. the spectacular entry of the chorus) and typical routines which always occur somewhere (e.g. comic monologues, slapstick, patter songs) as well as traditional costumes (e.g. the actors wearing the *phallos*). The traditional structure of Old Comedy was as follows:

1 The prologue: the actors come in, and, in a series of often irrelevant and farcical routines, introduce the plot and themselves and prepare for the entry of the chorus.

2 The *parodos:* this is the long-awaited and often highly spectacular entry of the chorus (e.g. a chorus of birds in *Birds* and clouds in *Clouds*). It is normally the signal for the start of the main action, out of which a conflict develops, often between actors on the one side and the chorus on the other.

3 The *agōn* ('conflict'): this is a traditional, stylised form of alternating speeches and songs which always include a *pnīgos* (a tongue-twisting, breath-taking *tour de force* in the shape of a patter song).

4 The *parabasis:* the chorus comes forward and gives what purports to be serious political advice, frequently entirely unconnected with anything in the play.

5 Various farcical scenes and self-contained sketches in which the consequences of the *agōn* are worked out.

6 The *exodos:* the 'departure', in which events reach a climax, often involving celebrations, or a wedding, to hail the end of the dispute.

But just as characteristic as the formal structure of Aristophanēs' plays is the nature of the plots. They usually follow this sort of pattern: (1) a great and fantastic idea is put forward (the more outrageous the better), frequently involving salvation for oneself, one's family or the whole of Greece. The originator of this idea becomes the hero(ine). (2) The idea is advanced and after a series of minor setbacks, the main struggle takes place, after which the 'great idea' is realised. (3) The consequences of the success of the 'great idea' are worked out.

8.74   In common with other playwrights of Old Comedy, Aristophanēs was prepared to sacrifice consistency of e.g. character, logic, time, place to the needs of the moment and the episode. Fantasy was an important ingredient of his art. In *Birds*, Euelpidēs and Peisetairos escape from Athens and found a new city, with none of its vices, in the clouds above, amongst the birds of the air, and call it Cloudcuckooland (*Nephelokokkūgiā*). In *Peace*, Trygaios harnesses a dung beetle and soars up to heaven to bring Peace back to earth. Making matters laughable in the eyes of the audience, not representing the world as it is, was the Aristophanic priority. Scholars tend to emphasise how in *Clouds* Sōkratēs is made into a typical 'intellectual', dealing in all the sort of claptrap which was commonly associated with intellectuals, whether it bore any relation to Sōkratēs' own views or not (cf. on Sōkratēs 8.33, and on misunderstanding intellectuals at 8.14). But the same foisting of traits commonly associated with a class of persons onto an individual representative of that class was likely to apply equally to the politician Kleōn.

8.75   Aristophanēs had a keen ear for verbal dexterity. His language was (as far as we can tell) colloquial, but it was shot through with parody of and allusions to any discipline he cared to abuse (e.g. he freely uses medical and tragic diction, the language of decrees and prophecies, philosophical jargon and rhetorical tricks), as well as rich in invented words, outrageous puns and extended alliteration. He was especially adept at parodying tragedy and tragic diction. But this does not imply that the audience, in order to laugh at the parody, was acutely aware of the nuances of tragedy. *Frogs*, for example, reaches its climax with a contest between Aiskhylos and Euripidēs about who wrote the best tragedy. It is full of allusions to their plays and parody of their language (especially Euripidēs'), but the actors could easily have signalled parody by their use of tone and gesture, and the quotations themselves might have been well-known enough for the average man to pick up.

8.76   One striking feature of Aristophanēs' language is its wealth of obscenity and outrageously inventive metaphors for the sexual parts and act, e.g. metaphors for the male genitals include: eel, finger, dried fig, acorn, chickpea, soup-ladle, oar, handle, rope, peg, ram, pole, goad, beam, wing, tail, sparrow. Outside the Ionian iambic poetry of Arkhilokhos (8.1, 5) and cult practices (especially in worship of Dionȳsos or Dēmētēr), such obscenity is found only in Old Comedy. This obscenity, which brought social taboos out into the open and made public fun of them (contrast modern pornography, which encourages retreat into a private fantasy world), added great emphasis and power to Aristophanēs' attacks on people, ridiculing, exposing and degrading them. In the following passage, combining lyricism and filth, an old hag takes advantage of a new law passed by the women in parliament – that if a young man wants to make love to his girl, he must make love to an old woman first:

> *Girl:* Come here my dear,
> Come here, come here
> And spend all the night in my bed with me.
> For my head it just whirls
> At your beautiful curls
> And I'm wholly on fire
> With the strangest desire.
> Love, give me relief from my torment and grief
> And make sure that you bring him to bed with me.
> *Boy:* Oh open, my dear,
> Your door and come here
> Or I'll fall on your doorstep and lie there.
> Oh why *am* I so mad about you, dear, oh why?
> For what I am longing to do is to lie
> Head nicely at rest on your bosom
> And hands caressing your dear little bottom.
> Love, give me relief from my torment and grief
> And make sure that you bring her to bed with me.
> That's really a very moderate expression
> Of all the torment I suffer from my passion.
> So open the door and give me a kiss,
> As it is you are simply tormenting me.
> You're the song in my heart,
> My treasure, my bliss,
> My sweet honey-bee,
> My love and my flower
> My delicate luxury miss.
> *Hag:* Hi! Who's knocking? Are you looking for me?
> *Boy:* Not likely.
> *Hag:* You knocked on my door.
> *Boy:* Damn me if I did.
> *Hag:* Who are you looking for with that torch?
> *Boy:* Someone from Wankborough.
> *Hag:* Who?
> *Boy:* Not the screwdriver whom you are perhaps expecting.
> *Hag:* Well you've got to do me whether you want or not.
> *Boy:* But we're not dealing with the over-sixties now. We're leaving them till later and trying the under-twenties.
> *Hag:* That was under the old regime, love. Now you must take us on first.

> *Boy:* But the rule is you can take your choice.
> *Hag:* Oh no you can't. It's table d'hôte, not à la carte.
> *Boy:* You don't understand. I've got a girl to knock here.
> *Hag:* But you've got to knock at my door first.
> *Boy:* We don't want soiled goods.
> *Hag:* Oh I know I'm desirable. Are you surprised to find me out of doors?
>   Come on, give us a kiss.
> *Boy:* No, no: I'm afraid of your lover.
> *Hag:* Who?
> *Boy:* The best of artists.
> *Hag:* And who's that?
> *Boy:* The undertaker's man. Be off in case he sees you.
> *Hag:* I know what you want.
> *Boy:* And I know what you want.
> *Hag:* I vow by Aphrodītē, whose devotee I am, that I will not let you go.
> *Boy:* You are mad.
> *Hag:* Nonsense. I'll get you to bed yet. (Aristophanēs, *Ekklēsiazousai* 952ff.)

8.77 Aristophanēs had an enviable capacity to integrate effortlessly the fantastic plot on stage with contemporary life. His characters did not step outside themselves to make topical allusions; instead they drew the subjects of their allusions (people, places, events, issues) into the plot. Thus when Dikaiopolis at the start of *Akharnians* laments the Athenians' refusal to take seriously the question of ending the war (see 6.10), he alludes to real people and real occasions, yet the plot itself is outrageously absurd – one man's fight to forge a personal peace treaty with Spartē. In *Birds*, Peisetairos is founding a new city in the clouds (Cloudcuckooland), but finds the usual charlatans coming to make some money. First is an oracle-monger (cf. 3.20):

> *Peisetairos:* Eh? Who are you?
> *Soothsayer:* An oracle-monger.
> *Pei.:* Get lost.
> *S.:* O think not lightly, friend, of things divine; you see, I've an oracle of
>   Bakis, bearing on your Cloudcuckoolands.
> *Pei.:* Eh? Then why did you not tell me the oracle that before I founded my
>   city here?
> *S.:* The Force forbade me.
> *Pei.:* Well, well, there's nowt like hearing what it says.
> *S.:* 'Nay, but if once grey crows and wolves shall be banding together
>   Out in the midway space, twixt Corinth and Sikyon, dwelling,—'
> *Pei.:* But what in the world have I to do with Corinth?
> *S.:* Bakis is riddling: Bakis means the Air.
>   'First to Pandōra offer a white-fleeced ram for a victim.
>   Next, who first shall arrive my verses prophetic expounding,
>   Give him a brand-new cloak and a pair of excellent sandals.'
> *Pei.:* Are sandals in it?

> *S.:* Take the book and see.
>   'Give him moreover a cup and fill his hands with the innards.'
> *Pei.:* Are innards in it?
> *S.:* Take the book and see.
>   'Youth, divinely inspired, if thou dost as I bid, thou shalt surely
>   Soar in the clouds as an Eagle; refuse, and thou ne'er shalt become an
>   Eagle, or even a dove, or a woodpecker tapping the oak-tree.'
> *Pei.:* Is all that in it?
> *S.:* Take the book and see.
> *Pei.:* Well well! How unlike your oracle is to mine, which from Apollo's words
>   I copied out:
>   'But if a cheat, an impostor, presume to appear uninvited,
>   Troubling the sacred rites, and lusting to taste of the inwards,
>   Hit him betwixt the ribs with all your force . . .'
> *S.:* You must be joking . . .
> *Pei.:* Take the book and see.
> 'See that ye spare not the rogue, though he soar in the clouds as an Eagle,
> Yea, be he Lampōn himself or even the great Diopeithēs *[both seers]*.'
> *S.:* Is all that in it?
> *Pei.:* Take the book and see. Get out!
> *[Strikes him]*
> *S.:* Aagh!
> *Pei.:* Take that! Now get out of here and soothsay somewhere else.
>   (Aristophanēs, *Birds* 959ff. (Rogers, adapted))

8.78 Aristophanēs generally pulled no punches and took no hostages. It is true he never called for a change in the radical democratic constitution of fifth-century Athens, nor did he (in his surviving work) seriously attack public figures such as Nīkiās or Alkibiadēs. But apart from these, all was grist to his mill: the audience, the gods, politicians, intellectuals, homosexuals, jurors, bureaucrats, students, the military. In all this, his purpose was to win first prize; but the appeal to his audience, which included farmers, city men, the poor, sailors, soldiers, the successful and the disillusioned, the educated and the illiterate, surely resided in the *hope* he gave them. Aristophanēs' heroes like Dikaiopolis were all little people of no importance, but still individuals who felt passionately about something probably close to the heart of the audience and who made heroic efforts to achieve their ends – usually successfully. In the strongly competitive world of Athenian society (cf. 4.8), this reassertion of the little man's will to win and to overcome his superiors must have been as reassuring as the discomfiture of the high and mighty (cf. on Kleōn 8.72).

8.79 But where did Aristophanēs stand in all this? It is extremely difficult to know what were Aristophanēs' own views. His aim was to make people laugh and to win a prize. There is no reason why anything he said should reflect anything other than this end and the audience's prejudices. It is true that in the *parabasis* of his plays the chorus sometimes gives what is apparently serious advice (though frequently this is purely generalised, on a 'good of all mankind' level, rarely does it seem contentious, and often it is interspersed with jokes as well). It is true too that there are some constant themes running through this work which may suggest to us that we can define some of his serious concerns. In the following passage from the *parabasis* of *Frogs*, Aristophanēs reminds the Athenians how they had granted freedom to those slaves who had fought at the battle of Arginoussai and urges them to grant a pardon to those who had been deprived of their rights for their 'one mishap' in becoming involved in the oligarchic coup of 411. Phrȳnikhos had played a major part in the coup. Plataians had been given Athenian citizenship after the destruction of their own city in 427 (1.56):

> Well it suits the holy Chorus evermore with counsel wise
> To exhort and teach the city; this we therefore now advise—
> End the townsmen's apprehensions; equalise the rights of all;
> If by Phrȳnikhos's wrestlings some perchance sustained a fall,
> Yet to these 'tis surely open, having put away their sin,
> For their slips and vacillations pardon at your hands to win.
> Give your brethren back their franchise. Sin and shame it were that slaves,
> Who have once with stern devotion fought your battle on the waves [i.e.
>   Arginoussai],
> Should be straightway lords and masters, yea 'Plataians' fully blown—
> Not that this deserves our censure; there I praise you; there alone
> Has the city, in her anguish, policy and wisdom shown—
> Nay but these, of old accustomed on our ships to fight and win
> (They, their fathers too before them), these our very kith and kin,
> You should likewise, when they ask you, pardon for their single sin.
> O by nature best and wisest, O relax your jealous ire,
> Let us all the world as kinsfolk, and as citizens acquire,
> All who on our ships will battle well and bravely by our side.
> If we make our city haughty, narrowing her with senseless pride,
> Now when she is rocked and reeling in the cradles of the sea,
> Here again will after ages deem we acted brainlessly. (Aristophanēs, *Frogs*
>   686ff. (Rogers))

If we were to risk ascribing any views to Aristophanēs, it would be that he resented what he saw as the misuse of power by people like Kleōn, he despised the *dēmos* when it encouraged such 'unworthy' individuals (cf. 1.58; 6.17), and he wanted an end to the Peloponnesian War – but only if it brought glory to Athens. When it comes to his frequent attacks on e.g. intellectuals and jurors, it is more difficult to decide. Perhaps he saw such trends and institutions as symptomatic of some vague and indefinable threat to the solidity and moral fibre of the Athenian people. Certainly, in Plato's *Sumposion* Aristophanēs sits most comfortably discoursing among the leading intellectuals of the day (including Sōkratēs), which suggests that Plato wished us to suppose that Aristophanēs did not have an ineradicable prejudice against everything new. On top of the problem of trying to determine Aristophanēs' 'views', there are (probably irresolvable) problems about how 'serious' he was. Did his comedies set out policies in which he believed? Did the audience expect to have their views changed by them? Or is one-off comic fantasy at a festival an inappropriate medium for political persuasion? Granted that the comedies start from a situation, often political, that is actually facing the Athenian people at the time, how far does Aristophanēs offer a genuine solution to it?

8.80 Aristophanēs' later plays are not like his earlier ones. His last play, *Ploutos* (*Wealth*), lacks almost entirely the outrageousness of insult, fantasy and obscenity so characteristic of earlier work (and present, as the quotation at 8.76 illustrates, even in *Ekklēsiazousai* three years earlier). Part of the explanation for this is likely to lie in what was happening at Athens. The two oligarchic coups and the loss of the Peloponnesian War and of the empire had seriously rocked Athenian self-confidence. The nature of political participation changed, and fourth-century politics had a flavour distinct from that of the fifth century. The assumption of superiority to other Greeks, so apparent in Periklēs' speeches in Thucydides, and above all in the Funeral Oration, was one that no Athenian could ever make again. The period we call Middle Comedy (380–320) is almost entirely undocumented, but by the time of what we call New Comedy (320 onwards), of which we have substantial work by the Athenian Menander, Greek comedy was an entirely different animal.

(c) New comedy

8.81 The language of New Comedy was plain, typical of ordinary conversation; lyrics were confined to song and dance routines between the acts (the chorus had no part in the plot of the play at all and the playwright merely wrote 'choral song' as a stage direction at the act-divisions, so that none of the songs survives). The formal structure of Old Comedy was replaced by a five-act unit; the grossness of Old Comedy costume was modified in favour of more decency; and, most important of all, the plays moved from the disorganised, fantastic, obscene (but in many ways fundamentally serious) chaos of Aristophanēs to a world where ordinary human affairs, played out by carefully drawn, ordinary human characters, held the stage. It was a world which we recognise as the origin of drawing-room comedy or the comedy of manners, where humour arises from misunderstandings and 'double-takes', and where the crises to be resolved are more or less familiar domestic crises. It is this style of comedy (which reached Western Europe through its Roman adaptations, above all by Plautus and Terence), not that of Aristophanēs, which was to have such an important effect on the development of European comedy. The plays of Menander stand behind those of Molière and *The Importance of Being Earnest*.

8.82 Here is a typical extract from New Comedy. In it Farmer Knēmōn (the bad-tempered old man of the title, *Dyskolos*), after a life of surliness, has fallen

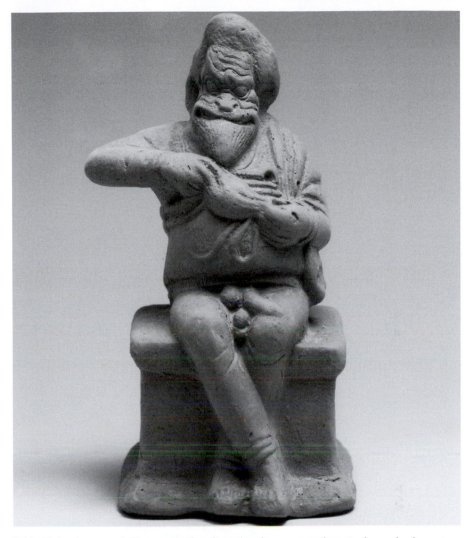

8.11–12 (and see over) Terracotta figurines showing more or less stock comic characters became quite popular in the fourth century and give us some of our best evidence not only for comic costume (note the masks and the comic phallus) but also for the poses struck by actors.

down a well and is rescued in the nick of time. He abandons his responsibilities to his son Gorgiās, who is to ensure that he marries off Knēmōn's daughter Myrrhinē to someone suitable. Gorgiās ensures that Sōstratos, the leisurely, aristocratic young neighbour who is in love with Myrrhinē but has been going through hell trying to win her (e.g. pretending to be a farmworker), should be the groom:

> *Knēmōn:* What's the matter, young man? Whether I die now – I'm in a bad
> way and think I shall – or whether I survive, I adopt you as my son; so

8.12

consider my whole estate yours. As for my daughter Myrrhinē, I make you
her guardian. Find her a husband. Even if I get well again I could never
find one for her myself – not to satisfy me. If I do live, let me live as I like.
Take things over and run them as you like – thank god you have some
sense, and you are the proper guardian for your sister. Divide the property
in half – give her one half for dowry, keep the other half and look after
your sister and me.

Now help me lie down, Myrrhinē. Talking more than necessary is no
occupation for a man, I reckon. But there's one thing I'd like you to know,
son. I'd like to say a few words about myself and my ways. If everyone was
like me there would be no law-courts, no imprisonment, no war. Everyone
would have enough and be satisfied. But I guess people like things better as

they are. Carry on then, this cantankerous old malcontent will soon be out
of your way.

Gorgiās: Thank you, father, for all that. But you must help us to find a
husband for the girl as quick as we can, if you agree.

Knēmōn: Look, I've told you what I want. For goodness' sake, don't
bother me.

Gorgiās: There's someone here who wants to meet you.

Knēmōn: No, no, for God's sake.

Gorgiās: He wants to marry the girl.

Knēmōn: That's nothing to do with me now.

Gorgiās: But it's the man who helped rescue you.

Knēmōn: Who's he?

Gorgiās: There he is. Here, Sōstratos!

Knēmōn: He's nicely sunburnt. Is he a farmer?

Gorgiās: He certainly is. He's tough, not the sort you find idling round all day.

Knēmōn: Very well; give her to him. Carry me indoors. (Menander, *Duskolos*
729ff.)

That is an example of typical New Comedy moralising, and humour based
on character. For a more slapstick style of humour, involving cooks (traditional figures of fun in New Comedy) who are trying to borrow some uten-
sils from Knēmōn, see *Dyskolos* 441ff.

Greek Art

Background to the classical achievement

8.83 We cannot translate the word 'art' into Greek, and no Greek discussed the
painted pottery, sculpture, and architecture, which appear together in
books about 'Greek Art', as if they were all engaged in the same enterprise.
This was not because there was no notion of beauty, or no awareness that
some craftsmen were able to produce more beautiful objects than were
others. But the craftsmen of myth, the god Hēphaistos and Daidalos, were
associated both with the creation of beautiful objects and with the creation
of cunning devices. Their ability was to provide what was needed in particular circumstances, and aesthetic qualities were simply one resource
among several which enabled them to perform the role expected of them
(e.g. the enchantment produced by high quality workmanship, or the aura
which came from the identification between the work of art and the
divine or mythical figure it represented). Modern scholars often write a
history of Greek art in terms of the evolution of art from geometric styli-
sation, through the archaic creation of human images of particular types
freighted with heavy symbolic meaning, to classical naturalism. In so
doing, they tell only the latest form of the story Greeks themselves, very
conscious of competition between potters, painters and sculptors, might

8.13 The most magnificent of all eighth-century grave-markers, this belly *amphorā* dating to c. 750 shows the laying out of the corpse of a woman, surrounded by mourners. (Compare figs. 1.3, 5.28 above)

tell about the way works of art got better and better at fulfilling the roles expected of them.

8.84 As far as we know, Athens had not been a significant producer of pottery during the bronze age. But the style of pottery known as 'Protogeometric', which prevailed during the earlier part of the dark age (1100–900), was developed by Athenian potters; and it was in Athens also that pioneering figure decoration appeared on pottery, not far off 800 (1.13–15). During the eighth century, Athenian potters developed painted decoration on pottery whose style and choice of subject matter (i.e. iconography) were distinct from the

8.14 This Proto-Attic *amphorā* from the first half of the seventh century was used to bury a young boy's body in. It shows on the neck the blinding of Polyphēmos and on the body the sisters of the Gorgō(n) Medousa pursuing her killer Perseus.

painting on pots made in other parts of Greece (e.g. in Argos or on Euboia). In particular, around 750 it became fashionable in Athens, or at least in one particular Athenian cemetery (the Dipylon cemetery), to mark graves with pots of colossal size (belly *amphorā*s for women's graves, neck *amphorā*s or *krātēr*s for men's graves) decorated with scenes of the laying out of the corpse and with other scenes, many of them involving ships. Occasional use of large marker vases persisted after 700, and Athens continued to be a place with a strong tradition of large pots. But seventh-century pottery (of a style known as 'Proto-Attic' and then early 'black-figure') for the first time shows scenes

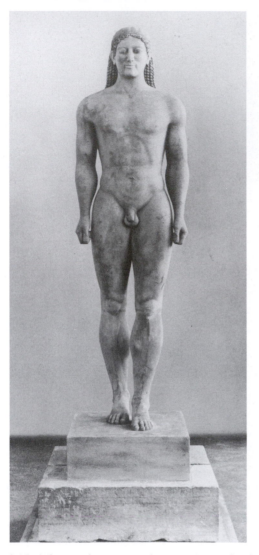

8.15 A *kouros* that was used as a grave-marker in a cemetery in southern Attikē, c. 520.

that can be directly linked to Greek myths, as well as decorative motifs and a style of animal drawing influenced from the Near East.

8.85 By contrast to the potters' distinguished tradition, Athenian sculptors and architects do not seem to have been trail-blazers. Bronze figurines of eighth-century date have indeed been excavated on the Athenian Akropolis, but not many of them, nor in a distinctive style. We know little of Athenian buildings in the period 800–600; but the marked advances in building technology from 700, including the use of 'dressed' stone walls (i.e. whose stones had been squared to fit) and clay roof-tiles, seem to have been made elsewhere in Greece. It was almost certainly in the Peloponnese that the 'Doric order' of architecture was developed, with its distinctive

8.16 A surviving figure from a late sixth-century pediment on the Athenian Akropolis.

arrangement of fluted columns without bases, triglyph and metope frieze, and hawksbeak mouldings. More or less coincident with the invention of the Doric order was the development of the life-size or over-life-size stone sculptures of naked youths or clothed maidens, known respectively as *kouroi* and *korai*. The earliest large stone *korai* come from the seventh-century Cyclades, but the monumental *kouroi* from Sounion and Athens seem to be as early as any monumental *kouroi*. Again, these were produced at least partly under the influence of Near Eastern (in this case specifically Egyptian) examples.

8.86 Attikē was unusual in using both *kouroi* and *korai* as grave-markers between 600 and 480. But even in Attikē, *kouroi* and *korai* were mostly placed sanctuaries as dedications to the gods, and between 550 and 490 a large number of *korai* and some *kouroi* were dedicated on the Athenian Akropolis. Scholars have long debated whether *korai* and *kouroi* should be seen as in some way representing those who dedicated them, or as representing the deity to whom they were dedicated; but dedication of *kouroi* to female deities and of *korai* by men suggests that these figures should not be thought of in that way. *Korai* are frequently referred to in dedications as 'a very beautiful thing of delight' (*perikalles agalma*) and it is arguably the beauty of *korai* that made them seem appropriate offerings to the gods. That beauty is explored in great variety in the late archaic *korai* from the Akropolis, which display both a wide range of facial features and very different clothing and decoration. But the use of *kouroi* and *korai* also on graves suggests that their beauty was not the only factor in their popularity. Standing still and staring straight ahead as they do, and engaging in no action (or some minimal gesture of offering), these statues provoke the viewer who meets their gaze to compare and contrast himself or herself with them, to measure up to the achievements, and sympathise with the lot, of the dead person commemorated, or ask about their own relationship to the god.

8.87   The sixth-century Akropolis was occupied not simply by sculptural dedications but also by temples with sculpted pediments. The exact sequence and placing of the various Doric temples from which sculpture survives is still disputed, but the most important temple seems to have been the temple of *Athēnē Polias*, built c. 560 and rebuilt c. 510, which stood in the space between the later Parthenōn and Erekhtheion (see fig. 1.50). Although by the end of the century there were other sanctuaries in Attikē with cult buildings, no other sanctuary seems to have approached the Akropolis either for the wealth of sculpted dedication or for architectural sculpture. But in cemeteries, where in the eighth century Athens seems to have been unmatched for its funerary monuments, the rest of Attikē put up strong competition, with important *stēlai* (in relief) found in cemeteries across the Attic countryside, as well as *kouros* and *kore* funerary monuments (see fig. 2.7).

8.88   Around 600, something of a revolution occurred in Athenian pot production. This revolution was partly a revolution of technique. As mentioned above, the black-figure technique was adopted in Athens, almost certainly from Corinth, c. 620. In this technique, figures were not *painted* as solid silhouettes, or *drawn* in outline; rather, a painted black silhouette figure had details incised into it, so that the lines of the lighter clay showed through. This enabled much finer drawing than could be done with a brush, and hence enabled all sorts of details to be painted. Initially this technique was adopted in the Attic large pot tradition, but very rapidly Athenian potters also took up potting and painting smaller vessels, and in particular drinking cups. Again, the inspiration here came from Corinth, as did certain iconographic choices, but quickly a quite distinct Attic tradition developed. Athenian potters offered both a range of shape and a variety of iconography which was much greater than that offered by Corinthian products. The result was that, in the course of the sixth century, Athenian pottery, which had hardly been exported at all in the seventh century, came to be the pottery of choice throughout the central Mediterranean. Indeed, the vast bulk of Athenian pottery on show in museums outside Greece today comes from tombs in Etruria, where local burial customs meant that large pots were not only deposited in tombs but tended to survive there intact. Some of that pottery seems to have been made and specially decorated with the Etruscan market in mind. For example, Etruscans seem to have had more of a taste for scenes involving bloodshed than did Athenians; but since they did not themselves do athletics naked, some Athenian potters produced athletes wearing loin cloths specially for them. Nevertheless, merchants serving the Etruscan market seem on the whole to have bought up *anything* that was on offer in Athens to sell on.

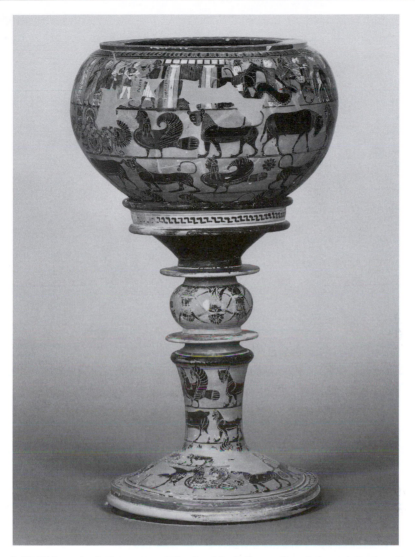

8.17 This early sixth-century Athenian black-figure *dīnos* (wine-mixing bowl) and stand by an artist named Sophilos shows in its upper frieze the gods coming to the wedding of Pēleus and Thetis. All the figures are carefully named.

8.89   In the course of the sixth century, Athenian pot painters explored a very wide range of iconographic possibilities. Some of the pots they painted were highly 'interactive', i.e. they exploited the appearance of the pot, as it was being used, in various ways. For instance, it became popular to decorate drinking vessels with eyes, so that when the vessel was tipped up to be drained it became a sort of face-mask for the drinker. Other pots explored mythological themes, or took mythological characters and constructed scenes involving them which required viewers to use their knowledge of mythology to understand their significance (cf. figs. 3.13, 4.1, 2). The most serious of all sixth-century

8.18 Exēkiās' intricately detailed scene of Akhilleus and Aiās playing dice, painted on an *amphorā* in the middle of the sixth century.

Athenian potters and painters was an artist named Exēkiās, active in the middle of the century and highly influential (fig. 1.6). Exēkiās seems to have been particularly interested in the figure of Aiās, depicting Aiās carrying off the dead body of Akhilleus from the battlefield, Aiās' suicide (after the Greeks failed to award him the arms of Akhilleus) and – a scene which he seems to have made up – Aiās playing dice with Akhilleus. Exēkiās particularly painted *amphorā*s and specialised in carefully balanced compositions which lead the viewer to concentrate on the motivations and feelings of the figures involved. Twice he painted Akhilleus killing the Amazon Penthesileia on the battlefield. In one example, he put such emphasis on the burning glance Akhilleus throws, even through his helmet, that scholars have speculated that he is alluding to a tradition that Akhilleus fell in love with Penthesileia even at the moment that he fatally wounded her (though that version of the story is attested in literature only much later). Other artists were very much lighter-hearted, painting weddings or scenes of grape-gathering or of the hunt (see figs. 2.4, 10, 3.4–6, 5.2–4, 16, 20, 7.8, 8.10). Particularly fascinating in this regard is Exēkiās' contemporary known as the Amasis Painter (because he paints for a potter named Amasis, itself an Egyptian name, or nickname). Competition among pot painters is apparent. For example, several of the Amasis Painter's pots seem

8.19 This mid-sixth-century black-figure *amphorā* attributed to the Amasis Painter shows the god Dionȳsos surrounded by dancing worshippers.

to have been painted with an Exekian pot in mind; the Amasis Painter has used Exekian compositional techniques to depict scenes – e.g. of the god Dionȳsos – which Exēkiās himself never painted.

8.90 Around 520 Athenian pot painters invented a completely new technique of painting, red figure. In this technique, the figures were not black, with incised detail, on a background made up of the red clay of the pot; the *background* was now filled in in black, and the figures were left in the red colour of the clay. Further, the details of the figures were not incised but painted in, with very finely drawn lines, in an extremely dense paint. The new technique had the advantage that it made it much easier to suggest that the figures were not flat but occupied space – though the disadvantage was that the black background inevitably itself

8.20 A young boy performs a dance with a spear to the music of the double pipes
played by a symposiast on this red-figure cup of c. 500.

seemed flat. With the new technique came some new iconographies. Scenes of
athletics, for instance, became much more popular; and in general scenes related
to daily life (including soldiers and the symposium; figs. 4.7, 9, 5.5, 9–10, 12–15,
17–19, 22, 6.9, 7.3–5, 8.1) came to outnumber scenes telling a story from myth
(see figs. 1.11, 3.1–2, 4.4–6, 8.6–8). Although the symposium was an institution
dating back before 600 and perhaps before 700, the frequency of sympotic
images at this period suggests that the symposium increased in popularity in the
late archaic period. The symposium ('drinking party') was an important aristocratic male institution, which put those who participated, and their behaviour,
under the spotlight. An important feature of it was to ask participants to
perform in one way or another. That many of the cups used at symposia themselves showed scenes of symposia suggests that there was a heavy concentration
by those present on *how* they and other guests performed, rather than upon the
substantive content of what was said. Status meant little in this context; what
mattered was how well one performed on the night. The competitive element to

this is typical (4.2); but it is attractive to associate the willingness to be exposed to such challenges with the keen desire to have opportunities to participate in public politics which the new Kleisthenic democracy offered.

8.91 In 480 the Persians sacked the Athenian Akropolis, burning down the temple of *Athēnē Polias*, damaging another temple which was under construction to its south, and wreaking havoc among the monuments in the Kerameikos cemetery. When the Athenians returned to the city, they buried the damaged sculpture on the Akropolis, and employed much of the damaged funerary sculpture to construct themselves new town walls (1.41). This clearing away of the old not only preserved many late archaic monuments for us; but, after thirty years in which the Athenians left visible the signs of Persian desecration (because they had other things to do), it also led to a concentrated period of reconstruction from the 450s. It was this that brought about the extraordinary legacy that is the classical Athenian Akropolis. As a result, it allows us to see the astonishing degree of real change that can be seen in sculpture in the first forty years of the fifth century.

Classical Athenian art

(a) Sculpture and the Parthenōn

8.92 One of the final dedications on the Athenian Akropolis before the Persian sack was a figure in the basic *kouros* tradition, i.e. naked, and with one leg slightly advanced. But whereas for the *kouros* this pose is static, this figure is moving. What gives the impression of movement is partly the twist of the hips, partly the slight turn of the head. At the same time, while all *kouroi* are beardless, this figure is definitely young, as his flesh and his undeveloped genitals show. Because the head has similarities to the copies of a sculpted pair attributed to Kritios and Nēsiōtēs (see also fig. 1.7), this figure has become known as the Kritian Boy. Not only does his fine condition suggest that he was the last dedication before the Persians came, he was also the last *kouros*. The body of the traditional *kouros* may have had the advantage of not seeming to invite the viewer to tell any particular story to account for it or make any particular emotional or critical response; but the Kritian Boy unquestionably demands both a particular story and a particular response.

8.93 Ten or twenty years later we see the full possibilities, and problems, presented by this new, wholly committed sculpture in the figures known as the Riace Bronzes. These two bronzes were recovered from the sea off Riace Marina at the southern tip of Italy, and there has been much discussion of their original location. There is a good chance that they were part of a victory monument in a Greek sanctuary, and at least a chance that they were the work of Pheidiās, the sculptor who oversaw the sculptures associated with the Parthenōn. These are two extraordinary figures, since they show the ability of an early classical artist to imbue figures which have virtually identical

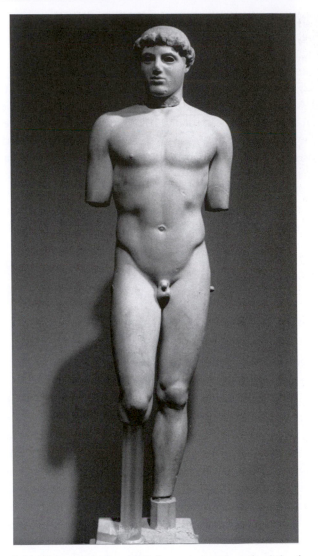

8.21 This statue of a young boy excavated on the Athenian Akropolis is ascribed to the sculptor Kritios because of its similarities to the copies of the statues of the tyrannicides (above fig.1.7).

poses with a quite different ethos. Riace A is fit, alert and ready to go; his keen glance has just a hint of aggression, but there is a strong sense that this is a person with whom what you see is what you get. Riace B has seen slightly better days and is beginning to go to seed. His flesh is thin and he has lost muscle tone. There is a certain slight weariness about him, but also a strong sense of a man who keeps his own counsel; it would not be good to try to take advantage of him. Interpretations of character such as this would seem absurd for any *kouros*, and even the very facially varied *korai* invite only the most basic classification into character types. The Riace Bronzes express

8.22 Warrior A from the bronzes recovered from the sea off Riace Marina in southern Italy.

character with their whole bodies. One is no longer looking simply at men, but at particular men, whose past history is written on their bodies.

8.94 The expressive power displayed in the Riace Bronzes had enormous potential. There is a similarly strong sense of character expressed on the body of the seer in the scene shown in the sculptures of the east pediment of the temple of Zeus at Olympiā, completed in the early 450s. It was the expression of anxiety on the face of the seer that provided the viewer with the key to the story of the race between Pelops and Oinomaos shown there and of its fateful outcome. But that expressive power was not desirable in all circumstances. When it came to showing many mythological battles, it was more important

8.23 Warrior B from Riace.

that those battling might be seen to share features with the viewer than that
they should be distanced from the viewer as distinct individuals. If, then, the
sculptor wanted to encourage individual citizens to act, like the mythical
figures, in concert together, he had to minimise the differences, not emphasise
them. The challenge to the sculptors commissioned in the 440s to work on
the sculptures for the temple that was to be the chief glory of the reconstructed Akropolis was to exploit the expressive powers newly developed to
display not remarkable individuals but good players in a team.

8.95 The Parthenōn was a product of megalomania. The gold and ivory cult statue
of Athēnē which it was built to house established a quite new trend in cult
statues (Olympiā immediately decided that it too needed a gold and ivory

8.24 The west frieze of the Parthenōn *in situ*, running across not the columns of the exterior but those that front the rear porch.

statue for its temple of Zeus). The massive cult statue demanded a spacious room, and to achieve this the Parthenōn was given eight columns across the façade, not six. But the cult statue also needed to be seen, not to be stuck at the back of a long dark room. So the architect gave the room only the shallowest of porches and also two eastern windows, bringing the cult statue much further forward than a visitor would expect, and making it unusually well lit. This had the incidental advantage of making space for a second closed room at the west end of the temple, which could be used as a treasure store. The whole building was then decorated with sculpture, much of it, courtesy of Lord Elgin, now in the British Museum. Not only did the Parthenōn have sculpture in its pediments, as was normal for major Doric temples, but also on all its ninety-two metopes (Olympiā had sculpture on just twelve metopes). In addition, unprecedentedly, there were further decorations in a continuous frieze around the outside of the inner building and around the inside of the front porch (figs. 3.16, 7.2).

8.25–7 (and see over) Three adjacent metopes from the south side of the Parthenōn give an indication of the range of different centaurs with which the sculptors face the viewer.

8.96   But the Parthenōn was not simply megalomaniac. The sculptures offered ways of thinking about Athens' patron goddess, Athēnē, whose birth was shown in the east pediment and whose struggle with Poseidōn to be patron deity of Athens was shown in the west pediment. They also offered ways of thinking about conflict, both with barbarians and with other Greeks, in their presentation of a series of mythical battles on the pediments. The east metopes showed battles of gods and giants, the west battles of Greeks and Amazons (a scene repeated on the shield of the cult statue), the south battles between lapiths and centaurs, and the north the sack of Troy. The south metopes are the best preserved. There we can see the sculptors using the recently developed expressive powers to explore how the viewer's sense of the conflict might change, according to whether one stresses the bestiality of the horse-man hybrid centaurs or their humanity. The north metopes are less well preserved, but enough can be recovered to show that rather than showing only fighting (in fact they might not have shown any fighting *at all*), they

8.26

largely depicted the Trojans leaving the city and Helen seeking refuge at the statue of Athēnē. The emphasis was therefore on the suffering of the sacked city, rather than on the glory of conquest. And those who viewed the metopes caught at the same time glimpses through the colonnade of the continuous frieze, so that its representation of Athenians processing at the Panathēnaic festival produced a counterpoint to the violence of the metopes. Like the reader of the description of the shield of Akhilleus in *Iliad* book 18, the visitor to the Parthenōn was presented with a view of the city at peace and a view of the city at war.

8.97 Just as the expressive possibilities developed by classical sculptors were exploited to raise questions over the brutishness of the centaurs of the south metopes, so in the Parthenōn frieze they were deployed to render vivid the particular individual circumstances of the young horsemen on parade. The technical skill, both of planning and of execution, which enabled the sculptors, who were working in very shallow relief, to create a picture of serried ranks of more or less orderly cavalry, is extraordinary. But the delicate

8.27

balance of order and flexibility on show in the cavalry formations carries also an ideological overtone. The young men are shown coping with distinct immediate circumstances, as they control their variously docile or spirited mounts, and they are distinct also in their choice of clothing and equipment, with no single military uniform imposed. But the facial features of the young men, in complete contrast to the centaurs of the metopes, are near-identical. The viewer receives no encouragement to compare and contrast different individuals or to reconstruct different life histories. Rather the sculptures suggest a world where the human material is uniform, though men meet different particular circumstances. The classical 'idealism' which has rightly been detected in the images of these young men carries with it a particular view of how men should relate to one another and live in the world.

8.98 Round about 500, the Athenians seem to have legislated against sculpted grave markers, but around 430 sculpted reliefs (*stēlai*) reappear. Scholars have sometimes wondered whether the legislation was changed so that sculptors trained on the Parthenōn could find employment. This seems implausible, since

8.28 The use of drapery to model form is particularly clear in this figure of Īris, messenger of the gods, from the west pediment of the Parthenōn.

neither Athens nor any other classical city interfered to any great extent in economic matters. Nevertheless, the funerary reliefs reproduce the same sculptural style as the Parthenōn frieze: the men and women on classical funerary reliefs, in other words, are idealised, not individualised, the emphasis not on the particular person but on their situation. That is, whereas archaic reliefs had almost always shown just one person, most classical reliefs show the dead person with one or more people in attendance; they present the dead person as lost to a social group, not simply as individuals.

8.99   The sculptural style of the Parthenōn frieze and of grave reliefs was not, however, the only style being deployed in the late fifth century. The pediments of the Parthenōn show an exuberant exploration of the ways in which drapery can be employed to make the female form visible underneath the clothing – quite different from the demure fall of the clothing worn by the women on the frieze. That possibility for revealing the form beneath the drapery is taken still further in the reliefs showing Nīkē (Victory) which formed the balustrade to the little Temple of Athēnē Nīkē (this was erected in the 420s on a bastion right by the new monumental gateway to the Akropolis, the newly completed Propylaia). In the most famous of these reliefs, Nīkē is shown bending to remove her sandal, an unmotivated action chosen for the possibilities it affords of showing a woman bending and pulling her lightweight garment taut across her body. There can be little doubt that this sculpture was designed to produce an erotic thrill, and that the parallel between erotic thrills and the thrill of victory is here deliberately invoked. These sculptures do not simply reproduce the outer form of the human body, but give the impression of a body lying under and giving form to the drapery, when in reality all there is is a simple block of stone. Such 'tricking' of the eye raises more sharply than ever before the issues of what seems to be and what really is, and of the relationship between convention and nature, which are so much explored by intellectuals and writers at this period (8.32).

(b) Pottery

8.100 The history of painted pottery in the fifth century shows some parallels with the history of sculpture, but is no simple mirror of that history. Painters had been exploring the body in action already at the end of the sixth century, well before the Kritian Boy was produced. But although painters were quite capable of producing figures that conveyed a sense of a substantial living presence, they largely restricted such figures to particular situations, and in particular to the portrayal of figures in the underworld – that is, figures whom literary texts treat precisely as *in*substantial (cf. 3.10, 8.29). Potters do sometimes raise questions about just how bestial satyrs, those other horse-man hybrids, should be thought to be in the same way as the Parthenōn does; but on the whole, there is very little in painting to parallel the particularism of the Riace Bronzes. But pot painters do develop a particular interest in the possibility which their medium gives of moving in and out of a fantasy world. This takes a number of forms, e.g. converting a 'genre (i.e. wholly typical, everyday) scene' into a mythological scene by the simple addition of a name label; showing 'real' tombs with figures presumably meant to represent the dead sitting in front of them; and depicting men *dressed up* as actors in satyr plays next to 'real' satyrs, or in one case creating a female satyr (fig. 8.31; cf. figs. 7.11, 8.5, 8.9). Once again we can see the links between these games played on pots and the big issues of nature and convention aired not only among sophists and their pupils but also on the Athenian stage, both in Aristophanic comedy and in such Euripidean tragedies as *Helen*.

8.101 The end of the fifth century constitutes quite a marked break in the history of Athenian, and to some extent more generally of Greek, art. Pot painting developed new iconographies and new techniques (with more use of added colour), but lost further ground in the markets of the Mediterranean, particularly in Italy where local schools of pot painting grew very strong. Athens became so poor that, for the best part of half a century, there was little public building, and architectural sculpture was never again significant. We

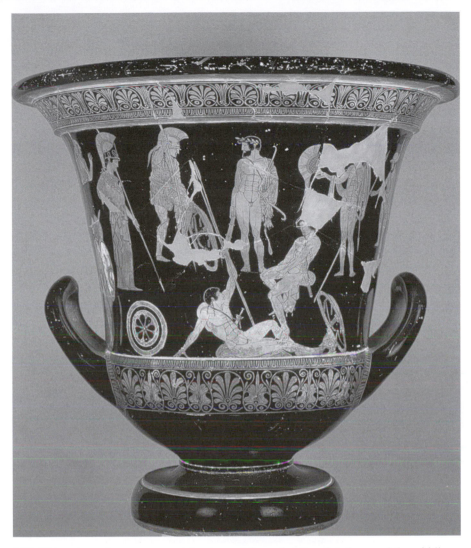

8.29 This enigmatic scene on an Athenian red-figure *krātēr* painted around the middle of the fifth century, in which the pensive figures seem to look past one another, is thought to have been influenced by wall-painting and perhaps to show figures in the underworld.

know little about the tradition of free-standing sculptures in the fifth century (particularly as dedications in sanctuaries) because they were largely made of bronze, which did not survive melting down. In the fourth century, however, we know a little more because marble was adopted once again for some free-standing statues, and was, in particular, championed by the Athenian sculptor Prāxitelēs. His use of it to represent female flesh made a particular stir with his naked Aphrodītē, now known only from later copies, which ended up in a temple at Knidos.

8.30 The serpent coiled round the tree on the lower frieze of this water jug (*hydriā*) ascribed to the Meidiās Painter identifies that scene as the Garden of the Hesperides. Above we see the carrying off by Kastōr and Polydeukēs of the daughters of Leukippos.

8.102 The greatest continuity is presented by grave reliefs. These were made in their thousands for the great cemeteries of Athens itself, the Peiraieus, and the demes of Attikē. Imposing funerary enclosures dominated several of the roads into Athens, the road from the sanctuary to the settlement and fort at Rhamnous, and no doubt elsewhere. Although many reliefs are conservative in their iconography, there is a tendency over time for the more elaborate monuments to show ever higher relief and larger groups of figures (figs. 1.15, 8.32). Part of the reason for this is artistic. High relief enabled effects which

8.31 The painter of this early fourth-century Athenian red-figure cup gives satyr-style shorts to a woman to create the 'impossible' female satyr.

could not be achieved in shallow relief. So the striking sense of the tangible presence of the naked young man on the famous *stēlē* recovered from near the river Īlīsos is very closely related to the depth of the relief. This presence is essential to the effect of the *stēlē* on which is also depicted a young weeping slave boy and an older man whose gaze stares through and past, rather than at, the dead man. The effect of this is to make the untimely dead seem to continue to be present for, while actually absent from, those closest to them. But high relief was also a feature of grand monuments. This suggests that Athenians now had a greater tolerance of 'undemocratic' individual display, a tolerance that can be measured both in the sheer scale of some monuments and the way in which some *stēlai* 'heroise' the individual dead person. That not everyone at Athens felt comfortable with this brash display of superiority is suggested by the sudden end of all sculpted *stēlai*, as a result of a ban brought in by the philosopher tyrant, Dēmētrios of Phalēron, in 317.

8.103 The loss of fourth-century tragedy, of Middle Comedy, and of many works of history written in fourth-century Athens, is partly a matter of chance, partly a matter of quality. The absence of fourth-century Athenian pot painting and, particularly, sculpture is much more a direct consequence of the difference between fourth- and fifth-century Athens. The public commissions

8.32 A mid-fourth-century Athenian grave *stēlē* recovered from the river Īlīsos.

which produced the enduring monuments of the fifth century have no parallels in the fourth. But the changes in art, as in literature, are unlikely to be a
simple product of changed economic situation. Even though the Athenians
restored democracy after the oligarchic coup which followed directly on the
loss of the Peloponnesian War, that democracy was operated by individuals
whose experiences of war and political revolution had seriously altered the
way they thought about each other and about their place in the world. Bouts
of imperial ambition in the fourth century never produced the rebirth of that
arrogant self-confidence which not only enabled the Athenians to win and
run an empire but also enabled them to face up squarely to the big moral and
conceptual issues about the place of man in the world. Classical Athenian art,
like the history of Thucydides, the comedy of Aristophanēs, and the tragedy
of Sophoklēs and Euripidēs, displays both that overwhelming confidence and
something of the imperial arrogance.

9 Postscript: The world of Athens and other worlds

9.1 This book has claimed and attempted to describe 'the world of Athens'. For no other Greek city, and for no period of ancient Greek history except the classical, could such a description be constructed. From classical Athens we have a very large amount of literature across a large number of different literary genres. Tragedy and comedy survive only from the pens of Athenian writers; we have around a hundred speeches written by Athenians or by Greeks resident in Athens, whereas we have only a handful of short pamphlets written outside Athens; classical painted pottery is dominated by Athenian production, and we have more sculpture from classical Athens than from anywhere else, and we know more about the contexts in which that sculpture was displayed. More famous philosophers were born outside Athens than were Athenian, but of the classical philosophers who have left us substantial written work, Plato was Athenian and Aristotle and Theophrastos spent very significant portions of their time working and teaching in Athens (8.15). When it comes to the writing of history, Thucydides and Xenophōn were both Athenian, and although Hērodotos was not, Athens plays an absolutely central role in his account (8.41–3). Other cities as well as Athens recorded public decisions on stone, but Athens had more public business to record and probably recorded more of it, and from an earlier date, than any other city. Works of non-Athenian writers whose viewpoint was formed entirely outside Athens do survive (Aineiās the Tactician, a fourth-century resident of the Peloponnese who wrote a manual on 'How to survive a siege', is one good example (7.33)); but they are few and far between, and even if we marshal all the literary and epigraphic evidence that we have, it affords at best tiny glimpses of what the world of any other city was like.

9.2 Athenians knew that being Athenian was different. They constructed their world as distinctive not least by contrasting themselves with others. They contrasted themselves with their northern neighbours, the Boiotians, proverbially regarded as 'pigs', but most consciously they contrasted themselves with their most serious enemies, the Persians and the Spartans. Hērodotos engaged in serious research to discover the truth about both Persia and Spartē, affording Spartē an ethnographic description without parallel in his treatment of Greek states, and Thucydides also worked hard, on his own account (cf. book 5.68) to discover the truth about Spartē. But Athenians in general derived their picture neither from Hērodotos and Thucydides nor from careful research or systematic comparison of their own. Rather they depended upon isolating particular features which were then taken to stand for the people as a whole. Those features could no doubt often be found, but their prevalence is very much more open to doubt. Not all Spartans were blindly obedient to orders (see above 7.12), slow of thought, and brief in their oral expression; not all Persians were effeminate and soft, just as not all Athenians were, as the Spartans held them to be, quick to embrace innovation but inconstant.

9.3   The ways in which other people are described always says as much about the person doing the description as about those who are the object of the portrait. We see a nice example of this when Hērodotos, beginning his description of the Persian empire, gives a sketch of the marriage customs of the Enetoi:

> Once a year in each village the girls of age to marry were collected all together into one place; while the men stood round them in a circle. Then a herald called up the girls one by one, and offered them for sale. He began with the most beautiful. When she was sold for no small sum of money, he offered for sale the one who came next to her in beauty. All of them were sold to be wives. The richest of the Babylonians who wished to wed bid against each other for the loveliest girls, while the humbler wife-seekers, who were indifferent about beauty, took the more homely girls with marriage-portions. For the custom was that when the herald had gone through the whole number of the beautiful girls, he should then call up the ugliest – a cripple, if there chanced to be one – and offer her to the men, asking who would agree to take her with the smallest marriage-portion. And the man who offered to take the smallest sum had her assigned to him. The marriage-portions were furnished by the money paid for the beautiful girls, and thus the fairer girls portioned out the uglier. No one was allowed to give his daughter in marriage to the man of his choice, nor might any one carry away the girl whom he had purchased without agreeing really and truly to make her his wife; if, however, it turned out that they did not agree, the money might be paid back. All who liked might come even from distant villages and bid for the women. This was the best of all their customs, but it has now fallen into disuse. They have lately hit upon a very different plan to save their girls from violence, and prevent their being torn from them and carried to distant cities, which is to bring up their daughters to be prostitutes. This is now done by all the poorer of the common people. (Hērodotos, *Histories* 1.196)

What makes Hērodotos select precisely these features to describe in this way is his expectations about what marriage customs should be like, derived from the way Greeks conducted marriages. In Greek marriage customs (cf. above 5.17–24) money or property was exchanged, in the form of a dowry, at the point of marriage; but the question of dowry followed the selection of the bride and any bargaining that went on was very much out of the public domain. The customs of the Enetoi confuse, to a Greek way of thinking, both the sorts of exchange involved in marriage with the sorts of exchange involved in prostitution, and the sorts of bargaining used in the market-place with the sorts of discussions that occur privately within and between house-holds. They also treat an exchange in which, for a Greek, the family back-ground of the bride and her social position were vital elements in her marriageability, as an exchange where all that matters is the physical attrac-tions of the bride. Revealingly, the closest parallel with the customs of the Enetoi is to be found in the fantasy scene in Aristophanēs' *Ekklēsiazousai* (lines 877–1111) in which, once women have taken charge, the customary rules regarding sexual relations are overturned.

9.4   The Athenians themselves show by their actions that they are aware of the shallowness of many of the stereotypes with which they operated. Although when we compare Aiskhylos' stereotypical depiction of the Persians in our earliest extant tragedy, *Persai*, with Hērodotos' treatment, we can see how Hērodotos writes against Aiskhylos' presentation (8.49, 60), the Athenians were far from demonising the Persians. Indeed, it is notable that they seem to have adopted elements of Persian dress as festival dress throughout the fifth century, and particularly in the later years of the century. But there is no doubt that they stressed the differences between themselves and the Persians, and saw the differences as the reason for Persian inferiority. To an Athenian, what the Persians did was not so much beyond the pale as out of place: the freeborn population were treated as slaves; extravagance which should be reserved for the gods was displayed in secular contexts; decisions which should be made in public were made in secret, and domestic matters deter-mined political decisions. It is not difficult to see that in stressing these aspects of life in Persia, the Athenians were reasserting what were to them core values: the strong distinction between free men and those who had been acquired with money in order to provide services; the strong distinction between behaviour appropriate between and towards men and women, and behaviour appropriate between and towards the gods; and the strong dis-tinction between both what it was appropriate to decide publicly and what privately, and what considerations should be relevant to public and private decision-making.

9.5   We can observe something rather similar in the way the Athenians articulated their attitudes to the Spartans. Both archaeology and poetry give us quite rich pictures of archaic Spartē, which emerges as a community much like other archaic Greek communities, though with some distinctive practices. But for classical Spartē, the archaeological evidence is weak; few inscribed texts survive; and all the literary discussions are written by non-Spartans. Only one of these writers, the Athenian Xenophōn, who wrote a *Constitution of the Spartans* as well as an *Agēsilāos* and gave a full treatment of Spartē in his *Hellēnika*, had himself spent significant amounts of time in Spartē and knew individual Spartans, including the king Agēsilāos, well (8.43). The Athenian picture of Spartē stresses lack of initiative on the part of the Spartans themselves, licence on the part of Spartan women, and cruelty and deceit in Spartan treatment of their servile population, the helots. Different literary genres presented different aspects of this picture: Thucydides emphasised the contrasts between how decisions concerned with war were taken and executed in Spartē and at Athens, and his discussion of the campaign of Brasidās in northern Greece presents Brasidās as the exception who proves the rule; Euripidēs in *Andromakhē* stressed Spartan cruelty and deceit; Aristophanēs in *Lysistratē* stressed Spartan slow-wittedness and the manliness and freedom of Spartan women. But we can see how, once again, the traits singled out for comment relate to values on which the Athenians put central emphasis: they were proud of their initiative, unusually restrictive in the rights that they gave to freeborn women, careful to protect women from men outside the household, and, while wishing to maintain a clear difference between free and slave, afforded slaves at least minimal protection in law against the arbitrary actions of their owners.

9.6   These simplified and distorted pictures helped the Athenians to articulate and to reinforce their own values. But the way in which one people represents another to itself affects the way in which it acts towards that people. We see this happening when the Athenians misjudge Brasidās and what he might do because of their assumptions about Spartan slowness and lack of initiative. It is an appropriate irony that the Athenian commander who underestimated Brasidās' speed of action and ability to talk others round, and so arrived too late to liberate the strategically crucial city of Amphipolis, was none other than the historian Thucydides. While simplification and distortion are unavoidable features of anyone's view of any group or individual, the form that the distortion takes is precisely shaped by and revealing of assumptions. States, ancient and modern, have all at various times encouraged or discouraged particular distortions. In recent history in times of war, simplified and distorted views of the enemy have often been encouraged by all régimes; in times of peace, extremist political régimes, whether of the left or of the right, have devoted much energy to persuading their people to take their caricatures of others as a true reflection of reality, while liberal régimes in an age of political correctness often attempt to mitigate popular distortions. It is unlikely to be by chance that the most strongly distorted pictures of Spartē and of Persia offered in Athenian writers are offered in the context of war – Aiskhylos' *Persai*, the picture of Spartē offered by various speakers in Thucydides, and the Spartē of the plays of Euripidēs and Aristophanēs. One of the reasons is that Athenians negotiated their way through the conflicts of the fifth and fourth centuries narrated in chapter one by convincing themselves that the Spartans and Persians were quite other than themselves.

9.7   One of the key intellectual debates of the period of the Peloponnesian War arose out of the way Athenians thought that Spartans and others differed from themselves. Athenians tended to stress cultural differences (*nomos*) rather than human nature (*phusis*). In general, though not invariably (compare the attitude to Spartan women), Athenians also stressed ways in which the Spartans were illiberal. In both these respects, Athenian portraits of others strongly resemble ways in which modern Western states portray others, and indeed Athenian caricaturing of Persia is an important predecessor of modern 'orientalism' (i.e. superior attitudes to eastern cultures). In modern Western societies, popular attitudes which put the emphasis on nature, not culture, and which charge other peoples with being morally lax rather than with being too morally restrictive, often lurk behind official or intellectual positions. In Athens too we can find traces of similar popular attitudes. Athenian painted pottery, which was relatively cheap and, in some shapes at least, widely distributed among the population, offers some striking evidence here. Visual representations not surprisingly tend to focus on bodily forms rather than e.g. dress or style, and so on nature rather than culture (figs. 5.23, 7.6, 8.4). When one Athenian painter chooses to show a unique victim of torture by satyrs to be a woman of distinctive black African appearance, it is hard to know where the observation is directed – at the behaviour of the satyrs, or at treating a woman of that origin like that – and what degree of approval or condemnation is expected. But one interesting class of Athenian pottery may give us more evidence. This is the 'head-vase', whose body was moulded into the shape of a head, or sometimes of two faces (fig. 8.2). These head-vases show various heads, representing e.g. black Africans, satyrs, Persians, Dionȳsos, Hēraklēs and Greek women. What they never show is the head of a Greek man. The systematic absence of the ordinary Greek male from these images suggests that the potters are not simply exploring the variety of physiognomical types. Rather they are selecting among physiognomical types those which contrast with the (never represented) Greek male. That simple act of selection is, in terms of *modern* legislation, 'racist' and 'sexist'.

9.8 Not the least valuable feature of the world of Athens is that it is in some very important ways similar to our own world. Complaining about the immorality of Greek slavery does not help us to understand that practice, and complaining about the racism implicit in portrayals of black Africans does not help us to understand the causes or consequences of that habit. Observing the dubious morality of the Athenians has value in as far as it encourages us to look more carefully at our own practices. But it is also important for us to understand the degree to which the Athenians constructed for themselves, and operated according to, a highly selective picture of Spartans and Persians, because it leads us to see that they were just as selective about the picture they drew of themselves.

9.9 Much of the evidence which has been used in this book has been the evidence of Athenians. The historian has little choice but to assume that, in general, what you see in the ancient sources is (part of) what you got in everyday Athenian life. But just as the Athenians emphasised selected features of others, so what the Athenians saw in themselves was highly selective. The account of the world of Athens given in the earlier chapters has attempted to combat this selectivity by describing not just the Athenians as they saw themselves but the Athenians as we might see them, deploying modern categories of analysis and not simply the Athenians' own categories. With that account in mind it is now possible for us to look back at the most famous of all Athenian descriptions of what it was to be Athenian, and to see it for the partial and distorted, if also inspiring, picture that it is. Thucydides puts the description into the mouth of Periklēs on the occasion of the public burial of those who had died in the first year of the Peloponnesian War. Parallels with other orations at the public funeral of the war dead which survive or are known in part suggest that much of the structure of the speech and many of the particular claims were commonplaces. There is reason, therefore, to think that this was not an isolated or peculiar vision of Athens, but one which would have been more or less familiar to those who heard it, and which the Athenians had largely already internalised. At least in part the Athenians were who they were because they had come to believe that the Athens invented in this and other funeral orations was the city in which they lived.

We offer Crawley's (1876) translation (slightly adapted) of this speech at the end of this book not because it somehow summarises the description of the world of Athens which we have created in earlier chapters, but because, read against that description, it enables us the better to understand how all descriptions are of their time. Periklēs' repeated claims (below 2.37, 2.39) that the Athenians do not 'spy jealously on one another' and 'live exactly as we please' contrast starkly with the litigiousness of a legal system which relied on citizens prosecuting one another (above 6.39–58). His presentation (below 2.39) of Athenian military success as achieved through natural courage and without toil contrasts with the stress Thucydides himself gives on the importance of long Athenian experience in their naval success (above 7.34–41). His claim (below 2.41) that no subject of Athens could question that the Athenians had merited their rule sits ill with the sense of allies terrorised by Athenian interference offered by Aristophanēs' *Birds* (above 6.83–4). His picture (2.42 below) of Athenians so devoted to their city that personal interest would never affect their public service has to stand against the career of Alkibiadēs whose public actions at every turn can be seen to promote primarily his private interests (above 1.69–79, 4.9, 6.16). Scholars debate whether Thucydides himself, in relaying this speech, intended contemporary readers to see the irony of so many of the claims, sooner or later undermined by his own narrative. But we surely miss the point of the speech in Thucydides' history if we see only irony and not also a driving and uplifting vision. And so also, as we hope that the rest of this book will act as it were as a commentary on this speech, so this speech is offered here also as a commentary on the rest of this book, each of them revealing the degree to which the other has been constructed with the blindnesses and insights with which its moment of composition confronts the world:

'. . . But what was the road by which we reached our position, what the form of government under which our greatness grew, what the national habits out of which it sprang; these are questions which I may try to solve before I proceed to my panegyric upon these men; since I think this to be a subject upon which on the present occasion a speaker may properly dwell, and to which the whole assemblage, whether citizens or *xenoi,* may listen with advantage.

37. Our constitution does not copy the laws of neighbouring states; we are rather a pattern to others than imitators ourselves. Its administration favours the many instead of the few; this is why it is called a *dēmokratiā.* If we look to the laws, they afford equal justice to all in their private differences; if to social standing, advancement in public life falls to reputation for capacity, class considerations not being allowed to interfere with *aretē;* nor again does poverty bar the way. If a man is able to serve the state, he is not hindered by the obscurity of his condition. The freedom which we enjoy in our government extends also to our ordinary life. There, far from spying jealously on each other, we do not feel called upon to be angry with our neighbour for doing what he likes, or even to indulge in those hard looks which cannot fail to be offensive, although they inflict no positive penalty. But all this ease in our private relations does not make us lawless as citizens. Against this, fear is our chief safeguard, teaching us to obey those in office and the laws, particularly such as regard the protection of the injured, whether they are actually on public display, or belong to that code which, although unwritten, yet cannot be broken without acknowledged disgrace.

38. Further, we provide plenty of means for the mind to refresh itself from business. We celebrate games and sacrifices all the year round, and the elegance of our private establishments forms a daily source of pleasure and helps rid us of irritations; while the size of our city draws the produce of the world into our harbour, so that to the Athenian the fruits of other countries are as familiar a luxury as those of his own.

39. If we turn to our military policy, there also we differ from our enemies. We throw open our city to the world, and never by alien acts exclude *xenoi* from any opportunity of learning or observing, although the eyes of an enemy may occasionally profit by our openness, trusting less in system and policy than to the native spirit of our citizens; while in education, where our rivals from their very cradles by a painful discipline pursue courage, at Athens we live exactly as we please, and yet are just as ready to encounter every legitimate danger. In proof of this it may be noticed that the Spartans do not invade our country alone, but bring with them all their allies; while we Athenians advance unsupported into the territory of a neighbour, and fighting upon a foreign soil usually defeat with ease men who are defending their homes. Our united force was never yet encountered by any enemy, because we have at once to attend to our navy and to dispatch our citizens by land upon a hundred different services; so that, wherever they engage with some such fraction of our strength, a success against a detachment is magnified into a victory over the nation, and a defeat into a reverse suffered at the hands of our entire people. And yet if, given as we are to ease, not toil,

and to natural, not enforced, courage, we are still willing to encounter danger, we have the double advantage of escaping the experience of hardships in anticipation and of facing them in the hour of need as fearlessly as those who are never free from them.

40. Nor are these the only points in which our city is worthy of admiration. We cultivate refinement without extravagance and knowledge without effeminacy; wealth we employ more for use than for show, and place the real disgrace of poverty not in owning up to the fact but in declining to fight it. Our public men have, besides politics, their private affairs to attend to, and our ordinary citizens, though occupied with their own business, are still fair judges of public matters; for, unlike any other nation, regarding him who takes no part in these duties not as unambitious but as useless, we Athenians are at least able to judge, even if we cannot originate, and instead of looking on discussion as a stumbling-block in the way of action, we think it an indispensable preliminary to any wise action at all. Again, in our enterprises we present the singular spectacle of courage combined with careful calculation, each carried to its highest point, and both united in the same persons; although among others decision is usually the fruit of ignorance, while reflection leads to hesitation . . .

41. In short, I say that as a city we are the school of Hellas; while I doubt if the world can produce a man, who where he has only himself to depend upon, is equal to so many emergencies, and graced by so happy a versatility, as the Athenian. And that this is no mere boast thrown out for the occasion, but plain matter of fact, the power of the state acquired by these habits proves. For Athens alone of her contemporaries is found when tested to be greater than her reputation, and alone gives no occasion to her enemies to blush at the antagonist by whom they have been defeated, or to her subjects to question her title by merit to rule. Rather, the admiration of the present and succeeding ages will be ours, since we have not left our power without witness, but have shown it by mighty proofs; and far from needing a Homer for our panegyrist, or other of his craft whose verses might charm for the moment only for the impression which they gave to melt at the touch of fact, we have forced every sea and land to be the highway of our daring, and everywhere, whether for evil or good, have left imperishable monuments behind us. Such is the Athens for which these men, in the assertion of their resolve not to lose her, nobly fought and died; and well may every one of their survivors be ready to suffer in her cause.

42. Indeed if I have dwelt at some length upon the character of our country, it has been to show that our stake in the struggle is not the same as theirs who have no such blessings to lose, and also that the panegyric of the men over whom I am now speaking might be by definite proofs established. That panegyric is now in a great measure complete; for the Athens that I have celebrated is only what the heroism of these and their like have made her, men whose fame, unlike that of most Hellēnes, will be found to be only commensurate with their deserts. And if a test of worth be wanted, it is to be found in their closing scene, and this not only in the cases in which it set the final seal upon their merit, but also in those in which it gave the first

intimation of their having any. For there is justice in the claim that steadfastness in his country's battles should be as a cloak to cover a man's other imperfections; since the good action has blotted out the bad, and his merit as a citizen more than outweighed his demerits as an individual. But none of these allowed either wealth with its prospect of future enjoyment to unnerve his spirit, or poverty with its hope of a day of freedom and riches to tempt him to shrink from danger. No, holding that vengeance upon their enemies was more to be desired than any personal blessings, and reckoning this to be the most glorious of hazards, they joyfully determined to accept the risk, to make sure of their vengeance and to let their wishes wait; and while committing to hope the uncertainty of final success, in the business before them they thought fit to act boldly and trust in themselves. Thus choosing to die resisting, rather than to live submitting, they fled only from dishonour, but met danger face to face, and after one brief moment, while at the summit of their fortune, they passed away from the scene, not of their fear, but of their glory.

43. So died these men as became Athenians. You, their survivors, must determine to have as unfaltering a resolution in the field, though you may pray that it may have a happier issue. And not contented with ideas derived only from words of the advantages which are bound up with the defence of your country, though these would furnish a valuable text to a speaker even before an audience so alive to them as the present, you must yourselves realise the power of Athens, and feed your eyes upon her from day to day, till you become an *erastēs* of her; and then when all her greatness shall break upon you, you must reflect that it was by courage, sense of duty, and a keen feeling of honour in action that men were enabled to win all this, and that no personal failure in an enterprise could make them consent to deprive their country of their *aretē*, but they laid it at her feet as the most glorious contribution that they could offer. For this offering of their lives made in common by them all they each of them individually received that renown which never grows old, and for a sepulchre, not so much that in which their bones have been deposited, but that noblest of shrines wherein their glory is laid up to be eternally remembered upon every occasion on which deed or story shall call for its commemoration. For heroes have the whole earth for their tomb; and in lands far from their own, where the column with its epitaph declares it, there is enshrined in every breast a record unwritten with no tablet to preserve it, except that of the heart. These take as your model, and judging happiness to be the fruit of freedom and freedom of courage, never decline the dangers of war. For it is not the worthless that would most justly be unsparing of their lives; these have nothing to hope for; it is rather they to whom continued life may bring reverses as yet unknown, and to whom a fall, if it came, would be most tremendous in its consequences. And surely, to a man of spirit, the degradation of cowardice must be immeasurably more painful than the unfelt death which strikes him in the midst of his strength and patriotism!

44. Comfort, therefore, not condolence, is what I have to offer to the parents of the dead who may be here. Numberless are the chances to which, as they know, the life of man is subject; but fortunate indeed are they who

draw for their lot a death so glorious as that which has caused your mourning, and to whom life has been so exactly measured as to terminate in the happiness in which it has been passed. Still I know that this is a hard saying, especially since we talk of those of whom you will constantly be reminded by seeing in the homes of others blessings of which once you also boasted: for grief is felt not so much for the want of what we have never known, as for the loss of that to which we have been long accustomed. Yet you who are still of an age to beget children must bear up in the hope of having others in their stead; not only will they help you to forget those whom you have lost, but will be to the state at once a reinforcement and a security; for never can a fair or just policy be expected of the citizen who does not, like his fellows, bring to the decision the interests and apprehensions of a father. While those of you who have passed your prime must congratulate yourselves with the thought that the best part of your life was fortunate, and that the brief span that remains will be cheered by the fame of the departed. For it is only the love of honour that never grows old; and honour it is, not gain, as some would have it, that rejoices the heart of age and helplessness.

45. Turning to the sons or brothers of the dead, I see an arduous struggle before you. When a man is gone, all are accustomed to praise him, and however outstanding your *aretē* should become, you will still find it difficult not merely to overtake, but even to approach their renown. The living have envy to contend with, while those who are no longer in our path are honoured with a goodwill into which rivalry does not enter. On the other hand, if I must say anything on the subject of female *aretē* to those of you who will now be in widowhood, it will be all comprised in this brief exhortation. Great will be your glory in not falling short of your natural character; and greatest will be hers who is least talked of among the men whether for good or for bad.

46. My task is now finished. I have performed it to the best of my ability, and in word, at least, the requirements of the law are now satisfied. If deeds be in question, those who are here interred have received part of their honours already, and for the rest, their children will be brought up till manhood at the People's expense: the state thus offers a valuable prize, as the garland of victory in this race of valour, for the reward both of those who have fallen and their survivors. And where the rewards for *aretē* are greatest, there are found the best citizens. And now that you have brought to a close your lamentations for your relatives, you may depart. (Thucydides, *Peloponnesian War* 2.36–46)

Glossary of terms (with Greek alphabet)

Alphabet and simplified pronunciation

Minuscule		Transliteration	Capitals
α	(alpha) pronounced 'c*u*p' or 'c*a*lm'	a, ā	A
β	(beta) pronounced 'b' as in English	b	B
γ	(gamma) a hard 'g', like 'got'	g	Γ
δ	(delta) a clean 'd', like 'dot'	d	Δ
ε	(epsilon) short 'e', like 'p*e*t'	e	E
ζ	(zeta) like 'wi*s*dom'	z	Z
η	(eta) pronounced as in 'h*ai*r'	ē	H
θ	(theta) – blow a hard 't' ('*t*are')	th	Θ
ι	(iota) like 'b*i*n' or like 'b*ea*d'	i, ī	I
κ	(kappa) a clean 'k' like 's*k*in'	k	K
λ	(lambda) like '*l*ock'	l	Λ
μ	(mu) like '*m*ock'	m	M
ν	(nu) like '*n*et'	n	N
ξ	(xi) like 'bo*x*'	x	Ξ
ο	(omicron) a short 'ŏ', like 'p*o*t'	o	O
π	(pi) a clean 'p', like 's*p*ot'	p	Π
ρ	(rho) a rolled 'r', like '*rr*at'	r	P
σ, ς	(sigma) a soft 's', like '*s*ing'	s	Σ
τ	(tau) a clean 't', like '*t*ing'	t	T
υ	(upsilon) French 'l*u*ne'	u,y	Υ
	or German 'M*ü*ller'	ū ȳ	
φ	(phi) – blow a hard 'p', like '*p*ool'	ph	Φ
χ	(khi) – blow a hard 'c', like '*c*ool'	kh	X
ψ	(psi) as in 'la*ps*e'	ps	Ψ
ω	(omega) like 's*aw*'	ō	Ω

Note: 'clean' indicates no 'h' sound; 'blow hard' indicates plenty of 'h' aspiration (e.g. 'ph' as in 'to*p-h*ole'). Greek words have accents which indicate change in pitch. They are best ignored.

Diphthongs and double consonants

		Transliteration
αι	as in 'h*i*gh'	ai
αυ	as in 'h*ow*'	au
ει	as in 'fianc*é*e'	ei

ευ   (pronounce both elements *separately*)   eu
οι   as in 'b*oy*'   oi
ου   as in 't*oo*'   ou
γγ   as in 'fi*n*ger'   gg

Dwell on all double consonants, e.g. ττ as 'ra*t-t*rap', λλ as 'who*ll*y' etc.

Sigma and iota subscript

Observe that ς is used at the *end* of words, while σ is used elsewhere (see next example). Sometimes ι is printed *underneath* a preceding α (ᾳ), η (ῃ) and ω (ῳ). Transliterations are ai, ēi, ōi.

Breathings

'above a vowel indicates the presence of an 'h' sound:' above a vowel indicates the absence of 'h' sound, e.g.

ὅσος = 'hosos'
οἷος = 'oios'

Names, institutions and terms

Academy (*Akadēmos*, originally *Hekadēmos*): a grove of Athens, where Plato (c. 385) established a school.

Agamemnōn: leader of Greek expedition to Troy, who sacrificed his daughter Iphigeneia to get the wind for the journey. Quarrelled with Akhilleus. Murdered on his return home by his wife Klytaimēstrā.

agōn: trial, contest, struggle (cf. 'agony'). Used of any contest e.g. at law, the Olympic games, between playwrights competing for prizes at festivals, to describe the central struggle in a comedy, etc.

agorā: lit. 'gathering-place'. Came to mean the market-place and civic centre of any town.

Agoraios: 'of the *agorā*', a title used for gods in their capacity as protector of the *agorā* of Athens.

agorānomoi: in Athens, there were five for the city, five for the Peiraieus. Collected market dues, checked quality and weight of goods.

Aiskhylos (*Aiskhulos*) c. 525–459: Athenian tragedian, most famous for our sole surviving trilogy, the *Oresteia*, the story of Agamemnōn's murder by his wife Klytaimēstrā after his return from Troy, and subsequent revenge by his son Orestēs.

Akhilleus (Achilles): Greece's greatest fighter at Troy. Subject of Homer's *Iliad*, when he withdrew from the fighting, to return only when his companion Patroklos had been killed by the Trojan Hektōr. Akhilleus killed Hektōr, only later releasing the body to Hektōr's father Priam, king of Troy.

Akropolis: lit. 'the top of the city', usually the high spot of a town where temples and final defences were built. In Athens, it was where the temple of Athēnē, the Parthenōn, and the temple of Erekhtheus, the Erekhtheion (and others) were built. The Parthenōn served as the Athenians' treasury.

Alkibiadēs c. 450–404: Athenian general and statesman, close associate of Periklēs and Sōkratēs. Wealthy, handsome, enigmatic figure; accused of complicity in the mutilation of the Hermai; joined the Spartan side briefly during the Peloponnesian War, but returned to Athens later. Later he was rejected again, and died at the hands of a lesser satrap.

Andokidēs c. 440–390: Athenian politician and speech-writer. Implicated in the Hermai incident and wrote and delivered a speech *On the Mysteries* at a later date, which is an important source of information about it. Spent much time out of Athens because of the incident.

Anthestēria: festival in honour of Dionȳsos.

Antiphōn c. 480–410: Athenian speech-writer and politician, who came to the fore during the oligarchic coup of 411, but was later executed.

Aphroditē: goddess of love.

Apollo (*Apollōn* 'the destroyer'): god of prophecy (his major shrine was at Delphi), medicine and music.

archaic period: 700–500 BC.

Areopagus (*Areios Pagos*, 'Crag of Arēs'): Athens' most ancient council, consisting of ex-*arkhontes*. It once held great power, but in the fifth century it oversaw religious functions and had jurisdiction in murder trials.

Arēs: god of war.

aretē: manliness, courage; then it came to mean goodness, excellence, virtue – in general, what is admirable in a man or thing.

Aristeidēs (nicknamed 'the Just'): Athenian statesman and soldier. Fought at Marathōn, Salamīs and Plataia. Fixed the contribution for each state in the Delian League to make.

Aristophanēs (c. 445–c. 385): greatest Athenian comic playwright. Eleven of his 40 or so plays survive, including *Wasps* (about the law-courts), *Acharnians* (where Dikaiopolis ends the Peloponnesian War for *himself* by making a personal truce with the Spartans), *Frogs* (literary criticism of Aiskhylos and Euripidēs) and *Lȳsistratē* (a sex-strike by the women to end the war). Much obscenity, social and political comment.

Aristotle (*Aristotelēs*) 384–322: born in Stageira (Khalkidikē). Joined Plato's Academy. Settled eventually in Athens and founded his own school, the Lykeion (Lyceum), a great research centre. Aristotle wrote works on physics, metaphysics, zoology, ethics, politics, rhetoric, poetics, logic, astronomy. Probably the single most influential figure of the ancient world.

arkhē: official state position; Athenian empire; guiding philosophical principle. Generally, rule, control or beginning.

arkhōn (pl. *arkhontes*): there were nine *arkhontes* in all. They were chosen by lot annually, and joined the Areopagus at the end of their term of office. Originally the leading officers of state, after the sixth century they were left with mainly religious and judicial functions. The 'king' *arkhōn* presided over the Areopagus, and was in charge of homicide and impiety cases; the *polemarkhos* (originally the war *arkhōn*) was in charge of non-Athenians resident in Athens; the 'eponymous' *arkhōn* (so-called as the year was named after him) was in charge of family property disputes, inheritance etc., especially orphans and heiresses. For the other six *arkhontes*, see *thesmothetai*.

Athēnaios c. 200 AD: his account of a cultured conversation over dinner spans 15 books and is an invaluable source of information. He cites c. 1,250 authors and quotes c. 10,000 lines of verse, much of it not extant from any other source.

Athēnē: goddess of the arts, and crafts, of war (frequently depicted in full armour), and patron goddess of Athens. The Parthenōn (so called after *parthenos*, virgin) was dedicated to her. Ten Treasurers controlled the payments to the goddess.

atīmiā: dishonour, disenfranchisement, i.e. loss of some or all civic rights.

aulos: a sort of pipe whose sound was produced by means of a double reed (rather like an oboe). Generally, a player played two at once. Provided the music for dramatic performances, accompanied personal poetry and kept lines of hoplites in step.

boulaios: 'of the *boulē*', often used of a god in his capacity as overseer of the *boulē*'s decisions.

boulē: council (of 500: see *bouleutai*). Open to all citizens over 30. It met daily (except for holidays) and had the vital task of preparing the agenda for the *ekklēsiā*, presiding over it, and seeing that its decisions were carried out. It oversaw state officials and finance.

bouleutai: members of the *boulē* (councillors). There were 500 of them, 50 from each *phūlē*, selected by lot. They served for a year, and could not serve more than twice.

bouleutērion: council chamber, the place where the *boulē* met.

classical period: 500–323 BC.

cleruchy (*klēroukhiā*): a settlement of Athenian citizens granted a piece of land (*klēros*) in conquered territory. They kept all their rights as Athenian citizens.

Dareios (Darius): father of Xerxēs and king of Persia (c. 522–486) when the Persians sent an expedition against the Greeks which was repulsed at Marathōn (490).

Delian League: an alliance of states of which Athens was the predominant member, formed after the Persian Wars to guarantee Greek security against further Persian invasion. Members paid Athens in money or ships. The treasury was moved from Dēlos to Athens in 454.

Delphic oracle: the sanctuary of Apollo at Delphi, where it was possible to consult the god. The most influential oracle in the ancient world.

deme (*dēmos*, pl. *dēmoi*): local communities (villages, wards of town) which formed the basis of Kleisthenēs' political reforms. Membership of a deme was a requirement for citizenship. Athenians usually identified themselves by deme name and father's name.

Dēmētēr: the Greek corn goddess, who governed the fruits of the earth. She was a central figure of the Mysteries at Eleusīs and of the female festival in Athens, the *Thesmophoria*.

dēmokratiā: democracy, lit. 'the rule of the *dēmos*', where *dēmos* = all Athenian citizens (i.e. males over 18 with Athenian mother and father).

dēmos: a variety of meanings: (i) the whole adult male citizen body, (ii) the poorer (as against aristocratic) citizens, (iii) the democratic constitution, (iv) democrats as against those favouring other constitutions, (v) the democratic state of Athens, (vi) the People of Athens in the *ekklēsiā*, (vii) the local division, the deme.

Dēmosthenēs: (i) a fifth-century soldier who captured the Spartans on Sphaktēriā in 425 and was killed later in the Sicilian expedition: (ii) a fourth-century orator and politician who urged all Greeks to unite against the threat of King Philip of Makedōn. He also wrote many private speeches for litigants on a wide range of topics.

dikastērion (pl. *dikastēria*): the law-courts.

dikastēs (pl. *dikastai*): dikast, juror. Empanelled from Athenian citizens over 30. 6,000 a year could be called up for duty in the courts. They were paid for attendance.

dikē: justice, law, right; penalty. Also a private lawsuit brought by an individual against another, cf. *graphē*.

Diodōros fl. c. 40: wrote a *World History*, using sources now largely lost to us. Of the 40 books, 4–6 cover Greece and Europe and 7–17 from the Trojan War up to Alexander the Great.

Dionȳsia: in Athens the Lesser (or Rural) *Dionȳsia* was a smaller rustic festival than the Greater (or City) *Dionȳsia* in honour of Dionȳsos, at which a statue of the god was carried from Eleutherai and the major tragic and comic competitions were staged.

Dionȳsos: god of all things living and god of transformation (hence patron god of the theatre) and of destruction. Associated with the frenzy brought on by wine. In their ecstasy his followers were said to kill and devour animals raw to get the living god inside them.

dokimasiā: an examination which state officials and *bouleutai* underwent before taking up office. It asked them about their rights to citizenship, care of family burial grounds, etc.

dokimastēs: the state official (in fact a slave) whose duty it was to test the purity of the coinage.

drakhmē: a unit of money, within the following system:
obol
drakhmē (six obols)
mnā (100 *drakhmai*)
talent (60 *mnā*s)

eisphorā: a special tax on capital, often levied when the state was at war, applicable to citizens and metics.

ekhthroi (s. *ekhthros*): personal enemies.

ekklēsiā: the *ekklēsiā* (lit. 'called out', 'selected'), open to all Athenian (male) citizens over the age of 18. It sat regularly four times a month, of which one session was the *kūria* (sovereign) *ekklēsiā*, with a fixed agenda. It could be summoned at other times. It was the sovereign body of the state. It voted on all major questions and elected the most important officials. Its agenda was prepared by the *boulē*, but the *ekklēsiā* could reject the *boulē*'s proposals and demand that the *boulē* do what *it* wanted.

Eleven, the (*hoi hendeka*): this board dealt with ordinary criminals, charging and punishing them. They also oversaw prisons.

Ēliaiā (often given as 'Hēliaiā'): the body of 6,000 *dikastai* empanelled to serve on the juries for a year. (A juror can be called (*h*)*ēliastēs* as well as *dikastēs*.)

ephebes (*ephēboi*): Athenians aged 18–19 who undertook training in units based on the ten *phūlai* to become hoplites. This training was formalised in the 330s.

epistatēs: chairman of the *prutaneis* and of the *ekklēsiā*. Served for one day. Since there were 50 *prutaneis* serving for a period of 35–6 days, there was a good chance that any given *prutanis* would serve as *epistatēs*.

'eponymous' *arkhōn*: see *arkhōn*.

erastēs: lover. Used especially of the older, active partner in a homosexual relationship. Cf. *erōmenos*.

Erekhtheion (Erechtheum): a temple of Erekhtheus on the Akropolis, housing the venerable statue of Athēnē Polias as well as other sacred objects.

Erekhtheus: mythical king of Athens, a son of Earth and reared by Athēnē.

erōmenos: 'the [male who is] loved', used of the younger, passive partner in a homosexual relationship. Cf. *erastēs*.

Euripidēs c. 485–406: Athenian tragic playwright, with a reputation for especially provocative analyses of Greek myth and of the human motivation which made the characters act as they did. Contemporary intellectual issues seem to surface in his plays more than in those of other tragedians.

euthūnai: audit, review. This was the term applied to outgoing state officials, who were subject to *euthūnai* to check they had not abused their position (especially with regard to finance).

exēgētai (pl.): lit. 'expounders', 'interpreters'. A body of men concerned with unwritten, sacred law and with some specific issues (especially purification and burial). They had connections with Apollo at Delphi.

genos (pl. *genē*): a descent group responsible for providing priests of a particular cult.

graphē: a lawsuit on a matter of public importance brought by an individual against another (there was no such thing as a public prosecutor in Athens). Cf. *dikē*.

graphē paranomōn: a lawsuit brought by an individual against another, alleging that the defendant had been responsible for proposing a measure which was illegal.

hawksbeak: a moulding characteristic of the Doric order of architecture. used generally at the top of an architectural element, this moulding takes its name from its profile, which is that of a hawk's beak.

hēgemōn: leader, cf. hegemony.

Hektōr: Trojan hero of the Trojan War, who killed Akhilleus' companion Patroklos and was killed in turn by Akhilleus. His maltreated body was eventually returned by Akhilleus to his father Priam, king of Troy.

Hellas: the Greek word for 'Greece', i.e. the Greek world (*not* a state or country).

Hellēnes (s. *Hellēn*): men of Hellas, Greeks.

Hellēnotamiai: state treasurers in charge of funds used for administering the Athenian empire (after 411 they absorbed also the work of the *kōlakretai*, till then in charge of domestic funds). Like *stratēgoi*, they could be re-elected every year.

Hēphaistos: god of fire, husband of Aphrodītē; the craftsman's god.

Hēra: wife of Zeus, goddess of marriage and women's life. Strong connections with Argos.

Herkeios: 'concerned with the household', often used of Zeus in his role as protector of the house.

Hermēs: god of travel, escort of the souls of the dead, god of heralds and thieves. Hermai (s. Herm) were representations of the god consisting of a stone block, with a head on the top and phallus half-way up the block, placed outside houses in Athens.

Hērodotos c. 480–420: fifth-century historian from Halikarnassos, who lived for some time in Athens. Said to have travelled widely around the Mediterranean compiling his *Histories* in 9 books of the way in which Greeks and Persians came into conflict in the Persian Wars: 'the father of history'.

Hesiod (*Hēsiodos*): poet writing about 700 in an adapted epic style. His two major works, *Works and Days* (a farmers' calendar and instruction manual) and *Theogony* (the birth of the gods), are the earliest poems in which a poet talks about himself.

hiereus: priest, or 'one in charge of sacred matters (*hiera*)'.

Hikēsios: 'concerned with supplication', used of Zeus in one of his roles as protector of suppliants.

hippeis: see *pentakosiomedimnoi*.

Hippokratēs: the famous doctor from Kōs, lived during the fifth century. Virtually all medical treatises were ascribed to him. The probable founder of scientific medicine.

Homer (*Homēros*): epic poet to whom the *Iliad* and *Odyssey* were ascribed. Came from Ionian coast. Nothing else known about him. The poems reached more or less the form we have shortly after 700.

Hoplites (*hoplītai*): Greek warriors, fighting with shield, spear, sword and full heavy armour. The hoplite formation gained its strength from its unity, rank upon rank of closely linked fighting men.

hubris (hybris): an act of violence or aggression, whose main purpose was to degrade or humiliate.

hubristēs: one who commits an act of *hubris*, criminal.

Iliad (*Īliās*): Homer's epic version of the wrath of Akhilleus during the Trojan war, his withdrawal from battle but eventual return on the death of his companion Patroklos; how Akhilleus killed Patroklos' slayer Hektōr and maltreated his body but eventually returned it to his father, King Priam.

Isaios c. 420–350: Athens' leading speech-writer in cases concerned with wills and inheritance.

Isokratēs 436–348: treatise-writer and educationist, who insisted that utility in education was of more importance than abstract thought. In a number of his treatises he glorified the great days of Athens' past.

isonomiā: equality under the laws, rule of equals, democracy.

keleustēs: the bo'sun of a trireme, who gave the time for the rowers to keep to.

Kerameikos: Potters' Quarter in Athens (cf. 'ceramic'); also the site of an important cemetery.

kērux (pl. *kērukes*): herald, messenger.

khorēgos (choregus) (pl. *khorēgoi*): the wealthy (male) citizen who, as part of a *leitourgiā*, met all the expenses of a tragic or comic writer's entry at a play festival.

Kīmōn: aristocratic, wealthy Athenian statesman and soldier who greatly developed the Athenian empire between 476 and 460, though in some conflict with radical democratic leaders like Periklēs.

Kleisthenēs: Athenian statesman who in 507 reformed the Athenian constitution in a way that was to lead to the full democracy of the fifth century under Periklēs.

Klytaimēstrā (Clytaem(n)estra): wife of Agamemnōn. She married her lover Aigisthos and killed Agamemnōn on his return from Troy. She in turn was killed by their son Orestēs.

kratos: might, rule, sway, control.

Ktēsios: 'concerned with property', applied to Zeus in his role as protector of the home and its wealth.

kubernētēs: the steersman of a trireme, the most important figure in the control of the ship.

kūrios (pl. *kūrioi*): valid, sovereign, empowered. Used of male heads of the household who controlled the house's people and property; also used of the 'sovereign' *ekklēsiā* with a fixed agenda meeting once a month. Cf. *kūrieia:* control, sovereignty.

Lakedaimonians = Spartans.

leitourgiā (pl. *leitourgiai*) (liturgy): state duty imposed annually on the wealthiest men of Athens, who had to pay for, e.g., play productions at the festivals (cf. *khorēgos*), the expenses of running a trireme, etc.

logistai: thirty state auditors, who checked the financial dealings of all outgoing state officials as part of their *euthūnai*.

Lykeion (Lyceum): the grove in Athens sacred to Apollōn Lykeios where Aristotle established his school.

mantis: seer, prophet.

medimnos (pl. *medimnoi*): Attic grain-measure of approximately 12 gallons.

Menander (*Menandros*) c. 342–290: writer of so-called New Comedy, set in contemporary Greece and dealing largely with domestic situations. Forerunner of 'drawing-room' comedy.

metoikos (pl. *metoikoi*) (metic): resident alien (i.e. non-Athenian citizen who lived more than one month in Athens). Liable to military service and special taxes; not able to own landed property in Attikē. Resident aliens were responsible for much trade.

metope: a square or almost square panel, either plain or bearing painting or relief sculpture, which, alternating with triglyphs (s.v.), makes up the upper part of the section of the temple between the columns and the roof or pediment (gable).

Minoan world: i.e. Crete between 1800 and 1400 (so called after the legendary King Mīnōs). At this time Crete was a power in the Mediterranean, before it was destroyed c. 1400, probably by Mycenaean Greeks.

mnā (mina): unit of money; see *drakhmē*.

mustai: initiates into the Mysteries of Eleusīs.

Mycenaean period: 'Mycenaean' culture (so called because Mycenae seems to have been the most powerful city of the time) flourished in Greece between 1600 and 1100 BC. After its destruction there was a 'dark age' of nearly 200 years. Homer's poetry reflects elements of Mycenaean culture.

Nīkiās 470–413: Athenian politician and general, frequently elected *stratēgos*. Negotiated the peace of 421 with Spartē in the Peloponnesian War. Reluctantly led the Sicilian expedition, on which he was killed.

nomos: law, custom, observance, habit. Frequently contrasted with *phusis*, when *nomos* comes to take on the idea of what is conventionally right.

nomothetai: law-makers, who were called in to draft new laws (as needed) for the *boulē* and *ekklēsiā* to approve.

obol: see *drakhmē*.

Odyssey (*Odusseia*): Homer's epic tale of Odysseus' return from Troy: how, after 10 years' wandering, he eventually returned home to Ithaka and killed the 108 suitors courting his wife Penelope.

oiketēs: slave, or free house servant; also (slave) aide to state official.

oikos (pl. *oikoi*): household (including property and slaves).

orkhēstrā: circular dancing-floor in the Greek theatre where the chorus in plays danced and sang.

ostracism (*ostrakismos*): an act of the *ekklēsiā* in banishing someone from Attikē for 10 years (though with no loss of property rights).

ostrakon: the potsherd on which names for ostracism were written down.

paean: battle song, chant; song of triumph, usually to Apollo.

palaistrā: a wrestling-ground, found both in association with gymnasia and independently; a place where leisured Greeks 'worked out' and relaxed.

Panathēnaia: an all-Athenian festival in honour of Athēnē's birthday, celebrated every year, and with special magnificence every fourth year (the Great *Panathēnaia*). There were processions, sacrifices, and games.

Parthenōn: the temple of Athēnē Parthenos ('the virgin'), constructed on the Akropolis in Athens 447–432.

Patrōios: 'of the father/ancestors'; used of gods in their roles as protectors of family and people.

Peiraieus (Piraeus): the harbour town of Athens.

Peisistratos (Pisistratus): sixth-century sole ruler (*tyrannos* = tyrant) of Athens, who did much to establish a sense of Athenian identity by instituting various festivals and building programmes.

peithō: persuasion by argument, sometimes personified as a goddess.

Peloponnesian War (Second): the war fought between Athens with her allies and Spartē with hers for domination of Greece. Athens was a sea-based power, Spartē a land-based one. It lasted from 431 to 404. Athens was defeated in the end.

peltast (*peltastēs*): Greek soldiers named from the small round shield they carried (*peltē*), who, originally skirmishers, were turned into a formidable fighting force in the fourth century.

pentakosiomedimnoi: a property class, of people who had an estimated annual income of not less than 500 *medimnoi* of grain, or its equivalent. This was the top property class, followed by: *hippeis*: 'knights' with annual income of 300–500 *medimnoi* or equivalent; *zeugītai*: 200–300 *medimnoi* annual income; *thētes*: less than 200 *medimnoi* annual income.

Periklēs c. 495–429: statesman and soldier, guiding spirit behind Athenian democracy and imperialism. Elected *stratēgos* every year from 443 till his death. Close friend of many leading intellectuals of the day.

Persephonē (Proserpinā): daughter of Dēmētēr and wife of Hādēs, god of the dead.

Persian Wars: the wars fought between the Greeks and Persia between 490 and 479, particularly the battles at Marathōn, Thermopylai, Salamīs and Plataia. The Persians were driven back in 490 and were finally repelled, under Xerxēs, in 479. Greeks looked back to these wars as a high point of Greek achievement. It was one of the few times when some (i.e. 31) Greek *poleis* forgot their differences to repel a common foe.

phallos (pl. *phalloi*): representation of the male reproductive organ, often carried in processions, particularly those associated with fertility, and worn by the chorus in comedies.

Pheidiās: one of the finest fifth-century Athenian sculptors. Responsible for the sculpture on the Parthenōn and for its cult statue.

Philip II, reigned 359–336: king of Makedōn, who unified Makedōn and made it the greatest fighting force of the fourth century. His victory over the Greeks at Khairōneia (338) ended Greek independence. Father of Alexander the Great.

philoi (s. *philos*): friends, allies; those with whom you presented a common front.

phoros: tribute paid by her allies to Athens for the maintenance of the empire.

phrātēr (pl. *phrāteres*): member of phratry.

Phrātriā (pl. *Phrātriai*) (phratry): a descent group, membership of which was part of what it was to be Athenian. New-born children were presented to it. As a body it was often called upon to witness to legitimacy and therefore rights of citizenship. The festival of the phratries was called the *Apatouria*.

Phrātrios: 'of the *Phrātriai*', a title applied to Zeus and other gods in their roles as protectors of the *Phrātria*.

phūlē (pl. *phūlai*): tribe; there were originally four of these, with various administrative and military functions. Kleisthenēs, while allowing these to remain for religious functions, created ten new *phūlai* in his democratic reforms, and these became the basis of state administration. There were ten *stratēgoi;* committees of the *boulē* often consisted of ten members; the *boulē* itself was made up of fifty members drawn from each of the ten *phūlai* (cf. *prutaneis*).

phusis: nature, natural law, often contrasted in Greek thought with *nomos*, conventional law.

Pindar (*Pindaros*) 518–438: lyric poet from Boiōtiā, famous for his odes, in which he celebrates the victories of athletes at various games (e.g. Olympic).

Plato (*Platōn*) c. 429–347: very influential Greek philosopher who built on Sōkratēs' teaching about how we should live our life a whole theory of metaphysics; the Theory of Forms (or Theory of Ideas) has been particularly important. A bitter rival of the sophists.

Plutarch (*Ploutarkhos*) c. AD 50–120: biographical historian and student of antiquities. Unreliable in use of sources, but his *Parallel Lives* of great Greeks and Romans are important.

Pnyx: the place where the Athenian *ekklēsiā* met.

polemarkhos (polemarch): see *arkhōn*.

pōlētai: sellers. Ten (one from each *phūlē*) *pōlētai* sold off the right to carry out official state business e.g. collecting taxes, mining rights, buying and putting up *stēlai*, etc.

Polias: an epithet for Athēnē in her role as guardian of the city, especially used of her statue in the Erekhtheion.

polis (pl. *poleis*): the name given to the self-governing city-states of the Greek world. Each *polis* had its own laws of citizenship, coinage, customs, festivals, rites, etc. Athens, Corinth, Thebes, Spartē were all separate, autonomous *poleis*. They were quick to form alliances amongst themselves and prone to conflict over the best forms of constitution.

Poseidōn: God of the sea and earth (quakes).

presbeis (s. *presbeutēs*): envoy, ambassador.

Priam (*Priamos*): king of Troy.

probouleuma: a decree made by the *boulē* for the *ekklēsiā* to discuss and then accept, modify or reject.

probouleusis: the act of the *boulē* in reaching a decision about what motions to lay before the *ekklēsiā* for discussion.

Promētheus: Titan god who made man, gave him fire and ensured that man got all the good meat to eat at sacrifice (Zeus being left with bones and offal).

prostatēs: leader of the *dēmos;* patron of a *metoikos*, who would guarantee him before the *polemarkhos* when the *metoikos* applied to live in Athens.

proxenos: the title given to someone who, as a citizen of state A and residing in state A, represented state B's views.

prutaneis (s. *prutanis*): the fifty members of the *boulē* drawn from a single *phūlē* who lived for 35–6 days, 24 hours a day, in the *tholos* at state expense to receive all business and determine whether the *boulē* or *ekklēsiā* should be summoned to deal with it.

psēphisma (pl. *psēphismata*): decrees of state passed by the *ekklēsiā*.

Pȳthiā: the priestess through whom Apollo spoke at his oracle in Delphi.

rhapsode (*rhapsōidos*): a professional reciter of epic (especially Homer's) poetry at festivals.

rhētōr (pl. *rhētores*): lit. 'speaker', 'orator' (cf. rhetoric). Came to mean politician, i.e. someone who could speak effectively at meetings of the *ekklēsiā* and persuade the People as to the rightness of his own views.

Sicilian expedition: the Athenian expedition of 415–413, led by Nīkiās and Dēmosthenēs during the Peloponnesian War, to try to take Sicily. It failed disastrously, the whole fleet being lost.

skēnē: the stage building against which Greek drama was performed (cf. scene).

Sōkratēs 469–399: the philosopher most responsible for turning the trend of Greek philosophical enquiry away from questions of the nature of the physical world to questions of man's position and duties in it. He never wrote a word, versions of his thought being recorded for us by Plato and Xenophōn in dialogue form. Invented dialectic (question-and-answer technique).

Solōn: Athenian statesman and poet who, in the 590s, divided the citizen body into four classes by wealth (see *pentakosiomedimnoi*) and assigned a number of political responsibilities to them by class, opening up service in the courts to the lowest classes. Made other laws which were still observed in fifth-century Athens. A greatly revered figure.

sophistēs (pl. *sophistai*) (sophist): lit. 'wise men'; the term became applied to travelling lecturers who were prepared to impart knowledge of any number of subjects (but especially rhetoric, the ability to persuade people) for payment.

Sophoklēs c. 496–406: Athenian tragedian. Much-loved figure in Athens. Famous for *Oidipous Tyrannos*, which tells how Oidipous found out that he had killed his father and married his mother, and *Antigonē*, which tells how Antigonē went to her death for burying her brother, in defiance of an edict given by her uncle Kreon, the king.

sōphrōn: modest, sensible, prudent, discreet, law-abiding. *Sōphrosunē* is a virtue constantly recommended by Athenian writers to those who want to keep their noses clean. One of the officials appointed to look after the ephebes was known as the *sōphronistēs*.

stasis: internal revolution.

stēlē (pl. *stēlai*): inscribed stone monuments, especially grave-markers and upright slabs on which decrees and similar public documents were inscribed.

stoā: a building with a roof supported by columns, but especially a long, open colonnade. Usually it resembles a long hall with one side thrown open and supported by columns.

stratēgos (pl. *stratēgoi*): military commander. Ten of them, normally one from each *phūlē*, directly elected annually by the People; they could be re-elected. Apart from military duties, the *stratēgoi* were the most influential moulders of state policy.

sukophantēs (pl. *sukophantai*) (sycophant): a vexatious litigant, one who was alleged to exploit the Athenian reliance on private prosecution to his own advantage.

summoriā (pl. *summoriai*) (symmory): a group of tax-payers who, instead of paying individually for the upkeep of a trireme (*see* trierarch; *leitourgiā*), paid for it as a group. An institution of the 350s.

talent: *see drakhmē*.

Ten Treasurers of Athēnē: annual officials, drawn by lot from each of the *phūlai*. Superintended the funds of the goddess and her statue.

Themistoklēs c. 528–462: leading Athenian general of the Persian Wars, who later ensured that Athens was defended by fortified walls against Spartē. He sponsored the fortification of the Peiraieus and the holding of a fleet.

Theophrastos c. 370–285: successor to Aristotle as head of the Lykeion; researcher in botany and other scientific subjects. His *Characters* is a description of 30 or so people who exhibit extremes of behaviour.

Thēseus: legendary Athenian national hero. Supposed to have drawn all the communities of Attikē into one, with Athens at their head. Slaughtered the Cretan Minotaur.

Thesmophoria: women's festival in honour of Dēmētēr.

thesmothetai: six *arkhontes*, concerned with administering justice, fixing trial dates, etc.

thētes: see *pentakosiomedimnoi*.

Thirty Tyrants (or oligarchs), the Thirty: leaders of the oligarchic coup in Athens of 404.

tholos: the round meeting and dining room in the Athenian *agorā* where the *prutaneis* lived.

thrānītai: those who rowed from the highest point of the trireme, and therefore had to pull on the longest oars at the sharpest angle; paid more than the other ranks of rowers.

Thucydides (*Thoukudidēs*) c. 460–400: Athenian who wrote the history of the Peloponnesian War. He insisted on the care which he had taken to discover the truth, and can rarely be faulted on the accuracy of what he includes, though his omissions have caused much discussion.

tīmē: honour, worth, status, evaluation.

trierarch (*triērarkhos*): wealthy citizen chosen to pay for and captain a trireme (see *leitourgiā*).

triglyph: a rectangular panel divided in three by grooves which, alternating with metopes (s.v.), makes up the upper part of the section of the temple between the columns and the roof or pediment (gable).

Trojan War: the ten-year siege of Troy by the Greeks, and its eventual capture (c. 1200, if the war occurred at all). The Greeks wanted to win back Helen, the wife of the Greek leader Menelāos (brother of the expedition's leader Agamemnōn), who had been seduced back to Troy by Paris, son of the Trojan King Priam. The subject of much epic poetry, including Homer's *Iliad*.

Xenophōn 428–c. 354: Athenian soldier and writer of *Anabasis* (the expedition of a Greek mercenary force to and back from Mesopotamia 401–399); *Hellēnika* (history of Greece 410–362); *Memorābilia* (memoirs of Sōkratēs); *Sumposion* (recollections of a party); but not of *Constitution of Athens* (the work of the so-called 'Old Oligarch', almost certainly not Xenophōn), a not wholly damning critique of Athenian democracy; and perhaps *Constitution of Spartē*, in high praise.

xenos (pl. *xenoi*): alien (i.e. in Athens, a non-Athenian resident, cf. *metoikos*). Also, a guest-friend, i.e. one with whom one has obligatory, reciprocal ties of friendship.

Xerxēs: king of Persia; led the expedition against Greece in the 480s which resulted in battles at Thermopylai, Salamīs and Plataia, and eventual Persian defeat.

zeugītai: see *pentakosiomedimnoi*. *zugītai* is used for those who rowed in the middle rank of a trireme.

Suggestions for further reading

Chapter 1

Scholars write histories of Greece rather than histories of Athens, at least until the classical period. Good introductions to Greek history from the Bronze Age on are provided by Cartledge (1998) and Sparkes (1998).

1.1–4 Hērodotos' account of Kylōn is at 5.71, Thucydides' at 1.126. For further discussion of the source problems in archaic Greek history, see R. Osborne (1996a) ch. 1.

1.2 Hērodotos' account of Greek history before his time has attracted much attention, see Bakker, de Jong and van Wees (2002); Thucydides' allusions to events earlier than 480 have attracted no general attention.

1.3 On the local historians of Athens, see Harding (1994) 9–35.

1.5 For a general account of the archaeology of Athens and Attikē, see Camp (2001).

1.7 For the earliest occupants of Attikē (and Greece), see Perlès (2001). For the more general background in European prehistory, see Cunliffe (1994).

1.8–10 On bronze age Greece, see Dickinson (1994).

1.11 On Troy, see Latacz (2003).

1.12 On the continuity of epic, see Sherratt (1990), West (1988).

1.13 For a brief introduction to 'dark age' Greece, see Osborne (1996a) ch. 3, Morris (2000). In more detail, see Lemos (2003). On Athenian pottery, see Whitley (1991).

1.14 On eighth-century Athens, see Morris 1987, 2000.

1.15 On Greek settlement abroad, see R. Osborne 1996a, 2004a.

1.16 For the tradition about Athenian *sunoikismos*, see Thucydides 2.15. The complicated problems of the archaeology of seventh-century Attikē are discussed by R. Osborne (1989).

1.17 For the historical value of the evidence of the Homeric (and Hesiodic) poems, see R. Osborne (1996a) ch. 5, (2004b). For the history of the Athenian constitution, see Hignett (1951). For early officials in other Greek cities, see R. Osborne (1996a) 186–8.

1.18 For the text of Drakōn's law, see ML 86.

1.19 The classic account of Greek tyrants remains Andrewes (1956). See also Murray (1993) ch. 9, R. Osborne (1996a) 185–97, 271–85.

1.20 On Solōn, see Murray (1993) ch. 11. On Solōn as a political poet, see Irwin (2005).

1.21 On Peisistratos, see R. Osborne (1996a) 283–5, Sancisi-Weerdenburg (2000).

1.22 Athenian culture of the sixth century is discussed by Shapiro (1989) and Verbanck-Piérard and Viviers (1995). On the sculpture from the Akropolis, see Payne and Young (1936), Keesling (2003).

1.23 On Hippiās and Hipparkhos, see Lewis (1988).

1.24 On Spartē in the sixth century, see Murray (1993) 262–8, R. Osborne (1996a) 287–91.

1.25–6 On the Kleisthenic reforms, see R. Osborne (1996a) 292–314.

1.27 On the history of Persia from the Persian point of view, see P. Briant (2002). For the whole history of Athens' relations with Persia in the fifth century, see Miller (1997).

1.28 On the Ionian revolt, see Murray (1988).

1.29–39 On the Persian Wars, see Burn (1988), Lazenby (1993).

1.31 On ostracism, see de Ste Croix (2004) ch. 5, Brenne (2001), Forsdyke (2005) ch. 4.

1.32 On the Peiraieus, see Garland (1987).

1.37 On issues of ethnicity, see J. M. Hall (1997), (2002) and Harrison (2002).

1.40ff. The ancient sources for the Delian League and Athenian empire are collected in LACTOR 1⁴. For a brief survey of the issues, see also Rhodes (1993). The standard discussion remains Meiggs (1972). For an account of the years 478–431 from a Spartan point of view, see Powell (2001) ch. 3. For general narrative histories of period, see *Cambridge Ancient History* vol. 5, Davies 1993, Hornblower 2002, and Rhodes 2006.

1.45 On Ephialtēs, see Wallace (1989) ch. 3, Rihll (1995). On Periklēs' citizenship law, see R. Osborne (1997a).

1.48 The Athenian casualty list is ML 33.

1.51 On Athenian building on the Akropolis, see Hurwit (2004) (abridged from Hurwit (1999)). For the politics of these years, see Powell (1995a).

1.55 On the causes of the Peloponnesian War, see Ste Croix (1972).

1.58 On the 'demagogues', see Finley (1962), Connor (1971).

1.61 The treaties with Leontīnoi and Rhēgion are ML 63 and 64.

1.64 The tribute reassessment decree is ML 69. The Standards Decree, now generally agreed to date to the 420s, is ML 45.

1.69 For the complex ancient traditions surrounding Alkibiadēs, see Gribble (1999).

1.73 On the Mutilation of the Hermai, see R. Osborne (1985a); on the affair of the Mysteries, see Murray (1990b).

1.77–8 On the oligarchic coup of 411, see Hignett (1951), Gomme, Andrewes and Dover (1981), Rhodes (1981) 362–415, Osborne (2003).

1.80 On the Arginoussai trial, see Andrewes (1974).

1.82–4 On the Thirty, see Rhodes (1981) 415–74, Wolpert (2002), R. Osborne (2003).

1.85 The full picture of the events of these years has to be pieced together from allusions in the orators as well as from the Aristotelian *Constitution of the Athenians*. See in the first instance Rhodes (1981) 474–80, Strauss (1986) ch. 4.

1.86 On the trial of Sōkratēs, see Stone (1988), Ober (1998) 165–79.

1.87ff. For full discussion of Spartē in the generation after the Peloponnesian War, see Cartledge (1987).

1.88 The literary impact of Xenophōn's account of the 10,000 is discussed in Rood (2004).

1.90–3 On the Corinthian War, see Seager (1994).

1.91 Athenian honours for Dionȳsius and Euagorās are RO 10 and 11

1.94 The Athenian treaty with Chios is RO 20.

1.95 The Athenian prospectus for their new League is RO 22. On that league, see Cargill (1981).

1.97 The Theban monument celebrating Leuktrā is RO 30.

1.98 Athenian dealings with Kea can be traced in RO 39 and 40. The Athenian alliance of 362/1 with Arkadiā, Akhaia, Ēlis and Phleious is RO 41.

1.101 On Philip of Makedōn, see Ellis (1976), Cawkwell (1978) and Borza (1990).

1.102–5 On Athens and Makedōnia, see E. M. Harris (1995).

1.103 On the Sacred War from the Phocian point of view, see McInerney (1999).

1.107–10 On Alexander the best short introduction is Hornblower (2002) ch. 19. The most reliable of monographs is Bosworth (1988).

1.110–11 For Athens under Alexander and the Lamian War, see Habicht (1997) chs. 1–2.

Chapter 2

2.2 On the geology of Greece, see Higgins and Higgins (1996).

2.5 On climate, see R. Osborne (1987a) 27–34.

2.6 On the interplay of geography and history, see Cary (1949) ch. 2 on Greece in general, pp. 75–9 on Attikē, Zimmern (1911) Part I, chs. 1–3.

2.7–9   On Attic mineral resources and their exploitation, see R. Osborne (1985b) chs. 5–6. On stone, see also Wycherley (1978).

2.8   On Greek clays, see Sparkes (1991a) 8–13, Hemelrijk (1991).

2.9   On mining, see Healy (1978).

2.10   On the natural vegetation of classical Greece, see Rackham (1990). For the productive use of the wild landscape, see Forbes (1997). On terraces, see Nixon and Price (2005).

2.12   On the tendency to overestimate how poor Attic land was, see Garnsey (1985). Thucydides' verdict is at 1.2.5, Xenophōn's at *Ways and Means* 1.3.

2.13ff.   On Greek agriculture, see R. Osborne (1987a) ch. 2, Sallares (1991) ch. 3, Isager and Skydsgaard (1992), Burford (1993), Hanson (1995).

2.17   For getting draught animals from Boiōtiā, see RO 94.

2.18   On travel, see Casson (1974).

2.19   For ancient shipping, see Casson (1986). For triremes, see Morrison, Coates, and Rankov (2000).

2.20   For the spreading of news in the Greek world, see Lewis (1996).

2.21   The precise mix of villages and isolated farms in Attikē continues to be debated. See R. Osborne (1985b) ch. 2 for the case for a village-dominated pattern. On the way the Athenians imagined the space of Attikē, see von Reden (1998).

2.22   On these sites in Attikē, see Camp (2001), Goette (2001).

2.23   On the Peiraieus, see Garland (1987), von Reden (1995), Roy (1998).

2.26, 37   On the archaeology of Athens, see Camp (2001).

2.27, 29, 33, 35   On the Athenian *Agorā*, see Camp (1986); for life in the *Agorā*, see Millett (1998).

2.30, 34   On the Athenian Akropolis, see Hurwit (1999).

Chapter 3

Recent years have seen a number of excellent introductions to Greek religion published. Foremost among them is Bremmer (1999) with invaluable guide to further bibliography. Note also Price (1999). Athenian religion is magisterially covered by Parker (1996) and (2005).

3.1   Two helpful approaches to how different Greek religion is from the Judaeo-Christian tradition are Gould (1985) and Kearns (1995).

3.2   On polytheism, see Rudhardt (1966), Detienne and Sissa (2000). For commentary on Hesiod's *Theogony*, see West (1966). On the logic of cosmogony, see Burkert (1999). For the theology of mythology, see Buxton (1994) and (2004). For introduction of new divinities, see Garland (1992).

3.3   On Zeus, see Arafat (1990). For Xenophōn's relations with Zeus, see Xenophōn, *Anabasis* 3.1.12, 3.2.9, 6.1.22, 7.6.44, 7.8.4. For Xenophōn's religion in the *Anabasis*, see Parker (2004). On heroes and heroines, see Lyons (1997) 28–34. On hero cults in Attikē, see Kearns (1989). On the archaeology of the hero, see Snodgrass (1988).

3.4   On reciprocity in Greek religion, see Parker (1998). On belief, see Veyne (1988).

3.5   On the manifestation of Greek gods, see Gordon (1979). On offerings, see van Straten (1992). On prayer, see Pulleyn (1997). On priests, see Garland (1990).

3.6   On intellectual critics of religion, see Price (1999) chapter 7.

3.7   On religion and agriculture, see R. Osborne (1987a) ch. 8; on religion and human fertility, see Cole (2004) ch. 5.

3.8   On illness and the gods, see Lloyd (1966), (1979) and (1987); Price (1999).

3.9   On Hērodotos and the gods, see Gould (1994), Harrison (2000a).

3.10   On mythology, see above on 3.2.

3.11–12   On Hesiod on Promētheus, see Vernant (1980) ch. 8.

3.14   On dreams, see Price (1986).

3.16   On the introduction of the cult of Asklēpios to Athens, see Parker (1996) 175–87. On the Amphiareion, see RO 27.

3.17   On Athens and the Delphic oracle, see Parker (1985), Bowden (2005) and RO 58.

3.18   On the wooden walls oracle, see R. Osborne (1996a) 353–4.

3.19–20   See Parker (2004). On *manteis*, see Bowden (2003) 257–64, Parker (2005) 116–20.

3.21   See Parker (2005) ch. 6. On magic in general, see Fowler (1995), Graf (1998), Ankarloo and Clark (1999), Dickie (2001). On curses, see Gager (1992). On necromancy, see Ogden (2001).

3.22   Lloyd (1979) ch. 1.

3.23   On Hērodotos and Croesos, see Harrison (2000a) 33–45.

3.24   On the gods in tragedy, see Parker (1997).

3.25   On impiety, see Plato *Euthyphro*, Dover (1975).

3.26   On blood-guilt, see Parker (1983) ch. 4.

3.27   On oaths, see Parker (1983) 186–8, (2005) 102–3, Cole (2004) 120–2.

3.28–32   On sacrifice, see Bremmer (1999) 40–43, Burkert (1983), Jameson (1988) and (1999), R. Osborne (1987a) 174–84, (1993), Peirce (1993), van Straten (1995), RO 62.

3.31   On distinctions between hero cults and Olympian cults, see Scullion (1994).

3.32, 39   On sacrificing communities at Athens, see Parker (2005) chs. 2 and 3, RO 37, 46, 63.

3.33   On purification, see Parker (1983), RO 97.

3.34   See Pulleyn (1997).

3.35–6   On supplication, see Gould (1973).

3.37   On placing of sanctuaries, see Polignac (1995), Alcock and Osborne (1994). On sanctuaries generally, see Marinatos and Hägg (1993), Pedley (2005).

3.38   On temples, see Spawforth (2006). On the Athenian Akropolis, see Hurwit (1999).

3.40   On Athenian festivals, see Parker (2005) chs. 8–16.

3.41   On festival days, see Mikalson (1975).

3.42   On the *Panathēnaia*, see Parker (2005) ch. 12, Neils (1992), RO 81.

3.43   On processions, see Kavoulaki (1999).

3.44   On games at festivals compare RO 73. On *chorēgiā,* see Wilson (2000).

3.45   For obligations placed on Athenian allies and colonies, see ML 46.41–2, 49.11–13, RO 29.

3.46   See on 3.42

3.47   On the *Anthestēria*, see Parker (2005) ch.14, Humphreys (2004) ch. 6.

3.48   On Dionȳsos generally, see McGinty (1978), Henrichs (1982), Carpenter and Faraone (1993).

3.49   On Dionȳsos and women, see Osborne (1997b), Goff (2004).

3.50–52   On the Eleusinian Mysteries, see Parker (2005) ch. 15.

3.53   On the *Apatouria*, see Lambert (1993), Parker (2005) 458–61, RO 5.

3.54   On deme festivals, see Parker (2005) 73–8, Humphreys (2004) ch. 4, Parker (1987), Whitehead (1986) ch. 7.

Chapter 4

Study of Greek values outside the philosophers was long dominated by Adkins (1960) and Dover (1974). There has been a recent marked interest in the exploration of values in tragedy, in particular in Williams (1993), Blundell (1989).

4.1   The importance of competitive values is stressed by Adkins (1960). For an effective response with regard to the Homeric poems, see Cairns (1993b).

4.2   On helping friends and harming enemies, see Blundell (1989). Various aspects of reciprocity are explored in Gill, Postlethwaite and Seaford (1998). The historical development of reciprocity and its control by the structures of the city are explored in Seaford (1994) On friendship, see Konstan (1996). For this view of the courts, see R. Osborne (1985c).

4.3   For funerary legislation, see Seaford (1994) ch. 3. On use of the lot, see Headlam (1933).

4.4   On honour, see Dover (1974) ch. 5B, Cohen (1991) 79–83, 139–44, (1995) chs. 4 and 5.

4.5, 4.7   On Akhilleus and Agamemnōn, see Postlethwaite (1998).

4.6   On *aidos*, see Cairns (1993a).

4.7   On the value of good advice in Homer, see Schofield (1986).

4.8   On games, see Golden (1998), Phillips and Pritchard (2003).

4.9   See Gribble (1999), esp. ch. 1.

4.10   On the importance of envy (*phthonos*), see Hornblower (1983) ch. 2, D. Cohen (1995) 31–3, 81–5.

4.11   On *philotīmiā*, see Whitehead (1983).

4.12   On *atīmiā*, see Todd (1993) 142–3, 365, Forsdyke (2005) 10–11, 78–9, 212–15. On ostracism, see on 1.31.

4.13   On who prosecuted whom and for what reasons, see R. Osborne (1985c). On motives for stasis, see D. Cohen (1995) ch. 2. On morality and inter-state relations, see Low (2007).

4.14   On reciprocity and friendship, see on 4.2. On Mēdeia's morality, see Foley (2001) ch. 3.5.

4.15   On guest friendship, see Herman (1987), Mitchell (1997).

4.17   On *hubris*, see Fisher (1992), Wilson (1992), D. Cohen (1995) ch. 6

4.18   For the virtues singled out for public honour, see Whitehead (1993).

4.19   On *sōphrosunē*, see Dover (1974) 66–9.

4.20   On the chorus of tragedy, see Gould (1996).

4.21   On the question of shared values and the courts, see Todd (1990a).

4.22   On Klutaimēstrā, see Foley (2001) ch. 3.4.

4.23   On attitudes to female sexuality, see D. Cohen (1991) ch. 6, Fantham et al. (1994) ch. 3.

4.24   On Teiresiās, see Loraux (1995).

4.25   On whether the Greeks thought in terms of 'rights', see Tuck (1979), Sorabji (1993) 134–57.

4.27   For a discussion of how Athenian values compare to the values of modern liberal ideal states, see Liddel (2007).

Chapter 5

5.1   On the development of citizenship at Athens, see Manville (1990); on Periklēs' citizenship law, see R. Osborne (1997a).

5.2, 5.5., 5.6   On the population of Athens, see Gomme (1933), Hansen (1985) and (1988). On participation in democracy, see Sinclair (1988). For the full range of classical Greek city-states, see Hansen and Nielsen (2004).

5.3   On Athenian autochthony, see Loraux (1986) and (1993), Rosivach (1987).

5.4   On the ideology of the metic at Athens, see Whitehead (1977). On the rise of one banking family from slave to citizen, see Davies (1971) 427–42, Trevett (1992). On slavery, see Garlan (1988), Fisher (1993).

5.5–8   See above on 5.2

5.9ff.   For another account of the topics treated in the rest of this chapter, see Davidson (2000).

5.9   On the *oikos*, see MacDowell (1989). On the family, see Patterson (1998). On Athenian women generally Gould (1980) remains classic.

5.10–12   On the *oikos* in law and Athenian inheritance, see Todd (1993) ch. 11; on the household and property, see Foxhall (1989). On family and burial, see Humphreys (1980).

5.11   For Aristotle's ideas of slavery, see Garnsey (1996) ch. 8.

5.12   On bastardy at Athens, see Ogden (1996).

5.13–14   On Dēmosthenēs 57, see R. Osborne (1985b) 146–51. On the Athenian deme, see Whitehead (1986), R. Osborne (1985b) and (1990b). On the Athenian phratry, see Lambert (1993).

5.15   For a collection of citizenship grants, see M. Osborne (1981–3). On adoption at Athens, see Rubinstein (1993). On the proportion of children orphaned, see R. Osborne (1988b) 308–9.

5.16   On *epiklēroi*, see Todd (1993) 228–31, Karabélias (2002).

5.17–19 On marriage, see Vernant (1980) ch. 3, Oakley and Sinos (1993), Foley (2001) ch. 2. On infanticide, see Patterson (1985).

5.20   On Athenian double standards of sexual morality, see D. Cohen (1991) ch. 6, Omitowoju (2002).

5.22–3   See Gould (1980). On the separation of women, see Schnurr-Redford (2003), Wagner-Hasel (2003), Lewis (2002). On the evidence of houses themselves, see Nevett (1994) and (1995).

5.24   On tragic women, see Goldhill (1986) ch. 5, Foley (2001).

5.25–7   See Lewis (2002) and Reeder (1995) for the visual evidence, and Lissarrague (1990a) for the symposium.

5.26   On women's religious life, see R. Osborne (1993), Dillon (2002), Cole (2004), Goff (2004).

5.28   See above on 5.22–3. On women's dress, see Llewellyn-Jones (2002) and (2004).

5.29   On food, see Wilkins et al. (1995), Garnsey (1999).

5.30–31 On prostitutes, see Davidson (1997).

5.31   On Xenophōn's treatment of Theodotē, see Goldhill (1998).

5.32–5   On homosexuality, see Dover (1978), Foucault (1986), D. Cohen (1991) ch. 7, Davidson (2001). On the ages of boys, see Davidson (2006). On the gymnasium, see Fisher (1998).

5.34–5   On the Tīmarkhos case, see Winkler (1990) ch. 2, Fisher (2001).

5.37–43 For an introduction to classical education, see Morgan (1998) 9–21. The classic treatments are Marrou (1956), Beck (1964) and (1975). For recent contributions, see Too (2001).

5.39   On literacy, see Thomas (1989) and (1992), W. V. Harris (1989). On music, see Murray and Wilson (2004).

5.42.   On athletics, see Kyle (1987), Golden (1998).

5.44–8   On the sophists, see Wallace (1998), Ford (2001), Kerferd (1981).

5.49   On Isokratēs and education, see Livingstone (1998), Too (1995).

5.50   On attitudes to labour, see Burford (1972) chs. 1–2, Finley (1973) 40–42, 79–82. On the source of these attitudes, see Scheidel (2002).

5.51   On agriculture, see R. Osborne (1987a), Wells (1992), Burford (1993), Horden and Purcell (2000) chs. 6–7. On the settlement pattern of Attikē, see R. Osborne (1985b) ch. 2. On cereal production, see Garnsey (1985).

5.52   On slaves and agriculture at Athens, see Jameson (1977), (1992) and (1994), R. Osborne (1995). On patterns of landholding in Attikē, see R. Osborne (1985b) ch. 3. On the way olive oil etc. can become not staples but semi-luxuries, see Foxhall (1998).

5.53   For the distribution of landowning among rich and poor in Athens, see R. Osborne (1992), Foxhall (1992). On the property of Dēmosthenēs, see Davies (1971) 113–39.

5.54   On manufacturing, see Burford (1972), R. Osborne (1994a), E. M. Harris (2002).

5.55   On coinage, see Howgego (1995), Kim (2001), Trevett (2001), Seaford (2004), ML 45.

5.56   On the grain trade, see R. Osborne (1987a) 97–104, Garnsey (1988), and RO 26. On Kean ruddle, see RO 40.

5.57   On traders at Athens, see Millett (1983), Reed (2003) (but Reed's conclusions about the wealth/poverty of traders are insecure and those about the absence of Athenian traders achieved by ruling out the (good) evidence).

5.58   For the Peiraieus, see 2.23 above.

5.59   On maritime loans, see Millett (1983) and (1991) ch. 8, E. E. Cohen (1992) ch. 5.

5.61   On attitudes to slavery, including Aristotle's, see Garnsey (1996). For general discussions, see Garlan (1988), Fisher (1993). For slaves in utopia, see Aristophanēs *Ekklēsiazousai* with Vidal-Naquet (1981).

5.62–3   On the rights of slaves, see Todd (1993) 184–94; on slaves and the law in practice, see Hunter (2000), R. Osborne (2000b). For the Attic Stelai, see ML 79.

5.63   For the slave *dokimastēs*, see RO 25. On wealthy slaves, see E. E Cohen (2000) ch. 5. On slaves and the household, see Hunter (1994) ch. 3.

5.64–6   On slave occupations and the politics of slavery, see R. Osborne (1995). On slaves and the Erekhtheion, see Randall (1953).

5.66   On slavery and technology, see Finley (1959).

5.67–8   On metics, see Whitehead (1977), Todd (1993) 170–74, 194–9.

5.69   On exile, see Forsdyke (2005).

5.70   On Pāsiōn and his family, see above on 5.4.

5.71   On the *Bendideia*, see Parker (1996) 170–5, on the Egyptian and Kitian foundations, see Parker (1996) 160–1, 243.

5.72–7   On Greek medicine, see Lloyd (1979) and (1983), King (1998) and the Hippokratic texts collected in Lloyd (1978).

5.73   On Asklēpios, see Edelstein (1945), Parker (1996) 175–85, and RO 102.

5.77   On medicinal use of plants, see Lloyd (1983) 119–35.

5.78   On death and burial, see Garland (1985), Kurtz and Boardman (1971).

5.79   On the public burial of the war dead and the orations given at it, see Loraux (1986).

5.80–83   See Seaford (1994) chs. 3–4 on archaic funerals, Oakley (2004) on classical Athens.

5.83   On death and pollution, see Parker (1983) ch. 2; on the power of the unburied dead, see Johnston (1999).

Chapter 6

6.1   For introductions to the democracy as a philosophical and historical problem, see respectively T. R. Harrison (1993) and Dunn (2005).

6.2–3   On the question of when Athens became a democracy, see Hansen (1994), R. Osborne (2006).

6.3–4   On the terms used in antiquity for 'democracy', see Ostwald (1969), Hansen (1986).

6.4–5   On the Persian debate, see Pelling (2002).

6.5   On critics of democracy, see Jones (1957), Farrar (1988), Ober (1998).

6.6   The classic treatment of fourth-century Athenian democratic practice is Hansen (1991). For the Aristotelian *Constitution of the Athenians*, see Rhodes (1981).

6.7   On the Athenian Assembly, see Hansen (1983), (1987) and (1989). On the Arginoussai trial, see Andrewes (1974).

6.8   On the political context of Philip's seizure of Elateia, see Harris (1995) ch. 7.

6.9, 6.11–12, 19–22 On the *boulē*, see Rhodes (1972).

6.9   On the Pnyx, see Forsén and Stanton (1996).

6.12   On the relationship between what was said and what was inscribed, see R. Osborne (1999).

6.13   On participation, see Sinclair (1988), R. Osborne, (1985b) ch. 4, Taylor (2007). On Assembly pay, see Markle (1985).

6.14   On the extent to which politics was in the hands of an élite, see Ober (1989).

6.16   On *rhētores* in fourth-century Athens, see Hansen (1989) ch. 2. On the authority of generals, see Hamel (1998).

6.17   On political groups at Athens, see Strauss (1986) ch. 1, Calhoun (1913); on 'demagogues', see Finley (1962), Connor (1971).

6.18   For what Athenians took decisions about, see Hansen (1991) 155–8.

6.19   On meeting days, see Mikalson (1975).

6.20   On the Kleisthenic arrangements, see Traill (1975), R. Osborne (1996a) 294–308.

6.23   On the changes to the way of choosing archons, see Badian (1971).

6.24–5   On Athenian generals, see Hamel (1998).

6.25   On politicians and generals, see Hansen (1989) ch. 2.

6.26   On the election of generals, see Rhodes (1981) 535–7, 676–82.

6.28   On election by lot, see Headlam (1933).

6.29   On the number of officials, see Hansen (1980).

6.31   On the Eleven and the Scythian archers, see Hunter (1994) 144–8.

6.33–37   On ambassadors and diplomacy, see Mosley (1973), Adcock and Mosley (1975), Herman (1987), Mitchell (1997).

6.38–58   On Athenian law and courts, see MacDowell (1978), Todd (1993), Christ (1998), Lanni (2006).

6.38   On the Areopagus council, see Wallace (1989).

6.39   For Aristotle's definition, see *Politics* 1275a22–3. For discussion, see Miller (1995) 143–53. For the debated relationship between courts and Assembly, see Hansen (1987) 94–107.

6.40   On the Ēliaiā (conventionally, but wrongly, called the Hēliaiā), see Boegehold (1995) 18–20, 159–152. The dikastic oath is quoted by Dēmosthenēs 24.149–51. See Todd (1993) 54–5.

6.41   On jury pay, see Markle (1985).

6.42   On who prosecuted whom, by what procedure and for what, see R. Osborne (1985c), Todd (1993) chs. 7 and 9, D. Cohen (1995) chs. 5 and 6, Christ (1998).

6.43   On the *graphē paranomōn*, see Hansen (1974), Todd (1993) 298–300.

6.46   On bystanders, see Lanni (1997), on noise in the courts, Bers (1985). On *sunēgoroi*, see Rubinstein (2000).

6.47   On witnesses in Athenian courts, see Todd (1990b).

6.48   On women in Athenian courts, see Goldhill (1994), Foxhall (1996). On slaves, see Todd (1993) 184–94. On torture, see duBois (1991).

6.49–50   On arbitration, see Todd (1993) 123–5, 128–9.

6.51   On the selection of jurors in the fourth century, see [Aristotle] *Constitution of the Athenians* 63–9 with Rhodes (1981).

6.52   On execution of judgement, see Todd (1993) 144–5.

6.54   On the *sukophantēs*, see R. Osborne (1990a), Harvey (1990), Christ (1998).

6.55   On Athenian attitudes to law, see Thomas (1994).

6.56–8   For *atīmiā*, see on 4.12.

6.59   On Athenian resources and how these were affected by the Peloponnesian War, see Strauss (1986) ch. 2.

6.60   On taxation, see Jones (1974).

6.61   On the Athenian silver mines, see Conophagos (1980), R. Osborne (1985b) ch. 6, Shipton (2001).

6.62   On liturgies, see Davies (1967), Davies (1971) xvii–xxiv, Davies (1981), R. Osborne (1991), Wilson (2000).

6.64   On the *eisphorā*, see Brun (1983) 3–73.

6.65–9   On the Athenian grain supply all modern debate starts from Garnsey (1985); see also Garnsey (1988), and for the general context Sallares (1991), Horden and Purcell (2000).

6.68   The 374/3 grain tax law is RO 26. Note also RO 95, 96.

6.69   On Athenian links with the Kimmerian Bosporos, see RO 64.

6.70   On democracy and imperialism, see Boedeker and Raaflaub (1998).

6.71ff.   On the history of the Athenian empire, see on 1.40ff.

6.73–4   On Thucydides' account of the Athenian empire, see LACTOR 1⁴ 3–5.

6.74ff.   On the profits, and losses involved in the Athenian empire, see Finley (1978), Nixon and Price (1990), LACTOR 1⁴, Rhodes (2006) ch. 15.

6.76   On changing relations with Persia, see Miller (1997) ch. 1

6.78   The crucial inscriptions are ML 45–6; for current views on their dates, see LACTOR 1⁴ nos. 190, 198. On the language of Athenian inscriptions, see Low (2005).

6.79   On the Akropolis building programme, see Hurwit (1999) and (2004).On allies' festival obligations, see on 3.45. On the Megarian decree, see de Ste Croix (1972), MacDonald (1983). On Athens and the Black Sea, see Braund (2005). For the checkpoint at the Hellēspont, see ML 65.

6.80   Periklēs' statement about Athenian resources is at 2.13 (cf. above 5.6). The epigraphic evidence for increasing financial pressure on allies is ML 68–9. The Standards Decree is ML 45. The decree about Eleusīs is ML 73.

6.81 For Athenians with property abroad, see ML 79. For allied involvement in the Sicilian expedition, see Thuc. 7.57.

6.82 For the *eisphorā* of 428, see Thuc. 3.19. On Athenian settlements abroad, see Brunt (1966).

6.83 For commentary on *Birds*, see Dunbar (1995).

6.84–5 The classic discussion of the popularity of the Athenian empire is de Ste Croix (1954–5).

6.87 On proxeny, see Walbank (1978).

6.89–90 On Athenian politics immediately after the Peloponnesian War, see Strauss (1986), Hornblower (2002) ch.15.

6.91 On the Second Athenian Confederacy, see Hornblower (2002) ch. 16, Rhodes (2006) ch. 18.

6.93 On Athens and Keōs, see Lewis (1962), RO 39, 40.

Chapter 7

7.1 Good recent introductions to Greek warfare are to be found in (in order of increasing detail) Sidebottom (2004), Lendon (2005), van Wees (2004); see also van Wees (2000). The classic account of the experience of warfare in ancient Greece is Hanson (1989). The most thorough treatment of Greek warfare is Pritchett (1971–91).

7.2 On war and religion, see Jacquemin (2000), Jameson (1991), Jackson (1991). On *manteis*, see Bowden (2003).

7.3 On the Athenian fleet, see Morrison, Coates and Rankov (2000), Gabrielsen (1994), Strauss (1996).

7.4 On 'Common Peace', see Ryder (1965).

7.7 On ravaging and its effects, see Hanson (1983).

7.10 On the conduct of generals in battle, see Wheeler (1991).

7.11, 31 On the Athenian *ephebeia*, see RO 88, 89.

7.13 What exactly happened when armies met has been much debated of late. See van Wees (2004) ch. 13.

7.14 On logistics, see van Wees (2004) ch. 8.

7.16–17, 22–6 On light troops, see van Wees (2004) ch. 5; on cavalry, see Bugh (1988), Spence (1993). On their representation, see Lissarrague (1990b).

7.19. On arms and armour, see Snodgrass (1967).

7.20 On the representation of warfare in art, see Lissarrague (1989). On what happened in battle, see above on 7.13.

7.27 On fourth-century developments, see Lendon (2005) ch. 5.

7.28 On mercenaries, see van Wees (2004) 71–6.

7.32–3 On developments of siegecraft, see Garlan (1974), Lawrence (1979), R. Osborne (1987a) ch. 7. On Aineiās Tacticus, see Whitehead (1990).

7.34–5 See Morrison et al (2000).

7.37–41 See van Wees (2004) ch. 15.

7.42–8 See Gabrielsen (1994).

Chapter 8

8.1 For general histories of Greek literature, see Taplin (2000), Rutherford (2005). For reasons to believe in the antiquity of some Homeric epic, see West (1988).

8.2–3 For the earliest Greek writing, see Jeffrey (1961), B. B. Powell (1991).

8.4 On use of verse for law, see Thomas (1996) 14; for philosophy, see C. Osborne (1998).

8.5 On the survival of Greek texts, see Reynolds and Wilson (1968). The 'Cologne Epode' of Archilochos was published in 1974: see Merkelbach and West (1974) for the first publication, Stehle (1997) 242–5 for recent discussion. For the new Simōnidēs, see Boedeker and Sider (1996).

8.6   On orality and its consequences, see Lloyd (1979) 239–40, Lloyd (1990), Thomas (1992).

8.7–9   On pre-Socratic philosophy, see C. Osborne (2004); and for a translation of source material, see Barnes (1987).

8.10–12   On polarity and analogy, see Lloyd (1966).

8.13   On early Greek theology, see Price (1999) ch. 7.

8.14   The importance of contact with the Near East for the development of Greek culture has been much debated in the recent past. For material culture, see S. Morris (1992); for poetry, see West (1997).

8.16   On literacy, see above on 5.39.

8.17   On dissemination of news, see Lewis (1996).

8.17ff.   For the development of rhetoric, see Kennedy (1963), Carey (2000a), Goldhill (2002). For the place of Homer in Athenian culture, see Ford (1999) 232–41. On the experience of tragedy, see Cartledge (1997).

8.18   On the importance of counsel and persuasion in Homer, see Schofield (1986).

8.19–21   For the philosophical side of the development of rhetoric, see Wardy (1996).

8.20   On the question of whether the Athenians did think seduction worse than rape, see Harris (1990), Carey (1995), Omitowoju (2002) 63–70.

8.22ff.   On the sophists, see on 5.44–8.

8.23   On the sophists and education, see Ford (2001).

8.24   On Aristophanēs and Sōkratēs, see Nussbaum (1980). On the context, see Carey (2000b).

8.25–6   On Pythagorās and Zēnōn, see Hussey (1997).

8.27   On Plato's *Kratulos*, see Sedley (2003).

8.28   On tragedy's interest in persuasion, see Buxton (1982). On arguments from probability, see Carey (1994a) and (1994b). On the Melian dialogue, see Macleod (1975), Hussey (1985) 126–8.

8.29   On Prōtagorās' myth, see Farrar (1988) 81–98.

8.31   On issues of evidence, see Thomas (2000) ch. 6.

8.32   On Hērodotos and *nomos*, see Humphreys (1987), Thomas (2000) ch. 4.

8.33–6   The picture we create of Sōkratēs depends on which sources we privilege. The current orthodoxy on this is Vlastos (1991).

8.35   On the *Lakhēs, see* Balot (forthcoming).

8.36   On Socratic 'midwifery', see Burnyeat (1977).

8.37   On development of medical science, see Lloyd (1979) ch. 1 and (1987) chs. 1–2.

8.38   On the limitations of Greek medicine, see Lloyd (1987) ch. 3.

8.39   On Asklēpios, see on 5.73.

8.40   On early Greek mythographers, see Fowler (2000).

8.41   On differences between Hērodotos and his predecessors, see Fowler (1996). On Hērodotos and his contemporaries, see Thomas (2000). Extensive and up-to-date discussion of all aspects of Hērodotos are found in Bakker et al. (2002), Dewald and Marincola (2006).

8.42   Recent work on Thucydides has been primarily interested in the construction of his text. See especially Rood (1998). For a general discussion of Thucydides the man and his intellectual affinities, see Hornblower (1987).

8.43   For *Hellēnika Oxyrhynchia*, see McKechnie and Kern (1988). For Xenophōn, see Gray (1989), Dillery (1995).

8.45–7   For the dramatic festivals at Athens, see Csapo and Slater (1995). On the judging procedure, see Marshall and van Willigenburg (2004). On the Athenian theatre, see Wiles (1997). On the context of drama, see Winkler and Zeitlin (1990).

8.46   On actors, see Easterling and Hall (2002). For the *khorēgos*, see Wilson (2000).

8.49ff.   On tragedy, see generally Taplin (1978), Goldhill (1986), Easterling (1997a). For a stimulating argument about the development of tragedy, see Seaford (1994) chs. 7–10. On *Persians*, see E. Hall (1989) and (1996), Pelling (1997b), Harrison (2000b).

8.50   On ritual in the *Bacchae*, see Foley (1985).

8.51   On the chorus, see Henrichs (1995), Gould (1996), Calame (1999). On song in tragedy, see E. Hall (1999).

8.52   On the Dionysiac festivals and tragedy, see Winkler and Zeitlin (1990), Seaford (1994), Easterling (1997b), Scullion (2002).

8.53–5 On tragedy and myth, see Burian (1997). On what myth did for the Greeks more generally, see Buxton (1994).

8.56–7 On tragedy and history, see Pelling (1997a) and (2000). On *Trojan Women*, see Croally (1994) esp. 232–4.

8.58   For a classic exposition of this approach to the tragic hero in Sophoklēs, see Knox (1964).

8.59   On the different attitudes of tragedy and comedy to the audience the classic exposition is Taplin (1986).

8.60   For an introduction to formal issues, see Taplin (1978), Easterling (1997c).

8.61   On stichomythia, see Collins (2005) 3–29.

8.64–5 See Wiles (1997), Taplin (1978).

8.66   On tragedy as text, see Goldhill (1986) ch. 11.

8.67   The best short introduction to Athenian comedy (which effectively means Aristophanic comedy) is Cartledge (1990). See also Dover (1972), Bowie (1993).

8.69   For what we know of non-Aristophanic Old Comedy, see Harvey and Wilkins (2000).

8.71   On the politics of Old Comedy, see McGlew (2002).

8.75   On the language of Aristophanēs, see Colvin (1999), Willi (2002).

8.79   On Aristophanēs' own politics, see de Ste Croix (1972), Cartledge (1990), Goldhill (1991) ch. 3.

8.81   On Menander, see Wiles (1991), Lape (2004), Fantuzzi and Hunter (2004) 404–32.

8.83ff. For a general introduction to Greek art, see R. Osborne (1998); on a larger scale, see Robertson (1975). For a fine bibliographical survey, see Sparkes (1991b). On the invention of art, see Tanner (2006).

8.84   On early Athenian pottery, see Boardman (1998).

8.85   On Greek architecture, see Coulton (1977); on the development of the orders, see Barletta (2001). On Greek sculpture, see Stewart (1990).

8.86   On *korai*, see Karakasi (2003). On the Athenian Akropolis *korai*, see Keesling (2003). On Akropolis marble dedications neither the text nor the photographs of Payne and Young (1936) have been surpassed. I argued the case for the gaze of the *kouros* in R. Osborne (1988a).

8.87   On the sixth-century Akropolis, see Hurwit (1999).

8.88   On Athenian black-figure pottery, see Beazley (1951), Boardman (1974). On the Etruscan market, see R. Osborne (2001).

8.89   On the portrayal of myth on Greek vases, see Henle (1973), Woodford (2003). On Exēkiās, see Boardman (1978). On the Amasis Painter, see von Bothmer (1985).

8.90   On early red-figure vases, see Boardman (1975), Robertson (1992), with D. Williams (1991) on technique and Neer (2002) on politics. On vase painting as the image of the city, see Bérard et al. (1989).

8.91   On the 'Greek Revolution' in art, see Elsner (2006).

8.92   On the Kritian Boy, see Hurwit (1989). On classical Greek sculpture, see Boardman (1985).

8.93   On the Riace Bronzes, see E. Harrison (1985).

8.94–6 On Olympiā and the Parthenōn, see Ashmole (1972).

8.95–7 On the sculptures of the Parthenōn, see Brommer (1979), Boardman and Finn (1985). I develop the reading offered here in R. Osborne (1987b), (1994b) and (1994c).

8.99   On the variety of styles in use in the late fifth century, see Ridgway (1981). For different readings of the Nīkē, see Pollitt (1972), R. Osborne (1996b).

8.100 On later fifth-century pot-painting, see Boardman (1989).

8.101 On fourth-century sculpture, see Boardman (1995).

8.103   For an exploration of the cultural changes occurring at the end of the fifth century, see R. Osborne (2007).

Chapter 9

9.2   On Athenian self-conscious construction of difference, see Loraux (1986).

9.3   On Aiskhylos' *Persians*, see above on 8.49ff. On Athenian use of Persian dress, see Miller (1997) ch. 7.

9.4   On the construction of Spartē in antiquity and since, see Rawson (1969), Powell and Hodkinson (1994), Hodkinson (2000) chs. 1–2.

9.6   My comments here are drawn from an undergraduate thesis by Helen Chambers. See also Snowden (1983), Miller (1997) 212–14, E. Cohen (2000). See also Lape (forthcoming).

9.8.   The starting point for all discussion of Periklēs' Funeral Oration is now Loraux 1986. Note also Ziolkowski (1981), Macleod (1983) 149–53, Hussey (1985) 123–5.

Bibliography

ML R. Meiggs and D.M. Lewis *Greek Historical Inscriptions to the end of the Fifth Century BC*. Oxford.

RO P.J. Rhodes and R. Osborne *Greek Historical Inscriptions 404–323 BC*. Oxford.

Adcock, F.E. and Mosley, D.J. (1975) *Diplomacy in Ancient Greece*. London.

Adkins, A.W.H. (1960) *Merit and Responsibility: a Study in Greek Ethics*. Oxford.

Alcock, S. and Osborne R. eds. (1994) *Placing the Gods: Sanctuaries and Sacred Space in Ancient Greece*. Oxford.

Andrewes, A. (1956) *The Greek Tyrants*. London

—(1974) 'The Arginusae trial', *Phoenix* 28: 112–22.

Ankarloo, B. and Clark, S. eds. (1999) *Witchcraft and Magic in Europe*, vol. 2: *Ancient Greece and Rome*. London.

Arafat, K.W. (1990) *Classical Zeus: A Study in Art and Literature*. Oxford.

Ashmole, B. (1972) *Architect and Sculptor in Classical Greece*. London.

Badian, E. (1971) 'Archons and *strategoi*', *Antichthon* 5: 1–34.

Bakker, E., de Jong, I. and van Wees, H. eds. (2002) *Brill's Companion to Herodotus*. Leiden

Balot, R.K. (forthcoming) 'Democracy and the Platonic *Laches*', in Balot, *Courage and its Critics in Democratic Athens*.

Barletta, B. (2001) *The Origins of the Greek Architectural Orders*. Cambridge.

Barnes, J. (1987) *Early Greek Philosophy*. Harmondsworth.

Beazley, J. (1951) *The Development of Attic Black-Figure*. Berkeley.

Beck, F.A.G. (1964) *Greek Education, 450–350 BC*. London.

—(1975) *An Album of Greek Education*. Sydney.

Bérard, C. et al. (1989) *The City of Images: Iconography and Society in Ancient Greece*. Princeton.

Bers, V. (1985) 'Dikastic *thorubos*', in Cartledge and Harvey (1985) 1–15.

Blundell, M.W. (1989) *Helping Friends and Harming Enemies: a Study in Sophocles and Greek Ethics*. Cambridge.

Boardman, J. (1974) *Athenian Black-Figure Vases: a Handbook*. London.

—(1975) *Athenian Red-Figure Vases: the Archaic Period*. London.

—(1978) 'Exekias', *American Journal of Archaeology* 82: 18–24

—(1985) *Greek Sculpture: the Classical Period: a Handbook*. London.

—(1989) *Athenian Red Figure Vases: the Classical Period: a Handbook*. London.

—(1995) *Greek Sculpture: the Late Classical Period and Sculptures in Colonies and Overseas: a Handbook*. London

—(1998) *Early Greek Vase Painting 11th–6th centuries BC: a Handbook*. London.

Boardman, J. and Finn, D. (1985) *The Parthenon and its Sculptures*. London.

Boedeker, D. and Raaflaub, K. eds. (1998) *Democracy, Empire and the Arts in Fifth-Century Athens*. Cambridge, MA.

Boedeker, D. and Sider, D. eds. (1996) *The New Simonides*. Baltimore.

Boegehold, A.L. (1995) *The Law-courts at Athens: Sites, Buildings, Equipment, Procedure, and Testimonia. The Athenian Agora*, vol. 28. Princeton.

Borza, E. (1990) *In the Shadow of Olympus: the Emergence of Macedon*. Princeton.

Bosworth, A.B. (1988) *Conquest and Empire: the Reign of Alexander the Great*. Cambridge.

Bowden, H. (2003) 'Oracles for sale', in P.S. Derow and R.C.T. Parker eds. *Herodotus and his World*. Oxford: 256–74.

—(2005) *Classical Athens and the Delphic Oracle: Divination and Democracy*. Cambridge.

Bowie, A.M. (1993) *Aristophanes: Myth, Ritual, and Comedy*. Cambridge.

Braund, D. (2005) 'Pericles, Cleon and the Pontos: the Black Sea in Athens c. 440–421', in D. Braund ed. *Scythians and Greeks: Cultural Interactions of Scythia, Athens and the Early Roman Empire* (*Sixth Century* BC – *First Century* AD). Exeter.

Bremmer, J. (1999) *Greek Religion*. Greece and Rome New Surveys in the Classics, no. 24. Oxford.

Brenne, S. (2001) *Ostrakismos und Prominenz in Athen*. Vienna

Briant, P. (2002) *From Cyrus to Alexander: a History of the Persian Empire*, trans. P. T. Daniels. Winona Lake, IN.

Brommer, F. (1979) *The Sculptures of the Parthenon*. London.

Brun, P. (1983) *Eisphora, syntaxis, stratiotika: recherches sur les finances militaires d'Athènes au IVe siècle*. Paris.

Brunt, P.A. (1966) 'Athenian settlements abroad in the fifth century BC', in E. Badian ed. *Ancient Society and Institutions: Studies presented to Victor Ehrenberg*. Oxford: 71–92. Reprinted in P.A. Brunt *Studies in Greek History and Thought*. Oxford, 1991: 112–36.

Bugh, G. (1988) *The Horsemen of Athens*. Princeton.

Burford, A. (1972) *Craftsmen in Greek and Roman Society*. London.

—(1993) *Land and Labor in the Greek World*. Baltimore.

Burian, P. (1997) 'Myth into *muthos*: the shaping of tragic plot', in Easterling (1997a) 178–208.

Burkert, W. (1983) *Homo Necans*. Berkeley.

—(1999) 'The logic of cosmogony', in Buxton (1999) 87–106.

Burn, A.R. (1988) *Persia and the Greeks*, revised by D.M. Lewis. London.

Burnyeat, M.F. (1977) 'Socratic midwifery, Platonic inspiration', *Bulletin of the Institute of Classical Studies* 24: 7–16.

Buxton, R. (1982) *Persuasion in Greek Tragedy: a Study of Peitho*. Cambridge.

—(1994) *Imaginary Greece: the Contexts of Mythology*. Cambridge.

—ed. (1999) *From Myth to Reason: Studies in the Development of Greek Thought*. Oxford.

—ed. (2000) *Oxford Readings in Greek Religion*. Oxford: 191–223.

—(2004) *The Complete World of Greek Mythology*. London.

Cairns, D.L. (1993a) *Aidos*. Oxford.

—(1993b) 'Affronts and Quarrels in the *Iliad*', *Papers of the Liverpool Latin Seminar* 7: 155–67. Reprinted in D.L. Cairns ed. *Oxford Readings in Homer's* Iliad. Oxford, 2001: 203–19.

Calame, C. (1999) 'Performative aspects of the choral voice in Greek tragedy: civic identity in performance', in Goldhill and Osborne (1999) 125–53.

Calhoun, G.M. (1913) *Athenian Clubs in Politics and Litigation*. Austin, TX.

Camp, J. (1986) *The Athenian Agora*. London.

—(2001) *The Archaeology of Athens*. New Haven and London.

Carey, C. (1994a) 'Rhetorical means of persuasion', in I. Worthington ed. *Persuasion: Greek Rhetoric in Action*. London: 26–45. Reprinted in A.O. Rorty ed. *Essays on Aristotle's Rhetoric*. Berkeley, 1996: 399–415.

Carey, C. (1994b) 'Artless proofs in Aristotle and the orators', *Bulletin of the Institute of Classical Studies* N.S. 39: 95–106.

—(1995) 'Adultery and rape in Athenian law', *Classical Quarterly* 44: 407–17.

—(2000a) 'Observers of speeches and hearers of action: the Athenian orators', in Taplin (2000) 192–216.

—(2000b) 'Old comedy and the sophists', in D. Harvey and J.M. Wilkins eds. *The Rivals of Aristophanes*. Swansea: 419–36.

Cargill, J. (1981) *The Second Athenian League: Empire or Free Alliance?* Berkeley.

Carpenter, T.H. and Faraone, C.A. eds. (1993) *Masks of Dionysus*. Ithaca, NY.

Cartledge, P.A. (1987) *Agesilaos and the Crisis of Sparta*. London.

—(1990) *Aristophanes and his Theatre of the Absurd*. Bristol.

—(1997) ' "Deep plays": theatre as process in Greek civic life', in Easterling (1997a) 3–35.

—ed. (1998) *The Cambridge Illustrated History of Ancient Greece*. Cambridge.

Cartledge, P.A. and Harvey, F.D. eds. (1985) *CRUX. Essays in Greek History Presented to G.E.M. de Ste Croix*. London.

Cartledge, P.A., Millett, P.C. and Todd, S.C. (1990) *Nomos: Essays in Athenian Law, Politics and Society*. Cambridge.

Cartledge, P.A., Millett, P.C. and von Reden, S. eds. (1998) *Kosmos: Essays in Order, Conflict and Community in Classical Athens*. Cambridge.

Cartledge, P.A., Cohen, E.E. and Foxhall, L. eds. (2002) *Money, Labour and Land: Approaches to the Economies of Ancient Greece*. London.

Cary, M. (1949) *The Geographic Background of Greek and Roman History*. Oxford.

Casson, L. (1974) *Travel in the Ancient World*. London.

—(1986) *Ships and Seamanship in the Ancient World*. Princeton.

Cawkwell, G.L. (1978) *Philip of Macedon*. London.

Christ, M.R. (1998) *The Litigious Athenian*. Baltimore.

Cohen, B. ed. (2000) *Not the Classical Ideal: Athens and the Construction of the Other in Greek Art*. Leiden.

Cohen, D. (1991) *Law, Sexuality and Society: the Enforcement of Morals in Classical Athens*. Cambridge.

—(1995) *Law, Violence and Community in Classical Athens*. Cambridge.

Cohen, E.E. (1992) *Athenian Economy and Society: a Banking Perspective*. Princeton.

—(2000) *The Athenian Nation*. Princeton.

Cole, S.G. (2004) *Landscapes, Gender, and Ritual Space*. Berkeley.

Collins, D. (2005) *Master of the Game: Competition and Performance in Greek Poetry*. Cambridge, MA.

Colvin, S. (1999) *Dialect in Aristophanes: the Politics of Language in Ancient Greek Literature*. Oxford.

Connor, W.R. (1971) *The New Politicians of Fifth-Century Athens*. Princeton.

Conophagos, C. (1980) *Le Laurium antique*. Athens.

Coulton, J.J. (1977) *Greek Architects at Work: Problems of Structure and Design*. London.

Croally, N.T. (1994) *Euripidean Polemic*: The Trojan Women *and the Function of Tragedy*. Cambridge.

Csapo, E. and Slater, W.J. (1995) *The Context of Ancient Drama*. Ann Arbor.

Cunliffe, B. ed. (1994) *The Oxford Illustrated Prehistory of Europe*. Oxford.

Davidson, J. (1997) *Courtesans and Fishcakes: the Consuming Passions of Classical Athens*. London.

—(2000) 'Private life', in R. Osborne (2000a) 139–69.

—(2001) 'Dover, Foucault and Greek homosexuality: penetration and the truth of sex', *Past & Present* 170: 3–51. Reprinted in R. Osborne (2004c) 78–118.

—(2006) 'Revolutions in human time: age-class in Athens and the Greekness of Greek revolutions', in Goldhill and Osborne (2006) 29–67.

Davies, J.K. (1967) 'Demosthenes on liturgies: a note', *JHS* 87: 33–40.

—(1971) *Athenian Propertied Families 600–300 BC.* Oxford.

—(1981) *Wealth and the Power of Wealth in Classical Athens.* New York.

—(1993) *Democracy and Classical Greece.* 2nd edn. London.

Detienne, M. and Sissa, G. (2000) *The Daily Life of the Greek Gods.* Stanford.

Detienne, M. and Vernant J.-P. eds. (1989) *The Cuisine of Sacrifice among the Greeks.* Chicago.

Dewald, C. and Marincola, J. (2002) *The Cambridge Companion to Herodotus.* Cambridge.

Dickie, M.W. (2001) *Magic and Magicians in the Greco-Roman World.* London.

Dickinson, O. (1994) *The Aegean Bronze Age.* Cambridge.

Dillery, J. (1995) *Xenophon and the History of his Times.* London.

Dillon, M. (2002) *Girls and Women in Classical Greek Religion.* London.

Dover, K.J. (1972) *Aristophanic Comedy.* Berkeley.

—(1974) *Greek Popular Morality in the time of Plato and Aristotle.* Oxford.

—(1975) 'The freedom of the intellectual in Greek society', *Talanta* 7: 24–54. Reprinted in K.J. Dover *The Greeks and their Legacy.* Oxford, 1988: 135–58.

—(1978) *Greek Homosexuality.* London.

duBois, P. (1991) *Torture and Truth.* London.

Dunbar, N. (1995) *Aristophanes* Birds *Edited with Introduction and Commentary.* Oxford.

Dunn, J.M. (2005) *Setting the People Free: the Story of Democracy.* London.

Easterling, P.E. ed. (1997a) *The Cambridge Companion to Greek Tragedy.* Cambridge.

—(1997b) 'A show for Dionysus', in Easterling (1997a) 36–53.

—(1997c) 'Form and performance', in Easterling (1997a) 151–77.

Easterling, P.E. and Hall, E.M. (2002) *Greek and Roman Actors: Aspects of an Ancient Profession.* Cambridge.

Edelstein, E.J. and Edelstein, L. (1945) *Asclepius: a Collection and Interpretation of the Testimonia.* Baltimore.

Ellis, J.R. (1976) *Philip II and Macedonian Imperialism.* London.

Elsner, J. (2006) 'Reflections on the "Greek Revolution" in art: from changes in viewing to the transformation of subjectivity', in Goldhill and Osborne (2006) 68–95.

Fantham, E., Foley, H.P., Kampen, N.B., Pomeroy, S.B. and Shapiro, H.A. (1994) *Women in the Classical World.* Oxford.

Fantuzzi, M. and Hunter, R.L. (2004) *Tradition and Innovation in Hellenistic Poetry.* Cambridge.

Farrar, C. (1988) *The Origins of Democratic Thinking.* Cambridge.

Finley, M.I. (1959) 'Was Greek civilization based on slave labour?' *Historia* 8: 145–64. Reprinted in Finley (1981) ch. 6

—(1962) 'The Athenian demagogues', *Past and Present* 21: 3–24. Revised version in Rhodes (2004) 163–84.

—(1973) *The Ancient Economy.* Berkeley.

—(1978) 'The Athenian empire: a balance sheet', in P. Garnsey and C.R. Whittaker eds. *Imperialism in the Ancient World.* Cambridge: 103–26. Reprinted in Finley (1981) 41–61.

—(1981) *Economy and Society in Ancient Greece*, ed. B.D. Shaw and R.P. Saller. London.

Fisher, N.R.E. (1992) *Hybris.* Warminster.

—(1993) *Slavery in Classical Greece.* London.

—(1998) 'Gymnasia and democratic values of leisure', in Cartledge, Millett and von Reden (1998) 84–104.

—(2001) *Aeschines Against Timarchus.* Oxford.

Foley, H.P. (1985) *Ritual Irony: Poetry and Sacrifice in Euripides*. Ithaca, NY.

—(2001) *Female Acts in Greek Tragedy*. Princeton.

Forbes, H.A. (1997) 'A "waste" of resources: aspects of landscape exploitation in lowland Greek agriculture', in P.N. Kardulias and M.T. Shutes eds. *Aegean Strategies: Studies of Culture and Environment on the European Fringe*. Lanham, MD. 187–214.

Ford, A. (1999) 'Reading Homer from the rostrum: poems and laws in Aeschines' *Against Timarchus*', in Goldhill and Osborne (1999) 231–56.

—(2001) 'Sophists without rhetoric: the arts of speech in fifth-century Athens', in Too (2001) 85–109.

Forsdyke, S. (2005) *Exile, Ostracism and Democracy: the Politics of Expulsion in Ancient Greece*. Princeton.

Forsén, B. and Stanton, G.R. eds. (1996) *The Pnyx in the History of Athens*. Helsinki.

Foucault, M. (1986) *The Uses of Pleasure. The History of Sexuality*, vol. 2. London.

Fowler R.L. (1995) 'Greek magic, Greek religion', *Illinois Classical Studies* 20: 1–22. Reprinted in Buxton (2000) 317–43.

—(1996) 'Herodotus and his contemporaries', *Journal of Hellenic Studies* 116: 62–87.

—(2000) *Early Greek Mythography*, vol.1: *Text and Introduction*. Oxford.

Foxhall, L. (1989) 'Household, gender and property in classical Athens', *Classical Quarterly* 39: 22–44.

—(1992) 'The control of the Attic landscape', in Wells (1992) 155–9.

—(1996) 'The law and the lady: women and legal proceedings in classical Athens', in Foxhall, L. and Lewis, A.D.E. eds. *Greek Law in its Political Setting: Justification not Justice*. Oxford: 133–52.

—(1998) 'Cargoes of the heart's desire: the character of trade in the archaic Mediterranean world', in Fisher. N. and van Wees, H. eds. *Archaic Greece: New Approaches and New Evidence*. London: 295–310.

Gabrielsen, V. (1994) *Financing the Athenian Fleet*. Baltimore.

Gager, J. (1992) *Curse Tablets and Binding Spells from the Ancient World*. Oxford.

Garlan, Y. (1974) *Recherches sur le poliorcétique grecque*. Paris.

—(1988) *Slavery in Ancient Greece*. Ithaca, NY.

Garland, R. (1985) *The Greek Way of Death*. London.

—(1987) *The Piraeus: from the Fifth to the First Century BC*. London.

—(1990) 'Priests and power in classical Athens', in M. Beard and J. North eds. *Pagan Priests*. London: 75–91.

—(1992) *Introducing New Gods: the Politics of Athenian Religion*. London.

—(1985) 'Grain for Athens', in Cartledge and Harvey (1985) 62–75. Reprinted with addendum in P. Garnsey *Cities, Peasants and Foods in Classical Antiquity*. Cambridge: 183–200.

—(1988) *Famine and Food Supply in the Graeco-Roman World: Responses to Risk and Crisis*. Cambridge.

—(1996) *Ideas of Slavery from Aristotle to Augustine*. Cambridge.

Garnsey, P. (1999) *Food and Society in Classical Antiquity*. Cambridge.

Gill, C., Postlethwaite, N. and Seaford, R. eds. (1998) *Reciprocity in Ancient Greece*. Oxford.

Goette, H.R. (2001) *Athens, Attica and the Megarid: an Archaeological Guide*. London.

Goff, B.E. (2004) *Citizen Bacchae: Women's Ritual Practice in Ancient Greece*. Berkeley.

Golden, M. (1998) *Sport and Society in Ancient Greece*. Cambridge.

Golden, M. and Toohey, P. (2003) *Sex and Difference in Ancient Greece and Rome*. Edinburgh.

Goldhill, S. (1986) *Reading Greek Tragedy*. Cambridge.

—(1991) *The Poet's Voice: Essays on Poetics and Greek Literature*. Cambridge.

—(1994) 'Representing democracy: women at the Great Dionysia', in Osborne and Hornblower (1994) 347–69.

—(1998) 'The seductions of the gaze: Socrates and his girlfriends', in Cartledge, Millett and von Reden (1998) 105–24.

—(2002) *The Invention of Prose*. Greece and Rome New Surveys in the Classics, no. 32. Oxford.

Goldhill, S. and Osborne, R. eds. (1994) *Art and Text in Ancient Greek Culture*. Cambridge.

—eds. (1999) *Performance Culture and Athenian Democracy*. Cambridge.

—eds. (2006) *Rethinking Revolutions through Ancient Greece*. Cambridge.

Gomme, A. (1933) *The Population of Athens in the Fifth and Fourth Centuries BC*. Oxford.

Gomme, A., Andrewes, A. and Dover, K.J. (1981) *A Historical Commentary on Thucydides*, vol. 5. Oxford.

Gordon, R.L. (1979) 'The real and the imaginary: production and religion in the Greco-Roman world', *Art History* 2: 5–34. Reprinted in R.L. Gordon *Image and Value in the Graeco-Roman World*. Aldershot, 1996.

Gould, J. (1973) 'Hiketeia', *Journal of Hellenic Studies* 93: 74–103. Reprinted with addendum in Gould (2001) 22–77.

—(1980) 'Law, custom, and myth: aspects of the social position of women in classical Athens', *Journal of Hellenic Studies* 100: 38–59. Reprinted in Gould (2001) 112–57.

—(1985) 'On making sense of Greek religion', in P. Easterling and J. Muir eds. *Greek Religion and Society*. Cambridge: 1–33. Reprinted in Gould (2001) 203–34.

—(1994) 'Herodotus and Religion', in S. Hornblower ed. *Greek Historiography*. Oxford: 91–106. Reprinted in Gould (2001) 359–77.

— (1996) 'Tragedy and collective experience', in M. Silk ed. *Tragedy and the Tragic: Greek Theatre and Beyond*. Oxford: 271–43. Reprinted in Gould (2001) 378–404.

—(2001) *Myth, Ritual, Memory and Exchange: Essays in Greek Literature and Culture*. Oxford.

Graf, F. (1998) *Magic in the Ancient World*. Cambridge, MA.

Gray, V. (1989) *The Character of Xenophon's Hellenica*. London.

Gribble, D. (1999) *Alcibiades and Athens: a Study in Literary Presentation*. Oxford.

Habicht, C. (1997) *Athens from Alexander to Antony*, trans. D.L. Schneider. Cambridge, MA.

Hall, E.M. (1989) *Inventing the Barbarian: Greek Self-Definition through Tragedy*. Oxford.

—(1996) *Aeschylus* Persians. Warminster.

—(1999) 'Actor's song in tragedy', in Goldhill and Osborne (1999) 96–122.

Hall, J.M. (1997) *Ethnic Identity in Greek Antiquity*. Cambridge.

—(2002) *Hellenicity: between Ethnicity and Culture*. Chicago.

Hamel, D. (1998) *Athenian Generals: Military Authority in the Classical Period*. Leiden.

Hansen, M.H. (1974) *The Sovereignty of the People's Court in Athens in the Fourth Century BC and the Public Action against Unconstitutional Proposals*. Odense.

—(1980) 'Seven hundred *archai* in classical Athens', *Greek, Roman and Byzantine Studies* 21: 151–73.

—(1983) *The Athenian Ecclesia: a Collection of Articles, 1976–83*. Copenhagen.

—(1985) *Demography and Democracy: the Number of Athenian Citizens in the Fourth Century BC*. Herning.

—(1986) 'The origin of the term *demokratia*', *Liverpool Classical Monthly* 11: 35–6.

—(1987) *The Athenian Assembly*. Oxford.

—(1988) *Three Studies in Athenian Demography*. Copenhagen.

—(1989) *The Athenian Ecclesia II: a Collection of Articles, 1983–89*. Copenhagen.

Hansen, M.H. (1991) *The Athenian Democracy in the Age of Demosthenes*. Oxford.

—(1994) 'The 2500th Anniversary of Cleisthenes' Reforms and the Tradition of Athenian Democracy', in R. Osborne and S. Hornblower eds. *Ritual, Finance, Politics: Athenian Democratic Accounts Presented to David Lewis*. Oxford: 25–37.

Hansen, M.H., and Nielsen, T.H. (2004) *An Inventory of Archaic and Classical Poleis*. Oxford.

Hanson, V.D. (1983) *Warfare and Agriculture in Classical Greece*. Pisa.

—(1989) *The Western Way of War: Infantry Battle in Classical Greece*. New York.

—ed. (1991) *Hoplites: the Classical Greek Battle Experience*. London.

—(1995) *The Other Greeks: the Family Farm and the Agrarian Roots of Western Civilization*. New York.

Harding, P. (1994) *Androtion and the Atthis*. Oxford.

Harris, E.M. (1990) 'Did the Athenians regard seduction as a worse crime than rape?' *Classical Quarterly* 40: 370–77.

—(1995) *Aeschines and Athenian Politics*. Oxford.

—(2002) 'Workshop, marketplace and household: the nature of technical specialization in classical Athens and its influence on economy and society', in Cartledge et al. (2002) 67–99.

Harris, W.V. (1989) *Ancient Literacy*. Cambridge, MA.

Harrison, E. (1985) 'Early classical sculpture: the bold style', in C. Boulter ed. *Greek Art: Archaic into Classical*. Leiden: 40–65.

Harrison, T.E. (2000a) *Divinity and History: The Religion of Herodotus*. Oxford.

—(2000b) *the Emptiness of Asia: Aeschylus'* Persians *and the History of the Fifth Century*. London.

— ed. (2002) *Greeks and Barbarians*. Edinburgh.

Harrison, T.R. (1993) *Democracy*. London.

Harvey, F.D. (1990) 'The sycophant and sycophancy: vexatious redefinition?' in Cartledge, Millett and Todd (1990) 103–21.

Harvey, F.D. and Wilkins, J. eds. (2000) *The Rivals of Aristophanes*. London.

Headlam, J.W. (1933) *Election by Lot at Athens*. 2nd edn. Cambridge.

Healy, J.F. (1978) *Mining and Metallurgy in the Greek and Roman World*. London.

Hemelrijk, J.M. (1991) 'A closer look at the potter', in T. Rasmussen and N. Spivey eds. *Looking at Greek Vases*. Cambridge.

Henle, J. (1973) *Greek Myths: a Vase-Painter's Notebook*. Bloomington.

Henrichs, A. (1982) 'Changing Dionysiac identities', in B.F. Meyer and E.P. Sanders eds. *Jewish and Christian Self-Definition*, vol. 3: *Self-Definition in the Graeco-Roman World*. London: 137–60, 213–36.

—(1995) 'Why should I dance?' *Arion* 3: 56–111.

Herman, G. (1987) *Ritualised Friendship and the Greek City*. Cambridge.

Higgins, M.D. and Higgins, R.A. (1996) *A Geological Companion to Greece and the Aegean*. London.

Hignett, C. (1951) *A History of the Athenian Constitution*. Oxford.

Hodkinson, S. (2000) *Property and Wealth in Classical Sparta*. London.

Horden, P. and Purcell, N. (2000) *The Corrupting Sea: a Study of Mediterranean History*. Oxford.

Hornblower, S. (1983) *The Greek World 478–323 BC*. London.

—(1987) *Thucydides*. London.

—(2002) *The Greek World 478–323 BC*. 2nd edn. London.

Howgego, C. (1995) *Ancient History from Coins*. London.

Humphreys, S.C. (1980) 'Family tombs and tomb cult in ancient Athens: tradition or traditionalism?' *Journal of Hellenic Studies* 100: 96–126. Reprinted in S.C. Humphreys *The Family, Women and Death: Comparative Studies*. London, 1983.

Humphreys, S.C. (1987) 'Law, custom and nature in Herodotus', *Arethusa* 20: 211–20.

—(2004) *The Strangeness of Gods: Historical Perspectives on the Interpretation of Athenian Religion*. Oxford.

Hunter, V.J. (1994) *Policing Athens: Social Control in the Attic Lawsuits, 420–320 BC*. Princeton.

—(2000) 'Introduction: status distinctions in Athenian law', in Hunter and Edmonson (2000) 1–30.

Hunter, V.J. and Edmonson, J.C. eds. (2000) *Law and Social Status in Classical Athens*. Oxford.

Hurwit, J.M. (1989) 'The Critias Boy: discovery, reconstruction, and date', *American Journal of Archaeology* 93: 41–80.

—(1999) *The Athenian Acropolis: History, Mythology, and Archaeology from the Neolithic Era to the Present*. Cambridge.

—(2004) *The Acropolis in the Age of Pericles*. Cambridge.

Hussey, E. (1985) 'Thucydidean history and Democritean theory', in Cartledge and Harvey (1985) 118–38.

—(1997) 'Pythagoreans and Eleatics', in C.C.W. Taylor ed. *From the Beginning to Plato. Routledge History of Philosophy*, vol. 1. London: 128–74.

Irwin, E. (2005) *Solon and Early Greek Poetry*. Cambridge.

Isager, S. and Skydsgaard, J.E. (1992) *Ancient Greek Agriculture: an Introduction*. London.

Jackson, A.H. (1991) 'Hoplites and the gods: the dedication of captured arms and armour', in Hanson (1991) 228–49.

Jacquemin, A. (2000) *Guerre et religion dans le monde grec (490–322 av. J.-C)*. Liège.

Jameson, M.H. (1977) 'Agriculture and slavery in classical Athens', *Classical Journal* 73: 122–45.

—(1988) 'Sacrifice and ritual: Greece', in M. Grant and R. Kitzinger eds. *Greece and Rome. Civilization of the Ancient Mediterranean*, vol. 2. New York: 959–79.

—(1991) 'Sacrifice before battle', in Hanson (1991) 197–227.

—(1992) 'Agricultural labour in ancient Greece', in Wells (1992) 135–46.

—(1994) 'Class in the ancient Greek countryside', in P.N. Doukellis and L. Mendoni eds. *Structures rurales et sociétés antiques*. Paris.

—(1999) 'The spectacular and the obscure in Athenian religion', in Goldhill and Osborne (1999) 321–40.

Jeffrey, L.H. (1961) *The Local Scripts of Archaic Greece*. Oxford (revised edn. with a supplement by A.W. Johnston,1990).

Johnston, S.I. (1999) *The Restless Dead: Encounters between the Living and the Dead in Ancient Greece*. Berkeley.

Jones, A.H.M. (1957) *Athenian Democracy*. Oxford.

—(1974) 'Taxation in antiquity', in A.H.M. Jones (ed. P.A. Brunt) *The Roman Economy: Studies in Ancient Economic and Administrative History*. Oxford: 151–86.

Karabélias, E. (2002) *L'Épiclérat attique*. Athens.

Karakasi, A. (2003) *Archaic Korai*. Los Angeles.

Kavoulaki, A. (1999) 'Processional performance and the democratic polis', in Goldhill and Osborne (1999) 293–320.

Kearns, E. (1989) *The Heroes of Attica*. Bulletin of the Institute of Classical Studies, Supplement 57. London.

—(1995) 'Order, interaction, authority: ways of looking at Greek Religion', in Powell (1995a) 511–29.

Keesling, C.M. (2003) *The Votive Statues of the Athenian Acropolis*. Cambridge.

Kennedy, G. (1963) *The Art of Persuasion in Greece*. Princeton.

Kerferd, G. (1981) *The Sophistic Movement*. Cambridge.

Kim, H. (2001) 'Archaic coinage as evidence for the use of money', in Meadows and Shipton (2001) 7–22.

King, H. (1998) *Hippocrates' Woman: Reading the Female Body in Ancient Greece*. London.

Knox, B. (1964) *The Heroic Temper: Studies in Sophoclean Tragedy*. Berkeley.

Konstan, D. (1996) *Friendship in the Classical World*. Cambridge.

Kurtz, D.C. and Boardman, J. (1971) *Greek Burial Customs*. London.

Kyle, D.G. (1987) *Athletics in Ancient Athens*. Leiden.

Lambert, S.D. (1993) *The Phratries of Attica*. Ann Arbor.

Lanni, A. (1997) 'Spectator sport or serious politics? οἱ περιεστηκότε and the Athenian law-courts', *Journal of Hellenic Studies* 117: 183–9.

—(2006) *Law and Justice in the Courts of Classical Athens*. Cambridge.

Lape, S. (2004) *Reproducing Athens: Menander's Comedy, Democratic Culture, and the Hellenistic City*. Princeton.

—(forthcoming) *Racial Athens*. Cambridge.

Latacz, J. (2003) *Troy and Homer*. Oxford.

Lawrence, A.W. (1979) *Greek Aims in Fortification*. Oxford.

Lazenby, J.F. (1993) *The Defence of Greece 490–79 BC*. Warminster.

Lemos, I. (2003) *The Protogeometric Aegean*. Oxford.

Lendon, J. (2005) *Soldiers and Ghosts: a History of Battle in Classical Antiquity*. New Haven and London.

Lewis, D.M. (1962) 'The federal constitution of Keos', *Annual of the British School at Athens* 57: 1–4. Reprinted in D.M. Lewis *Selected Papers in Greek and Near Eastern History* (ed. P.J. Rhodes). Cambridge, 1997: 22–8.

—(1988) 'The tyranny of the Peisistratidae', in *Cambridge Ancient History*, vol.4. 2nd edn. Cambridge: 287–302.

Lewis, S. (1996) *News and Society in the Greek Polis*. London.

—(2002) *The Athenian Woman: an Iconographic Handbook*. London.

Liddel, P. (2007) *Civil Obligation and Individual Liberty in Ancient Athens*. Oxford.

Lissarrague, F. (1989) 'The world of the warrior' in Bérard (1979).39–52.

—(1990a) *The Aesthetics of the Greek Banquet*. Oxford.

—(1990b) *L'Autre Guerrier: archers, peltastes, cavaliers dans l'imagerie attique*. Paris.

Livingstone, N. (1998) 'The voice of Isocrates and the dissemination of cultural power', in N. Livingstone and Y.L. Too ed. *Pedagogy and Power: Rhetorics of Classical Learning*. Cambridge.

Llewellyn-Jones, L. ed. (2002) *Women's Dress in the Ancient Greek World*. London.

—(2004) *Aphrodite's Tortoise: the Veiled Woman of Ancient Greece*. Swansea.

Lloyd, G.E.R. (1966) *Polarity and Analogy*. Cambridge.

—(1978) *Hippocratic Writings*. Harmondsworth.

—(1979) *Magic, Reason and Experience: Studies in the origin and development of Greek Science*. Cambridge.

—(1983) *Science, Folklore and Ideology: Studies in the Life Sciences in Ancient Greece*. Cambridge

—(1987) *The Revolutions of Wisdom: Studies in the Claims and Practice of Ancient Greek Science*. Berkeley.

—(1990) *Demystifying Mentalities*. Cambridge.

Loraux, N. (1986) *The Invention of Athens: the Funeral Oration in the Classical City*. Cambridge, MA.

—(1993) *Children of Athene: Athenian Ideas about Citizenship and the Division between the Sexes*. Princeton.

—(1995) *The Experiences of Tiresias: the Feminine and the Greek Man*. Princeton.

Low, P.A. (2005) 'Looking for the language of Athenian Imperialism', *Journal of Hellenic Studies* 125: 93–111.

—(2007) *Interstate Relations in Classical Greece: Morality and Politics*. Cambridge.

Lyons, D. (1997) *Gender and Immortality: Heroines in Ancient Greek Myth and Cult*. Princeton.

MacDonald, B.R. (1983) 'The Megarian Decree', *Historia* 32: 385–410.

MacDowell, D.M. (1978) *The Law in Classical Athens*. London.

—(1989) 'The *oikos* in Athenian law', *Classical Quarterly* 39: 10–21.

McGinty, P. (1978) *Interpretation and Dionysos: method in the study of a god*. The Hague.

McGlew, J.F. (2002) *Citizens on Stage: Comedy and Political Culture in the Athenian Democracy*. Ann Arbor.

McInerney, J. (1999) *The Folds of Parnassus: Land and Ethnicity in Ancient Phokis*. Austin, TX.

McKechnie, P.R. and Kern, S.J. (1988) *Hellenika Oxyrhynchia*. Warminster.

Macleod, C.W. (1975) 'Form and meaning in the Melian dialogue', *Historia* 23: 385–400. Reprinted in C. Macleod *Collected Essays*. Oxford, 1983: 52–67.

Manville, P.B. (1990) *The Origins of Citizenship in Classical Athens*. Princeton.

Marinatos, N. and Hägg, R. (1993) *Greek Sanctuaries: New Approaches*. London.

Markle, M. (1985) 'Jury pay and Assembly pay at Athens', in Cartledge and Harvey (1985) 265–97.

Marrou, H.I. (1956) *History of Education in Antiquity*. London.

Marshall, C.W. and van Willigenburg, S. (2004) 'Judging Athenian dramatic competitions', *Journal of Hellenic Studies* 124: 90–107.

Meadows, A. and Shipton, K. eds. (2001) *Money and its Uses in the Ancient Greek World*. Oxford.

Meiggs, R. (1972) *The Athenian Empire*. Oxford

Merkelbach, R. and West, M.L. eds. (1974) 'Ein Archilochos-Papyrus', *Zeitschrift für Papyrologie und Epigraphik* 14: 97–113.

Mikalson, J. (1975) *The Sacred and Civil Calendar of the Athenian Year*. Princeton.

Miller, F.D. (1995) *Nature, Justice, and Rights in Aristotle's Politics*. Oxford.

Miller, M.C. (1997) *Athens and Persia in the Fifth Century BC: a Study in Cultural Receptivity*. Cambridge.

Millett, P.C. (1983) 'Maritime loans and the structure of credit in fourth-century Athens', in P. Garnsey, K. Hopkins and C.R. Whittaker eds. *Trade in the Ancient Economy*. London: 36–52.

—(1991) *Lending and Borrowing in Ancient Athens*. Cambridge.

—(1998) 'Encounters in the *Agora*', in Cartledge, Millett and von Reden (1998) 203–28.

Mitchell, L.G. (1997) *Greeks Bearing Gifts: the Public Use of Private Relationships in the Greek World, 435–323 BC*. Cambridge.

Morgan, T.J. (1998) *Literate Education in the Hellenistic and Roman Worlds*. Cambridge.

Morris, I.M. (1987) *Burial and Ancient Society*. Cambridge.

—(2000) *Archaeology as Cultural History*. Oxford.

Morris, S.P. (1992) *Daidalos and the Origins of Greek Art*. Princeton.

Morrison, J.S., Coates, J.F. and Rankov, N.B. (2000) *The Athenian Trireme: the History and Reconstruction of an Ancient Greek Warship*. Cambridge.

Mosley, D.J. (1973) *Envoys and Diplomacy in Ancient Greece. Historia* Einzelschriften 22.

Murray, O. (1988) 'The Ionian Revolt', in *Cambridge Ancient History*, vol 4. 2nd edn. Cambridge: 461–90.

—ed. (1990a) *Sympotica*. Oxford.

—(1990b) 'The affair of the Mysteries: democracy and the drinking group', in Murray (1990a) 149–61.

—(1993) *Early Greece*. 2nd edn. London.

Murray, O. and Price, S. eds. (1990) *The Greek City from Homer to Alexander*. Oxford.

Murray, P. and Wilson, P.J. eds. (2004) *Music and the Muses: the Culture of Mousike in the Classical Athenian City*. Oxford.

Neer, R.T. (2002) *Style and Politics in Athenian Vase-Painting: the Craft of Democracy, ca. 530–460 BCE*. Cambridge.

Neils, J. (1992) *Goddess and Polis: the Panathenaic Festival in Ancient Athens*. Princeton.

Nevett, L. (1994) 'Separation or seclusion? Towards an archaeological approach to investigating women in the Greek household in the fifth to third centuries BC', in M. Parker Pearson and C. Richards eds. *Architecture and Order: Approaches to Social Space*. London: 98–112.

—(1995) 'Gender relations in the classical Greek household', *Annual of the British School at Athens* 90: 363–81.

Nixon, L. and Price, S.R.F. (1990) 'The size and resources of Greek cities', in Murray and Price (1990) 137–70.

—(2005) 'Ancient Greek agricultural terracing: evidence from texts and archaeological survey' *American Journal of Archaeology* 109: 665–94.

Nussbaum, M.C. (1980) 'Aristophanes and Socrates on learning practical wisdom', *Yale Classical Studies* 26: 43–97.

Oakley, J.H. (2004) *Picturing Death in Classical Athens: the Evidence of the White Lekythoi*. Cambridge.

Oakley, J.H. and Sinos, R.H. (1993) *The Wedding in Ancient Athens*. Madison, WI.

Ober, J. (1989) *Mass and Elite in Democratic Athens*. Princeton.

—(1998) *Political Dissent in Democratic Athens: Intellectual Critics of Popular Rule*. Princeton.

Ogden, D. (1996) *Greek Bastardy in the Classical and the Hellenistic Periods*. Oxford.

—(2001) *Greek and Roman Necromancy*. Princeton.

Omitowoju, R. (2002) *Rape and the Politics of Consent in Classical Athens*. Cambridge.

Osborne, C. (1998) 'Was verse the default form for Presocratic philosophy?' in C. Atherton ed. *Form and Content in Didactic Poetry*. Bari: 23–35.

—(2004) *Presocratic Philosophy: a Very Short Introduction*. Oxford.

Osborne, M.J. (1981–3) *Naturalization in Athens*. 4 vols. Brussels.

Osborne, R. (1985a) 'The erection and mutilation of the Hermai', *Proceedings of the Cambridge Philological Society* n.s. 31: 47–73.

—(1985b) *The Discovery of Classical Attica*. Cambridge.

—(1985c) 'Law in action in classical Athens,' *Journal of Hellenic Studies* 105: 40–58.

—(1987a) *Classical Landscape with Figures: The Ancient Greek City and its Countryside*. London.

—(1987b) 'The viewing and obscuring of the Parthenon frieze', *Journal of Hellenic Studies* 107: 98–105.

—(1988a) 'Death revisited; death revised: the death of the artist in archaic and classical Greece', *Art History* 11: 1–16.

—(1988b) 'Social and economic implications of the leasing of land and property in classical and Hellenistic Greece', *Chiron* 18: 279–323.

—(1989) 'A crisis in archaeological history: the seventh century in Attica', *Annual of the British School at Athens* 84: 297–322.

—(1990a) 'Vexatious litigation in classical Athens: sycophancy and the sycophant', in Cartledge, Millett, and Todd (1990) 83–102.

—(1990b) 'The Demos and its divisions', in Murray and Price (1990) 265–94.

—(1991) 'Pride and prejudice, sense and subsistence: exchange and society in the Greek city', in J. Rich and A. Wallace-Hadrill eds. *City and Country in the Ancient World*. London: 119–45.

—(1992) 'Is it a farm? The definition of agricultural sites and settlements in ancient Greece', in Wells (1992) 21–7.

—(1993) 'Women and sacrifice in classical Greece' *Classical Quarterly* 43: 392–405. Reprinted in Buxton (2000) 294–313.

—(1994a) 'The economy and trade', in J. Boardman ed. *Cambridge Ancient History: Plates to Vols. 5 and 6*. Cambridge: 85–108.

—(1994b) 'Democracy and imperialism in the Parthenon procession: the Parthenon Frieze in context', in W. Coulson et al. eds. *The Archaeology of Athens and Attica under Democracy*. Oxford: 143–50.

—(1994c) 'Framing the centaur', in Goldhill and Osborne (1994) 52–84.

—(1995) 'The economics and politics of slavery at Athens', in Powell (1995a) 27–43.

—(1996a) *Greece in the Making, c. 1200–479 BC*. London.

—(1996b) 'Desiring women on Athenian pottery', in N. Kampen ed. *Sexuality in Ancient Art*. Cambridge: 65–80.

—(1997a) 'Law, the democratic citizen and the representation of women in classical Athens', *Past and Present* 155: 3–33 Reprinted in Osborne (2004c) 38–60.

—(1997b) 'The ecstasy and the tragedy: varieties of religious experience in art, drama and society', in Pelling (1997a) 187–212.

—(1998) *Archaic and Classical Greek Art*. Oxford.

—(1999) 'Inscribing democracy', in Goldhill and Osborne (1999) 341–58.

—ed. (2000a) *Classical Greece: The Short Oxford History of Europe,* vol.1. Oxford.

—(2000b) 'Religion, imperial politics and the offering of freedom to slaves', in Hunter and Edmonson (2000), 75–92.

—(2001) 'Why did Athenian pots appeal to the Etruscans?' *World Archaeology* 33.2: 277–95.

—(2003) 'Changing the discourse', in K.A. Morgan ed. *Popular Tyranny: Sovereignty and its Discontents in Ancient Greece*. Austin, TX: 251–72.

—(2004a) *Greek History*. London.

—(2004b) 'Homeric Society', in R.L. Fowler ed. *Cambridge Companion to Homer*. Cambridge: 206–19.

—ed. (2004c) *Studies in Ancient Greek and Roman Society*. Past and Present Series. Cambridge.

—(2006) 'When was the Athenian democratic revolution?' in Goldhill and Osborne (2006) 10–27.

—ed. (2007) *A Cultural Revolution in Classical Athens? Art, Literature, Philosophy and Politics 430–380 BC*. Cambridge.

Ostwald, M. (1969) *Nomos and the beginning of the Athenian Democracy*. Oxford.

Parker, R.C.T. (1983) *Miasma: Pollution and Purification in Early Greek Religion*. Oxford.

—(1985) Greek states and Greek oracles', in Cartledge and Harvey (1985) 298–326. Reprinted in Buxton (2000) 76–108.

—(1987) 'Festivals of the Attic Demes', in T. Linders and G. Nordquist eds. *Gifts to the Gods*. Uppsala: 137–47.

—(1996) *Athenian Religion: a History*. Oxford.

—(1997) 'Gods cruel and kind: tragic and civic theology', in Pelling (1997a) 143–60.

—(1998) 'Pleasing thighs: reciprocity in Greek Religion', in Gill, Postlethwaite and Seaford (1998) 105–26.

—(2004) 'One man's piety: the religious dimension of the *Anabasis*', in R. Lane Fox ed. *The Long March: Xenophon and the Ten Thousand*. New Haven: and London 131–53.

Parker, R.C.I. (2005) *Polytheism and Society at Athens*. Oxford.

Patterson, C. (1985) ' "Not worth rearing": the causes of infant exposure in ancient Greece', *Transactions of the American Philological Association* 115: 105–23.

—(1998) *The Family in Greek History*. Cambridge, MA.

Payne, H. and Young G.M. (1936) *Archaic Marble Sculpture from the Acropolis*. London.

Pedley, J. (2005) *Sanctuaries and the Sacred in the Ancient Greek World*. Cambridge.

Peirce, S. (1993) 'Death, revelry and *thysia*', *Classical Antiquity* 12: 219–66.

Pelling, C.B.R. (1997a) *Greek Tragedy and the Historian*. Oxford.

—(1997b) 'Aeschylus' *Persai* and history', in Pelling (1997a) 1–20.

—(2000) *Literary Texts and the Greek Historian*. London.

—(2002) 'Speech and action: Herodotus' debate on the constitutions', *Proceedings of the Cambridge Philological Society* 48: 123–58.

Perlès, C. (2001) *The Early Neolithic in Greece*. Cambridge.

Phillips, D. and Pritchard, D. eds. (2003) *Sport and Festival in the Ancient Greek World*. Swansea.

Polignac, F. de (1995) *Cults, Territory, and the Origins of the Greek City-State*. Chicago.

Pollitt, J.J. (1972) *Art and Experience in Classical Greece*. Cambridge.

Postlethwaite, N. (1998) 'Akhilleus and Agamemnon: generalized reciprocity', in Gill, Postlethwaite and Seaford (1998) 93–104.

Powell, A. ed. (1995a) *The Greek World*. London.

—(1995b) 'Athens' pretty face: anti-feminine rhetoric and fifth-century controversy over the Parthenon', in Powell (1995a) 245–70.

—(2001) *Athens and Sparta: Constructing Greek Political and Social History from 478 BC*. London.

Powell, A. and Hodkinson S. eds. (1994) *The Shadow of Sparta*. London.

Powell, B.B. (1991) *Homer and the Origin of the Greek Alphabet*. Cambridge.

Price, S.R.F. (1986) 'The future of dreams: from Freud to Artemidorus', *Past & Present* 113: 3–37. Revised version in Osborne (2004c) 226–59.

—(1999) *Religions of the Ancient Greeks*. Cambridge.

Pritchett, W.K. (1971–91) *The Greek State at War*. 5 vols. Berkeley.

Pulleyn, S. (1997) *Prayer in Greek Religion*. Oxford.

Rackham, O. (1990) 'Ancient Landscapes', in Murray and Price (1990) 85–112.

Randall, R.H. (1953) 'The Erechtheum workmen', *American Journal of Archaeology* 57: 199–210.

Rawson, E. (1969) *The Spartan Tradition in European Thought*. Oxford.

Reed, C.M. (2003) *Maritime Traders in the Ancient Greek World*. Cambridge.

Reeder, E. ed. (1995) *Pandora: Women in Classical Athens*. Princeton.

Reynolds, L.D. and Wilson, N.G. (1968) *Scribes and Scholars : a Guide to the Transmission of Greek and Latin Literature* (3rd edn. 1991). Oxford.

Rhodes, P.J. (1972) *The Athenian Boule*. Oxford.

—(1981) *A Commentary on the Aristotelian* Atheneion Politeia. Oxford.

—(1993) *The Athenian Empire*. Greece and Rome New Surveys in the Classics, no. 17. Revised with addenda. Oxford.

—(2006) *A History of the Classical Greek World*. Oxford.

Ridgway, B.S. (1981) *Fifth Century Styles in Greek Sculpture*. Princeton.

Rihll, T.E. (1995) 'Democracy denied: why Ephialtes attacked the Areiopagus', *Journal of Hellenic Studies* 115: 87–98.

Robertson, C.M. (1975) *A History of Greek Art*. Cambridge.

—(1992) *The Art of Vase-Painting in Classical Athens*. Cambridge.

Rood, T. (1998) *Thucydides: Narrative and Explanation*. Oxford.

—(2004) *The Sea! The Sea! The Shout of the Ten Thousand in the Modern Imagination*. London.

Rosivach, V.J. (1987) 'Autochthony and the Athenians', *Classical Quarterly* 37: 294–306.

Roy, J. (1998) 'The threat from the Peiraieus', in Cartledge, Millett and von Reden (1998) 191–202.

Rubinstein, L. (1993) *Adoption in Fourth-Century Athens*. Copenhagen.

—(2000) *Litigation and Co-operation: Supporting Speakers in the Courts of Classical Athens*. Stuttgart.

Rudhardt, J. (1966) 'Considérations sur le polythéisme', *Revue théologique et philosophique* 99: 353–64.

Rutherford, R.B. (2005) *Classical Literature: a Concise History*. Oxford.

Ryder, T.T.B. (1965) *Koine Eirene*. Oxford.

Ste Croix, G.E.M. de (1954–5) 'The character of the Athenian empire', *Historia* 3: 1–41.

—(1972) *The Origins of the Peloponnesian War*. London.

—(2004) *Athenian Democratic Origins and Other Essays*. Oxford.

Sallares, R. (1991) *The Ecology of the Ancient Greek World*. London.

Sancisi-Weerdenburg, H. ed. (2000) *Peisistratos and the Tyranny: a Reappraisal of the Evidence*. Amsterdam.

Scheidel, W. (2002) 'The hireling and the slave: a transatlantic perspective', in Cartledge et al. (2002) 175–84.

Schnurr-Redford, C. (2003) 'Women in classical Athens – their social space: ideal and reality', in Golden and Toohey (2003) 23–9.

Schofield, M. (1986) '*Euboulia* in the *Iliad*', *Classical Quarterly* 36: 6–31. Reprinted in D. Cairns ed. *Oxford Readings in Homer's* Iliad. Oxford, 2001: 220–59.

Scullion, S. (1994) 'Olympic and Chthonian', *Classical Antiquity* 13: 75–119.

—(2002) '"Nothing to do with Dionysus": tragedy misconceived as ritual', *Classical Quarterly* 52: 102–37.

Seaford, R. (1994) *Reciprocity and Ritual: Home and Tragedy, in the Developing City-State*. Oxford.

—(2004) *Money and the Early Greek Mind*. Cambridge.

Seager, R. (1994) 'The Corinthian War', *Cambridge Ancient History*, vol. 6 2nd edn: 97–119

Sedley, D.N. (2003) *Plato's* Cratylus. *Cambridge*.

Shapiro, H.A. (1989) *Art and Cult under the Tyrants in Athens*. Mainz.

Sherratt, E.S. (1990) '"Reading the texts": archaeology and the Homeric question', *Antiquity* 64: 807–24.

Shipton, K.M. (2001) 'Money and the elite in classical Athens', in Meadows and Shipton (2001) 129–44.

Sidebottom, H. (2004) *Ancient Warfare: a Very Short Introduction*. Oxford.

Sinclair, R.K. (1988) *Democracy and Participation in Athens*. Cambridge.

Snodgrass, A.M. (1967) *Arms and Armour of the Greeks*. London.

—(1988) 'The archaeology of the hero', *Annali dell' Istituto Universitario Orientale di Napoli, sezione di archeologia e storia antica* 10: 19–26. Reprinted in Buxton (2000) 180–90.

Snowden, F.M. (1983) *Before Color Prejudice: the Ancient View of Blacks*. Cambridge, MA.

Sorabji, R. (1993) *Animal Minds and Human Morals: the Origins of the Western Debate*. London.

Sparkes, B.A. (1991a) *Greek Pottery: an Introduction*. Manchester.

—(1991b) *Greek Art*. Greece and Rome New Surveys in the Classics, no. 22. Oxford.

—ed. (1998) *Greek Civilization: an Introduction*. Oxford.

Spawforth, A.J.S. (2006) *The Complete Greek Temples*. London.

Spence, I. (1993) *The Cavalry of Classical Greece: a Social and Military History*. Oxford.

Stehle, E. (1997) *Performance and Gender in Ancient Greece*. Princeton.

Stewart, A. (1990) *Greek Sculpture*. 2 vols. New Haven and London.

Stone, I. (1988) *The Trial of Socrates*. Boston.

Strauss, B. (1986) *Athens after the Peloponnesian War: Class, Faction and Policy 403–386 BC*. London.

Strauss, B. (1996) 'The Athenian trireme: school of democracy', in J. Ober and C. Hedrick eds. *Demokratia: a Conversation on Democracies, Ancient and Modern*. Princeton.

Tanner, J.J. (2006) *The Invention of Art History in Ancient Greece: Religion, Society and Artistic Rationalisation*. Cambridge.

Taplin, O. (1978) *Greek Tragedy in Action*. London.

—(1986) 'Fifth-century tragedy and comedy: a *synkrisis*', *JHS* 106: 163–74.

—ed. (2000) *Literature in the Greek and Roman Worlds: a New Perspective*. Oxford.

Taylor, C.E. (2007) 'A new political world', in R. Osborne ed. *A Cultural Revolution in Classical Athens? Art, literature, philosophy and politics 430–380 BC*. Cambridge.

Thomas, R. (1989) *Oral Tradition and Written Record in Classical Athens*. Cambridge.

—(1992) *Literacy and Orality in Ancient Greece*. Cambridge.

—(1994) 'Law and the lawgiver in the Athenian Democracy', in Osborne and Hornblower (1994) 119–33.

—(1996) 'Written in stone? liberty, equality, orality, and the codification of law', in Foxhall and Lewis (1996) 9–31.

—(2000) *Herodotus in Context: Ethnography, Science and the Art of Persuasion*. Cambridge.

Todd, S.C. (1990a) '*Lady Chatterley's Lover* and the Attic orators', *Journal of Hellenic Studies* 110: 146–73.

—(1990b) 'The purpose of evidence in Athenian courts', in Cartledge, Millett and Todd (1990) 19–39.

—(1993) *The Shape of Athenian Law*. Oxford.

Too, Y.L. (1995) *The Rhetoric of Identity in Isocrates: Text, Pedagogy and Power*. Cambridge.

—ed. (2001) *Education in Greek and Roman Antiquity*. Leiden.

Traill, J.S. (1975) *The Political Organization of Attica*. Hesperia Supplement 14. Princeton.

Trevett, J.C. (1992) *Apollodorus Son of Pasion*. Oxford.

—(2001) 'Coinage and democracy in Athens', in Meadows and Shipton (2001) 23–34.

Tuck, R. (1979) *Natural Rights Theories: their Origin and Development*. Cambridge.

van Straten F.T. (1992) 'Votives and votaries in Greek sanctuaries', in A. Schachter ed. *Le Sanctuaire grec*. Entretiens Fondation Hardt 37. Geneva: 247–84. Reprinted in Buxton (2000) 191–223.

—(1995) *Hiera Kala: Images of Animal Sacrifice in Archaic and Classical Greece*. Leiden.

van Wees, H. (2000) 'The city at war', in Osborne (2000a) 81–110.

—(2004) *Greek Warfare: Myths and Realities*. London.

Verbanck-Piérard, A. and Viviers, D. (1995) *Culture et cité: l'avènement d'Athènes à l'époque archaïque*. Brussels.

Vernant, J.-P. (1980) *Myth and Society in Ancient Greece*. Hassocks.

Veyne, P. (1988) *Did the Greeks Believe in their Myths?* Chicago.

Vidal-Naquet, P. (1981) 'Slavery and the rule of women in tradition, myth and utopia', in R.L. Gordon ed. *Myth, Religion and Society*. Cambridge: 187–200. Reprinted in Vidal-Naquet (1986).

—(1986) *The Black Hunter: Forms of Thought and Forms of Society in the Greek World*. Baltimore.

Vlastos, G. (1991) *Socrates: Ironist and Moral Philosopher*. Ithaca, NY.

von Bothmer, D. (1985) *The Amasis Painter and his World*. Los Angeles.

von Reden, S. (1995) 'The Piraeus – a world apart', *Greece and Rome* 42: 24–37.

—(1998) 'The well-ordered *polis*: topographies of civic space', in Cartledge, Millett and von Reden (1998) 170–90.

Wagner-Hasel, B. (2003) 'Women's life in oriental seclusion? On the history and use of a topos', in Golden and Toohey (2003) 241–52.

Walbank, M.B. (1978) *Athenian Proxenies of the Fifth Century BC*. Toronto.

Wallace, R.W. (1989) *The Areopagus Council to 307 BC*. Baltimore.

—(1998) 'The sophists in Athens', in Boedeker and Raaflaub (1998) 203–22.

Wardy, R.B. (1996) *The Birth of Rhetoric: Gorgias, Plato and their Successors*. London.

Wells, B. ed. (1992) *Agriculture in Ancient Greece*. Stockholm.

West, M.L. (1966) *Hesiod: Theogony*. Oxford.

—(1988) 'The rise of Greek epic', *Journal of Hellenic Studies* 108: 151–72.

—(1997) *The East Face of Helicon: West Asiatic Elements in Greek Poetry and Myth*. Oxford.

Wheeler, E. (1991) 'The general as hoplite', in Hanson (1991) 121–70.

Whitehead, D. (1977) *The Ideology of the Athenian Metic*. Cambridge Philological Society Supplement 4. Cambridge.

—(1983) 'Competitive outlay and community profit: φιλοτιμία in classical Athens', *Classica et Mediaevalia* 34: 55–74.

—(1986) *The Demes of Attica 508/7 BC–ca. 250 BC: a Political and Social Study*. Princeton.

—(1990) *Aineias Tacticus: How to Survive under Siege, Translated with Introduction and Commentary*, Oxford.

—(1993) 'Cardinal virtues: the language of public approbation in democratic Athens', *Classica et Mediaevalia* 44: 37–76.

Whitley, J. (1991) *Style and Society in Dark Age Greece*. Cambridge.

Wiles, D. (1991) *The Masks of Menander: Sign and Meaning in Greek and Roman Performance*. Cambridge.

—(1997) *Tragedy in Athens: Performance Space and Theatrical Meaning*. Cambridge.

Wilkins, J., Harvey, D. and Dobson, M. eds. (1995) *Food in Antiquity*. Exeter.

Willi, A. ed. (2002) *The Language of Greek Comedy*. Oxford.

Williams, B.A.O. (1993) *Shame and Necessity*. Berkeley.

Williams, D. (1991) 'The invention of the red-figure technique and the race between vase-painting and free painting', in T. Rasmussen and N. Spivey eds. *Looking at Greek Vases*. Cambridge: 103–18.

Wilson, P.J. (1992) 'Demosthenes 21 (*Against Meidias*): democratic abuse', *Proceedings of the Cambridge Philological Society* 37: 164–95.

—(2000) *The Athenian Institution of the Khoregia: the Chorus, the City and the Stage*. Cambridge.

Winkler, J.J. (1990) *The Constraints of Desire: the Anthropology of Sex and Gender in Ancient Greece*. London.

Winkler, J.J. and Zeitlin, F.I. eds. (1990) *Nothing to do with Dionysus? Athenian Drama in its Social Context*. Princeton.

Wolpert, A. (2002) *Remembering Defeat: Civil War and Civic Memory in Ancient Athens*. Baltimore.

Woodford, S. (2003) *Images of Myths in Classical Antiquity*. Cambridge.

Wycherley, R.F. (1978) *The Stones of Athens*. Princeton.

Zimmern, A.E. (1911) *The Greek Commonwealth*. Oxford.

Ziolkowski, J.E. (1981) *Thucydides and the Tradition of Funeral Speeches at Athens*. Salem, NH.

Acknowledgements for Photographs and Drawings

Chapter 1

1.1 The entrance of the Mycenaean beehive tomb at Akharnai. Courtesy of James Watson.

1.2 An example of so-called 'Protogeometric' pottery from Athens. Courtesy of Deutsches Archäologisches Institut, Athens, neg. no. KER 4247. All rights reserved.

1.3 Athenian monumental wine-mixing bowl (*krātēr*). Courtesy of the Metropolitan Museum of Art, Rogers Fund, 1914 (14.130.15). Image © The Metropolitan Museum of Art.

1.4 Panathenaic *amphorā*. Courtesy of the Metropolitan Museum of Art, Rogers Fund, 1914 (14.130.12). Image © The Metropolitan Museum of Art.

1.5 The foundations of the late sixth-century temple of Athēnē Polias on the Athenian Akropolis. Photo: Alison Frantz, A7-36. Courtesy of the American School of Classical Studies.

1.6 Mid-sixth-century 'eye-cup' by Exēkiās. Courtesy of Hirmer Fotoarchiv, Munich. AM 2044/4

1.7 Marble copies of the statues of the 'tyrannicides', by Kritios and Nēsiōtēs. Courtesy of Deutsches Archäologisches Institut, Rome. All rights reserved.

1.8 Relief from the Persian city of Persepolis. Courtesy of the Oriental Institute of the University of Chicago.

1.9 *Ostrakon*. Courtesy of Deutsches Archäologisches Institut, Athens, neg. nos. KER 16171(a), 16172(b). All rights reserved.

1.10 Bronze statuette of a hoplite. Courtesy of Staatliche Museen zu Berlin Preußischer Kulturbesitz Antikensammlung, Misc. 7470.

1.11 Early fifth-century cup. Courtesy of the Metropolitan Museum of Art, Purchase, Joseph Pulitzer Bequest, 1953 (53.11.4). Image © The Metropolitan Museum of Art.

1.12 The Athenian Akropolis seen from the west. Photo: Alison Frantz, 8544-4. Courtesy of the American School of Classical Studies.

1.13 Fifth-century marble head of a herm. Athens, Agora S211. Courtesy of the American School of Classical Studies.

1.14 Silver tetradrachm with the head of the Persian satrap Tissaphernēs. © Copyright the Trustees of the British Museum.

1.15 The monument to the young cavalryman Dexileos. Courtesy of Hirmer Fotoarchiv, Munich, 562.0559.

1.16 Copy of the third-century statue of Dēmosthenēs. Courtesy of Ny Carlsberg Glyptotek, Copenhagen. 436a. Photograph © Jo Selsing.

1.17 Copy of a statue of Aiskhinēs. Courtesy of Deutsches Archäologisches Institut, Rome, neg. no. 85.486. All rights reserved.

1.18 The memorial to the Makedonian victory at Khairōneia. Courtesy of Hirmer Fotoarchiv, Munich. 562.0591.

1.19 Marble head of Alexander. Athens Akropolis 1311. Courtesy of Deutsches Archäologisches Institut, Athens, neg. no. AKA 2368.

Chapter 2

2.1 The face of an ancient quarry on Mount Pentelikon. Courtesy of Robin Osborne.

2.2 An ancient washery compound. Courtesy of John Ellis Jones.

2.3 Late sixth-century terracotta group. Paris, Louvre CA 352.

2.4 Athenian black-figure *amphorā*. Paris, Louvre AM 1008.

2.5 Early fifth-century red-figure cup attributed to the Antiphōn Painter. Photograph © 1992 Museum of Fine Arts, Boston, 10.199.

2.6 Red-figure *loutrophoros*. Courtesy of Staatliche Museen zu Berlin Preußischer Kulturbesitz Antikensammlung, F 2372.

2.7 Late sixth-century grave *stēlē*. Courtesy of Hirmer Fotoarchiv, Munich, 56i.0422.

2.8 Late sixth-century theatre at Thorikos. Courtesy of Robin Osborne.

2.9 Plans of the classical city of Athens and the Peiraieus.

2.10 Sixth-century water jug. B 330. © Copyright the Trustees of the British Museum.

2.11 Sixth-century boundary stone. Athens, Agora I 5510. Courtesy of the American School of Classical Studies.

Chapter 3

3.1 Early fifth-century red-figure cup. Paris, Louvre G115.

3.2 Early fifth-century Athenian red-figure cup. Courtesy of Bildarchiv Preußischer Kulturbesitz/Antikensammlung Staatliche Museen zu Berlin F 2293.

3.3 Mid-fifth-century *krātēr*. E 467. © Copyright the Trustees of the British Museum.

3.4–6 Mid-sixth-century black-figure *lekythos*. Courtesy of the Metropolitan Museum, Fletcher Fund, 1931 (31.11.10). Photograph, all rights reserved, The Metropolitan Museum of Art.

3.7 Ruins of the temple of Apollo at Delphi. Courtesy of James Watson.

3.8 Late sixth-century black-figure *amphorā*. B 171. © Copyright the Trustees of the British Museum.

3.9 Fifth-century red-figure column *krātēr*. Photograph © 2008 Museum of Fine Arts, Boston, 1970.567.

3.10 Mid-fifth-century red-figure bell *krātēr*. Photograph © 2008 Museum of Fine Arts, Boston, 00.346.

3.11 Mid-fifth-century Athenian bell *krātēr*. Courtesy of Museum für Vor- und Frühgeschichte, Frankfurt-am-Main, VF Beta 413.

3.12 Black-figure *hydriā*. Courtesy Sopprintendenza Archeologica per Etruria Meridionale, 65063.

3.13 Sixth-century *amphorā*. 97.7–27.2. © Copyright the Trustees of the British Museum.

3.14 Late sixth-century oil flask. Photograph © 2008 Museum of Fine Arts, Boston, 13.169.

3.15 Part of the frieze from the temple at Bassai. 524. © Copyright the Trustees of the British Museum.

3.16 Part of the east frieze of the Parthenon. Photo: Alison Frantz, EU 136. Courtesy of the American School of Classical Studies.

3.17 Remains of the fourth-century altar of Zeus Phrātrios and Athēnē Phrātriā. Athens, Agora I 3704. Courtesy of the American School of Classical Studies.

3.18 Early fifth-century Athenian red-figure cup. Paris, Louvre G138.

3.19 Panathenaic *amphorā*. Courtesy of the Metropolitan Museum of Art, Rogers Fund, 1914 (14.130.12). Image © The Metropolitan Museum of Art.

3.20 Fifth-century Athenian red-figure *stamnos*. E 439. © Copyright the Trustees of the British Museum.

Chapter 4

4.1 Late sixth-century Athenian black-figure *hydriā*. Photograph © 2008 Museum of Fine Arts, Boston, 63.475.

4.2 Fifth-century red-figure *skyphos*. Courtesy of the Kunsthistorisches Museum, Vienna, 3710.

4.3 Early sixth-century Athenian *krātēr*. Florence, Museo Archeologico 4209, photograph courtesy of Hirmer Fotoarchiv Munich, 591.2140.

4.4–5 Early fifth-century red-figure cup. Courtesy of the Kunsthistorisches Museum, Vienna, 3695.

4.6 Early fifth-century red-figure cup. Courtesy of The J. Paul Getty Museum, Villa Collection, Malibu, California. Attributed to the Brygos Painter, Attic Red-figured *Kylix* c. 490 BCE, 86.AE.286.

4.7 Early fifth-century red-figure cup. E52. © Copyright the Trustees of the British Museum.

4.8 Array of *ostraka* cast against Themistoklēs and Hippokratēs. Courtesy of the American School of Classical Studies (Agora Excavations).

4.9 Early fifth-century Athenian red-figure cup. Courtesy of Karlsruhe, Badisches Landesmuseum, 70/395.

Chapter 5

5.1 *Ostrakon* inscribed in the late fifth century. Courtesy of the American School of Classical Studies (Agora Excavations). P 27594.

5.2–4 Mid-sixth-century oil flask. Courtesy of the Metropolitan Museum of Art, Purchase, Walter C. Baker Gift, 1956 (56.11.1). Image © The Metropolitan Museum of Art.

5.5 Red-figure Athenian cup. Courtesy of Toledo Museum of Art (1972.55).

5.6 Mid-fifth-century red-figure *amphorā*. E 284. © Copyright the Trustees of the British Museum.

5.7 Early fifth-century red-figure cup. Courtesy of Antikensammlung Staatliche Museen zu Berlin Preußischer Kulturbesitz, F2289.

5.8 Fifth-century red-figure cup. Courtesy of Brussels, Musées Royaux, A 890.

5.9–10 Athenian red-figure *pelikē*. Courtesy of Bernisches Historisches Museum, Berne (12227).

5.11 Late sixth-century terracotta group. Photograph © 2008 Museum of Fine Arts, Boston, 01.7788.

5.12 Early fifth-century cup. Reproduced with the permission of the Master and Fellows of Corpus Christi College and of the Fitzwilliam Museum Cambridge. © Fitzwilliam Museum, Cambridge.

5.13 Early fifth-century cup. E 51. © Copyright the Trustees of the British Museum.

5.14–15 Late sixth-century red-figure cup. Courtesy of The J. Paul Getty Museum, Malibu, California. Attributed to the Carpenter Painter, Attic Red-figure *Kylix*, 515–510 BCE (85.AE.25).

5.16 Sixth-century Athenian black-figure *amphorā*. Courtesy of the Martin von Wagner Museum der Universität Würzburg, Würzburg 241. Photo: K. Oehrlein.

5.17 Early fifth-century red-figure cup. Courtesy of Bildarchiv Preußischer Kulturbesitz/ Antikensammlung Staatliche Museen zu Berlin, F2285.

5.18 Early fifth-century Athenian red-figure cup. Courtesy Kunsthistorisches Museum, Vienna, 3698.

5.19 Late sixth-century red-figure cup. Courtesy of The J. Paul Getty Museum, Malibu, California. Attributed to the Carpenter Painter, Attic Red-figure *Kylix*, 515–510 BCE (85.AE.25).

5.20 Mid-sixth-century Athenian black-figure cup. 1906.12–15.1. © Copyright the Trustees of the British Museum.

5.21 Model of an Athenian farm. Courtesy of Professor Dr Hans Lohmann.
5.22 Athenian red-figure cup of c. 500. B8785. © Copyright the Trustees of the British Museum.
5.23 Fifth-century water jug. Paris, Louvre CA2587.
5.24 Late fifth-century tombstone. Athens National Museum 3472. Courtesy of Hirmer Fotoarchiv, Munich 561.0443.
5.25–6 Fifth-century red-figure pot. Paris, Louvre CA 2183.
5.27 Fourth-century relief. Photograph: Welter, courtesy of the Deutsches Archäologisches Institut, Athens, Neg. Piräus 92. All rights reserved.
5.28 Red-figure *loutrophoros* from c. 470. Athens National Museum 1170. Courtesy of Hirmer Fotoarchiv, Munich 561.0266.
5.29 Late fifth-century Athenian grave *stēlē*. Athens National Museum. Courtesy of Hirmer Fotoarchiv, Munich 3624.

Chapter 6

6.1 Late fourth-century relief. Courtesy of the American School of Classical Studies, Athens (Agora Excavations) I 6524.
6.2 The Pnyx hill. Photo Alison Frantz. Courtesy of the American School of Classical Studies, Athens.
6.3 A model of the west side of the *agorā*. Courtesy of the American School of Classical Studies, Athens.
6.4 *Ostraka* cast against Kīmōn and Themistoklēs. Courtesy of the Deutsches Archäologisches Institut, Athens, Kerameikos 266186. All rights reserved.
6.5 Reconstruction drawing of the Athenian state prison. Drawing by John Travlos.
6.6 Official Athenian weight. Courtesy of the American School of Classical Studies, Athens. (Agora Excavations) B 495.
6.7 A range of official Athenian measures of capacity. Courtesy of the American School of Classical Studies, Athens (Agora Excavations).
6.8 Reconstructed model of an Athenian water-clock. Courtesy of the American School of Classical Studies, Athens (Agora Excavations) P 2084.
6.9 Fifth-century red-figure cup. Photograph © Musée des Beaux Arts de Dijon, CA 1301.
6.10 Fourth-century Athenian bronze ballots. Courtesy of the American School of Classical Studies (Agora Excavations) B 146, 728, 1055, 1056, 1058.
6.11 Fourth-century bronze *pinakion*. Courtesy of the American School of Classical Studies, Athens (Agora Excavations) B822.
6.12 Fragment of an inscription. Courtesy of the American School of Classical Studies, Athens (Agora Excavations) I 7307.

Chapter 7

7.1 Mid-fifth-century Athenian red-figure *pelikē*. Photograph © 2008 Museum of Fine Arts, Boston, 20.187.
7.2 Part of the Parthenōn frieze. Photo Alison Frantz, AT 189, Courtesy of the American School of Classical Studies.
7.3 Late sixth-century Athenian red-figure *kratēr*. Courtesy of the Metropolitan Museum of Art, New York, 1972.11.10. Image © The Metropolitan Museum of Art.
7.4 Late sixth-century Athenian red-figure cup. Courtesy of the Institut für klassische Archäologie und Antikenmuseum, Leipzig, 7487.
7.5 Fifth-century Athenian red-figure *amphorā*. E 285. © Copyright the Trustees of the British Museum.
7.6 Early fifth-century 'negro alabastron'. Photo M. and P. Chuzeville. Paris, Louvre CA 4193.

7.7 The relief from the public funerary monument to Athenian cavalrymen who died in combat in 394. Courtesy of Athens National Museum 2744.

7.8 Athenian black-figure cup of c. 530. Paris, Louvre F123.

7.9 Reconstruction of a trireme. Courtesy of Professor Boris Rankov.

7.10 Aerial view of the Peiraieus. © 1989 Loyola University of Chicago Archives, R. V. Schoder, SJ, photographer.

7.11 Early fifth-century red-figure *lekythos*. Courtesy of the Metropolitan Museum of Art, New York, 25.189.1. Image © The Metropolitan Museum of Art.

Chapter 8

8.1 Early fifth-century Athenian red-figure cup. Courtesy of Staatliche Museen zu Berlin Preußischer Kulturbesitz Antikensammlung, F2285.

8.2 'Head vase' from Athens, c. 500. Photograph © 2008 Museum of Fine Arts, Boston, 00.332.

8.3–4 Early fifth-century so-called '*negro alabastra*' from Athens. Courtesy of Bildarchiv Preußischer Kulturbesitz/Antikensammlung Staatliche Museen zu Berlin, V.I. 3382.

8.5 Fifth-century Athenian red-figure *hydriā*. Photograph © 2008 Museum of Fine Arts, Boston, 03.788.

8.6–7 Athenian red-figure calyx *krātēr*. Photograph © 2008 Museum of Fine Arts, Boston, 63.1246.

8.8 Water jar from c. 500. Courtesy of Bildarchiv Preußischer Kulturbesitz/Antikensammlung Staatliche Museen zu Berlin, 1966.18.

8.9 Fifth-century Athenian red-figure *pelikē*. Courtesy of Bildarchiv Preußischer Kulturbesitz/Antikensammlung Staatliche Museen zu Berlin, 3223.

8.10 Mid-sixth-century Athenian black-figure *amphorā*. Courtesy of Bildarchiv Preußischer Kulturbesitz/Antikensammlung Staatliche Museen zu Berlin, F 1697.

8.11–12 Terracotta figurines. Courtesy of the Metropolitan Museum of Art, New York, 13.225.18, 13.225.28.

8.13 Eighth-century belly *amphorā*, used as a grave-marker. Courtesy of the Hirmer Fotoarchiv, Munich.

8.14 Early seventh-century Proto-Attic *amphorā*. Courtesy of the Hirmer Fotoarchiv, Munich.

8.15 *Kouros* used as a grave-marker in southern Attikē, c. 520. Courtesy of the Hirmer Fotoarchiv, Munich.

8.16 A surviving figure from a late sixth-century pediment on the Athenian Akropolis. Photograph: Hege, courtesy of the Deutsches Archäologisches Institut, Athens, Neg. 1902. All rights reserved.

8.17 Early sixth-century Athenian black-figure *dīnos*. © Copyright the Trustees of the British Museum.

8.18 Mid-sixth-century *amphorā* by Exēkiās. Courtesy of the Hirmer Fotoarchiv, Munich, 591.2016.

8.19 Mid-sixth-century black-figure *amphorā* attributed to the Amasis Painter. Courtesy of Antikensammlung Basel und Sammlung Ludwig. Inv. Kä 420.

8.20 Red-figure cup of c. 500. Reproduced with the permission of the Master and Fellows of Corpus Christi College and of the Fitzwilliam Museum Cambridge, loan 103.18. © Fitzwilliam Museum, Cambridge.

8.21 Statue of a young boy, excavated on the Athenian Akropolis. Courtesy of Jeffrey Hurwit.

8.22 Bronze Warrior A recovered from the sea off southern Italy. Courtesy of the Alinari Archives, Florence.

8.23 Bronze Warrior B recovered from the sea off southern Italy. Courtesy of the Alinari Archives, Florence.

8.24 West frieze of the Parthenōn *in situ*. Photo Alison Frantz, AT 27. Courtesy of the American School of Classical Studies.

8.25–7   Metopes from the south side of the Parthenōn. Courtesy of the Hirmer Fotoarchiv, Munich.

8.28   Figure of Iris, from the west pediment of the Parthenōn. 303J. © Copyright the Trustees of the British Museum.

8.29   Mid-fifth-century Athenian red-figure *krātēr*. Paris, Louvre G 341.

8.30   *Hydriā*, ascribed to the Meidias Painter. E224. © Copyright the Trustees of the British Museum.

8.31   Early fourth-century red-figure cup. Corinth Museum. Courtesy of the American School of Classical Studies.

8.32   Mid-fourth-century Athenian grave *stēlē*. Athens National Museum. Courtesy of Hirmer Fotoarchiv, Munich, 561.0458.

General Index

Index of passages quoted